Anticipating *The Wealth of Nations*

Anders Chydenius (1729–1803) has sometimes been called "Scandinavia's Adam Smith" for his publications in the 1760s. Until now it has been impossible for non-Swedish readers to judge whether this is a reasonable epithet. This collection of Chydenius's writings provides the answer.

Bo Sandelin, University of Gothenburg, Sweden

Anders Chydenius, a clergyman and influential politician in the Swedish realm during the eighteenth century, advocated freedom of trade, the rights of the rural working class and the extension of the freedom of expression and the freedom of religion. He presented arguments for economic liberalism similar to those of his renowned contemporary Adam Smith. Chydenius's views have largely remained unnoticed owing to the fact that his writings have not been available to the international research community.

The book consists of 11 of the most important writings of Anders Chydenius, eighteenth-century pioneer of freedom and democracy. Thematically, they touch upon subject areas such as the freedom of trade and industry, emigration, the monetary system of the Swedish realm in the eighteenth century, freedom of the press (or, as Chydenius put it, the freedom of writing and printing), freedom of information, the rights of the rural working class and freedom of religion. The book also includes a comprehensive biography of Chydenius written by Lars Magnusson, together with commentaries and explanatory notes on each text.

For academic researchers and professionals of the history of economic thought and the history of ideas, both Smith scholars and others, this book provides valuable new source material that has not hitherto been available in English. This volume is also intended for members of the general public with an interest in, for instance, questions related to freedom of information and freedom of religion. This volume will serve as fruitful ground for future comparative studies, raise new intriguing questions and promote general discussion on these topics.

Maren Jonasson is Editor-in-Chief of the Collected Works of Anders Chydenius. She is currently employed by the University of Jyväskylä in Finland.

Pertti Hyttinen is Editor of the Collected Works of Anders Chydenius. He is currently employed by the University of Jyväskylä in Finland.

Lars Magnusson is full professor and chair in Economic History, Uppsala University, Sweden, member of the Royal Academy of Sciences and chairman of Swedish Collegium for Advanced Study (SCAS).

Routledge studies in the history of economics

Anticipating *The Wealth of Nations*

The selected works of Anders Chydenius
(1729–1803)

**Edited by Maren Jonasson and
Pertti Hyttinen, with an Introduction by
Lars Magnusson. Translated from the
original by Peter C. Hogg**

Routledge
Taylor & Francis Group

LONDON AND NEW YORK

First published 2012 by Routledge

2 Park Square, Milton Park, Abingdon, Oxon OX14 4RN
711 Third Avenue, New York, NY 10017, USA

Routledge is an imprint of the Taylor & Francis Group, an informa business

First issued in paperback 2016

British Library Cataloguing in Publication Data
A catalogue record for this book is available from the British Library

Library of Congress Cataloging in Publication Data
A catalog record has been requested for this book

ISBN: 978-0-415-55133-5 (hbk)
ISBN: 978-1-138-68642-7 (pbk)

Typeset in Times
by Wearset Ltd, Boldon, Tyne and Wear

Contents

Illustrations

Foreword

Anders Chydenius (1729–1803) is one of the most noteworthy politicians in the Swedish realm during the eighteenth century. He is most of all remembered as an outspoken, and sometimes even fierce, defender of freedom in all areas of life. Chydenius's views on freedom of trade and industry, for instance, were a consequence of his general ideology of freedom. According to him, democracy, equality and respect for human rights were the only way towards progress and happiness for the whole of society.

One of the initiators of this volume, the Anders Chydenius Foundation, brings together researchers, thinkers, decision makers and other influential persons to deliberate on the legacy of Anders Chydenius and its significance for the current discussions on freedom of trade, freedom of information and freedom of religion. Since 2007, 2 December has been celebrated in Finland and Sweden as "Freedom of Information Day" to highlight the Nordic principle of transparency (*offentlighetsprincipen*). The date has been chosen in order to mark the anniversary of the world's first Freedom of Information Act, promulgated on 2 December 1766, which was one of the greatest achievements of Anders Chydenius.

In 2005 the Foundation, in cooperation with the University of Jyväskylä/ Kokkola University Consortium Chydenius and the Support Association of the Chydenius Institute, launched a project to publish a scientific edition of Anders Chydenius's collected works during the years 2006–12. The complete works will be published in five volumes in the original Swedish in the coming years. All five volumes will thereafter be translated into and published in Finnish. In addition, the Foundation and its partners decided to publish the principal works of Chydenius and a comprehensive biography in English. The complete works will also be accessible on Internet at a later stage.

This volume contains the principal works of Anders Chydenius, translated into English by Peter Hogg. Peter Hogg spent most of his career at the Department of Printed Books of the British Museum Library in London, from which he retired as head of the Scandinavian Section. The biography of Anders Chydenius and the comments and explanatory notes to the texts are written by Professor Lars Magnusson of Uppsala University. He is Professor of Economic History there and has written extensively on general and Swedish economic history as well as on the history of economic thought and doctrines. Michael F. Metcalf,

Professor of History and Senior International Officer at The University of Mississippi and an expert on the Age of Liberty in Swedish history, has provided comments and suggestions regarding the translations of several of the documents in this volume. Docent Kaj Sandberg, former director of the Institutum Romanum Finlandiae in Rome, has offered his expertise on ancient Greek and Roman history. The Taylor & Francis Group (Routledge) has agreed to publish this volume. On behalf of the Anders Chydenius Foundation and its partners, I would like to express my warmest gratitude to these experts and to Routledge for their valuable efforts and smooth cooperation.

This volume is especially funded by the Bank of Finland. Substantial financial contributions to this project have also been given by the Finnish Ministry of Education and Culture, the Swedish Cultural Foundation in Finland (Svenska kulturfonden), the Bank of Sweden Tercentenary Foundation (Stiftelsen Rikbankens Jubileumsfond), the Royal Swedish Academy of Letters, History and Antiquities, the City of Kokkola, Alfred Kordelin Foundation, Föreningen Konstsamfundet, Nokia Corporation, Nordea Bank Finland, Pohjolan Voima Oy, Metso Corporation and Sanoma Corporation. The steering group, composed of representatives of the financing bodies, has followed the project with great interest. The editorial board, composed of Professors Bo Lindberg, Juha Manninen and Jari Ojala, Docent Henrik Knif and the editors, Maren Jonasson and Pertti Hyttinen at Kokkola University Consortium Chydenius, has been responsible for the final version of this volume.

On behalf of the Anders Chydenius Foundation and as the chairman of the steering group and the editorial board, I would like to express my warmest thanks to all institutions and persons who have made it possible to publish this volume in English for an international audience. It is our sincere hope that it will increase interest in Anders Chydenius and his works, and inspire a lively debate on issues of vital interest for the worldwide current discussions on democracy, openness and freedom in every field of human activity.

Gustav Björkstrand
Chairman of the Anders Chydenius Foundation
Kokkola, 31 March 2011

Bank of Finland

Preface

The research community worldwide has over the years directed several inquiries to the Anders Chydenius Foundation in Finland and other institutions involved in promoting Anders Chydenius's legacy concerning the availability of English translations of his texts. Until now, they have been forced to reply that only one text is available in English, *The National Gain*, originally written in 1765 and published in English in 1931 by Ernest Benn Ltd. The same edition appeared in facsimile in 1994. The availability of these editions is, however, highly limited. Therefore, the time has definitely come to give Anders Chydenius's thoughts and views the attention they deserve, and thereby also provide the international community with a reliable source on the fascinating world of Chydenius. The demand for a high-quality and annotated English edition has long been manifest. Reading Chydenius's texts today, one is astonished by how modern his thoughts still seem, in a world where democracy, freedom of information and freedom of religion are burning questions worldwide.

Anticipating The Wealth of Nations: *The Selected Works of Anders Chydenius (1729–1803)* is part of a trilingual publishing project launched in 2005, *The Collected Works of Anders Chydenius*. The complete works will be published in an annotated, critical edition in Swedish and in a Finnish translation. In this volume *a selection* of Anders Chydenius's most important works is presented, together with a comprehensive biography in English. Anders Chydenius, a clergyman and an influential politician in the Swedish realm during the eighteenth century, advocated freedom of trade, the rights of the rural working class and an extension of freedom of expression and freedom of religion. He presented arguments for economic liberalism similar to those of his renowned contemporary Adam Smith. However, Chydenius's views have often remained unnoticed, largely because his writings have not been available to the research community in any critical edition, and only minimally in reliable translations.

The members of the editorial board feel convinced that the views of Anders Chydenius, as an eighteenth-century pioneer of freedom and democracy, most certainly will find their international audience, as we are witnessing a growing interest in research into these fields. We hope to reach a readership primarily consisting of academic researchers and professionals in the history of economic thought and history of ideas, both Smith scholars and others, but this volume is also intended for members of the general public with an interest in, for instance, questions related to freedom of information and freedom of religion. We believe this volume can serve as fruitful ground for future comparative studies, can raise intriguing new questions within several fields of academic research and can promote general discussion on these topics.

The editorial board has selected 11 texts by Chydenius for this volume. Roughly 85 written documents (including both printed documents and manuscripts) by him have survived. Only 12 letters in his hand have survived, which is noteworthy considering that during his adult years he was probably a busy letter-writer. The selection has been made according to certain criteria. The editorial board wanted to include texts that most likely would appeal to an international audience, pieces that thematically touch upon universal issues such as freedom of movement, expression, religion and enterprise. The pieces dealing with Chydenius's views on economic matters perhaps dominate somewhat in this selection. Although he wrote extensively on religious matters, homiletics in particular, none of his theological texts has been included, partly because his views in this regard were fairly common, partly because of their sheer length. Another criterion in selecting the texts was their importance at the time they were written. Many times, Chydenius's political pamphlets caused quite a stir and they actively promoted the process towards an extension of many freedoms and rights. The last piece included is his autobiography, written in 1780. It was selected for this volume because it sheds light on how Chydenius himself regarded his work and his input.

In the case of these 11 texts, selecting the editions on which the translations were to be based caused almost no difficulties, because as a rule they were printed only once during Chydenius's lifetime, or, in the case of manuscripts, only one written copy has survived. Two of the texts, *The Source of Our Country's Weakness* and *A Remedy for the Country by Means of a Natural System of Finance*, were, however, printed twice. In both cases the second edition was published within weeks of the first edition and the differences between the two are minuscule, consisting mainly of the corrections of mistakes made by the printer or typesetter and differences in spelling, and thus only rarely having any consequences for the translation. In both cases it has been impossible to decide which of the two editions was the first, as there is no explicit information or indicators in the editions to distinguish them from each other. The editorial board has therefore decided to base the translations on the ones containing fewer obvious mistakes, well aware of the possibility that the selected edition might be the second and not the first edition.

The publishing project was fortunate enough to engage retired librarian Peter Hogg in this demanding and sometimes very difficult task of translating eighteenth-century Swedish into modern English. The aim has been to create a translation that is loyal to the original without being stiff and cumbersome to read. Something that has been a real headache for Mr Hogg and the editors is Chydenius's habit of being somewhat inexact in his use of pronouns, making certain sentences almost impossible to understand, or giving the reader and the translator several alternative meanings to choose from. The structural resemblance between Swedish and English has allowed us to stay fairly loyal to the original, not forcing us to change the order of phrases or clauses too much. We have, however, chosen to split up some of the sentences; a single sentence in Chydenius's texts can easily stretch over ten to fifteen lines, which of course was very common at the time but would cause today's readers unnecessary strain.

The biggest challenge has been to come up with good English equivalents for the many political and administrative terms used in the original texts, names for different committees and institutions, laws and ordinances, which were often specific to the conditions in the Swedish realm and therefore do not have natural equivalents in English. The editorial board has consulted several experts and academic works, articles and books written on eighteenth-century Swedish conditions and events, and has tried to use the same (or similar) terms as the authors of these. In many cases, however, there seems to be very little consensus on which terms to use, and we, like others, have found ourselves inventing new terms in English. Occasionally we have supplied the text with the original Swedish term in parenthesis for the case of clarity.

A more comprehensive list of English terms, together with definitions of the corresponding Swedish terms, is given in a glossary towards the end of this volume.

Subjects, place names and persons mentioned in the texts have been indexed for the convenience of the reader. Names of places and persons have been given their modern form and spelling both in the translation and in the index. In cases where cities and other locations in today's Sweden and Finland have an English version of their name, i.e. Gothenburg, Karelia and Lapland, that form of the name has been used, whereas other cities and locations in today's Sweden are given their present-day name in Swedish, and cities and locations in present-day Finland are given their name in Finnish. Many cities and locations in Finland have a parallel form of their name in Swedish. In these latter cases, the parallel form in Swedish is mentioned in parenthesis the first time the name appears. In the eighteenth century a person's name often had a parallel form in Latin. The principle here has been to present the names in their current form, the way they are spelled today in Swedish, unless there is an internationally established form, i.e. for royalty and renowned scientists. Eighteenth-century currencies, measures and weights have kept their original form in the translated text, owing to the impracticality and impossibility of finding exact equivalents in the past or present English measuring systems. The complicated monetary system is clarified in a separate appendix, where currencies and monetary terms used in this volume are given a definition. Measures and weights are converted to modern metric measures and weights in an appendix.

The structure of this volume is easy to follow. First, Anders Chydenius's life and work are presented in a comprehensive biography written by Professor Lars Magnusson. The biography is followed by the selected works. Each text by Chydenius is followed by a short commentary placing the text in its historical and thematic context. All 11 commentaries are written by Professor Magnusson.

The 11 texts are divided thematically and chronologically into four parts. The first part consists of four texts, all written during the important Diet of 1765–6. The second part presents three texts on the issue of freedom of writing and printing, and free access to official documents, which Chydenius very actively promoted during the same Diet. The third part, consisting of three texts written during the late 1770s, deals with freedom of trade and industry and human rights issues. The fourth part consists of only one text, the already mentioned autobiography. Notes to the biography, to the translated texts and to the commentaries have been placed after each text. At the end of the book, we have included appendices, a glossary, a list of Anders Chydenius's central writings, indexes, and a bibliography.

On behalf of the editorial board,
editors Maren Jonasson and Pertti Hyttinen

Key events in Anders Chydenius's life

Figure 1 Anders Chydenius (1729–1803). Oil painting, Per Fjällström 1770. Alaveteli
Church.

1729	Anders Chydenius is born on 26 February in Sotkamo.
1734	His father, Jakob, is appointed rector of Kuusamo.
1739–41	Anders and his brother Samuel attend school in Oulu.
1744	Anders and Samuel receive private tuition by Rector Johan Wegelius in Tornio.
1745	Anders and Samuel commence their studies at the Academy in Turku.
1746	His father is appointed rector of Kokkola.
1750–1	Chydenius studies in Uppsala.
1753	He graduates and is ordained as a priest. He moves to Alaveteli to adopt the post of preacher.
1754	His mother dies.
1755	He marries Beata Magdalena Mellberg, a merchant's daughter.
1757	His brother Samuel drowns in a river, the Kokemäenjoki.
1760	He is promoted to the post of chaplain in Alaveteli.
1761	He takes part for the first time in a writing competition announced by the Royal Academy of Sciences.
1763	He speaks at the provincial council meeting in defence of staple rights.
1765–6	Chydenius attends the Diet in Stockholm for the first time and publishes several important tracts and treatises.
1766	He is expelled from the Estate of Clergy. His father dies.
1769	He is elected to the Diet in Norrköping, but his letter of appointment is rejected on his arrival and he returns home.
1770	Chydenius is appointed rector of Kokkola.
1778–9	He attends the Diet in Stockholm for the second time.
1779	He obtains the titles of Dean and Doctor *honoris causa* in theology. He joins the Society of Arts and Sciences in Gothenburg.
1781	He is awarded the title of rural dean.
1782	He joins the Theological Homiletic Society in Uppsala and takes part in its writing competition.
1786	Chydenius gives a speech at the execution grounds of Kruunupyy. Work to refurbish the parish church begins.
1790	He sets up a provisional hospital in Kokkola for victims of epidemics caused by the Russo-Swedish War.
1792	He attends the Diet, in Gävle, for the third time.
1795	Work to refurbish the town church in Kokkola begins.
1797	He joins the Royal Finnish Economic Society in Turku.
1803	Anders Chydenius dies in Kokkola on 1 February.

Anders Chydenius's life and work

An introduction

Lars Magnusson

Half a century ago the American economist Carl G. Uhr described Anders Chydenius as the Finnish "predecessor of Adam Smith". As early as the mid-1760s, Uhr argued, Chydenius had presented in a preliminary form the essence of Smith's grand theory, stressing particularly the importance of freedom of contract and the dynamic role of competition and division of labour. Furthermore, Chydenius had identified the search for individual gain as the foundation for public wealth and happiness. In contrast to Smith, however, he had not based his version upon a systematic moral or social philosophy. Instead, it was grounded in common sense and founded upon a democratic attitude arriving naturally from a man from the periphery.[1] Uhr was, however, not the first biographer of Chydenius to compare him with the great Scotsman. This tradition was started by the Finnish medical doctor Frans Johan Rabbe, writing in 1857.[2] Some years later, in 1880, the liberal writer and politician E.G. Palmén stated that, in particular, Chydenius's pamphlet *The National Gain*, published in 1765, although much more condensed, should "be placed alongside the famous Adam Smith's *Wealth of Nations* published eleven years later".[3] More than 50 years later this was still the view of the Swedish economic historian Eli F. Heckscher, who found a "striking similarity" between Smith's and Chydenius's conceptualizations of social society, although they had arrived at their views from very different origins. Heckscher stressed that Chydenius was not a theoretician but rather a self-taught man who through sound instinct had come to the conclusion that economic freedom should be regarded as a general principle, and that the "invisible hand" was the best available analytical tool for understanding economic life in general.[4]

However, especially in Palmén's eyes, Chydenius was something more than just a precursor of liberal economic doctrine. Palmén was a great admirer of Chydenius and was writing in 1880, when there was still hope that Finland would be able to retain its independent status within the Russian Empire and gradually develop its economy and polity in a more liberal direction, hence his interpretation of the eighteenth-century writer was clearly biased. According to Palmén, Chydenius was a Finnish patriot as well as a forerunner of economic, political and religious liberal thinking in the nineteenth-century meaning of the word. In the same vein, he was a democrat living well ahead of his time. Georg

Schauman, too, another biographer writing around the turn of the twentieth century, emphasized that Chydenius was "the first precursor of modern democracy in Sweden and Finland".[5] The patriotic side of Chydenius had already been strongly underlined by Rabbe in the 1850s. A practising physician himself, he especially stressed the enlightened role Chydenius had played in introducing vaccination against smallpox as early as the 1760s.[6] Rabbe implies that the efforts to introduce modern methods of treating illnesses went hand in hand with Chydenius's democratic and liberal attitudes. In the eyes of later interpreters and biographers, the role he played in the introduction of the Swedish Ordinance on Freedom of Writing and Printing in 1766 made him a prototype of a "modern" democrat. Lastly, his pivotal contribution to the passing of the Ordinance on Religious Freedom at the Diet of 1778–9 further contributed to such a characterization. On the other hand, Chydenius's rather conservative Lutheran outlook and his dislike of Voltaire perhaps do not seem a perfect fit with the image of an enlightened modern man, as was noted particularly by Georg Schauman.[7] Nevertheless, most of his biographers have insisted that in general he was far ahead of his time.

Too often, the writing of history in terms of predecessors and anticipations of more "modern" doctrines leads to anachronisms. As we have indicated, Chydenius's posterity has not avoided such a fate.[8] On the contrary, he has often (intentionally or not) been used in order to illustrate the progress of liberal views and attitudes, particularly in economic thinking. In this field he has been hailed as an early and radical opponent of the old *dirigisme* and the doctrine of mercantilism, paving the way for the new liberal synthesis of Adam Smith and classical political economy. Moreover, in a general sense Chydenius has been used to demonstrate the triumph of liberal doctrines and modernization. In particular, the suggestion that Chydenius's ideas and views were home-grown and based upon empirical common sense was explicitly used to bolster the rationale of economic and political liberal doctrine and policy as a logical step in the march of civilization. The way in which he *combined* liberal views on the economy as well as in polity and religion seemed to fit especially neatly into this picture.

However, such anachronisms most often lead us to misconceive and take out of context what historical actors – writers of economic pamphlets, for example – really wanted to say and argue. Hence, it is not possible to comprehend what a writer and political activist such as Anders Chydenius said and meant if we merely acknowledge him as a *predecessor* to something that arrived only later. Instead, we must stress that he most certainly was a man of his own time. As such, he took part in contemporary debates and political struggles clearly aware of what he wrote and what his intentions were; neither was he the "unconscious" tool of common sense suggested by later interpreters such as Heckscher and Uhr.[9] Hence, it is highly unfruitful to interpret his texts as immediately reflecting practical matters of the day. Instead, Chydenius was clearly involved in the intense intellectual discussions taking place during his time, for example with regard to moral philosophy. To emphasize that Chydenius was *not* a nineteenth-century democrat (or for that matter a Finnish patriot in its late-nineteenth-century meaning) does not diminish him or his work. As we will see later on, he was a radical even when seen in his own historical context. Moreover, we can still acknowledge his great intellectual qualities at the same time as we insist on placing him within his own historical and intellectual context. A man of great gifts he surely was; one contemporary, the Swedish historiographer royal Anders Schönberg, characterized him as "[t]his clergyman who was born with more wits than are needed in a chaplain's head".[10]

The Swedish realm in the eighteenth century

Anders Chydenius was born in 1729 in the small parish of Sotkamo, at present located in the region of Kainuu (Kajanaland) in northern Finland. The region was, and still is, sparsely populated and has a harsh climate. Before the twentieth century, its short summers and long winters created the basis of a meagre agriculture, sometimes of the primitive slash-and-burn type. On the other hand, other natural resources such as wood for charcoal, masts, planks and tar were plentiful, as were game and fish. Hence, in order to earn a living the peasant population combined agriculture with working in the woods, as well as engaging in a multitude of different handicrafts and taking part in petty trading. Tar in particular was an important export product of this region. In general, the few, and small, towns in this area (the county of Ostrobothnia) on the coast of the Baltic Sea, such as Oulu (Uleåborg) and Raahe (Brahestad), were located far apart and it could take days to reach them on foot or horseback. Hence, rivers and lakes played an important role in communication in this area. Against this background, making rivers and streams navigable was one of the most intensely debated issues of the day and led to a number of different plans and projects that Anders Chydenius would later in his life also take a keen interest in.

In 1734 Chydenius's father, Jakob Chydenius, was appointed rector (*kyrkoherde*) of the huge parish of Kemin Lappi (Kemi Lappmark), which was even further north than Sotkamo, and settled in Kuusamo near the present-day Russian border and only a little south of the Arctic Circle. Here the climate was even harsher and the economic conditions more primitive. The inhabitants were to a large degree dependent upon reindeer-rearing and what the woods and streams could provide in terms of game and fish.[11] Kuusamo was even further than Sotkamo from any town. It was here that Chydenius spent most of his childhood until his father was appointed rector of Kokkola (Gamlakarleby – today Karleby) further south in the heartland of Ostrobothnia. Later in life, Chydenius would recall, "I was ten years old before I saw any town".[12]

Finland as we know it today consisted of a number of provinces that had belonged to the Swedish realm since medieval times – and the provinces would remain in this position until 1809, when they were formed into an autonomous grand duchy within the Russian Empire. In contrast to the conditions under Russian rule – Russia accepted Finland's autonomy (up until the end of nineteenth century, at least) – the provinces were, in legislative, administrative and political terms, completely integrated into Sweden. This did not stop many Finns

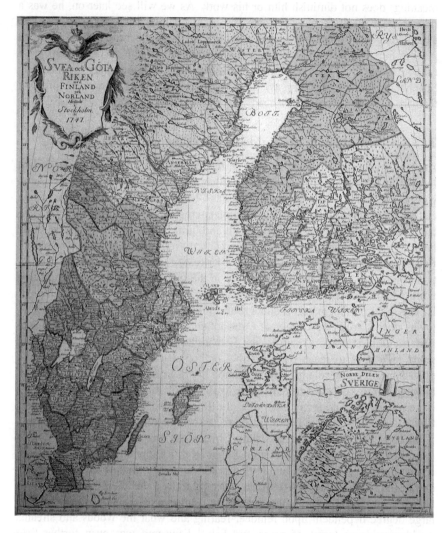

Figure 2 Map of Sweden, 1747. Copper engraving, G. Biurman. The National Board of
Antiquities, Finland.

– undoubtedly including Chydenius[13] – from feeling that they belonged to a less
privileged nation, one neglected by the Swedish Crown. That their native region
was more or less mistreated was a view voiced quite frequently. It was often said
that the Swedish kings were more eager to conscript Finnish males into their
armies than Swedish ones. Without doubt, there was more than a grain of truth
in such lamentations. The eastern part of the Swedish realm was generally speaking less developed than the southern and western parts. It had less industry and
its towns were even smaller. It housed only one town of significance, Turku
(Åbo), which had a population of less than 10,000 in the mid-eighteenth century.

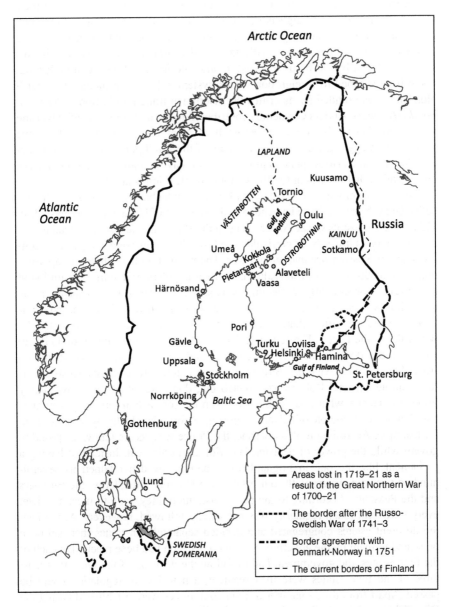

Figure 3 The Swedish realm during the eighteenth century: the most important border changes and places of importance in Anders Chydenius's life and works. Map by Jari Järvinen.

It was regarded as particularly unfair that the eastern part, or Finland, had only a few towns with so-called staple rights: apart from Turku, the only ones were Helsinki (Helsingfors) and Hamina (Fredrikshamn), while Sweden south of Stockholm had 20 towns with such privileges. A lack of staple rights meant that it was forbidden for the townsmen to export produce from that region on their own ships directly to foreign ports. In the north of Finland no town had such rights until 1765. According to the existing system of regulation, exportable produce from this region (especially tar but also timber, planks, various handicrafts, etc.) first had to be transported to and sold in Stockholm. Only after that could it be shipped to foreign ports. This system, which also included Swedish Norrland, was branded by its critics the "Bothnian trade prohibition" (*Bottniska handelstvånget*). Anders Chydenius contributed to its abolition in 1765. Over the years, it has been debated how effective this system in fact was, especially as we know that smuggling was frequent in many of the small ports. However, the fact that the system's critics spent so much effort on having it abolished at least gives an indication that it was not totally without practical importance.[14]

After the wars with Russia, Denmark and Brandenburg-Prussia *et al.* (the so-called Great Northern War) had ended with the Peace of Uusikaupunki (Nystad) in 1721, Sweden lost its Great Power status in the Baltic area and now instead had to turn its energies inwards. In particular, the Finnish regions were ravaged as a consequence of Russian occupation and war. The population here shrank to approximately 330,000 (the Swedish realm had a total population of some 1.8 million at the time).[15] Consequently, agriculture was suffering from a loss of hands at the same time as trade and commerce lay idle. The so-called political and constitutional "revolution" after Charles XII's death in 1718 replaced absolute monarchy with rule by the Diet.[16] The founding fathers of the new constitution of 1719–20 were without doubt influenced by contract and constitutional theory stemming from Hugo Grotius, Algernon Sidney and other natural law theorists. However, as for example Michael Roberts has pointed out, domestic influences were equally important. Hence, what was established was not a contractual form of governance based upon any principle of balance of power, as formulated later by Montesquieu, for example. According to this doctrine, the Prince was, as we know, supposed to govern while the power of decision lay with the parliament. Instead of having a parliament like the one in England, for example, Sweden retained its several-hundred-year-old system with four estates: the Nobility, the Clergy, the Burghers and the Peasants. According to the new constitution, they were to meet at a Diet every third year (such regularity was not strictly followed, however). At the Diet the different estates congregated and decided separately on issues that had been presented to them by the government. After a decision had been reached in each of the four estates, the government had to follow the decision of the Diet. If at least three of the four estates were in agreement, a new law or regulation could be passed. Apart from this, a number of joint committees were established during the Diets. They consisted of members from the different estates and their task was to prepare new legislation. As we will see, Chydenius took part in a number of them during the Diet of 1765–6.

As a main result of the constitution of 1719–20, the estates congregated at the Diets became the overwhelmingly dominating power. This meant that the monarch had very little legislative power; if indeed any.[17] The estates were regarded as corporations and had one vote at the Diet. This meant, for example, that no consideration was taken of the fact that the fourth estate, the Peasants, represented 80 per cent or more of the Swedish population. Also, the delegates in the estate chambers were elected by corporations: towns, hundreds (*härader*, local legal corporations outside the towns) and dioceses. In contrast to this, all noble families had the right to participate and vote in their estate (which meant that their gatherings at the House of Nobility (*Riddarhuset*) could be extremely crowded). Moreover, it was a strongly held principle that each member of an estate was responsible only to it. The idea that members might respond to or represent their own local constituencies was stigmatized as an extremely dangerous doctrine – the so-called doctrine of principalship (*principalatsläran*) – and had been strictly forbidden by law since 1744.[18] Of course, the king could exercise at least some power between the Diets, but the executive power, too, was by and large dominated by the estates. This meant, for example, that the king's government, or the Council of the Realm (*Riksrådet*), was responsible before the Diet for its decisions.

During the 1730s, two opposing interest groups with supporters in all four estates came into being: the famous parties of the Hats and the Caps.[19] Certainly they were not political parties in the modern sense of the word. They had no formal membership or clearly defined roles to play in the estates or at Diets. Even so, they had distinct political programmes and agendas. Furthermore, they also had their base in different socio-economic groupings. Typically, the Hats found their followers among the nobility, but perhaps even more so among wealthy burghers (especially the merchants in Stockholm, the so-called *Skeppsbroadeln*), owners of ironworks and steel manufacturing plants (*brukspatroner*), as well as state officials of higher ranking. The ranks of the Caps, on the other hand, were swollen by men of lower status: peasants, petty burghers from the small towns, as well as clergymen. Up to the 1750s, however, the nobility was still able to dominate the Cap party. It was also identified as the "English" party, in contrast to the Hats, who were considered to be "French". Accordingly, the two parties differed in their views on contemporary foreign policy and Sweden's position in the European power system. To what extent their policies were based upon principled arguments can be debated. According to malicious reports, at least, the two parties' finances were heavily dependent upon secret funding stemming from France or England (and Russia). During the 1760s the Cap party was in reality split between the more radical "younger Caps", dominated by people of lower ranking, and the conservative "older Caps", still to a large degree dominated by noblemen.[20]

However, there were many exceptions to this stylized picture (for example, many bishops were Hats, while the lower clergy voted for the Caps), and it was not unusual for individuals to change their sympathies during one and the same Diet. Moreover, in order to guarantee that law, order and social hierarchy were preserved, a special Secret Committee (*Sekreta utskottet*) was inaugurated. The Estate of Peasants was excluded from the Secret Committee, which dealt with the most important matters, such as Sweden's foreign policy. Up until the dramatic events at the Diet of 1765–6 (to which Anders Chydenius vividly contributed), the Secret Committee was dominated by the Nobility and the Hat party.

Hence, there is little to suggest that the Swedish constitutional and political order after the fall of absolutism was democratic in any modern sense of the word. In particular, the stubborn resistance to making members of the Diets responsible to their local constituencies, as well as the estates' dominance of both the legislative and the executive power, argue against such a conclusion. On the other hand, the increased role given to the estates led contemporaries during this period to speak of an "Age of Liberty".[21] In Swedish and Finnish historiography this age is generally defined as the period beginning in 1719 and ending with the *coup d'état* of Gustavus III in 1772. By and large, it is this political context to which Anders Chydenius refers in his texts. Increasingly over time – as we will see – he becomes critical of the very foundation upon which political rule during the Age of Liberty was founded. He came to dislike in principle a polity made up of competing parties. More and more he leaned towards a system with a strong monarch. Hence, his political attitudes were quite complex and perhaps not so "modern" as has often been suggested – an issue we will return to.

While the Age of Liberty was not "democratic" in a modern sense, the term might nevertheless be accurate from another perspective. The 1730s in particular saw the opening up of a lively public debate dealing with political, economic, social and scientific issues.[22] In books, pamphlets and journals – made possible by a generous attitude towards the freedom of the press – proposals for promoting economic development and modernization were presented. Not everything was allowed, of course (as the case of Chydenius during the Diet of 1765–6 clearly illustrates). Until the Ordinance on Freedom of Writing and Printing was passed, in 1766, every printed text had to be approved by a censor; at the time of the stormy Diets in the 1760s, this position was held by a professor from Lund, Niclas von Oelreich. On the whole he seems seldom to have used his power to censor: according to the gossip, the censor's libertarianism was said to derive from the fact that he was paid for every pamphlet and book that he allowed to be published. The system was therefore rather flexible and could easily be manipulated. Censorship was, however, used as a force in the political battle between the Hats and the Caps, as the printed media could be used to expose the flaws and errors of the opposing party. Although political tracts and treatises could be published rather freely, religious literature was still eagerly scrutinized in order to detect blasphemous utterances and critique of the established Church dogmas.

During the Age of Liberty a clear ambition was to spread new scientific ideas, encourage the introduction of new methods and practices in agriculture, and find means and ways to establish more trade and manufactures. Swedish historians have often labelled this spirit, which dominated the public discussion during the Age of Liberty, as "utilistic".[23] Hence, the introduction and practical use of new knowledge was aimed at enhancing national honour and prosperity. In order to re-establish Sweden as a Great Power, the development of sciences and the spread of useful knowledge were essential. The patriotic aim was to strengthen Sweden's international power position through an enlarged and more productive agriculture as well as by more foreign trade and manufactures. An enlarged economy would in turn render possible a rapid growth of population. No state could grow strong and powerful without a large population, according to the prevailing view. Moreover, the Hats especially (the Caps in the 1760s mainly favoured agricultural improvements) insisted that the most prosperous state at the time, the Dutch Republic, could only have emerged as such because of its expanding foreign trade and its manufactured goods – which made possible a dense population. For Swedish patriotic writers, the lesson to be learned was clear: a poor country with a small population and without industry and trade could not compete with the other European states. To regain what had been lost in the Peace of Uusikaupunki, economic reforms and growth were necessary, and to that end the visible hand of the state was needed.[24]

In order to contribute to this development a number of initiatives were taken. First, to stimulate useful scientific research and spread innovations, a Swedish Royal Academy of Sciences was inaugurated in 1739. According to its statutes, its aim was to promote science in general, but in practice it developed into a society mainly for the improvement of agriculture with the intention of increasing the population level.[25] Almost immediately it began publishing learned letters and articles on a multitude of topics in order to spread novel and useful scientific ideas. It also launched prize competitions in which writers were asked to deliver answers to specified issues, competitions that were partly responsible for stimulating Chydenius to take up his political pen. Other learned societies with "utilistic" and patriotic aims, too, were established in order to stimulate improvements, including the Patriotic Society (*Patriotiska sällskapet*) in 1772. Moreover, starting in the 1790s, rural economy and agricultural societies (*Hushållningssällskap*) were established at the county level in order to introduce new tools, machines and methods of production in the farming sector.

Second, steps were also taken at the universities. At Uppsala University, the oldest in Sweden, the professor of botany in the Faculty of Medicine, Carolus Linnaeus (after his ennoblement in 1761 Carl von Linné), was a clear proponent of "utilism" in order to enhance the power and glory of Sweden. But the new chairs in the economic sciences were also established for practical purposes, the first being in Uppsala in 1741, followed by Turku in 1747 and Lund in 1750.[26] Much to the dislike of Linnaeus, the new chair in Uppsala was placed within the Faculty of Law rather than in Medicine, with the title *jurisprudentiae, oeconomiae et commerciorum professor*. Linnaeus insisted that economics was the principal science, upon which physics and all other natural scinces were dependent and upon which the temporal well-being of all humans rested.[27] But in Uppsala the first professor of the new subject, Anders Berch, concentrated his lecturing activities on economic legislation and governance (police or *polizey*). On the other hand, Berch was known for collecting models of new agricultural tools

Figure 4 Observations made on Pehr Kalm's travels to America were the starting point for Anders Chydenius's graduate thesis *American Birchbark Boats*. Chydenius believed that the bark canoe, used by the Native American Indians and later also by the French settlers, could well be suited also for conditions in Finland. Copper engraving by Anders Chydenius, 1753. The National Library of Finland.

J. J. N.

AMERICANſka
Näſwerbåtar,
Beſkrefna/

och med

Wederbörandes tilſtädielſe/

Under

Oeconomiæ PROFESSORENS, och Kongl. Wettenſk.
Academ. Ledamots/

Herr PEHR KALMS,
Inſeende/

För Magiſter Krantſens ärhållande

Utgifne/

Och til almänt ompröfwande öfwerlämnade i Åbo Academies
öfre Sal f. m. den 26. Maij 1753.

Af

ANDERS CHYDENIUS,
Öſterbottninge.

ÅBO Tryckt, hos Directeuren och Kongl. Boktr. i Stor-
Förſtendömet Finland, JACOB MERCKELL.

such as ploughs, harrows and threshing machines and putting them on display in his lecturing premises close to the Fyris River, the *Theatrum oeconomicum*. Hence, for him too, improvement of agriculture was part of the tutorial programme. In Lund and Turku the connection to agriculture was even more clearly expressed. In Lund the first professor, Clas Blechert Trozelius, advised his students to take up such mundane topics as cattle-rearing, bee-keeping and the proper way to build farmhouses and stables, while Pehr Kalm in Turku, who since 1747 had held a chair in *Professione scientiæ oeconomicæ*, was regarded as an economist even though he was most interested in his collection of stones and minerals.

Third, the stimulation of economic growth was also a cornerstone of economic policy and regulation during the Age of Liberty. While earlier regulations had been very strict on matters such as the division of farms – no doubt in order to hinder pauperization – the public discussion now took a new turn to stimulate reforms. Hence, in 1747 a more liberal regulation concerning the splitting up of farms (*hemmansklyvning*) was inaugurated. The aim was to stimulate farmers to take up new land through reforesting or by digging ditches in order to reclaim wetlands that previously had not been in use. As a consequence, the legislators hoped, population would increase considerably. Another important step was the introduction of the great redistribution of landholdings, which started in the 1750s. The General Redistribution Act of 1757 (*storskiftet*) was followed by other acts of redistribution in 1803 and 1827. The idea was to stimulate individual initiative in order to introduce more effective methods of production. Rightly or wrongly, it was taken for granted that the old collectivist strip-farming was detrimental to productivity (as well as to the reclaiming of more land). To what extent such reforms contributed to the undisputed growth of agriculture which started in the 1720s and lasted until the 1770s is not easy to say. Perhaps the more peaceful conditions that dominated during most of the Age of Liberty played an even more pivotal role – a population growth that led to more hands becoming available, which in turn meant more land could be put under the plough.[28] This progress was temporarily halted in the 1770s during the reign of Gustavus III with the emergence of what has been described as the last Malthusian crisis in Swedish agriculture.[29] The suggested reason for the hunger crisis was that the increase of population had not been matched by an increase of production sufficiently great to support it. Despite all attempts and suggestions for improvement, productivity had remained low and the traditional agricultural methods had exhausted the resource base. However, when the wheels began to turn again at the beginning of the nineteenth century, after some decades of agricultural crisis, this was perhaps the most important long-term effect of the reform activities initiated during the Age of Liberty.

High hopes and reform activity were not restricted to the agricultural sector. As in many other European countries during the eighteenth century, the authorities in the Swedish realm were more than willing to support the establishment of manufactories. The aim was to establish centralized enterprises for the production of industrial wares such as cloth, paper, glass and other useful items of consumption, but also luxuries such as tobacco, silk, porcelain, etc. Although their actual organization often differed – most manufactories both in Sweden and elsewhere combined centralized proto-factory production with putting-out activities (the *Verlag* system) – they were clearly distinguishable from the old crafts practised in the towns. Most pertinently, they had a distinct legislative status and were governed by particular laws and privileges.[30] Moreover, manufactory owners were not members of guilds or other town corporations; quite often they carried out their operations in premises located outside towns. The aim of supporting such manufactories was, as elsewhere in Europe, to contribute to economic modernization and growth, to increase population and to strengthen political and military power (many manufactories concentrated on producing supplies for the army and the fleet). The basic idea was to replace expensive imports by domestic production and develop an industrial policy strategy that in later times has been named "import substitution". Clearly, the motive was not only to increase economic growth but also to strengthen military and national power. Developing a domestic industry meant that a state would no longer have to rely on foreign imports, which could be especially beneficial during periods of war and conflict – no doubt an almost endemic situation during the middle of the eighteenth century.

In the Swedish realm, special legislation based upon far-reaching privileges for the iron and steel industry had developed during the seventeenth century. At the end of that century, similar kinds of privileges were also granted to owners of manufactories. However, the breakthrough for such a policy occurred following the Diet of 1738–9, when the Hat party came to power. At this Diet a financial fund for the support of manufactories was established, the *Manufakturfonden*. Simultaneously, an office was inaugurated in order to monitor the exclusive legislative framework put forward by the government, the Manufactures Office (*Manufakturkontoret*). From now on, generous subsidies poured out of the state coffers in order to establish enterprises producing wool and linen (also silk) textiles, paper, porcelain, glass and other items. Best known became the manufactories established by Jonas Alströmer in a small town in the west of Sweden, Alingsås. With the help of subsidies he established a whole set of manufactories there, including both textile manufactories and a tobacco-spinning factory, an oddity in Sweden at the time, producing tobacco from home-grown plants. When this policy of protection and financial support began to receive severe criticism in the 1760s, it was easy to point to the case of Alströmer.[31] To some extent such a critical attitude must be said to have been justified: without the support of the state, many manufactories withered away when the Caps took over power after 1765.[32] No doubt the established manufacture policy was looked upon by many as a typical feature of corrupting tendencies and rent-seeking activities on the part of wealthy merchants, speculators and money-jobbers, who constituted the leading circle of the Hat party – a group which would be attacked fiercely at the Diet of 1765–6, not least by Chydenius.

It is largely against this background of the introduction of an economic policy of regulation – most specifically regarding the manufactories – that the specific economic discussion during the Age of Liberty should be contextualized. Those who favoured state regulation as a means to achieve economic growth have been named "mercantilists" by later historians of economic doctrines from Sweden and Finland, while those more critical of such regulation have been labelled "reform-mercantilists".[33] For example, E.F. Heckscher found in the textbook *Inledning til almänna hushålningen* (1747), by Anders Berch, the first professor of economy at Uppsala, a full programme of conservative "mercantilist" regulation that he regarded as typical for the time.[34] Clearly inspired by German and Austrian cameralists such as von Rohr, Dithmar, Lau and others, Berch divided his subject matter into three parts: "police" (*polizey*), "cameralism" and "economy". Berch was in principle favourable towards state intervention in order to steer the economy in the right direction. At times he went so far as to propound policies not too far from what we today would label as leading to a "planned economy". Thus, arguing for a yearly calculation to be carried out by the state concerning the number of young people needed in each trade and occupation, he wrote:

> No less mistaken is the view put forward ... that economic equilibrium could be accomplished by itself if only one had a free right to choose one's own occupation.... Why should we run the risk of making a detour instead of taking the short cut?[35]

Berch was in favour of most of the economic regulations that existed at the time, including the prohibitions against rural trade, and the privileges of cities. If the rural population were free to trade on its own, it would ruin the towns while the peasants neglected to tend to their fields, he maintained. Similarly, he was in favour of regulations concerning foreign trade including the staple system. The so-called Commodity Ordinance (*produktplakatet*) also belonged to this system of policy. Influenced by the English Navigation Acts from the middle of the seventeenth century, this ordinance was inaugurated in 1724 and made even more restrictive two years later. It was aimed at inhibiting foreigners from shipping to Sweden anything but their own produce. By this means, practical opportunities for foreign merchants to take part in the Swedish exporting were eliminated, which was intended to create opportunities for the Swedish merchant fleet to grow. Moreover, Berch favoured the policy of manufactories and regarded subsidies as essential for their establishment. In line with many others at the time, he regarded national manufactories as a most beneficial counterweight to "excessive" imports from abroad, especially of luxury items. On the other hand, like other debaters in the economic discussion during this period, he was very critical of the prevailing guild system. He designated the guilds as "monopolists" and, as such, as harmful as the opposite system of "polipoly" (free trade and competition), using the vocabulary of the seventeenth-century German economic writer Johann Joachim Becher. Other important "mercantilist" writers supporting the existent system of regulation were Eric Salander, Johan Fredrik Kryger (both of them high officials at the Manufactures Office) and the brothers Edvard Fredric and Ephraim Otto Runeberg, who were Finns by origin. While Kryger pointed out that free enterprise must lead to a situation in which "no one wants to be a labourer",[36] Salander emphasized that "all small craftsmen will be ruined because all would like to be masters".[37]

However, especially from the 1750s onwards many voices were raised against some of these regulations, or even against the logic of the system as a whole. As has been mentioned, this group of writers have been called "reform-mercantilists". They shared a number of viewpoints concerning, and criticisms against, the prevailing regulative system, in many cases based upon a specific philosophy of humankind and the natural order. It is within this intellectual context that Anders Chydenius must be placed. Hence, it was not mere intuition that led him to formulate his programme of economic and political freedom. Instead, he is better characterized as perhaps the most radical of the reform-mercantilists, drawing with great clarity and weight the conclusions that he believed followed only naturally from his moral-philosophical as well as religious premises.

Life and career up to 1765

Anders Chydenius was born in Sotkamo on 26 February 1729 as the second child of eight to the (at that time) curate Jakob Chydenius (1703–66) and his wife Hedvig, *née* Hornaeus (1699–1754). Both Jakob and Hedvig were born into clerical families with long-standing roots in the local Lutheran church. Since there were only a few persons or families of rank in the area surrounding Sotkamo, Chydenius at an early age learned to speak Finnish, the language of the peasantry in the area, as well as Swedish, his native language. Of his five brothers and sisters who survived to adult age, Anders' older brother Samuel (1727–57) studied in both Uppsala and Turku, where he subsequently became docent and assistant professor. He was also a junior member of the Royal Academy of Sciences in Stockholm. Samuel was regarded as a brilliant young scholar in various natural sciences such as chemistry, physics and mineralogy. He was a pupil of Christopher Polhem and became a renowned expert on inland traffic and the clearance of waterways to make them navigable. At the age of only 30, he was, sadly, drowned while investigating the possibility of using the Kokemäenjoki (Kumo älv), a river in south-western Finland, for navigation purposes. Given the important role of rivers for navigation and transport in this roadless region, this was a typical "useful" and patriotic subject for a young scholar at the Academy in Turku to take on, working under the auspices of Professor Pehr Kalm.[38]

Spending his childhood days in distant Lapland, Anders was sent with his older brother to study in Turku and Uppsala before the family moved to Kokkola in 1746. Hence, both Samuel and Anders matriculated at Turku during the autumn semester of 1745. The following years Anders mainly spent either at the university or at home in Kokkola helping his father with his priestly duties. In 1750 he followed Samuel to Uppsala but stayed only one year. In 1753 he graduated from the Academy in Turku by becoming consecrated as a priest and by

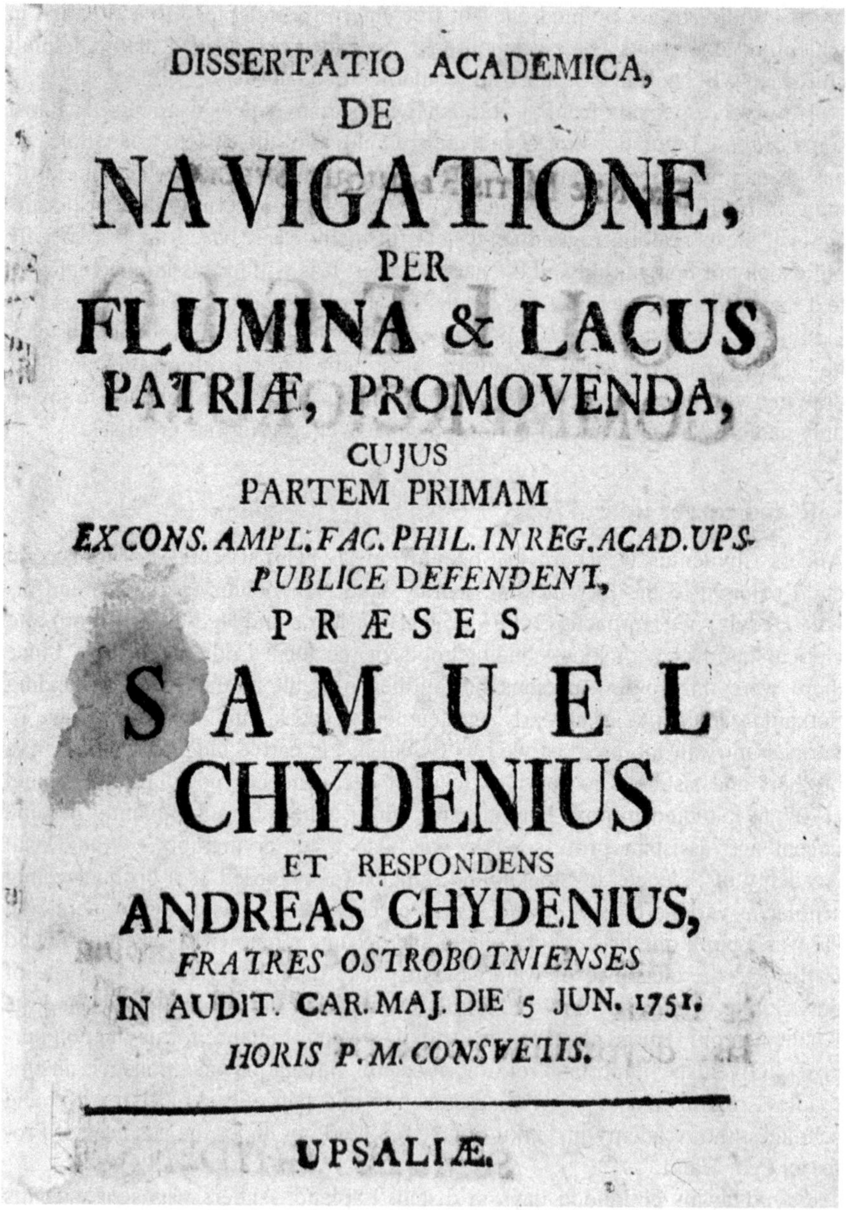

DISSERTATIO ACADEMICA,
DE
NAVIGATIONE,
PER
FLUMINA & LACUS
PATRIÆ, PROMOVENDA,
CUJUS
PARTEM PRIMAM
*EX CONS. AMPL. FAC. PHIL. IN REG. ACAD. UPS-
PUBLICE DEFENDENT,*
PRÆSES
SAMUEL
CHYDENIUS
ET RESPONDENS
ANDREAS CHYDENIUS,
FRATRES OSTROBOTNIENSES
IN AUDIT. CAR. MAJ. DIE 5 JUN. 1751.
HORIS P. M. CONSVETIS.

UPSALIÆ.

Figure 6 At Uppsala, Anders presented the counter-arguments to his brother Samuel's Master's degree dissertation, which was about the development of inland waterways. Samuel Chydenius was a versatile naturalist whose promising career was cut short by his accidental death at the age of 30. S. Chydenius, *De navigatione, per flumina & lacus patriae promovenda*, Upsaliæ, 1751. Kokkola University Consortium Chydenius.

taking a Master's degree under Professor Kalm. His dissertation, *Americanska näfwerbåtar* ("American birchbark boats") was written in Swedish, which was not so common at the time but very much in line with the passion for economics and "utilism" during the eighteenth century.[39] The choice of topic originated no doubt from his professor. As one of the famous student "apostles" of the great Linnaeus in Uppsala, Kalm was sent to North America in 1747 in order to collect plants and to investigate the area from an economic perspective, which included the economy of the native inhabitants. When he returned after three years he compiled *En resa till Norra Amerika* (1753–61), which was rapidly translated into German, Dutch and English. *Travels into North America* was published in London in 1770–2.[40]

When Chydenius in his autobiography 30 years later recalled his student years, for some reason he forgot to mention his theology studies. Instead, he seemed keener to mention his "fiddling around" with mathematics, astronomy, mechanics, etc. during his two semesters in Uppsala.[41] But his study of theology and particularly philosophy at Turku under Professor Johan Browallius without doubt had a profound influence on him – as we will note later. Browallius combined a keen interest in the natural sciences with the teaching of theology. He was not uncritical of the prevailing orthodoxy and was clearly influenced by the Prussian philosophy professor Christian Wolff, who at the time was very influential in the Swedish realm.[42] Although Browallius did not completely accept Wolffian rationalism, he agreed with Wolff that God had created a universal natural order which it was the duty of the (natural) sciences to grasp and categorize. This is the basis of the famous so-called physico-theology, which influenced a whole generation of Swedish scholars and writers – including in such subjects as economics.[43] Another profound influence upon Anders Chydenius was his teacher of philosophy at Turku, C.F. Mennander. Lecturing on Pufendorf's seminal *De officio hominis et civis*, Mennander emphasized natural law for grasping the duties and obligations of humankind. God had made all men equal in the sense that they were able to grasp his creation. More profoundly perhaps than Pufendorf, Mennander also emphasized that men were equal by birth.[44] Thus, existing inequalities in society were based upon a contract that men had made with each other, not on the natural order as such. This was of course a radical position during this period, and from it Chydenius would draw some disturbing conclusions from the point of view of current orthodox ideology.[45]

At the same time as Chydenius was consecrated into the Church, he was also appointed to his first position: to become a preacher at Alaveteli (Nedervetil), an arrangement that made him a subordinate under his father, the rector of Kokkola parish. His true feelings with regard to this we cannot be sure of, only that this arrangement seems at least partly to have been based upon his own choice. Although he failed to obtain a position as a university lecturer (docent), he could without doubt have stayed at the Academy in Turku. However, during his student years he had already spent time helping his father in the church, and possibly Chydenius felt obliged to assist the latter in view of his advancing years. However, in the Church hierarchy the position of preacher was the lowest

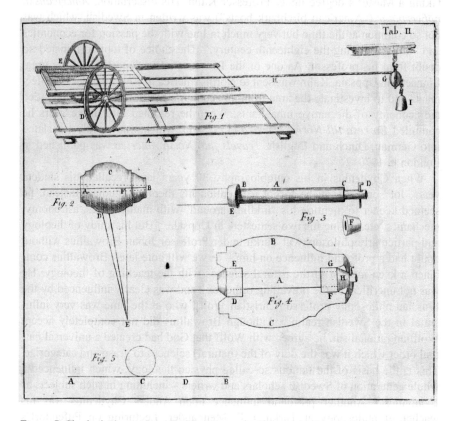

Tab. II.

Figure 7 Chydenius's essay on the improvement of carts gained second place in the prize
essay contest of the Academy of Sciences in 1764. Chydenius felt he had suffered a wrong and for a long time he was bitter about his defeat, which was
typical of his uncompromising attitude. Copper engraving by Anders Chydenius, 1764. Kokkola University Consortium Chydenius.

possible. His first step up the ladder was when he was appointed chaplain at
Alaveteli in 1760. Although carving out his existence on a meagre wage, he was
able to marry Beata Magdalena Mellberg in 1755, the daughter of a merchant
with some wealth from Pietarsaari (Jakobstad), who left a handsome 100,000
daler kmt when he died, in 1769.

Alaveteli at this time housed a small congregation of fewer than 600 inhabitants, mainly peasants and their families, together with a small number of craftsmen and soldiers. Chydenius's younger brother Jakob gave the following picture
of the situation in Kokkola (including Alaveteli) in 1754:

> The inhabitants seem in general to be quite proper and clean with regard to
> their houses and clothing. They are also in general sober, cheerful and
> industrious. They are diligent in different crafts, particularly woodworking,

and they are also ready to pick up new schemes when they feel there is something to gain from it. They are in general clever, polite and civil to the extent to be expected from mere peasants, as well as quite affluent.[46]

Besides his churchly duties and assisting his father, Chydenius spent most of his time trying to improve cultivation at his own farm. Rural clergymen in the Swedish realm were as much farmers as they were priests, and Anders Chydenius was no exception to this rule. In Chydenius's case this was even more necessary because the family could hardly survive on the small wage (disbursed by the congregation in barrels of grain, wool and other items) he received from his parish. By reclaiming new land, digging ditches and introducing new plants and crops, he seems to personify well the kind of diligent cultivator hailed in contemporary articles and letters published by the learned and patriotic societies in Stockholm. In 1766 he even started to grow tobacco and then some years later a novel crop: the potato. It was also during his time in Alaveteli that he began his medical activities, especially providing care for children. To improve health care in order to enable more children to survive (including introducing a state-controlled midwifery system) was part of the "utilistic" programme of the time and must be seen in relation to the political importance given to increasing the population. The early experimentation by Chydenius (together with his father) with vaccination against smallpox (perhaps starting in 1761) has already been mentioned. He was particularly proud of this, and it made him known to well-placed persons in Stockholm. He would return to this issue in one of the last pieces he wrote, published posthumously almost 40 years later.[47] He was also known for the extraction of a special liquid useful for healing sore eyes as well as for his surgical operations on eyes. He heard about new ideas regarding both the improvement of cultivation and medical treatments from the journals and books that were streaming out of the printing presses at the time. In Kokkola, Chydenius's father kept a not insignificant library, including books that had belonged to his oldest son, Samuel. The old man was also a keen subscriber to publications and journals issued by the Royal Academy of Sciences and other learned societies.

By around 1761, Chydenius had formed most of the radical political and economic ideas he would propound during the Diet of 1765–6 – and indeed for the rest of his life. An important influence here was his reading of some of Anders Nordencrantz's most important works. In his autobiography he particularly refers to the vitriolic attack on the Hat regime that Nordencrantz published in 1759, *Til riksens höglofl. ständer församlade wid riksdagen år 1760*. In a highly critical tone, Nordencrantz here held up to particularly close scrutiny the inflationary effects of the government's monetary policy. With the help of contemporary foreign literature (French *économistes* as well English moral philosophical works), he condemned economic *dirigisme* in a more general sense. The fact that Chydenius was especially influenced in his political and economic thinking by Nordencrantz was very well acknowledged by his contemporaries during the Diet of 1765–6, and this was also something he openly admitted. At times he spoke of Nordencrantz with great respect as his foremost "teacher".

The first proof of how much he had learned from Nordencrantz – and later perhaps superseded him – came in the written response that he presented to a prize question put 1763 by the Royal Academy of Sciences concerning "the cause of so many people annually emigrating from this country". However, this was not the first time he had taken part in such prize essay contests. In 1761 he had responded to a call from the same Academy with a piece titled "A response to the question regarding the best ways and means to cultivate moss-covered meadows". Two years later he returned with an answer to another Academy question, namely how a cart could be built to carry a considerably heavier load than the usual model. In this case his essay gained him a silver medal – although Chydenius himself thought he should have received the gold medal and complained to the Academy that the only reason why he had not won was because the Academy was biased in declaring one of its own members, Jacob Faggot, the winner.

Chydenius's essay on emigration included a general attack on the prevailing regulative system, including the Commodity Ordinance, the staple rights policy, the prohibition on rural trade, subsidies to manufactures, and much more. Many of his points echoed what Nordencrantz had said earlier, but there were also

Figure 8 Chydenius's contribution to the prize essay contest concerning the best ways and means to cultivate moss-covered meadows (1762) was published in German in Daniel Gottfried Schreber's *Neue Cameralschriften* (1765). The National Library of Finland.

some important additions, especially concerning the effects of the government's export policies. In all, the Royal Academy received 30 answers. Without any doubt Chydenius's piece stood out. It contained a full programme of radical reform-mercantilism written in a clear style and with precise arguments. But because of the Academy's consternation, in the end none of the contributions was rewarded with a prize and it refused to publish them. The competition had opened up a flood of critique – among which Chydenius's was by far the most radical – of a critical stance which the authorities had not expected.

The piece on emigration was not the first text Chydenius had written concerning economic matters. An unpublished manuscript most probably written in 1761 or 1762 was found by Georg Schauman when he was going through Chydenius's personal and domestic papers. It was written in a form presenting answers to three different questions concerning economic policy: first, whether it was beneficial or not for a nation to export money to other countries; second, whether the public's distrust of representative money (banknotes) was well-founded or not; and third, whether servants should be forced to go into service, or even be allocated to serve a particular master by local authorities, a discussion going on at the time. These were themes that Chydenius would return to in later texts. Especially in his discussion on servants, he formulates a belief in the natural freedom of men, a belief that he would return to again and again. In general this is something that starkly underlines his argumentation in the printed essay concerning the causes behind emigration from the Swedish realm.

One major political issue in the Finnish part of the Swedish realm at the time was the staple towns policy, which was felt to hamper the trade and economic development of this area. It was argued that a reform was necessary in order to make it possible for local merchants to trade directly with merchants in foreign ports. It was said that the trade of tar and other wood products in particular was negatively affected by the present system of regulation. Especially during the Diet of 1760–2, this topic became a heated issue, and a memorial was published by Per (Petter) Stenhagen, a merchant from Kokkola, backed up by the local representatives from three of the estates (the Burghers, the Peasants and the Clergy). This author argued for the establishment of no fewer than three staple towns in Ostrobothnia.[48] However, a positive decision in this direction was blocked by the Burghers (of whom the Stockholm representatives were the most active). Against this background, protest meetings were held in Ostrobothnia, and Chydenius made his political debut at one of the meetings held in Kokkola on 17 February 1763. He had written a manuscript for the occasion, which he read before an audience of angry protesters. This manuscript is lost, but it was very possibly an early version of the pamphlet he published in 1765.

In his autobiography, Chydenius depicts the February meeting in dramatic colours, suggesting that he was close to being arrested by the police – the likelihood of which has been put in doubt by his later biographers.[49] But however that may be, it was undoubtedly this gathering that made the chaplain from Alaveteli known to a wider audience, and ultimately earned him a ticket to Stockholm two years later as one of the representatives of the Ostrobothnian clergy.

The Diet of 1765–6

It was the issue of the staple rights – by far the most important political issue at the time from an Ostrobothnian perspective – that to a large extent paved the way for Chydenius's debut at the Diet of 1765–6. However, his road to becoming a delegate for his estate was a long and winding one. Initially, some influential leaders of the Cap party in Finland seem to have taken notice of the radical young chaplain. Among them the three brothers Per Niklas, Gabriel and Matthias Mathesius – sons of Nils Mathesius, the rector at Pyhäjoki – seem to have been the most important.[50] They were all radical opponents of the Hat government, and, together with other family members, present and past, active in the Estate of Clergy (Gabriel was appointed dean in Uppsala in 1766).[51] Chydenius was obviously successful in convincing the brothers Mathesius and others that he was the right man to send to Stockholm in order to work for a reform concerning the staple question. However, to become elected he had to be voted in by his corporation, and this was indeed a complicated process. It remained unclear until the beginning of the Diet whether or not the more humble chaplains were allowed to send a delegate of their own.[52] When Chydenius arrived in Stockholm it was first said that the clergymen in Ostrobothnia had made a mistake: chaplains were not worthy to become delegates. This did not, however, hinder Chydenius from being voted in by a majority of his estate. As we will see later on, he would take a very active part in the debates and activities during the Diet, and in this respect he could not have disappointed his patrons.[53] His first intervention, first delivered orally and then in a written memorial, clearly made many ponder how this novice from remote Ostrobothnia could speak up in such radical language: he starkly proclaimed that no one who had been the least involved in the affairs of the Bank of the Estates or the Ironmasters' Association or had handled the state finances in the past should be allowed to be a member of a Diet committee.[54]

Shortly after his arrival in Stockholm he published a short pamphlet, probably based on the manuscript written in 1763, arguing for the right of the citizens of Ostrobothnia and Västerbotten to sail wherever they wished with their products: "Refutation of the Reasons Employed to Deny the Towns in Ostrobothnia and Västerbotten as well as in Västernorrland a Free Navigation".[55] A struggle that had been going on for decades finally ended when the estates granted staple rights to two towns in Norrland and four towns in Ostrobothnia, including Kokkola. The right that was granted was of significant importance for the development of these towns later, during the nineteenth century.

It was his work in different committees and in the estate that stimulated Chydenius to write a number of his best-known tracts (all published in this volume), including "The Source of Our Country's Weakness" (*Källan til rikets wan-magt*, 1765), "The National Gain" (*Den nationnale winsten*, 1765) and "A Remedy for the Country by Means of a Natural System of Finance" (*Rikets hjelp, genom en naturlig finance-system*, 1766). Moreover, his contribution in helping to pass the ordinance for an extended freedom of printing in 1766 was without doubt decisive. Maybe he was a bit too active? As we will see, some may have thought that the young chaplain overstretched himself a little, and were quite relieved when he was suddenly excluded from the Diet and sent home during the summer of 1766. We will return to the causes of this dramatic event in a moment.

Without doubt, the Diet of 1765–6 formed the scene for the most formative moment in which Chydenius developed his main economic and political ideas. At this Diet one issue totally dominated all the others: the fact that the Swedish economy was in acute and severe crisis. A staggering rate of inflation hit the iron and steel industry especially hard, as it was extremely dependent on exports. Rising prices caused exports to fall, which in turn led to a negative trade balance; this was called "underweight" at the time. Less foreign demand for wares also caused falling demand for Swedish monies. A more modern view taking its point of departure from Hume's specie-flow mechanism would perhaps see this lowering of value as a positive counterbalancing force: cheaper money creates more demand from abroad. However, at this time the "raising"[56] of the exchange rate of Swedish money in Hamburg, Amsterdam and other foreign cities was looked upon as a problem caused by an "underweight" to which there existed no automatic countervailing or stabilizing forces. Hence, if foreign wares became dearer in exchange (a worsening of the nation's terms of trade), the effect would be a direct national loss. The supposition that Sweden had a negative trade balance with other countries had in fact been a mantra in the economic discussion since the 1730s. It served as one of the main arguments in favour of a policy of substituting foreign imports for domestic production, for example through state support of manufactories.[57] Moreover, the observation that inflation seemed to hurt some people (savers) but help others (spenders) – a common general effect of high inflation – was used as proof that criminal behaviour on the part of some speculating individual "capitalists" and money-jobbers was the *true* cause of the crisis.

More particularly, the Bank of the Estates (*Ständernas bank*) was blamed by contemporary critics. As the first central bank in Europe, it had started its operations in 1668. Formally it was owned and controlled by the estates, with its main task being to issue bonds or promissory notes in order to borrow money on behalf of the state. On request, the issued notes were to be exchanged for copper or silver monies. To some extent also, the bank was intended to be able to lend money to individuals. However, it was unable to refrain from issuing too many notes, which seems to be an eternal vice repeating itself through history. The result was inevitable: the notes fell in value. Bankruptcy would occur if there were a run for metallic money, and therefore the cashing in of notes had to be stopped in 1745, which in practice meant a transfer to a paper standard. Sweden's disastrous involvement in the Seven Years War in the 1750s had to a large extent been financed through the issuing of ever more notes. Consequently, their value rapidly deteriorated in relation to the silver Hamburg *riksdaler*, the main denominator at the time. Hence, a loan taken up in circulating money in the form of notes became an increasingly lighter burden over time. In fact, the relative value of the circulating so-called copper *mark* in relation to the Hamburg *riksdaler* sank from 1:36 in 1737 to 1:72 in 1761.[58] Not least, those who had bought notes at the Bank of the Estates at the higher rate felt utterly cheated. What they were able to receive in silver money when they cashed in their notes had rapidly dropped in value. This, more than anything else, caused alarm and bitterness during the Diet of 1765–6 and the situation reached boiling point; a scapegoat was clearly needed and was ultimately found.

Hence, for many observers it seemed clear that the directors of the Bank of the Estates as well as individuals connected with them through patronage were the people most responsible.[59] In particular, it was argued that this group had a private stake in lowering the value of the circulating money. According to this version, "insiders" had borrowed great sums from their own bank, which they could now pay back in money of less value than before. For their own private gain they had over-issued promissory notes as well as manipulated the Swedish exchange rate in order to make it fall in relation to foreign money. A critique against "evil speculators" such as Gustaf Kierman, Jean Henry Le Febure and the brothers Claes and Johan Abraham Grill had already started at the end of the 1750s but now escalated. Increasingly, the Hat leadership, to a large extent consisting of wealthy Stockholm merchants, nicknamed *Skeppsbroadeln*, was also now being targeted. In the eyes of the Cap opposition, which had grown considerably in size since the last Diet, that of 1760–2, they were responsible also for the unsuccessful war with Prussia and its allies. They were also accused of corrupt use of state means to support the manufactory industry. According to the radical critique, the whole system of regulation had been set in place in order to serve the interest of the rich merchants in Stockholm.

For one leading opponent of Kierman and the others, this turned into a private vendetta.[60] Hence, Anders Nordencrantz did not merely accuse the directors of the Bank of the Estates of having mismanaged the economy, but insisted that they had done so deliberately in order to gain personally. Nordencrantz's bitter diatribes against the Hat regime were undoubtedly coloured by the fact that he had lost a lot of money by selling some of his ironworks in the county of Uppland to persons in close relation to the Bank, namely the Stockholm merchant house of John Jennings and Richard Finlay. According to him, the buyers had been extremely slow to pay, which meant that inflation over time had diminished the agreed-upon price in real terms. However, it was not only the Bank that was involved in the alleged trickeries. Another object of Nordencrantz's harsh criticism was the Ironmasters' Association (*Järnkontoret*), of which he himself, ironically enough, had been the main initiator some decades ago. The aim behind the Association had been to organize iron and steel exports from Sweden in order to obtain the highest possible price. However, according to Nordencrantz, instead of carrying out this cartel function it operated in such a way as to benefit the leading merchant houses in Stockholm, as well as to use its position to provide loans to "insiders" which were repaid later with inflation-affected monies. On this basis he was ready to draw the conclusion that the directors of the Bank as well as some of the leading Hats were criminal speculators who had destroyed the kingdom's economy. Hence, it was not the "underweight" in the balance of trade that had caused Swedish money to fall in exchange, but the undertakings of "secret operations" and "manipulations by criminal speculators".[61]

The Diet of 1765–6 turned into an inquisition, as it were, with the Hat regime in general and a number of leading *Skeppsbroadel* merchants in particular being targeted. As a consequence, the Hats had to leave their leading positions in the estates as well as in the Council of the Realm. Moreover, some of those who seemed to have been most responsible for the operations in the Bank were put in jail while others had to pay fines; Kierman, who was regarded as the worst offender, was sentenced to life imprisonment at the Marstrand prison (however, he was released after only one year). Chydenius was one of the most aggressive spokesmen for punishing this group of *Wäxel-Associerade* ("exchange associates"). At a committee meeting he branded them as "traitors to their country" and "imposters". On top of the prison sentences he sensed that a "just" punishment would be for a number of those most involved to be pilloried in each of the towns they passed on their way from Stockholm to the prison in Marstrand, a distance of 500 kilometres with a dozen towns en route.[62]

Hence, Chydenius contributed to the inquisition against the high officials of the Bank to a substantial degree. By his critique of the main parts of the Hat regime's regulative framework, he had done his best to undermine its position. However, as we will see later, he was not at all satisfied with what the Caps had to offer in its place. In general he had supported Nordencrantz's critique against the Hat speculators and agreed with Nordencrantz's interpretations. But during the Diet he changed his mind to some extent. When the Caps suggested drastic measures that would cause prices to fall rather dramatically, Chydenius disagreed completely. He formulated his doubts in "A Remedy for the Country by Means of a Natural System of Finance" (1766) – which ultimately led to his exclusion from the Diet. The background was that the new Cap government had put forward a scheme by which the value of circulating money was to be gradually raised so that it would regain the value it had had in foreign silver *riksdaler* in 1737. This could of course only be achieved by drastically decreasing the number of banknotes, creating a shortage of money in circulation. Such a step, however, would, according to Chydenius, depress the economy and severely hurt most trades and industry – a not too unrealistic assumption, given what we know today about the effects of deflation. However, one problem with this interpretation was that it seemed to go against what he had said previously. Neither would it satisfy his old colleagues in the Cap party – or Nordencrantz, for that matter, his old teacher.[63]

Among his activities at the Diet of 1765–6 we must also mention Chydenius's important work regarding the abolition of censorship and the establishing of a more liberal attitude to the printing and publication of state and official papers. This historic effort was crowned with the establishment of a new ordinance on freedom of writing and printing in 1766 as well as the establishment of the principle of freedom of information. In Sweden this principle is more exactly called the "principle of public access to official records" (*offentlighetsprincipen*), and

Chydenius is rightly hailed as one of its most important instigators.[64] To quite an extent, Chydenius's contribution here was coloured by his own personal experiences during the Diet. The fact that it was not possible to publish (secret) state papers – or proceedings of the work in the estates – was regarded by Chydenius as well as others as a serious factor inhibiting their political work.

From the beginning of the 1760s, censorship of the press was increasingly challenged. An early voice demanding reform was that of Anders Nordencrantz (who had favoured reform since 1730), but later Christian König and Anders Johan von Höpken spoke out too. In the 1750s the journal "An Honest Swede" (*En ärlig swensk*) made some impact arguing for a more open attitude, and it is most possible that the suppression of the publication of "Thoughts on Civil liberty" (*Tankar om borgerliga friheten*) by the Uppsala philosopher and student of Linnaeus Peter Forsskål in 1759 worked in the same direction.[65] Even more important was probably the publication of Anders Nordencrantz's tract "Indefeasible thoughts on freedom in the use of reason, pens and print, and how far such a freedom should be extended in a free society, together with its consequences",[66] the printed copies of which were confiscated by the Board of Chancery, even though the censor, von Oelreich, had approved it. However, a couple of hundred copies had already been distributed. Here Nordencrantz used a proverb that Chydenius too cites on several occasions: "Freedom of speech is the apple of the eye of a people's freedom."[67] He argues for an almost total freedom of printing, with one exception: religious tracts and texts. This was also a line that Chydenius would follow some years later during his work towards reform of the system.

At the Diet of 1760–2 it was already clear that the question of the freedom of printing was linked to an even bigger issue: the downfall of the Hat government and the rise of the Caps. Nordencrantz's tract was now published, and almost everything that was written in opposition to the Hats was allowed to be printed by the censor, von Oelreich. During the Diet a special committee on the freedom of printing was appointed and the historiographer royal Anders Schönberg – later Chydenius's friend – was asked in 1761 to write a memorial. He presented a rather cautious proposal that suggested some steps forward, but at the same time regarded it as too dangerous to totally eliminate the possibility of censoring libellous political texts. However, not even this was accepted by a majority at the Diet, and the matter came to a standstill.

At the following Diet of 1765–6 the issue was once again taken up, and now with more force. In June 1765 Chydenius wrote a memorial (in fact signed by Anders Kraftman, a colleague of Chydenius in the Estate of Clergy). It was much more radical than, for example, Schönberg's piece, and Chydenius here argues for a total lifting of censorship for non-religious texts (and implicitly also for freedom of information). In August the same year a new Freedom of Printing committee, the so-called Third Committee, was appointed, with Chydenius as one of its most active members; the committee was in fact dominated by radical Caps from the Estate of Clergy. The work here resulted in new reports and memorials which ultimately led to the proposal for a new ordinance in the autumn of 1766. At that time Chydenius was of course already back in Finland, but it is clear that he perhaps more than anybody contributed to the launching of this ground-breaking reform.

Chydenius had arrived in Stockholm in the midst of political turmoil and a struggle between the Hats and the Caps. We will return to the particular circumstances concerning the discussions he was involved in – and which in most cases led to the publication of a treatise or pamphlet – as we introduce each of the texts from his pen included in this volume. Without doubt, Chydenius had some success but also met with some disappointments at what was indeed an eventful Diet. In his unpublished bucolic "Herda-qväde", which he wrote in a sombre mood after being sent home in 1766, he emphasized how naive he as a young chaplain from a remote part of the Swedish realm must have appeared only a year earlier.[68] In Stockholm, "everything was on display; a feeling of abundance filled all senses of the gazing spectators". Instead of allowing himself a relaxing night out with his colleagues, or alternatively a good night's sleep, he worked hard at his desk most nights in order to carry out what he saw as his duty:

> A stage full of sights that aroused my senses stood before me, and I did not know myself which person I was or how I wanted to act ... I was on top of the world: no honour or happiness so great that I did not have a chance to win it for myself. But it is easy for a fearless young man to fall for any folly, and hot blood was streaming through my young veins. I dreamed quite happily of all the opportunities I seemed to be able to catch as soon as I held out my hand, until I suddenly woke up in indignation over the fool I had been. I had fallen for the kind of false illusions that trick many a young man, making him forget that simplicity and humbleness instead of appearing under false colours is the key to his true fortune.[69]

After 1765–6

His exclusion from the Diet in 1766 meant that Chydenius was forbidden to take part in the next Diet, held in Norrköping in 1769. He did in fact travel there but was sent back home again. It is too much to say that after this his career in active politics was over: he would take part in the Diet of 1778–9, and he was a delegate of the Clergy in Ostrobothnia at the short and somewhat peculiar Diet of 1792. This was held in Gävle shortly before Gustavus III was assassinated in the early spring of 1792, following the unsuccessful war with Russia after which the king had made himself almost a dictator with the so-called Union and Security Act (*Förenings- och säkerhetsakten*) in 1789. Eyewitnesses present at the Diet depicted Gävle as a military camp swarming with police spies.[70]

At the same time, it is clear that Chydenius would never again play such an important role as during the Diet of 1765–6. This did not mean that he had lost interest in economic and political reform issues. He published his radical views on workers and servants in "Thoughts Concerning the Natural Rights of Masters and Servants" (*Tankar om husbönders och tienstehions naturliga rätt*, 1778),

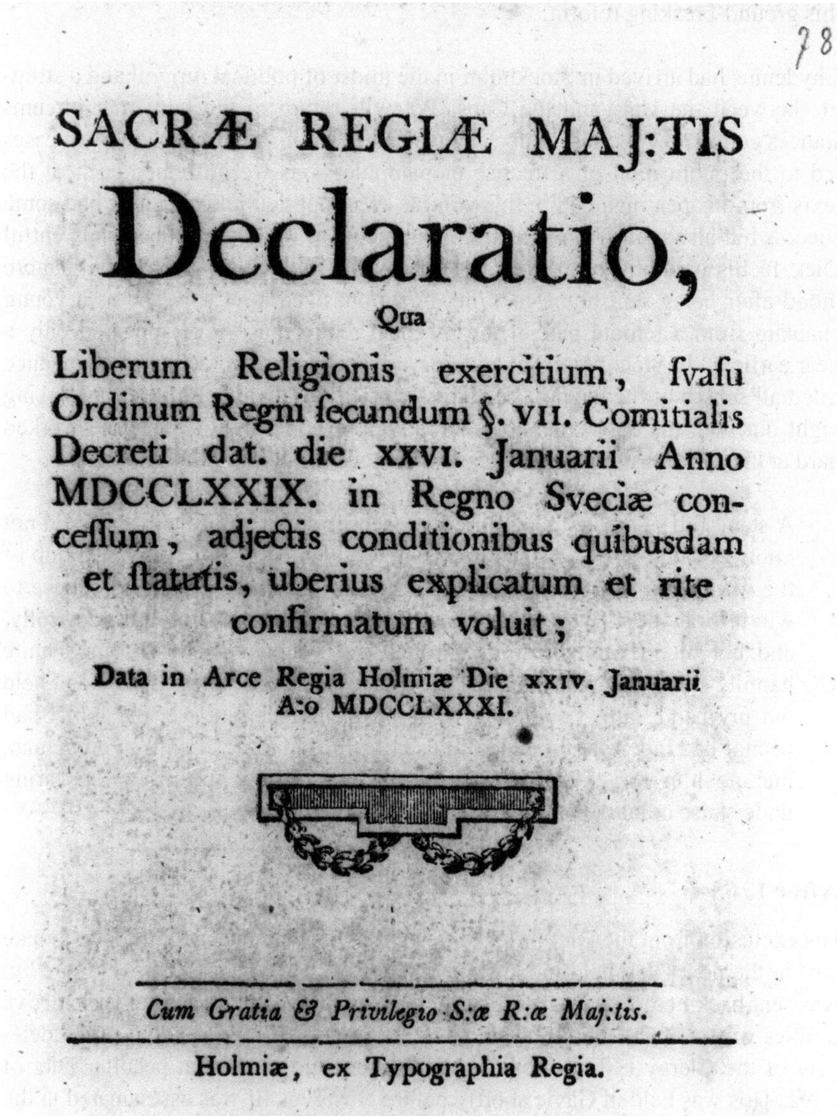

SACRÆ REGIÆ MAJ:TIS

Declaratio,

Qua

Liberum Religionis exercitium, fvafu
Ordinum Regni fecundum §. VII. Comitialis
Decreti dat. die XXVI. Januarii Anno
MDCCLXXIX. in Regno Sveciæ con-
ceffum, adjeais conditionibus quibusdam
et ftatutis, uberius explicatum et rite
confirmatum voluit;

**Data in Arce Regia Holmiæ Die XXIV. Januarii
A:o MDCCLXXXI.**

Cum Gratia & Privilegio S:æ R:æ Maj:tis.

Holmiæ, ex Typographia Regia.

Figure 9 By advocating an extension of the freedom of religious faith, Chydenius gained
the king's favour but called down the wrath of the clergy. Gustavus III, who
sought a reputation as an "enlightened" monarch, had his statute translated into
Latin and sent a copy of it to the Pope. The National Library of Finland.

and in "Whether Rural Trade Is Generally Useful or Harmful to a Country" (*Huruvida landthandel för et rike i gemen är nyttig eller skadelig*, 1777) he argued for the establishment of free enterprise, especially in the countryside. Much later in life he also wrote a piece titled "The Improvement of Finnish Agriculture" (*Finska lantbrukets upphjälpande*, 1799) in which he repeated many ideas and suggestions from his earlier works, but it was not printed during his lifetime.[71]

The pamphlet on the rights of servants mentioned above had directly to do with Chydenius's activities during the Diet of 1778–9. He published it in order to push for the replacement of the existing statute on servants – which made it a crime for a propertyless worker to be without a master and in general treated servants as second-class citizens in their own country – to a system building on free contracts between masters and servants. Most probably because of its radical content, the proposal was rejected by a majority of the Estates. While this must have been a disappointment, Chydenius was more successful with regard to another burning issue at this time: religious tolerance. He wrote the important "Memorial Regarding Freedom of Religion" (*Memorial, angående religionsfrihet*, 1779), in which it was suggested that while the Lutheran Church should still be the only recognized church in the Swedish realm, foreigners should have increased rights to practise their own religion. Moreover, it is clear that the king himself played an important role in having the memorial accepted. Ever since, it has been speculated whether or not Chydenius wrote it in response to a direct exhortation from Gustavus III.[72] Most probably, however, the initiative was taken by Chydenius himself, but possibly with the aim of gaining political favour with the monarch. On the other hand, there is no doubt that he from his own experience drew the conclusion that more religious freedom was beneficial. In Ostrobothnia at the time, Pietism was widespread and Chydenius was opposed to rash treatment of Pietists. Be that as it may, his engagement did not make him very popular among his clerical colleagues. By many in his Estate he was looked upon as a traitor against the unity of the Church and the true Lutheran evangelic gospel.[73] The fact that he was not elected to take part in any new Diet before 1792 was most certainly a consequence of this.

A more general factor behind his absence from the national political stage was Gustavus III's *coup d'état* in 1772. One of its effects was that the political system changed fundamentally, and the days of the Age of Liberty were over. From now on, the king would take a much more active part in ruling the country. As a consequence of the new constitution of 1772, the power of the Estates dwindled. Not even the Diets were what they once had been. No longer the power base of competing Hat and Cap politicians, this institution became less important and was transformed into a mere platform for royal power designed by the king himself. At the same time, it is clear that Chydenius in this situation changed his political sympathies. He was obviously no longer a Cap; his loyalty to the Caps' cause had abruptly ended in 1766 when he was excluded from the Diet. During the 1770s and 1780s he was mainly recognized by contemporaries as a follower of Gustavus III and loyal to the new order. Hence, at the same time as he was reconciled to being a "democrat" – perhaps even more so than before – he was also a "Gustavian". How this combination was possible we will return to in a moment.

When his father, Jakob, died in 1766, shortly before Anders Chydenius arrived home after the tumultuous events in the spring of 1766, he might have thought it only natural that he should succeed his father as rector at Kokkola. But when he was not put in the first place for the position, he himself at least drew the conclusion that this had to do with his exclusion from the recently finished Diet. However, a new opportunity appeared when his father's successor as rector, Johan Haartman, left Kokkola after just one year in active service. Hence, in 1770 Chydenius was installed at Kokkola, and would remain there for the rest of his life. Moving up the Church hierarchy, he became dean in 1779, and the same year he was awarded with the title of *doctor honoris causa* in theology. Two years later he also became a rural dean, which was the highest position one could reach in the Church hierarchy without becoming a bishop. Now that he was installed in his new duties, his energies turned in new directions. During the 1780s he published a number of theological works in the format of sermons. What seems to have sparked him off in this direction was once again the launching of a new prize competition; this time it was the Theological Homiletic Society in Uppsala (*Theologico-Homiletiska sällskapet*), which put up a prize for the best sermon concerning the topic of the Ten Commandments. Chydenius submitted in total 11 sermons on this topic and received a first prize. They were subsequently published in the Society's series *Homiletiska försök* (1781–2). Some years later he published another set of sermons in the same series concerning the articles of faith in which he elaborated on some themes taken from the Lutheran Catechism.[74]

While spending most of his time with duties that followed from his position as shepherd of his flock at Kokkola, he continued to take a keen interest in agricultural improvements and was always eager to try out new projects and schemes. However, during the 1780s he seems to have been particularly busy carrying out building projects: enlarging the parish church building as well as furnishing it with a new tower. Although times were not particularly good and a series of bad harvests had hit the Swedish realm during the 1770s, Kokkola had seen a rise in population which made the church too small. Chydenius was also able to engage in a pastime that he especially cherished: at Kokkola he had his own small orchestra, in which he seems to have been especially handy with the flute.[75] While not taking any part in national politics after his return from the Diet in Gävle 1792 – perhaps old age and the experience of the journey back from Gävle, when he and his travel companions had almost lost their lives trying to cross the frozen Gulf of Bothnia in the middle of winter had been deterrent enough – he continued to write on different political and economic subjects. In 1795 he sent a piece on the production of saltpetre in Ostrobothnia (*Saltpetter-sjuderierne, särdeles i Österbotten*) to a recently created society for the distribution of useful knowledge in Stockholm, *Sällskapet för allmänne medborgerlige kunskaper*. It was in fact printed as the first number in the society's series. In this

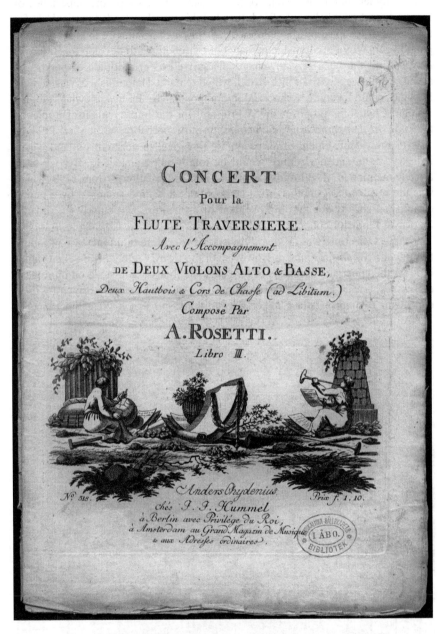

Figure 10 The collection of musical manuscripts and sheet music Chydenius had in his possession indicates that he was well aware of the musical trends in Europe at the time and that his orchestra most likely played the latest European music. The first foreign music shop in Finland, an agent of Hummel of Amsterdam, was established in Kokkola. Antonio Rosetti (*c.*1750–92), Flute Concerto in G major (Libro III). Sibelius Museum, Turku.

essay, Chydenius repeated some of his well-known views on the importance of free trade and establishment of industry, but this time he pleaded particularly for the repeal of the existing state monopoly on producing saltpetre in order to make gunpowder. Why not allow the peasants in Ostrobothnia to develop this trade, as they had all the necessary raw materials as well as a multitude of hands? he asked. Another essay from this period, which remained unpublished, was on how Lapland could become richer and more populated. In a somewhat utopian fashion, Chydenius proposes in "A Proposal for the Improvement of Lapland" (*Förslag til Lappmarkernes uphjelpande*, most probably written in 1794 or 1795)[76] the establishment of an economic free zone in northern Finland where industry, trade and agriculture would be totally unregulated. Lastly, we have already mentioned "The Improvement of Finnish Agriculture" from 1799, which was the result of yet another prize competition, this time launched by a newly established society for the improvement of agriculture particularly in Finland, the Royal Finnish Economic Society (*Kungliga Finska Hushållningssällskapet*). The subject this time was to identify obstacles to a more rapid increase of industry and agriculture in Finland. However, in the essay Chydenius dwelled rather little on the concrete conditions of Finland. The focus was instead on more general issues, particularly emphasizing that men everywhere were driven by their endeavour to improve their material conditions and that a great hindrance in

Figure 11 Kokkola's parish church was built at the beginning of the sixteenth century and was extended under the supervision of Chydenius in the 1780s. Painting by Conrad Sovelius, *c.*1870. The K.H. Renlund Museum – Provincial Museum of Central Ostrobothnia.

present society against such improvements was regulations put forward by "aristocratic conspiracies". Chydenius here also presents a critique of contemporary colonial plunder outside Europe practised by the mercantile powers, showing an outlook that was quite advanced for the period. Because the essay was so little concerned with Finland, it is perhaps no surprise that Chydenius did not receive a prize. However, the essay does include a small section discussing the national character of the Finns. Many criticize Finns for being lazy and drowsy and drinking too much, he says. But the real causes of their backwardness are political. Finland has been the most oppressed part of the kingdom, and Swedish economic regulations have particularly disfavoured the Finnish region, he believes. To this should also be added the consequences of the wars with Russia – the most recent having been waged by Gustavus III only ten years previously – which had led to occupation, devastation and an acute shortage of population. It is the voice of a disappointed Finn from the periphery that we can sense in his last political essay.

Chydenius as an economist

As we have already noted, a lively debate touching upon economic matters was opened up during the decades after the establishment of the Age of Liberty. Earlier scholars dealing with the history of Swedish economic thought and literature have tried to find theoretical propositions from these economic debates during the Age of Liberty that correspond to major themes in the history of economic doctrines at large. Hence, the first economics professor at Uppsala, Anders Berch, has often been depicted as a typical proponent of "mercantilism". To this group, such writers as Eric Salander, Johan Fredrik Kryger, Anders von Höpken, Johan Alströmer and Johan Låstbom (docent at Uppsala) are usually added. The young Anders Nordencrantz (or Bachmanson before he was ennobled) also seems to belong there, with his *Arcana oeconomiae et commercii* (1730). *Arcana* was in fact the first comprehensive treatise in economics ever printed in Sweden.[77] Especially in Berch's 1747 textbook *Inledning til almänna hushålningen*, all the ingredients of the mercantilist doctrine can be found, according to Eli F. Heckscher, including the theory of the favourable balance of trade.[78] In the same manner, Karl Petander finds traces of the "typical" mercantilist view that money is wealth in Bachmanson-Nordencrantz's text from 1730, as well as in texts written by Eric Salander. Moreover, because Thomas Mun's *England's Treasure by Forraign Trade* was translated into Swedish and published in two editions (1732 and 1745), Petander takes for granted that this archetypal mercantilist (according to Adam Smith) also had a great influence in Sweden.[79] However, to identify a "typical mercantilist" is not always so easy. With regard to Berch, it is, however, clear that he did *not* believe that money was identical to wealth, or that an inflow of currency would immediately increase the wealth of the nation. He was rather of the opinion that foreign trade should be organized in a manner that maximized the export of worked-up wares in order to increase jobs and population – a view which rather resembles that of late-seventeenth- and early-eighteenth-century English economic writers such as Charles Davenant and Charles King, to whom we will return.[80]

Hence, after more than a century of discussion it is not clear to what extent mercantilism really was a "school" of economic thought, as for example the French Physiocrats were. To a large extent the proposed theoretical foundations of the Colbert system, or *système mercantile*, which the French *économistes* criticized from the 1740s onwards, was rather something that Smith invented in his *Wealth of Nations* (1776) – mainly in order to contrast his own theories on economic value and growth. Hence, it is not generally true that "mercantilists" confused wealth with gold and silver. It is in fact difficult to find writers after the middle of the seventeenth century who wrote favourably of a positive balance of trade.[81] Certainly this still makes it possible to depict mercantilism or Colbertism as a particular strand of economic policy and practice founded upon certain ideas, for example regarding the positive role of the state in economic growth and improvement, or even with regard to how the economy worked and functioned during this age of perpetual trade wars. As was noted by David Hume in the 1750s, "jealousy of trade" was a prevailing state of affairs in Europe during the early eighteenth century.[82]

According to historians of economic doctrine, a stream of thought developed in Sweden from the 1720s onwards that was critical of mercantilism. Building upon writers from an earlier period like Christopher Polhem and Emanuel Swedenborg in the 1720s as well as Lars Salvius in the decade that followed, this "school" has conventionally been called "reform-mercantilism". Breaking with the *dirigisme* of old mercantilism, reform-mercantilism is said to build a bridge with the new economic liberal school of Adam Smith and classical political economy. It includes important figures such as the mature Anders Nordencrantz, Carl Leuhusen, Per Stenhagen, Carl Fredrik Scheffer (although Scheffer is most often described as a Swedish Physiocrat, perhaps the only true specimen[83]), the brothers Edvard Fredric and Ephraim Otto Runeberg from Finland – and Anders Chydenius. While it is clear that this group of writers were hostile to the economic policies of the Hat party, especially such regulations as particularly favoured manufactories in relation to other sectors in general and agriculture in particular, it is more difficult to find coherent theoretical principles behind their criticism. Karl Forsman – whose analytical contribution to the analysis of reform-mercantilism has been sadly neglected by later historians – especially emphasized the emergence of more "liberal" economic attitudes as a consequence of the combination of patriotic Gothicism (*göticism*), with roots in the seventeenth century (including the fantasies by Olof Rudbeck regarding Sweden as the sunken Atlantis and the home of the Hyperboreans), and natural rights theory. Moreover, Forsman particularly refers to the influence of French *économistes* and proto-Physiocrats such as Mirabeau the elder. This most certainly led the "reform-mercantilists" to agitate for "utilism" as developed by natural scientists like Linnaeus, while at the same time they argued for natural liberty and the importance of agriculture.

Most certainly Anders Chydenius must be placed within the group of Swedish "reform-mercantilists". As we will see later on, many of his ideas of reform were developed within a contemporary discussion concerning moral philosophy and natural liberty which strongly influenced his political preferences. But can we also distil some kind of economics from his texts? Where should he be placed in the history of economic discourse at large?

To begin with, it must be noted that Chydenius refers only sparsely to other economic writers, Swedish or foreign. We have already seen that he describes Anders Nordencrantz as his intellectual father figure. From him he picked up ideas propounded by the leading *philosophes* during this time, including Montesquieu (whom Chydenius read, at least in translation), Helvétius, Voltaire and Hume – as well as Mandeville.[84] Apart from these authors we do not know exactly from whom he received his ideas. He used the library of his father, of course, which included books his father had inherited from his son Samuel, who had died young. The library seems to have included some economic texts written by Carl Leuhusen, Pehr Niclas Christiernin, Abraham Sahlstedt and a few others.[85] Furthermore, from his autobiography we know that during his stay in Stockholm he frequently used the library of the book printer and economic writer Lars Salvius, which included many political and economic texts, both Swedish and foreign. As the French cultural and intellectual influence was very strong in Sweden during this period – what English writers wrote was often read in French translations – it is perhaps not surprising that such texts dominated. In fact, Nordencrantz was one of the very few who were able to read books and pamphlets in English. While Chydenius probably found handwritten memoranda by Polhem and Swedenborg – who had such an important influence on him – in the Diet archive, Salvius's library contained the bulk of what the leading Swedish authorities had written with regard to economic issues. Here Chydenius found most of the material for his tract *Rikets hjelp* ("A Remedy for the Country"). This also included Salvius's own *Tanckar öfver den swenska oeconomien* ("Thoughts on the Swedish Economy", 1738), which no doubt contains critical passages that influenced Chydenius profoundly, for example with regard to his thoughts concerning the iron industry. He must also have felt quite comfortable with Salvius's views on economic policy, which in general were quite liberal.[86]

As Heckscher pointed out, Chydenius in his perhaps most important text, *The National Gain*, takes his starting point from the notion that when "the value of exported commodities exceeds that of imported ones", this is "rightly called the profit of the nation".[87] This was of course commonplace at the time, although the definition of what this "profit" consisted of varied considerably between authors. However, nowhere can we see in Chydenius (or in Berch, as we saw above) any signs of the main "mercantilist prejudice", the idea that an export surplus in the form of hoarded money per se would be particularly gainful for a country. What he instead repeats several times is that the "wealth of the people" consists of the quantity or value of products brought forward with the help of the "number of workers and their diligence". On the other hand, he does not explicitly criticize the favourable balance of trade theory. Instead, his argument is rather in the negative: he argues that it does not make a nation any richer if the state, for example by means of export bounties, redirects trade from one branch to another. But nowhere does he fall into the "fallacy" that Adam Smith conceived as the kernel of the mercantile system: to confuse an export surplus with material wealth.

Making production and the stock of labour the basis of a nation's wealth, Chydenius instead defines "a favourable balance of trade" in a manner that became common, especially in England, from the 1690s and onwards, and which we find with other Swedish authors at the time, including Berch. While rejecting the simple idea of a pile of money as beneficial to the nation, English economic writers such as Josuah Child, Charles Davenant, Nicholas Barbon and Charles King instead emphasized such a gain in terms of exporting as much value added wares as possible, while importing products with less added value or raw materials. Especially by E.A. Johnson in a seminal work on the economic thinking of this era, this was called the theory of "foreign paid incomes", or the "labour balance of trade" theory. Hence, by selling worked-up wares the foreigner was supposed to "pay" the wage bill for the exporting country's workers. This led to more income for the country, more employment and – supposedly – a richer and stronger nation.[88] To what extent Chydenius agreed with this we cannot be sure. As we have seen, he regarded full employment as the cornerstone of wealth. On the other hand, Chydenius seems not in the first place to have pressed for more worked-up goods. Arguments for giving priority to trades that produced value-added wares for export were of course often used at the time in order to make the case for more manufactories, as well as for regulative measures in order to support and protect them at the expense of other branches, for example agriculture or peasant handicrafts. But Chydenius saw no point in giving exclusive privileges to the manufactories, even though they might be able to produce more value-added wares.

It has been suggested that Chydenius here took a realistic viewpoint: the idea that Swedish manufactories might be able to contribute to the country's exports lay at best in a very distant future. Sweden was much less economically developed and could not possibly compete on markets for advanced industrial products.[89] Instead, it was Chydenius's view that it should utilize its main "comparative advantage", namely, cheap labour and the ample resources of different raw materials. Hence, if the native workers were allowed to freely concentrate on production where they could receive the highest income, this would in turn increase exports and ensure that a maximum of hands were employed at home. Hence, Chydenius, like many of the English writers in the eighteenth century, including Charles King, Josiah Tucker and James Steuart, argued that a nation's wealth lies in a multitude of working hands. What an individual is able to gain through hard toil is also the profit of the nation – that was the conclusion he drew.

Although Chydenius played with concepts such as "favourable balance of trade", his preference for agriculture over manufactories makes it much more relevant to connect him to another stream of economic thought in the middle of the eighteenth century. Hence, while not exactly being a Finnish Adam Smith, Chydenius rather belongs to a broad school of writers often identified as proto-Physiocrats or *économistes*, many of them of French origin. In insisting upon this connection, Karl Forsman without doubt is on the right track. This implies that Chydenius belongs to a group of writers who certainly played a pivotal role in what Adam Smith would publish in his *Wealth of Nations* in 1776 – but, as we know, there were also great differences between Smith and the French *économistes* (and with the Physiocrats). This group of agriculture-friendly economists included Mirabeau the elder, Melon, Gournay and Forbonnais, but also Boisguilbert early in the century as well as Turgot later on. Accordingly, Heckscher quite accurately calls Chydenius "a Finnish Turgot".[90] In Salvius's library, Chydenius could for example have read the Swedish translation of Melon's *Essai politique sur le commerce*, published in 1751, or Mirabeau's *L'Ami des hommes* (published in an abridged Swedish translation in 1759). However, he could also have picked up viewpoints of the *économistes* through Swedish authors such as Carl Leuhusen and Johan Fischerström, writing in the early 1760s.[91] The latter in particular seems to have been well acquainted with the French literature, and he refers in his texts to authors such as Mirabeau, Savary, Montesquieu and Melon – but also to English authors such as Petty and Davenant. Moreover, both Leuhusen and Fischerström emphasized the role of agriculture in making a nation rich. With a strong voice they condemn "unnatural" regulations to support manufactories. They also proclaim themselves great friends of liberty with regard to trade and the establishment of enterprise. Leuhusen, for example, strongly argues in favour of a trade as unlimited as possible; his main focus here is the grain trade. Another writer, E.O. Runeberg, agreed, and regarded agriculture as the very cornerstone of economic wealth in general. The most pertinent problem with the inflation during the Hat regime was, according to most of these writers, that workers were drawn from agriculture to the "unnecessary" manufactories in Stockholm by the folly of luxury.[92] "Agriculture-friendly" Swedish authors during this period seldom went so far as to reject all kinds of state support. In general they disfavoured support for urban industry, including the manufactories, but were ready to accept regulations and bounties intended to develop the agricultural sector.[93] Chydenius had without doubt already come across the view that agriculture was more important than manufactories during his stay at the Academy in Turku in 1748. He would have heard Johan Kraftman emphasize in his lectures that as long as the Swedish realm was not self-sufficient in foodstuffs, no manufactories should be allowed.[94]

Did Chydenius add something beyond what this group of "proto-Physiocrats" had already said? To some extent the answer is yes. First, it is clear that Chydenius was more consequent in his free market views than perhaps anybody else in the Swedish realm at this time. He condemned economic regulation in principle, including with regard to agriculture, which was rather uncommon at the time. In a radical manner he scrutinized the "mercantilist" idea that only the political state can establish a correct balance between the different trades. In contrast, Chydenius argued that a true balance can only be achieved when every man is free to seek his opportunity wherever he finds it most suitable. However, this does not mean that Chydenius, ten years before Adam Smith, had "invented" the invisible hand argument[95] – especially as this by no means is something that originated with Smith. The paradox that "private vices" can be transformed into "public benefits" was well known before 1776 from authors such as Mandeville.[96] Moreover, the notion that some kind of *harmonia preaestabilita* existed in human society as well as in nature was a common theme in the prevailing moral philosophy discourse at the time. In Chydenius's case his definition of "liberty" and "happiness" was also coloured by his religious views, as we will see.

Chydenius's radical attitude especially shines through when discussing the rights of servants and workmen. His argument for a free contract between masters and servants is based upon the notion that the latter too are citizens of a free state. He emphasizes how the existing system of regulation builds on privilege and monopoly, as well as depicts the corruptive aspects of the mercantile system. He saw this system as being linked to vested interests, especially those of the elite of merchant capitalists in Stockholm. In his condemnation of the latter he is not at all far from Adam Smith's harsh critique formulated in *The Wealth of Nations* some ten years later. However, his critique of corruption and monopoly also has to be seen as part of a wider moral philosophical discussion, which we will return to shortly.

Lastly, Chydenius propounds the beneficial influence that a division of labour has on the nation's profit. He extends this argument to include trade with foreigners. Here he is more advanced than most of the proto-Physiocrats (who were not much concerned with international exchange). Like his contemporary Josiah Tucker in England – as well as Adam Smith later on – he develops a crude theory of comparative advantage in international trade. His view is that each country should export what it is best suited for. As we have seen, this argument was developed in order to make the case for free exportation from Ostrobothnia, rather than, in an "unnatural" fashion, support the export of Swedish manufactories that by themselves were unable to compete on the export markets.

Hence, it is clear that Chydenius held views that were close to what other "reform-mercantilists" of Swedish origin or French "proto-Physiocrats" were saying at the same time. But although he belonged to this broad group of economist writers, who certainly influenced the further development of economics, he also developed new ideas and insights within this framework. In this respect it is not unfair to regard him as a predecessor to Adam Smith. At the same time we must be more precise and acknowledge the very different context in which he wrote and in which his ideas must be placed. This will become even clearer when we later on discuss Chydenius's moral philosophy and theology.

We have seen that it was Chydenius's critique against the Caps' plan for monetary restoration that led to his early return home from Stockholm in 1766. As has also been pointed out, "A Remedy for the Country by Means of a Natural System of Finance" to a large extent corrected his own previous views. Earlier, he had largely followed Nordencrantz in his analysis of the causes behind the inflation and the lowering of the exchange rate. Like his "teacher", he had put

Figure 12 Chydenius lived in this rectory near the parish church of Kokkola from 1770 until his death in 1803. The white stone building opposite the rectory was built by Chydenius in the 1770s. The photograph is from the beginning of the twentieth century. The National Board of Antiquities, Finland.

the blame on "manipulating" and "criminal speculators", who with their malicious operations had caused the fall in value of circulating money. At the start of the Diet of 1765–6 he seems to have agreed upon the scheme put forward by the new ruling Cap party to gradually increase the value of the copper *mark* to what it had been in 1737; at least, he kept quiet when the plan was up for scrutiny at a Diet meeting in 1765 (although he afterwards seems to blame this on being too busy with other matters to take enough notice).[97] More probable is that he changed his mind as a consequence of his return to the old discussion between Nordencrantz and the *adjunct* in economics at Uppsala University, Pehr Niclas Christiernin, which started in 1761 with the publication of the latter's *Utdrag af föreläsningar angående den i Swea rike upstigne wexel-coursen* ("Excerpts from Lectures concerning the High Exchange Rate in Sweden"). At some point he must have come to the conclusion that Christiernin (influenced by John Locke as he was) had a strong case when basing his analysis on the quantity theory of money, arguing that not evil speculators but an over-issue of banknotes was the root of the problem. He must have realized that what he himself had written some years earlier (in his emigration pamphlet) in favour of the Caps' realization plan did not stand up to scrutiny. Apart from reading Christiernin, he heard arguments for such a revision from the Cap politician Christer Horn, as well as from reading an old memorandum by Emanuel Swedenborg written in 1722.

Swedenborg here describes the negative consequences of raising the value of money which had occurred at the beginning of the 1720s especially for the iron industry, but also for other trades, including agriculture.[98]

Eli F. Heckscher in particular has credited Chydenius for distancing himself from Nordencrantz's "not very clear" ideas about the causes of inflation and instead accepting Christiernin's "basically sound" use of the quantity theory of money. This may be easy to agree on from the point of view of modern theory. On the other hand, there may have been a grain of empirical truth in Nordencrantz's attacks on "capitalist speculators". Hence, it is not at all unlikely that special interests during this period speculated in the fall of money in order to gain for themselves or their clients when borrowing from the Bank of the Estates. Moreover, even though Chydenius used theory that is accepted today, this should not make us believe that he was more "modern" than he actually was. We must repeat that he was neither an Adam Smith without being conscious of it, nor someone who would have been better understood a hundred years later.[99] The angry reaction to his pamphlet – the eyewitness Daniel Tilas reported from a meeting with the Secret Committee that it was called a most "seditious" piece from which nothing good could be expected[100] – indicates that its message at this time was perhaps too well understood for his own good!

A philosophy of natural liberty

The historiographer royal, Anders Schönberg, called his friend Chydenius a "Swedish Rousseau".[101] Misleading as a general characterization, it is perhaps true in a more specific sense: like the famous philosopher living in Geneva, Chydenius was a "spirited democrat".[102] Like Rousseau, Chydenius took part in the broad intellectual movement known as the Enlightenment that flourished during the eighteenth century. There is in general no agreement among scholars concerning how broad the span of this movement was, but surely it included some who remained loyal to the Christian faith (as Chydenius did). In most of his texts he refers to "natural liberty" as a guiding policy for economic policy. It is to this liberty, which every man is born with, that he refers when he emphasizes that servants should have the right of movement and to be free members of society. Something he calls "natural liberty" is also a cornerstone when he argues that tenant farmers should have the right to sell their merchandise freely. Almost always it is with this weapon in hand that he attacks the regulatory system of the Cap regime.

As Carola Nordbäck suggests, when Chydenius refers to "natural liberty" or "the individual's right of happiness", such concepts must be understood in relation to his theology. "Natural liberty" was a state created by God, and by pursuing such a goal and striving for happiness, men fulfilled God's plan.[103] At the same time, his reference to "natural liberty" places him within a broad trend of European moral philosophy of natural rights based upon great authorities from the previous century such as Grotius and Pufendorf. As pointed out, a natural-rights-based discussion forms a link between early forms of civic humanist thought and the development of the radical visions of the Scottish Enlightenment: from Machiavelli and the Florentine tradition to David Hume and Adam Smith. Without doubt, both Grotius and Pufendorf had been well known to Chydenius since his early student days in Turku and Uppsala. However, concepts such as "natural rights" and "natural liberty" were open to very different interpretations from which, too, different policy conclusions were drawn. They could be used in order to defend absolute monarchy (as was for example the case in Denmark[104]), but also other forms of government. In Sweden, natural jurisprudence was used by those who wrote the new constitution after the downfall of absolutism in 1718 in order to argue for a social contract between the king and his subjects. Moreover, in the economic discussion during the Age of Liberty a natural rights vocabulary was used in order to defend *dirigisme* and strict regulation – but also to argue for more freedom of trade. In fact, the heated debates between the "mercantilists" and "reform-mercantilists" to a large degree took their point of departure from different interpretations of concepts such as "natural liberty" or "social contract".

Broadly speaking, there were at least two conclusions that were drawn in the moral philosophy discussion during the Age of Liberty. Both referred to a common base (except for a very few atheists): that God had created a natural order of the world which included minerals, plants, animals as well as men in perfect harmony with each other. Through empirical investigation it was possible to detect this "natural order" and decipher its codes. This broad ideological discourse, which dominated especially during the first decades of the Age of Liberty, is referred to as "physico-theology". An important influence regarding the breakthrough of such thinking in Sweden was the Prussian professor of philosophy Christian Wolff, whose programme to register and make a classificatory order of God's creation – Voltaire, who disliked him utterly, called him a pedantic collector of odds and ends – greatly impressed many Swedes, including the natural scientists Anders Celsius and Samuel Klingenstierna. Carolus Linnaeus too was influenced by him.[105] Wolffian philosophy was also a great stimulus to leading economic writers such as Anders Berch and J.F. Kryger. In his dissertation in philosophy *De felicitate patriæ per oeconomiam promovenda* (1731), which argued for the establishment of economics as an academic subject in Sweden, Berch followed Wolff quite closely (most of the dissertation was probably written by Celsius).[106] Even more apparent is the influence of Wolff with regard to Kryger, especially in his *Naturlig theologi* ("Natural theology"), published in three volumes between 1744 and 1753. Kryger explicitly speaks of "the system of nature" as a divine order uniting conflicting desires and interests to a concord which makes them "linked as in a chain".[107] As Tore Frängsmyr has pointed out, this was also the basis of the concept *Oeconomia Divina*, which Carl Gustaf Löwenhielm was the first to use in a lecture at the Swedish Royal Academy of Sciences in 1751.[108]

With Berch and Kryger, as we have seen, such views were entirely compatible with a rather authoritarian interpretation emphasizing the role of state regulation in pursuing economic and public prosperity. Hence, only a responsible statesman serving the public good was able to detect and draw the right conclusion (perhaps with the help of the impartial economist) concerning how this natural order was structured. As ordinary men fallen from Grace, they were not always able to understand the ways and means of the Creator. Hence, they needed steady advice from a visible and regulatory hand. Also, those who had read their Pufendorf would most probably agree upon the role of the state as an intermediator. In his version of natural law theory the state was a moral person who, for the good of all, established positive laws based on the knowledge of the laws of nature. From this it was of course easy to draw the conclusion that the economy must be governed in a fashion that fitted God's plans.[109]

However, this is not at all how Chydenius interpreted "natural law" or "natural liberty". Rather, he draws the opposite conclusion that men should not interfere in the natural order of things. As Forsman has pointed out, this was the "radical" interpretation of physico-theology. From the starting point of such a vision it was easy for Chydenius to condemn the bulk of economic legislation at his time, including the "unnatural" support for manufactures, the prohibitions against free exportation, etc. Such critical views based upon an alternative view regarding the implications of natural law discourse were shared by others among the "reform-mercantilists" and thus paved way for more liberal attitudes. This was certainly also the case with Anders Nordencrantz, who from the end of the 1750s developed a radical critique of the Caps based upon natural rights theory. On the other hand, one should not make the mistake of believing that Chydenius's insistence upon natural liberty as a ruling principle in economic policy was based upon an optimistic view of man and his social capabilities. On the contrary, he was a pessimist, emphasizing that man was corrupt by nature and driven by selfish interests and passions. In this regard he was far removed from an older "utilistic" view shared by the followers of Wolff and *Oeconomia Divina*. Hence, according to Nordencrantz the state was no impartial server of the common good; on the contrary, it was a promoter of private interests (perhaps not a strange conclusion to be drawn by somebody who saw the Hat government as a disguise for such private interests). This was also the reason why state power must be limited and checks and balances introduced in order to prevent corruption. Yet the absence of an omnipotent state did not mean that there should be no state at all. On the contrary, Nordencrantz and, perhaps especially, Chydenius saw the role of government as guaranteeing peace, order and religion. According to the latter, a ruler must be driven by the love of mankind. This also meant that that he must defend the poor against the rich and powerful.[110]

There is no doubt that Anders Chydenius to quite a large extent accepted Nordencrantz's critique of private interests and his fear of corruption (which would especially hurt the poor). As we have seen during the Diet of 1765–6, he was perhaps even more eager than his teacher to condemn the practices of evil speculators and speak out for harsh punishments. Late in life, he still continued to talk about the danger of "aristocratic conspiracies".[111] Such ways of thinking are most probably also the key to his sharp critique of special interests and his strong favouring of public participation in public affairs, even to the point that some were apt to call him an "enthusiast" or even "fanatic for democratic principles".[112] His pessimistic view of man can be detected in many of his texts. For example, in 1765 he wrote, in response to a critique of his "The Source of Our Country's Weakness": "The heart of Man is according to his nature a battlefield of numerous black vices which always and everywhere seek an opportunity to pop up."[113] It is perhaps accurate to say that such passages stem directly from his reading of the Bible; but that they also refer to the moral philosophy of Pufendorf (and Nordencrantz) seems beyond doubt.

Moreover, within the natural rights discussion during this period the question of the nature of man and his relation to state and society was especially pertinent. In the grand European debates, different views about the state of nature were often the starting point for such controversies. According to the theory of contract – which had also inspired the fathers of the constitution that was in operation during the Swedish Age of Liberty, as we have seen – men were born free. But in the state of nature they were primitive and apt to become victims of hunger and fear. While few would agree with the far-reaching conclusions Thomas Hobbes drew from this concering the need for a Leviathan, they were in general ready to accept that by joining an orderly society men had to give up some of their natural liberties. Social society could only be developed upon a restriction of liberty "in order to avoid strife and bloodshed", as for example J.F. Kryger pointed out in the Swedish discussion.[114] However, gradually an alternative view on the natural state developed during the eighteenth century, a view that had quite different implications. It was not so much Rousseau's vision of the noble savage and society as an enemy to natural man that became the main pathway; a well-read person like Nordencrantz in Sweden as well as most participants in the discussion on moral philosophy during the middle of the eighteenth century were explicitly critical of Rousseau. Rather, it was an interpretation based upon Pufendorf and later developed by David Hume and the Scots that would emerge as a main alternative: men did not have to give up their natural (God-given) rights when entering society because they were social already from birth. Hence, *sociabilitas* was part of their nature; they were born with a passion for forming societies for mutual cooperation as well as a passion to "trade and barter", as Adam Smith would emphasize so strongly in his *Theory of Moral Sentiments* (1759). The implication of this was clear enough: it was not necessary to establish the state in order to tame its subjects in order for them to become more social. More effectively, governance should be established which stimulated citizens to freely cooperate with each other. Men were born with both "good" and "bad" passions and sympathies. They were no angels; instead, they were prone to self-love and selfishness. However, by allowing men to compete with each other – freely and without fetters – their private vices could be turned into public benefits. The danger of corruption always lurked behind a strong state. The eighteenth-century natural rights moral philosophers condemned corruption as strongly as did the civic humanist tradition going back to Machiavelli; they saw it as the main reason for national decay and loss of happiness and prosperity (an obvious example here is Edward Gibbon[115]). This was certainly also

Nordencrantz's view, based upon what he had read, and some of this he trans-ferred to Chydenius. According to Nordencrantz, man is driven by a "natural" selfish instinct for private gain. Governments are prone to serve special interests and become corrupted (as became the fate of the political system at large during the Age of Liberty). Hence, a good constitution must be established which pre-vents certain men and interests from becoming too powerful.[116] Against this background the ideal society of Nordencranz was a small community of free men who minded their own business without much interference from bureaucra-cies and politicians; hence, he often nostalgically looks longingly back towards the old times when regulations were few and men uncorrupted. At the same time, we must emphasize that Nordencrantz was no republican. On the contrary, he gave a more elevated role to the Prince than was admitted under the constitution of 1720. In this respect too, Chydenius would follow in the footsteps of his old master – as we soon will see.

Lastly, it is commonplace to refer to Chydenius as an enlightened thinker influenced by new ideas from abroad emphasizing toleration and more freedom. To a large extent this is of course true: although he intensely disliked Voltaire for his alleged "deism" (or even "atheism"), and for the same reason remained critical towards belletrists such as Johan Henrik Kellgren and others among the Stockholm intelligentsia, he nevertheless favoured most parts of the broad Enlightenment programme. Hence, when Nils von Rosenstein sent him a copy of his programmatic defence of leading Enlightenment ideas, *Försök til en afhand-ling om uplysningen* (1793), Chydenius wrote a letter of thanks in which he emphasized that he had done his best all since 1765 to "work for enlightenment". Here he could of course especially point to his successful campaign to establish the Ordinance on Freedom of Writing and Printing in 1766 as well as the act on religious tolerance a decade later.[117] Moreover, as we have seen, his moral philo-sophy and emphasis on natural liberty rather point forward to ideas that became common after 1760 with the emergence of the Scottish Enlightenment as well as radical ideas propounded during the decades before the revolution in France. His critical points towards the role of special interest and corruption seem far removed from the perhaps more naive "utilism" dominating the scene earlier during the Age of Liberty.

A kingdom in concordance

To be an enlightened person in the mid-eighteenth century was seldom to be a democrat in the modern sense. Instead, most such people supported absolute monarchy – if it implied government according to law and the constitution (any-thing else was called arbitrary despotism) – in order that an enlightened rule could be inaugurated. Chydenius was no exception in this respect. By the end of the Diet of 1765–6 he had become increasingly critical towards the existing political system, most pertinently its party system. Saying farewell to the Caps – who of course had kicked him out – he raised a critique against the Age of Liberty as a whole. Certainly the verdict regarding this Age has differed among

Figure 13 In 1805, Chydenius's friends had an engraved portrait made of him. Stipple engraving and aquatint. J.F. Martin, 1805. The K.H. Renlund Museum – Provincial Museum of Central Ostrobothnia.

historians. While some have seen only its shortcomings, others have been more positive. In contrast to the absolutism that prevailed before 1718, the new constitution without doubt brought many new liberties. At least to some extent, a polity was introduced which resembled the English system after 1688: a system of checks and balances that could curb the abuse of governmental power. While the estates system did not constitute a parliament in the modern sense, it was nevertheless the case during the Age of Liberty that the estates were much more powerful than the monarch. In theory it resembled an order built upon the idea of a balance of power, as the new constitution defined that the estates were the lawmakers, while the monarch (including the Council of the Realm and the state administration) functioned as the executive power. In reality, of course, the divide between law-making and execution was crossed constantly by the estates, which were eager to govern directly.[118]

Against this background, most modern historians have described the Age of Liberty as semi-democratic, the embryo of a modern parliamentary system.[119] Others (scholars mainly of an older generation) have instead condemned it as corrupt, and dominated by self-interested elitist parties fighting over the spoils of government.[120] As we have seen, Chydenius was apt to agree with the latter characterization. Rather than an Age of Liberty, it was an age of bitter party strife and lack of concord, he thought.

This was the reason why Chydenius, following Gustavus III's *coup d'état* in 1772, was so ready to hail him as a liberator. Hence, right from the beginning and until his death he defended the new constitution of 1772, which emphasized monarchical power as a replacement for the rule of the estates that had held sway during the Age of Liberty. Chydenius became what in the Swedish realm at the time was called a Gustavian, a follower of an order that to a large extent resembled the kind of enlightened absolutism which was common in continental Europe during this period. Chydenius especially hailed the new regime for creating national concord and internal peace. In a speech given in Kokkola in 1778 at Gustavus's birthday, Chydenius depicted the old regime in dark colours: "Sweden was in a bad way when Gustavus took over the sceptre," he said. It was a time when "everybody wanted to rule but no one wanted to obey". But now a new time had emerged in all its glory. Gustavus has created the necessary concord, and unity now prevails in the nation, he insists. And he breaks into verse:

> Let out fire and thunder
> so that the Heavens shake,
> Our ship steers blissfully forward,
> As long as Gustavus illuminates our path.[121]

Chydenius's earlier biographers have often found it problematic that this prototype of a "modern" liberal could have been such a stern Gustavian. Even Virrankoski in his balanced analysis wonders whether or not Chydenius was an opportunist who defended the king in order to gain favour.[122] Without doubt his support was conditional: only to the extent that Gustavus defended the rights and liberties of his subjects was he the kind of ruler Sweden needed. At times, Chydenius seems to have doubted whether the king was really fulfilling this role; especially after his dramatic return from the Diet of 1792 in Gävle, which, as we have seen, was dominated by the king and his police. On the other hand, there is no doubt that Chydenius really did become a convinced Gustavian; standing for election in 1792 to participate in Gävle, he was openly recognized as belonging to the "royal party". While most of his colleagues in the Estate of Clergy in Ostrobothnia had left this party during the 1780s, Chydenius remained loyal to it.[123] He was certainly also horrified by the assassination of Gustavus at the opera house in Stockholm some months later, carried out by a group of conspiring noblemen.[124]

Perhaps we should not be surprised at Chydenius's support of the king. In fact, to regard monarchical rule as the best means of serving the common good was common during this period. First, the view that it was as a guarantee for concord and happiness in the state was part of an older popular ideology in Sweden connected with the Estate system defining a fair and just political order. In that country, as Michael Roberts has emphasized, "the peasants have always by tradition been positive to a strong monarch".[125] Hence, an older generation of historians such as Erik Gustaf Geijer spoke of "condemnation of aristocracy" (*aristokrati-fördömande*) as a prevailing political attitude among the lower estates in the Swedish realm all the way back to the medieval period. The reason was simple: a "just" monarch could maintain the existing privileges and the rights of the different orders in society. A weak monarch would leave the door open for private interest and rent-seeking.

Second, to hail absolute monarchs ruling according to the constitution as the best proponents of enlightened governance was widespread among radicals too during this period. In Denmark and Prussia this was a common view among friends of liberal reform. In France the economically liberal Physiocrats, headed by the king's personal physician, François Quesnay, were openly in favour of a strong monarchy which could guarantee that laws were protected within a constitution based upon natural liberty. In the Swedish realm, Chydenius was by no means alone in being a follower of Gustavus's revolution while at the same time propounding Enlightenment views. On the contrary, up to the mid-1780s there were very few who had a problem with this, while at the same time condemning the Age of Liberty for its corruption and party politics. One obvious example is Carl Fredrik Scheffer, Crown Prince Gustavus's tutor and friend, as well as one of the founding fathers of the new constitution of 1772. He was also the translator of French Physiocratic texts and was known for his hatred of the Age of Liberty constitution.[126] Another example is the finance minister Johan Liljencrants,[127] who more than any other politician at the time contributed to pushing forward a number of liberal economic reforms, which incidentally were in accordance with Chydenius's views during the 1780s. Lastly, the case of Chydenius's long-term friend and correspondent Anders Schönberg is highly illuminating. He was a warm friend of the coup in 1772, finding arguments for his support in Montesquieu's contract theory. In 1776 he published a fragment of a much longer piece which he as official historiographer royal had written concerning the history of government in Sweden. Here he condemned the Age of Liberty in clear language and hailed a system in which the king was the executive power while the estates should be the procurers of new legislation.[128]

Against this background it might seem peculiar that Chydenius at the same time was regarded as an enthusiastic democrat. However, this must also be understood in its contemporary and pre-modern meaning. Hence, what struck contemporaries was Chydenius's support for the common people against the nobility and big merchant capitalists. In particular, his taking the side of servants and workers – which involved him in a lengthy public debate in the Stockholm newspaper *Dagligt Allehanda* in 1778 and 1779 – has led at least some modern interpreters to question whether he was not in fact some kind of socialist.[129] However, this would certainly be a mistake. First and foremost, his insistence that all men were born free and should not be the property of other men stemmed from his interpretation of concepts such as natural law and natural liberty. The opinion that they should be able to move freely and to speak their minds independently merely followed from such a premise. Moreover, the fact that men were born with rights must be recognized by the ruler, he thought. All men should be equal under the constitution and the law. Hence, when he gives support to servants, he points to their problematic situation as semi-slaves under their masters. Accordingly, they were not free with regard to body and mind and hence able to use their freeborn rights. When he criticized the prohibitions against free peasant trade in Ostrobothnia, he insisted that such regulations violated the natural liberty of this group. As ordinances hindered the peasants from seeking opportunity and gain wherever they could, regulations of this kind upset the principle of natural liberty.

Defending the rights of common people, Chydenius also looked backwards to ideologies of an older origin. As in many parts of Europe, the estates' status as free corporations was still defended in the Swedish realm during the Age of Liberty. Ideally, the estates were regarded as the instruments for the corporate and collective will. One peculiarity, which we have already noted, was that the peasants too were allowed to form an estate in order to influence the political order in the kingdom. By the middle of the seventeenth century the Estates of Peasants and of Clergy had both become hothouses of radical ideas based on the notion of exclusive rights and privileges provided to them. With the exception of bishops and other higher clergy, perhaps, the Estate of Clergy often tended to take the peasants' view in their struggle against the noblemen and burghers; this was also to some extent the case at the Diet of 1765–6 and in the campaigns of the radical Caps from the clerical estate. Especially under the reign of Queen Christina (1644–54), both the peasantry and the clergy had defended the free status of the so-called tax-paying farmers (*skattebönder*) with allodial rights to their land against "feudal" conceptions (which the Swedish nobility had picked up when expanding their landowning in the Baltic area during the seventeenth century), which instead emphasized the subordinate position of all peasants.

While much of this radicalism disappeared during the period when Sweden was ruled by absolute monarchs up to 1718 and no Diets were held, this sense of estate exclusiveness returned during the Age of Liberty. However, as we have observed, at the end of the Age of Liberty a "party" of radical Caps emerged which was fiercely opposed to the Hat regime and saw itself as representing the people versus the elite. In general, its followers in the peasant or the clerical estate were especially vocal at the Diets of 1762, 1765–6 and 1769. Chydenius, as we have seen, belonged to such a Finnish network of radical Caps when he first entered the Diet of 1765–6. Moreover, at this Diet he was so outspoken in his critique against the noblemen and merchant capitalists that he gained the reputation of being a fierce radical. Especially regarding the nobility, he remained critical for the rest of his life. Hence, he supported all the reforms made during the reign of Gustavus III to strengthen the peasants' legal titles and ownership of land. When the nobility was stripped of its privilege to hold land with special rights, so-called *frälse-jord*, in 1789, he applauded loudly. Later in life, when he wrote his proposal on how to develop and populate Lapland, he spoke in favour of a system in which small peasants should be able to own their tilled land and from which all noble landowners should be excluded.[130]

When Chydenius defends the right of common people, he takes his point of departure from an ideology of rights developed within the old estate system – spiced up with the gospel of hard work as a moral obligation. This is the mixture he used when opposing the nobility as well as the rich merchant class. To some extent he transcended this ideology in order to advocate equal rights for all (including servants, which was seldom explicitly done at this time, as servants were often regarded as dependants in the same fashion as non-adults). However, all this took place still largely within a political idiom that was pre-modern in every sense of the word. Chydenius is in principle not affronted by an order that allocated different positions in society to different estates. It was only when such privileges violated the principle of natural rights – or, more profoundly, when the elite made use of their position of power to violate these rights – that his indignation is stirred.

Orthodox Lutheran and pietist

Chydenius's ancestors had been clergymen, and one of his nephews, whom he took care of when he was young, Jakob Tengström,[131] later became professor of theology and bishop of the Turku diocese. Chydenius himself never reached such a high position in the Church hierarchy; he became doctor *honoris causa* in theology (1779) and ended his career as rural dean (*kontraktsprost*) at Kokkola in 1781. Hence, for most of his life he served as an ordinary rector. We have already seen that his interest in theological issues developed even further after his participation in the Diet of 1778–9. To what extent his extensive publishing activities concerning theological issues had to do with the critique he received from colleagues when helping to push through the Ordinance on Religious Freedom shortly thereafter we can only guess.

Figure 14 After his death, Chydenius was largely forgotten about and he remained in oblivion until the end of the nineteenth century, when he was rediscovered by liberal historians and politicians. At the beginning of the twentieth century, Chydenius became one of the national heroes and most prominent figures in Finland's nation-building process. The bust of Chydenius, sculpted by Walter Runeberg, was unveiled in Kokkola in 1903.

We do not know whether Chydenius ever had the chance to read John Locke's text arguing for religious toleration; it had been translated into Swedish in 1721 but was not published until the 1790s because of resistance from the Church.[132] Nevertheless, Chydenius probably was familiar with its main arguments, especially the argument (put forward by many others apart from Locke at the time) that religious toleration was necessary in order to stimulate immigration of foreign workers in order to establish more industry and make the nation wealthier. However, as a general trait Chydenius was quite orthodox in his theology. Modern interpreters have often in vain searched for more radical viewpoints in his religious texts in an attempt to link his religious views with his radical politics. Instead, he was by and large faithful to the orthodox Lutheranism that was taught and preached during this time. Hence, according to his nephew Jakob Tengström, he was a "warm defender of the religious faith". In Church matters, according to one of his biographers, he was almost "dogmatic".[133] His religious texts, for example the extensive printed sermons, are filled with references to the sinful character of fallen man. He speaks against heresy and disbelief; men can find peace only in salvation and must seek salvation through repentance. This was also a time when the so-called *Hustavlan* (the Table of Duties in Luther's Small Catechism) was the ruling paternalistic ideology taught by the Lutheran Church in Sweden. Apart from insisting that servants should be subordinate to their masters, sons to fathers and women to men, etc., this ideology emphasized that a true Christian must work in the sweat of his brow. It is clear that Chydenius in general terms agreed with what was spelled out in Luther's catechism: "those who do not work shall not eat". As we have seen, such puritan views inspired him when he emphasized that hard work in order to pursue personal wealth and happiness was a natural right among the poor as well as others. Moreover, he was not, as were many of the reform-mercantilists, especially those inspired by Mirabeau and other pre-Physiocrats (for example, Fischerström and Leuhusen but also Scheffer), in favour of "luxury" as a means to increase the wealth of a nation – what Anders Johan von Höpken in 1740, clearly inspired by Mandeville, called "the utility of exuberance" (*yppighetens nytta*).[134] Instead, Chydenius favoured hard work as a means of increasing prosperity and regarded luxury consumption as vainglory or even as a sinister activity.

Chydenius was not only sceptical towards irreligious trends within the Enlightenment movement but also a clear enemy of some of the new religious ideas that spread during this period and gave rise to a number of sects, including a form of Pietism (radical Pietism) and the so-called Moravian Brethren (*herrnhutarna*), founded by the Danish count Nikolaus Ludvig von Zinzendorf in the 1720s. At his location in Ostrobothnia, Chydenius had most probably come into contact with people who knew the so-called Eriksson brothers and their followers (in all, sixty people, also known as *skevikarna*), who in the early 1730s had to leave the country. All these sects belonged to a Pietist trend of theological thinking and practice that had been developing since the late seventeenth century. Such sects shared a number of dogmas that differed from those of the established Church. They paid more attention to the sermon and the role of the priest to enliven the Christian gospel. They were sentimental devotees of Christ; Count Zinzendorf and his followers have been described as having an almost erotic relationship with Christ, worshipping his wounds and blood. What perhaps most irritated the orthodox state Church was their positive attitude towards more religious toleration. They were particularly critical of the Royal Proclamation against Conventicles (*konventikelplakatet*), which had been introduced in 1726 and forbade believers to congregate and have ceremonies led by anyone other than a consecrated clergyman. As we have seen, Chydenius was clearly in favour of more tolerance, including with regard to this issue. In his youth, living with his family in the forests of Lapland, he must have seen how difficult it was in practice to travel hundreds of miles to the closest parish church in order to attend services. As an established rector at Kokkola he was recognized for inviting members of his congregation to his home and giving special services there (perhaps with some music added). Moreover, he seems also to have been tolerant with regard to non-believers and heretics living in the parish, including, it seems, having a discussion on religious matters with a Pietist woman called Anna Stina Silahka.[135] Most probably his tolerance stemmed from the fact that Ostrobothnia housed both Pietists and orthodox Lutherans, and that harmony in such a situation was better than division and bitter struggle.

Given his tolerant views towards the Pietist movement, it has been discussed to what extent he should be described as an "orthodox" Lutheran or in fact as a Pietist in disguise. As Carola Nordbäck has argued, such concepts have been created much later and there is a danger that in trying to decide which of them we should use, we fall into the trap of anachronism. Instead, she argues that Chydenius mixed new (Pietist) views with old (orthodox) ones, in the same manner as he mixes theology with a moral philosophy of natural rights.[136] His orthodoxy is shown, for example, in his stern puritanical ethos of work. On the other hand, his inklings for new theological ideas are illuminated when he proposes that not the forms of worship but religious feeling should be the most important for a true Christian. Instead of preaching the dead letter, he emphasized the living religion. Moreover, he argued that living in faith must also include a willingness to perform good deeds; no one can reach salvation through faith alone if at the same time he lives sinfully. However, to the extent that he was influenced by Pietism, this was surely to an older form of Pietism closer to the views of the established Church. He was never a sectarian and was, as we have seen, openly critical of Zinzendorf in particular, whose teachings he regarded, according to Virrankoski, as dangerous and false doctrines.[137]

After the death of Chydenius in 1803, tumultuous changes occurred, taking the history of Sweden and Finland in new directions. The disastrous war with Russia which Gustavus III's son Gustavus IV waged during the so-called Fourth Coalition after the Tilsit peace between Napoleon and Tsar Alexander in 1807 led not only to his abdication in 1809, but also to the loss of Finland the same year. Finland was invaded by Russia, threatening the very existence of Sweden as a nation. In 1809, Alexander made Finland a grand duchy within his expanding empire and promised to maintain its laws and regulations and its Lutheran faith. In the case of Sweden, the year 1809 ended for ever whatever dreams it still had of playing an important role in European politics. Even more so than after 1721, it turned its energies inwards to foster neutrality in its foreign policies and industrial as well as social progress at home. Both in Sweden and Finland after 1809 the intellectual climate experienced a process of domestication. Only slowly was Sweden after 1830 able to see a return to a livelier debate on political and economic issues – and this came even later to Finland, where radical ideas had to be cautiously avoided in order not to upset its Russian rulers. Hence, most of Finland's energies became focused on developing the economy and on what later on during the nineteenth century was to be connected with the Fennoman movement: the quest for national language and culture and, in the long run, national independence. In Finland, Anders Chydenius became an icon for the search of national identity – an ideal modern type of man around which it would be possible to build a new liberal and democratic future. In Sweden, Chydenius to a large extent was forgotten. His struggle for freedom of the press and religious tolerance was sometimes recalled by nineteenth-century liberals, but his bowing to the absolutist ambitions of Gustavus III has been regarded by many as a blot on his memory. At the same time, reform-mercantilism of the late-eighteenth-century kind was transformed into national economy – more influenced by German cameralism than by French liberalism or English political economy. When liberal economic ideas returned to the Swedish discussion in the middle of the century, it was neither Adam Smith – whose ideas are subsumed in the form of an "industrial system", which emphasizes state help to establish industry in order to create economic prosperity – nor the classical political economy that was the big influence. Rather, as we have seen, a peculiar mixture appears, with harmony economics (formulated by Bastiat in France and Cobden in England), together with a belief in state intervention, being established as the leading economic doctrine. Hence, as we have noted, there is no straight line to be drawn from Chydenius to economic and political modernity, either in Sweden or in Finland. He was certainly an extraordinary man: someone we must always return to in order to grasp the richness of his own time, but also to make intelligible the variety and open character of the historical and intellectual process over time.

Notes

1 C.G. Uhr, *Anders Chydenius 1729–1803. A Finnish Predecessor to Adam Smith*, Meddelanden från Nationalekonomiska institutionen vid Handelshögskolan vid Åbo Akademi, no. 6, Åbo: Åbo Akademi, 1963, p. 10f.

2 F.J. Rabbe, "Anders Chydenius", in *Finlands minnesvärde män: samling af lefnadsteckningar*, vol. 2, Helsinki: J.C. Frenckell & Son, 1857, p. 321f.

3 E.G. Palmén, *Politiska skrifter af Anders Chydenius: Med en historisk inledning*, Helsinki: G.W. Edlunds förlag, 1880, p. LXV.

4 E.F. Heckscher, *Sveriges ekonomiska historia från Gustav Vasa*, II:2, Stockholm: Albert Bonniers förlag, 1949, p. 866.

5 G. Schauman, *Biografiska undersökningar om Anders Chydenius*, Skrifter utgifna af Svenska Litteratursällskapet i Finland 84, Helsinki: Svenska Litteratursällskapet i Finland, 1908, p. 490.

6 P. Virrankoski, *Anders Chydenius: Demokratisk politiker i upplysningens tid*, Stockholm: Timbro, 1995, p. 66.

7 Schauman, op. cit., p. 339f.

8 For a general discussion on this topic, see L. Magnusson, *The Tradition of Free Trade*, London: Routledge, 2004, pp. 1–19.

9 Heckscher, op. cit., p. 866; Uhr, op. cit., p. 11. For a theoretical and methodological approach that stresses the role of practice and historical context in intellectual history, see Q. Skinner, *Visions of Politics I: Regarding Method*, Cambridge: Cambridge University Press, 2002. See also Magnusson, op. cit., p. 12f. See also C. Nordbäck, *Lycksalighetens källa: Kontextuella närläsningar av Anders Chydenius budordspredikningar 1781–92*, Åbo: Åbo Akademis förlag, 2009, for an approach to Chydenius similar to mine.

10 In a letter from Schönberg to the publicist Carl Christoffer Gjörwell, cited in Schauman, op. cit., p. 235.

11 Virrankoski, op. cit., p. 38f.

12 A. Chydenius, "Herda-Qväde" [1766], published in Schauman, op. cit., p. 528.

13 Being from the periphery of the realm himself, Chydenius in his writings often emphasised the oftentimes unfavorable conditions the people in the more remote regions lived in. Cf. Virrankoski, op. cit., p. 102ff.

14 For this system, see G. Sundberg, *Partipolitik och regionala intressen 1755–1766: Studier kring det bottniska handelstvångets hävande*, Studia Historica Upsaliensia 104, Uppsala, 1978, ch. 1.

15 E.F. Heckscher, *Sveriges ekonomiska historia från Gustav Vasa*, II:1, Stockholm: Albert Bonniers förlag, 1949, p. 33.

16 L. Thanner, *Revolutionen i Sverige efter Karl XII:s död: Den inrepolitiska maktkampen under tidigare delen av Ulrika Eleonora d.y:s regering*, Uppsala: Almqvist & Wiksell, 1953, p. 193f. See also E. Ekegård, *Studier i svensk handelspolitik under den tidigare frihetstiden*, Uppsala, 1924, p. 128f.

17 M. Roberts, *The Age of Liberty: Sweden 1719–1772*, Cambridge: Cambridge University Press, 1986, p. 93f.

18 C.G. Malmström, *Sveriges politiska historia från Konung Karl XII:s död till statshvälfningen 1772*, del III, 2. uppl., Stockholm: P.A. Norstedts & söners förlag, 1897, p. 402f.

19 For this and the following, see P.-E. Brolin, *Hattar och mössor i borgarståndet, 1760–1766*, Uppsala: AB Lundquistska bokhandeln, 1953.

20 J. Nordin, "Frihetstidens radikalism", in M.-C. Skuncke and H. Tandefelt (eds), *Riksdag, kaffehus och predikstol: Frihetstidens politiska kultur 1766–1772*, Stockholm: Atlantis, 2003, pp. 55–72. See also P. Winton, *Frihetstidens politiska praktik: Nätverk och offentlighet 1746–1766*, Studia Historica Upsaliensia 223, Uppsala: Acta Universitatis Upsaliensis, 2006, p. 5ff.

21 Concerning how foreigners interpreted the new constitution, especially in Germany, see E. Nokkala, "Debatten mellan J. H. G. von Justi och H. L. von Heß om frihetstidens författning", in *Historisk Tidskrift för Finland*, issue 1, 2009, pp. 20–55.

22 T. von Vegesack, *Smak för frihet: Opinionsbildningen i Sverige 1755–1830*, Stockholm: Natur och Kultur, 1995, p. 27f.; E.F. Heckscher, *Sveriges ekonomiska historia från Gustav Vasa*, II:2, Stockholm: Albert Bonniers förlag, 1949, p. 812f.

23 S. Lindroth, *Svensk lärdomshistoria: Frihetstiden*, Stockholm: Norstedt, 1978, p. 91f.

24 See L. Magnusson, *Äran, korruptionen och den borgerliga ordningen*, Stockholm: Atlantis, 2001; K. Petander, *De nationalekonomiska åskådningarna i Sverige: Sådana de framträda i litteraturen*, vol. 1, Stockholm: P.A. Norstedt & söner, 1912; L. Magnusson, "Corruption and Civic Order: Natural Law and Economic Discourse

in Sweden during the Age of Freedom", *Scandinavian Economic History Review*, 1989, vol. 37:2, pp. 78–105.

25 Lindroth, op. cit., p. 48f.; K. Forsman, "Studier i det svenska 1700-talets ekonomiska litteratur", in *Skrifter utgivna av Svenska Litteratursällskapet i Finland*, vol. 312, Helsinki, 1947, p. 112f.

26 On the establishment of economics at Uppsala University and in Sweden, see S.-E. Liedman, *Den synliga handen: Anders Berch och ekonomiämnena vid 1700-talets svenska universitet*, Stockholm: Arbetarkultur, 1986.

27 Cit. from B. Hildebrand, *Kungl. svenska Vetenskapsakademin: Förhistoria, grundläggning och första organisation*, Stockholm: Kungl. Vetenskapsakademien, 1939, p. 381f.; cf. also Forsman, op. cit., p. 129.

28 See L. Magnusson, *An Economic History of Sweden*, London: Routledge, 2000, ch. 1; cf. C.-J. Gadd, *Det svenska jordbrukets historia*, vol. 3: *Den agrara revolutionen 1700–1870*, Stockholm: Natur och Kultur, 2000, p. 186f.

29 E.F. Heckscher, *Sveriges ekonomiska historia från Gustav Vasa*, II:1, Stockholm: Albert Bonniers förlag, 1949, p. 34f.

30 The classical reference here is still P. Nyström, *Stadsindustriens arbetare före 1800-talet: Bidrag till kännedom om den svenska manufakturindustrien och dess sociala förhållanden*, Stockholm: Tidens förlag, 1955.

31 A criticism that no doubt influenced Heckscher in his characterization of most of the manufactories as "hothouse flowers". See E.F. Heckscher, *Sveriges ekonomiska historia från Gustav Vasa*, II:2, Stockholm: Albert Bonniers förlag, 1949, p. 585f.

32 However, far from everything disappeared, especially with regard to the Stockholm textile manufactories. See the critique of Heckscher's "liberal bias" in Nyström, op. cit.

33 For example, Petander, op. cit.; Forsman, op. cit.; and Heckscher, op. cit., p. 857f.

34 Heckscher, op. cit., p. 826f.

35 A. Berch, *Tal om den proportion, som de studerande ärfordra til de ledige beställningar i riket...*, Stockholm, 1749, p. 15f.

36 J.F. Kryger, *Tankar om swenske fabriquerne upsatte af Johan Fredric Kryger*, Stockholm, 1755, p. 251f. About Kryger, see note 2, p. 115.

37 E. Salander, *Tal, om slögder, hållit för Kongl. Vetenskaps Academien af Eric Salander...*, Stockholm, 1754.

38 Virrankoski, op. cit., p. 35f.; Schauman, op. cit., p. 9f.

39 Dissertations were still most often written in Latin at this time, but in "utilistic" subjects such as economics they could be written in Swedish. This was done more often in Turku than in Uppsala and Lund.

40 A new translation has been published in E. Cormack (ed.), *The Linnaeus apostles: Global science & adventure. Europe, North & South America*, vol. 3: book 2, *Pehr Kalm*, London: IK Foundation, 2008.

41 Virrankoski, op. cit., p. 48f; Schauman, op. cit., p. 11f.

42 On this influence, see T. Frängsmyr, *Wolffianismens genombrott i Uppsala: Frihetstida universitetsfilosofi till 1700-talets mitt*, Uppsala, 1972.

43 Frängsmyr, op. cit.; see also T. Frängsmyr, "Den gudomliga ekonomin: Religion och hushållning i 1700-talets Sverige", *Lychnos*, 1971–2, pp. 217–44. See also p. 41.

44 Virrankoski, op. cit., p. 51f.

45 For an interpretation of the relationship between Pufendorf and Chydenius, see Nordbäck, op. cit., p. 217f.

46 J. Chydenius, *Sednare delen, om gamle Carleby, med wederbörandes minne, utgifwen af præses, Jacob Chydenius...*, Åbo, 1754. Citation from Schauman, op. cit., p. 20 (translation by the author).

47 A. Chydenius, *Tankar vid genomläsandet af Herr Professoren Doctor Gabr. Er. Haartmans Memorial till Kongl. Finska Hushållnings Sällskapet rörande min berättelse om Koppympningen* [1800], in Schauman, op. cit., p. 609f.

48 P. Stenhagen, *Tankar om Nödwändigheten af Stapel-Städers anläggande i Sweriges Norra Orter och i synnerhet Öster- och Wästerbottn*, Stockholm, 1762.

49 Virrankoski, op. cit., p. 106.

50 Winton, op. cit., p. 270f.

51 Virrankoski, op. cit., p. 97f.

52 See, for example, Winton, op. cit., p. 254f.

53 Cf. the discussion whether or not Chydenius was in fact the most active discussant in the Estate of Clergy: Schauman, op. cit., p. 108; Virrankoski, op. cit., p. 122.

54 Virrankoski, op. cit., p. 123.

55 A. Chydenius, *Wederläggning Af de Skäl, Hwarmed man söker bestrida Öster- och Västerbotniska Samt Wäster-Norrländske Städerne Fri Seglation*, Stockholm, 1765.

56 In eighteenth-century Sweden it was said that the exchange rate was "high" when an increased amount of Swedish money was needed to buy foreign currency. Today we would say "low".

57 J.W. Arnberg, *Anteckningar om frihetstidens politiska ekonomi*, Uppsala: W. Schultz förlag, 1868, p. 9ff.

58 Virrankoski, op. cit., p. 211.

59 About the Exchange Bill Office (*wäxel-contoir*), see note 12, p. 165.

60 On this, see Heckscher, op. cit., p. 769f., and Magnusson, "Corruption and Civic Order", p. 80.

61 Magnusson, "Corruption and Civic Order", p. 81.

62 Virrankoski, op. cit., p. 151. Cf. also Schauman, op. cit., p. 60f.

63 See further pp. 214–15.

64 This aspect is especially emphasized in J. Manninen, "Anders Chydenius and the Origins of the World's First Freedom of Information Act", in J. Mustonen (ed.), *The World's First Freedom of Information Act: Anders Chydenius' Legacy Today*, Kokkola, Finland: Anders Chydenius Foundation, 2006, pp. 18–53.

65 See P. Forsskål, *Thoughts on Civil Liberty: Translation of the Original Manuscript with Background*, Stockholm: Atlantis, 2009.

66 A. Nordencrantz, *Oförgripelige tankar, om Frihet i bruk af förnuft, pennor och tryck, samt huru långt friheten derutinnan i et fritt samhälle sig sträcka bör, tillika med påfölgden deraf*, Stockholm, 1756.

67 On the history of the freedom of printing in Sweden and particularly during the eighteenth century, see, for example, T. von Vegesack, *Smak för frihet: Opinionsbildning i Sverige 1755–1830*, Stockholm: Natur och Kultur, 1995; H. Eek, "1766 års tryckfrihetsordning, dess tillkomst och betydelse i rättsutvecklingen", *Statsvetenskaplig Tidskrift*, 1943, pp. 185–222.

68 For a presentation regarding Chydenius's time in Stockholm, see H. Knif, "Den farliga staden: Anders Chydenius och Stockholm", in M.-C. Skuncke and H. Tandefelt (eds), *Riksdag, kaffehus och predikstol: Frihetstidens politiska kultur 1766–1772*, Stockholm: Atlantis, 2003, p. 155f.

69 A. Chydenius, "Herda-Qväde" [1766]. Cited from Schauman, op. cit., p. 240 (translation by the author).

70 Schauman, op. cit., p. 389f.

71 Published in Schauman, op. cit., pp. 566–608.

72 Virrankoski, op. cit., p. 321f.

73 Virrankoski, op. cit., p. 323.

74 Virrankoski, op. cit., p. 347. These sermons are presented and analysed thoroughly in Nordbäck, op. cit.

75 Virrankoski, op. cit., p. 338.

76 Virrankoski, op. cit., p. 392.

77 Petander, op. cit.; G. Schauman, *Studier i Frihetstidens nationalekonomiska litteratur: Idéer och strömningar 1718–1740*, Helsinki, 1910, p. 80f; E.F. Heckscher, *Sveriges ekonomiska historia från Gustav Vasa*, II:2, Stockholm: Albert Bonniers

förlag, 1949, p. 806f; Magnusson, *Äran, korruptionen och den borgerliga ordningen*, op. cit., p. 51f.

78 Heckscher, op. cit., p. 826f.

79 Petander, op. cit., p. 19.

80 A. Berch, *Inledning til Almänna Hushållningen*, Stockholm, 1747, p. 55f.

81 L. Magnusson, *Mercantilism: The Shaping of an Economic Language*, London: Routledge, 1994, p. 147f.

82 I. Hont, *Jealousy of Trade: International Competition and the Nation-State in Historical Perspective*, Cambridge, Mass.: Harvard University Press, 2005, p. 5f.

83 Heckscher, op. cit., p. 824; L. Herlitz, *Fysiokratismen i svensk tappning 1767–1770*, Meddelanden från Ekonomisk-historiska institutionen vid Göteborgs universitet, vol. 35, Gothenburg, 1974, p. 9.

84 Nordencrantz's dependence upon Mandeville is especially emphasized by L. Herlitz, "Anders Nordencrantz", in *Sveriges Biografiska Lexikon*, vol. 27, Stockholm, 1990–1, p. 187f.

85 Virrankoski, op. cit., p. 43. The text by Sahlstedt was *Om frihet i näringar, i synnerhet wid swenska fabrikerna och handtwärken*, published in 1763.

86 On Salvius and Polhem, see L. Magnusson, "Mercantilism and 'reform' mercantilism: the rise of economic discourse in Sweden during the eighteenth century", *History of Political Economy*, 1987, vol. 19:3, pp. 415–33.

87 See p. 144.

88 E.A. Johnson, *Predecessors of Adam Smith: The Growth of British Economic Thought*, New York: Prentice Hall, 1937; L. Magnusson, *Mercantilism: The Shaping of an Economic Language*, London: Routledge, 1994, p. 134f.

89 Forsman, op. cit., p. 159.

90 Heckscher, op. cit., p. 863.

91 C. Leuhusen, *Tankar om de rätta och sanskyldiga Medel Til Sweriges Wälmåga*, 2 vols, Stockholm, 1761, 1763; J. Fischerström, *Påminnelser wid Sweriges Allmänna och enskylta Hushållning*, Stockholm, 1761.

92 Forsman, op. cit., p. 195.

93 Ibid., p. 201.

94 Ibid., op. cit., p. 172.

95 Heckscher, op. cit., p. 865; Uhr, op. cit., p. 41.

96 For a discussion on Smith's metaphor, see E. Rothschild, *Economic Sentiments: Adam Smith, Condorcet and the Enlightenment*, Cambridge, Mass.: Harvard University Press, 2001, p. 116f.

97 Schauman, op. cit., p. 211.

98 C. Horn, *Ödmjukt memorial af fri-herre Christer Horn til Höglofliga Ridderskapets och Adelen angående Höglofliga Secrete utskottets til Riksens Höglofligе Ständer upgifne berättelse om Banco-förwaltningen*, Stockholm, 1766; E. Swedenborg, *Oförgripelige Tanckar om Swenska Myntetz Förnedring och Förhögning*, Stockholm, 1722.

99 Uhr, op. cit., p. 7, 11.

100 Cited from Schauman, op. cit, p. 223.

101 Schauman, op. cit., p. 273.

102 Ibid., pp. 235, 273.

103 Nordbäck, op. cit., p. 346f.

104 K. Haakonssen and H. Horstbøll (eds), *Northern Antiquities and National Identities: Perceptions of Denmark and the North in the Eighteenth Century*, Copenhagen: Det Kongelige Danske Videnskabernes Selskab, 2007, ch. 10 and ch. 12.

105 T. Frängsmyr, *Wolffianismens genombrott i Uppsala: frihetstida universitetsfilosofi till 1700-talets mitt*, Uppsala, 1972, ch. 1; Liedman, op. cit., p. 30f.

106 G. Schauman, *Studier i Frihetstidens ekonomiska litteratur: Idéer och strömningar 1718–1740*, Helsinki, 1910, p. 52.

107 Cited from T. Frängsmyr, "Den gudomliga ekonomin: Religion och hushållning i 1700-talets Sverige", *Lychnos*, 1971–2, p. 230.

108 Ibid., p. 222.

109 On Pufendorf, see, for example, L. Krieger, *The Politics of Discretion: Pufendorf and the Acceptance of Natural Law*, Chicago: University of Chicago Press, 1965; and R. Tuck, *Natural Rights Theories: Their Origin and Development*, Cambridge: Cambridge University Press, 1979. On Pufendorf in Sweden, see B. Lindberg, *Naturrätten i Uppsala 1655–1720*, Uppsala: Acta Universitatis Upsaliensis, 1976.

110 Cf. Nordbäck, op. cit., p. 366.

111 See pp. 32–3.

112 G. Schauman, *Biografiska undersökningar om Anders Chydenius*, Skrifter utgifna af Svenska Litteratursällskapet i Finland 84, Helsinki: Svenska Litteratursällskapet i Finland, 1908, p. 329.

113 A. Chydenius, *Omständeligt Swar, På Den genom Trycket utkomne Wederläggning af Skriften, Kallad: Källan til Rikets Wanmagt*, Stockholm, 1765.

114 J.F. Kryger, *Tankar wid lediga stunder*, andra delen, Stockholm, 1763, p. 160.

115 For an analysis of Gibbon and his interpretation of the decline of the Roman Empire, see J.G.A. Pocock, *Barbarism and Religion*, vol. 1: *The Enlightenments of Edward Gibbon, 1737–1764*, Cambridge: Cambridge University Press, 1999.

116 For this interpretation, see L. Magnusson, "Corruption and Civic Order", op. cit., vol. XXXVII: 2, pp. 78–105; cf. also I. Hont, "The Language of Sociability and Commerce: Samuel Pufendorf and the Theoretical Foundations of the 'Four-Stages Theory'", in A. Pagden (ed.), *The Languages of Political Theory in Early-Modern Europe*, Cambridge: Cambridge University Press, 1987, p. 253f.

117 Schauman, op. cit., p. 412.

118 See Roberts, op. cit.

119 For a very positive view by a modern historian as well as an overview of the debate on the issue since the nineteenth century, see M.F. Metcalf, "The First Modern Party System? Political Parties, Sweden's Age of Liberty and the Historians", *Scandinavian Journal of History*, vol. 2, 1977, pp. 265–87. Cf. also M. Roberts, *Swedish and English Parliamentarism in the Eighteenth Century*, Belfast: Queen's University, 1973.

120 The main reference point is still the nineteenth-century debate between Erik Gustaf Geijer and Anders Fryxell. For an overview, see Metcalf, op. cit.; cf. F. Lagerroth, *Frihetstidens författning: En studie i den svenska konstitutionalismens historia*, Stockholm: Bonnier, 1915.

121 Cited from Schauman, op. cit., p. 535f. In Swedish: "Låt eld och åska åka fram / At Firmamentet ryser, / Wårt skepp går lika lyckligt an / Så länge Gustaf lyser" (translation by the author).

122 Virrankoski, op. cit., p. 262f.

123 See P. Virrankoski, "Anders Chydenius and the Government of Gustavus III of Sweden in the 1770s", *Scandinavian Journal of History*, 1988, vol. 13, pp. 107–19 at p. 119.

124 Schauman, op. cit., p. 392f.

125 Roberts, *The Age of Liberty*, op. cit., p. 267.

126 L. Magnusson, "Physiocracy in Sweden", in B. Delmas, T. Delmas and P. Steiner (eds), *La Diffusion internationale de la Physiocratie*, Grenoble: Presses Universitaires de Grenoble, 1995, pp. 281–99.

127 Permanent Secretary (*statssekreterare*) Johan Liljencrants (1730–1815) was King Gustavus III's financial adviser for many years.

128 H. Schück and K. Warburg, *Illustrerad svensk litteraturhistoria: Romantiken*, Stockholm: Hugo Gebers förlag, 1929, p. 144f.

129 Schauman, op. cit., p. 450f.

130 Ibid., p. 450.

131 Jakob Tengström (1755–1832) was the oldest son of Chydenius's sister Maria from her marriage with Johan Tengström the elder. See note 11, p. 347.
132 P. Virrankoski, *Anders Chydenius: Demokratisk politiker i upplysningens tid*, Stockholm: Timbro, 1995, p. 314.
133 Schauman, op. cit., p. 3.
134 Schück and Warburg, op. cit., p. 198.
135 Virrankoski, op. cit., p. 368.
136 Nordbäck, op. cit., p. 309f.
137 Virrankoski, op. cit., p. 368.

Part I

The tumultuous Diet of 1765–6

1 Answer to the Question Prescribed by the Royal Academy of Sciences

What May Be the Cause of So Many People Annually Emigrating from This Country? And by What Measures May It Best Be Prevented?

Submitted in 1763;
But now presented for public scrutiny

By
Anders Chydenius
Curate at Alaveteli Chapel in the parish of Kokkola

Quid liceat nescimus adhuc, sed aequa licere credimus…
Ovid[1]

Stockholm, Printed by Peter Hesselberg, 1765.

Price 2 *daler* 16 *öre kmt* per copy.
Imprimatur Niclas von Oelreich.

Honourable estates of the realm

Since the Royal Swedish Academy of Sciences stated the question regarding the cause of emigration by Swedish people and by what means it might best be prevented, three publications in particular have been printed on this subject which deserve attention. They are those of Commissioner Kryger,[2] of the Historiographer Schönberg[3] and of an anonymous author,[4] of which the first and last essentially agree that some very real disadvantages must exist to make a Swede dissatisfied with dwelling in Sweden, although they do not agree exactly in identifying these, while Mr Schönberg attributes that misfortune primarily to the want of a national way of thinking, which he describes on page 60 as consisting of such a love of the fatherland that it does not leave room for much consideration of the personal advantages that one may gain in another country and of the disadvantages in one's native land, and thus of a blind sentiment or enthusiasm that precludes the use of reason and clear thinking. The first two base themselves on reason, the latter on the imagination.

I am sure that among the many matters that at present occupy the blessed Estates of the Realm this is also one of the most important; specifying all the remedies for this corrosive disease will inevitably be in vain until its causes have been discovered. It can therefore only be perplexing to the honourable Estates of the Realm when learned, honest and sensitive men of our nation come to such different conclusions on a major subject.

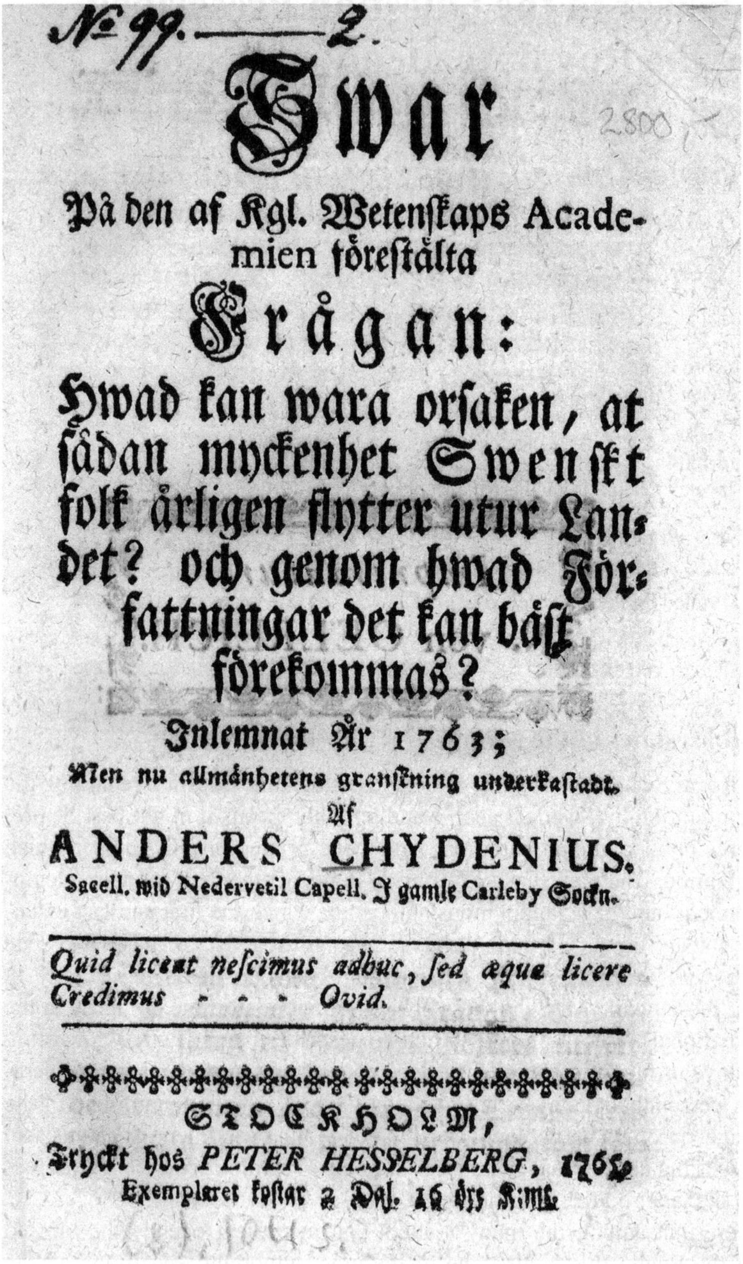

№ 99. —— 2.

Swar

På den af Kgl. Wetenskaps Academien förestålta

Frågan:

Hwad kan wara orsaken, at sådan myckenhet Swenskt folk årligen flytter utur Landet? och genom hwad Författningar det kan bäst förekommas?

Inlemnat År 1763;
Men nu allmänhetens granskning underkastadt.

Af

ANDERS CHYDENIUS.
Sacell. wid Nedervetil Capell. I gamla Carleby Sockn.

Quid liceat nescimus adhuc, sed æque licere Credimus - - - Ovid.

STOCKHOLM,
Tryckt hos PETER HESSELBERG, 1765.
Exemplaret kostar 2 Dal. 16 öre Kmt.

Figure 15 The title page of *Answer to the Question Prescribed by the Royal Academy of Sciences: What May Be the Cause of So Many People Annually Emigrating from This Country? And by What Measures May It Best Be Prevented?* (1765). Kokkola University Consortium Chydenius.

We all know what a large part rashness plays in all our activities. It often diverts us from the light of truth and draws us into actions that appal us as soon as we allow ourselves time to consider them more carefully. It is thus quite possible that an embittered person may in the heat of the moment run away from a blessed native land, but whether his feelings may become so constant that he will never come to his senses again and feel homesick once the ardour has passed I would not dare to assert.

Similarly, unless a national way of thinking is based on a careful comparison of advantages and disadvantages, it must remain a sentiment that inhibits the use of reason in a citizen. If it is a sentiment, it must soon pass; what will citizens then have to stop them from making such comparisons, so that neither their own distress nor the luxurious living of others will strike them? For my part, therefore, I can only conclude that such a national way of thinking in a free, enlightened and rational nation that consists of a blind and fierce passion, if sustained over several years, is a sheer contradiction, unless ignorance, as the true source of such passions, is first promoted. But how freedom may be preserved under those conditions is equally incomprehensible.

It is impossible to love something that is not real or is imagined to be good; to persuade people to credit what is not true is to act contrary to conviction, and to believe it is blindness. Wretched are those societies that have to be built on such weak foundations!

If the good is a genuine one, that is, if a Swede is as happy or happier in Sweden than elsewhere, then the remedy is easy, namely to make the nation aware of its well-being: to demonstrate to the farmer the security that he possesses in his land, the freedom available to his children, the respect he gains for his labour; to the workshops the freedom that activates them and the way in which a lively trade within the country and abroad makes everyone compete, in emulation of each other; that no one can be said to be oppressed in commerce and that no locality needs to languish for want of enterprise; that officials can enjoy promotion based on competence and merit; that the population in general is not oppressed by protracted legal proceedings, that everyone is secure in his or her property, and that those who are able to think and write anything to enlighten their fellow-citizens are free to do so.

But, in the absence of such things, to distract the nation from making such a comparison and to seek to implant a national way of thinking is hardly appropriate for an honest man and achieves still less.

Mr Schönberg and all honourable people along with him complain with good reason about the moral corruption among us; that luxuriance, voluptuousness, vindictiveness, self-interest, indolence and godlessness have become prevalent, no one can deny. But whether that moral corruption is the real source of Sweden's misfortunes or whether it is the enterprising offspring of an even worse mother – that is a major question. When the country is in need of assistance, it is necessary to find the true source of the evil, or else that assistance will never materialize. There are heathen states that have existed longer than Sweden, where people are as evil as we by nature, but are less tamed by religion, yet preserve civic virtues. We see still others that, without any external enemies, have been destroyed within a century or two by barbarous customs. But we also note a major difference between them. In the former the well-being is that of the nation but in the latter that of certain individuals within it.

When that is evenly distributed, no one can afford to be wasteful. It does not suffice for the maintenance of valuable horses, superfluous servants, costly carriages, concerts, balls and entertainments; neither luxuriance nor voluptuousness is able to defile the customs there. But when the wealth belongs to a select few, there are hundreds of ways to increase it, and the heart has an impressive ability to satisfy its impure desires by means of it, which spreads like a disease and infects the entire nation.

Neither Rome nor Carthage would have become so extravagant, through their extravagance immoral and out of immorality overthrown their governments, had their magnates not extracted excessive means from their citizens for their own enjoyment.

Oppression and licentiousness are thus also the real sources of our moral degeneration.

These always go together in a society, and when either of them has been destroyed, the other vanishes of its own accord. Licentiousness is exercised either against the state or the citizens, and whichever is subjected to it will remain in bondage. But where a lawful freedom reigns they must disappear, and then the real seed of immorality will have been destroyed.

How vain, then, are the fierce campaigns that are commonly waged against our moral corruption as long as the few through their licentiousness obtain as much wealth as they desire.

A relative equality in a free state is therefore the correct mechanism by which to set it in lively motion, so that one individual may not consume the sustenance of another nor become too fat by the emaciation of the latter. Mr Schönberg's wish that the children of the upper classes should engage in trades and crafts is an excellent one, but it is likely to remain unfulfilled unless we are not also allowed to wish the means, namely freedom, prosperity and respect for tradesmen. For few of them can be expected to show such a great enthusiasm out of a patriotic turn of mind that they will place them there as long as these are lacking.

The Royal Academy of Sciences has by means of this question, no less than in everything else, served our general interest excellently, by giving the nation an opportunity to think, speak and write about such an important subject. The honourable Estates of the Realm will certainly discover during their deliberations on this subject how much information may immediately, without the slightest cost, be obtained from all the answers received and will therefore encourage the Royal Academy to continue to raise such subjects, which truly concern our general economy.

When the Royal Academy formulated this question, the attractiveness of the subject tempted me to compose an answer to it. Here it is now delivered into the worthy hands of the honourable Estates of the Realm, which are at present busily

engaged in binding our wounds. I submit it to their most enlightened consideration with all the more confidence as I myself have the responsible honour of
being a lowly member of them and remain with profound reverence,

> the most humble and obedient servant
> of the Honourable Estates of the Realm,
> Anders Chydenius
> Stockholm, 16 March 1765.

§ 1

A country without inhabitants is a wasteland; a kingdom without subjects is a
shadow that frightens only those who believe that there are people living there.
Far-flung national borders look impressive on the map but mean nothing in
themselves, for otherwise Great Tartary in Asia would be the most powerful
kingdom in the whole world; a Palestine becomes a desert when labourers die
and move away, a Lapland a land of Canaan when it is inhabited by people.

How many thousands of Swedes have not died in order to extend our borders?
But how few have seriously considered the best way of filling the old ones with
inhabitants? An equal amount, however, may be achieved in both ways. We
have sometimes cut large patches off our neighbours, but before we have finished the game they have usually won the codille and the forfeit as well.[5] We
fight for the soil, of which we have enough, but risk losing that which is most
indispensable.

In ancient times the Nordic peoples gave rise to many others: they filled their
land with inhabitants and enriched those of others with the surplus. The climate
of Sweden, although it is regarded as harsh by southerners, not only is tolerable
to us out of habit, as Seneca believed,[6] but also it preserves its inhabitants from
many contagious diseases to which others are subject, makes the people fertile
and hardens the children's constitutions from the cradle. The pandemic plague
has not visited us in the North for more than 50 years now. Epidemics occur
rarely and are still tolerable.

Nor has a fortunate era failed to make our native land blessed. For more than
40 years Sweden has been spared the ravages of a dangerous neighbour, and
although we have twice since then taken to arms, not without serious consequences, yet the loss of those who on either occasion fell by the sword of the
enemy is not excessive. The freedom we have recovered is almost coeval with
that period of peace. Useful sciences have been nurtured, gained prestige and, to
the wonderment of all Europe, risen to such a height that our learned men have
seized from the hands of others laurels won without bribery and thus impartially
and have opened up paths of scholarship that others count themselves lucky to
be able to follow.

Crafts have been developed among us by considerable investments of money
and people, and the number of workshops has increased remarkably. We see in
our newspapers that much new land is being cleared for fields and meadows.

From all this, one would appear to be entitled to conclude how far such a fortunate society must have increased in inhabitants and wealth. Or who could believe anything else? But since, following the example of other nations, we have in recent times begun to record statistics for the entire population[7] every year or every third year, only then have we noticed the opposite. Here we recognize the cause of the fertility of the old Northmen in the ratio between births and deaths, but when we eagerly await the increase of population in Sweden that should naturally follow from that, the calculation proves wrong: people are born here, but when they ought to become productive, they are not to be found among the citizens.

Attempts have been made to forestall this by legislation, and the solicitude of the authorities extends to all the borders of the kingdom, to keep them guarded; nonetheless, it is difficult to keep anyone confined without chains and locks. Fetters, dungeons and bars are often unable to hold a single person. How, then, can one among millions control thousands who are unknown to anyone? Experience has also shown that all efforts to that end are fruitless.

Is it not, then, a matter of urgency to understand the true cause: *why such a multitude of Swedish people annually emigrate from this country and how it may best be prevented?*

The Royal Academy of Sciences has, out of zeal for the fatherland, presented this question to its compatriots and encouraged them to engage competitively with such an important subject.

Neither fear of not being listened to, nor that others will do it better, should make any well-disposed Swede hesitate to employ his energies on such a noble subject.

§ 2

The Creator has implanted in everyone a desire for perfection; we feel a concern and longing to improve our condition; we always find much in the present that impedes our bliss; all our activities are thus aimed partly at preserving the success that we have achieved and partly at achieving still more. We scarcely take a step without being guided by one of these aims. Whoever denies this proposition has not looked fully into the mainsprings of his own heart or has mistaken the means for his purpose.

The love of God, one's neighbour and the fatherland are nothing but means towards that end; but in order to make proper use of them, divine and human laws are required.

Bliss is either complete or relative; the former cannot be achieved during our earthly life. The latter is perceived by comparing one's own condition with that of others. When we evaluate our happiness, therefore, we examine the circumstances of others and those of our own; if we notice that we possess some advantages that another person lacks, we reckon ourselves fortunate, but if we observe them in others and lack them ourselves, we feel the opposite, and then a desire arises in us to achieve the same happiness. The satisfaction of these desires preoccupies us, and we spare neither mental nor physical efforts in the pursuit of it, for they are innate and ineradicable.

When we wish to know the real reason for something, it is in no way enough to limit ourselves to the factors that are always the immediate cause of some action; we must go to the actual source that gives rise to it, stop and consider that and, without haste and preconceived ideas, observe how large the rivulets may eventually become that flow from there. But if we intend to prevent something, we should take care above all not to build an expensive dam at the lower end of a stream with many falls in order to hold back the water. It may at first restrain a turbulent cataract, but as soon as the water has risen above the rim of the dam the stream will become as wide as it was before, and the water rushes along with greater vehemence and roaring more than ever before. Instead, one should examine at its very source, in case the spring itself cannot be dammed, where one can then best channel its flow to one's advantage.

If we approach the matter in this way, we can hardly miss the correct clue to the question before us.

We shall therefore first consider in general terms the reason why all migrations occur and explain that reason clearly with arguments drawn partly from individual households and partly also from the history of earlier and more recent times; we will then carefully examine whether and in what form such a reason may be present in our fatherland and finally the best means of counteracting it.

One thing alone occurs to me that threatens to bring my efforts to nought: the matter is too sensitive, for to flatter my fatherland in its distressed state would make me unworthy of being born a Swede, and to present a truth, however necessary, as nakedly as it appears to the general public will win no plaudits; but what encourages me is that I may do so in response to such a worthy invitation and to a society that has never yet deserved a reputation for partiality.

§ 3

As all the activities of human beings are directed towards their happiness, all migrations must be motivated by that and by no other cause. A seaman never goes on board a ship unless he expects to gain more thereby than he could be sure of earning at home; still less does any citizen venture to set foot on foreign soil, intending to stay there, unless he believes that he will in one way or another be more successful there.

On the one hand, he considers the circumstances under which he has hitherto lived and which he may in the future hope to enjoy at home, and he puts those in one scale of the balance; on the other hand, he acquaints himself with the condition that he might achieve in another country and what probability he may have of success there in the future, and he puts that in the other one. If the former preponderate, he will obviously remain, as long as he is human; if the balance remains in equilibrium, there is not yet any reason why he should emigrate; everyone prefers the known to the unknown when there is no difference in advantage; but if the balance tips the other way, then thoughts of going abroad begin to arise.

But one's fatherland also provides some particular attachments by which it seeks to remain preponderant, which a German author, Johann Reinhard Storck,[8] has neatly summed up in Latin: "*We love the country that received us when we came into the world*," he says, "*where we voiced our first complaint and played in childhood; were brought up and exercised in youth, whose air we have breathed, whose sky we have seen, with whose streams and fields we are familiar, where we can count numerous relatives, friends, properties,*[9] *companions and so many incentives to happiness that we vainly seek elsewhere.*"

If all these still cannot outweigh the other factors in someone's mind, then he must be regarded as lost to the fatherland: he is no longer a true citizen even though he lives within the borders of the country. All regulations are powerless to retain such an individual, except only for one that increases his advantages at home. Such citizens should be regarded as a precious wine in a leaky vessel which, although it cannot all flow out at once, will nevertheless seek a crack through which it will seep out. Prohibitions and overseers may prevent matters from proceeding so quickly, but they have the disadvantage that the longer such lost citizens are retained by force, to all the more people will they describe their anticipated happiness, and they take them with them once they get away.

In vain does one imagine the fatherland to be a magnet that holds its inhabitants in the same way as it attracts iron, or that it operates through some hidden means. It may have been appropriate for Homer to sing in his blessed Greece: *Nothing is dearer than one's fatherland.*[10] But Socrates and Democritus, who already saw that corruption was prevalent everywhere, only regarded the whole world as such. It was still acceptable for Cicero, who wished to defend the liberty of the Roman Republic that was just then being gambled with, to encourage everyone in his ethical writings to gladly die for the fatherland, though he himself was more suited to be an adviser to such heroes than their leader. Horace sings in the same mode: *Sweet it is*, he says, *and seemly to die for one's homeland,*[11] although the fatherland that Cicero had in mind, namely *liberty*, had already been lost in his lifetime. But 200 years later, when the domestic disasters had come to fruition, one no longer hears of anyone heeding such a call.

Could any of the early Romans, who during their period of expansion regarded it as virtually unthinkable to abscond from the fatherland, as they believed it would soon encompass the entire world, have been made to believe what nevertheless did happen, namely that their descendants would be transformed wholesale into barbarians?

It cost the Israelites many a bloodied shirt to seize Palestine and, in view of their powerful neighbours, even more to retain it as long as it was a land of Canaan. But once their towns, religious cult and trades were overthrown, no one was any longer inclined to risk so much for an unfortunate homeland.

But because this comparison of domestic and foreign advantages occurs in the mind of each separate individual, in accordance with that individual's understanding, prejudices, power of deduction and taste, innumerable errors are committed in this respect; experience nonetheless becomes an infallible teacher for such renegades.

If their hopes are fulfilled, they regard themselves as fortunate, and in relating their advantages to others, they lay dangerous traps for those who are experiencing the same as they previously did; but if their expectations are dashed, they regret their change of circumstances, return home more pleased with their fatherland than when they left it, or at least their disappointment deters others from following in their footsteps.

This allows me to conclude that the more freedom and opportunity each individual has to promote his happiness in his place of birth, especially in his early years, the less does he wish to exchange his fatherland with anyone else, and on the other hand, the less that he enjoys that freedom, the greater does he feel his misfortune and oppression to be, and the more he yearns to get away. And that *oppression*, or lack *of sufficient freedom to pursue his fortune in any honourable manner*, I venture to assert is the one and only cause of all emigration and thus also of that which occurs from our beloved Sweden. If that is denied, one must be capable either of loving something without regarding it as good or else of choosing that for which one feels revulsion.

Whatever else may be adduced as a cause of that is either none at all or merely part of it.

However, with regard to a subject that concerns the origin and destruction of entire states, it is by no means enough to limit oneself to deductions from thought and reason, but they should be made quite incontrovertible on the grounds of long experience; otherwise, it is very likely that the outcome will not match the expectation, and then it is often too late to correct an error that one would immediately have noticed if one had first consulted experience, the instructor of the simple-minded.

§ 4

We will therefore begin by considering a form of migration of which we are daily aware, is quite a delicate matter for us and of the causes of which no one is ignorant, in order to see whether that may not perhaps provide us with tangible reasons.

Servants constitute a significant part of Sweden's productive population, and as unimportant as many regard them, they are in fact indispensable to us. Under Swedish law they have one moving-day and in some places two every year, not in order that they necessarily have to move then but so that, should the master find himself dissatisfied with his servant or the latter with his or her master, they then both possess the freedom to terminate their relationship. In that regard a fair number of separations do take place every year, of servants from their former masters and of masters from their servants, for changing servants is in this respect nothing but a replacement of the social intercourse with those of whose services we have made use during the past year by one with others whom we have recently employed.

Now come! Let us look at the reasons for these moves. Before we give a servant notice at the time of St Laurence's Fair[12] we must have some objection to him or her and moreover entertain hopes of obtaining a better one as a replacement; otherwise we carefully avoid doing so. The servants must in that case have made us dissatisfied with their service because of their laziness, temper, arrogance, unreliability, the expense of their hire or something else; it would thus be a constraint to be bound to such an individual any longer.

The farmhand knows his master equally well from one or more years' personal experience, and from what has happened he draws conclusions concerning the future. He also acquaints himself with the manner in which various masters treat, feed and reward their servants. If he then discovers how amenable and reasonable his master is compared to the others, of which he becomes most aware by comparing them, he regards himself as lucky to be able to remain; but if he finds the situation to be the opposite, he cannot be retained unless he is offered better conditions than before or else is persuaded by fine promises to serve for a further year, which will probably be his last one with that master.

The advantages and inconveniences on both sides compared to each other thus provide both masters and servants with the true yardstick as to whether they are to part company or stay together.

If one now sees a master who is always approached by more people than he needs, while his neighbours suffer from a shortage of hired servants, then it is clear that they have more freedom and opportunity with the former to pursue their fortune, in any way whatsoever, than with any of the latter. He who suffers such a shortage may blame the shortage of working people or their wilfulness or whatever he chooses, yet every sensible person knows that it is oppressiveness that drives one away and oppressiveness that prevents another servant from taking his or her place. But if these men would only learn from their neighbours to treat their own people with more patience than rancour, more affection than blows, more guidance and freedom than servitude, they would soon share them equably with their neighbours.

If we believe that they are born to be bondsmen and we to be masters and imagine that we are in irrevocable possession of that superiority, never recalling that they can live without us but that we cannot do so without them, for they are able to maintain themselves and others by their work while we consume what several households are able to gather in by their sweat and toil, then it is not surprising that all the officers of the Crown are scarcely able to round up as many vagrants as are required to serve us, and if they do, it is even more difficult to persuade the latter to remain until the next moving-day; for beyond that it is impossible.

The issue is exactly the same in the question proposed. A kingdom is nothing but a large household or association of people, in which the Sovereign Power is the master and the subjects are his household servants. Several kingdoms in relation to one another are the same as several masters in this locality. If one observes extensive emigration, one may safely conclude that there must be some oppressiveness there; but if inhabitants congregate in some area, it is nothing but freedom that can be attracting them there. I am not really speaking here of a free constitution, for in so-called free societies the people are often in the deepest bondage, but on the other hand they enjoy protection and are treated considerately by astute monarchs.

§ 5

We shall now proceed and, in line with our plan, first consult the oldest annals and observe to what extent oppression even then gave rise to emigration and other disorders in societies.

The oldest and truest of them all narrates of the progenitor of God's people who, at the command of the Highest, settled in the land of Canaan, which was promised as an inheritance to his descendants in the future, that he had to move from there to Egypt, not for the sake of tranquillity or of a change but because he was forced to do so by hunger, as *the time was very hard in the land.*[13]

Out of the same necessity his grandson Jacob then moved there with his entire prolific family 212 years later. The Canaanites had developed splendid plantations, so that honey, spices, dates, almonds, balm, wine, oil, etc. etc. were to be found there. But however priceless all that was, the dearness of the times oppressed its inhabitants when there was no more bread. But the Egyptians were already cultivators at that time; their fields were covered with grain while those of the Canaanites were resplendent with splendid and artfully terraced wine, fruit and oil farms. But when famine arose they were glad to give their spices away to Egypt merely for permission to buy food there for themselves.

Had this numerous group enjoyed the freedom in Egypt that it was at first accorded, namely to settle down, occupy the land and be supported with food and subsidies for their pastoral settlements, it would within a few centuries have been able to make Egypt feared by the whole world as it then was; but things soon took on quite a different complexion. It was subjected to oppression; their lives were made bitter by bondage and heavy labour with clay and bricks; foremen were placed over them, with the aim of weakening this community, the growth of which attracted the attention of the Egyptians.

The bondage eventually became so severe that it led to murder and tyranny, but that was precisely a sign and cause of its not being sustainable for long, for the more the cries of an oppressed people are violently suppressed, the more dangerous will its eventual eruption be for a society. Tired of an unbearable yoke, the children of Israel themselves thus threw it off, gathered all the most precious of Egypt's treasures, moved away with them and settled down in freedom under the protection of an Almighty Power.

Carthage, a flourishing state in early times, had not only under its *suffetes* or annual rulers[14] grown in wealth and fame in its own freedom but had also subjected to itself the resources of the entire African coastline and had made extensive inroads in Europe into Spain, Sardinia, Corsica and Sicily, but a case of oppressiveness that in our age would be regarded as quite inconsequential almost overthrew all that.

Among the troops in their pay that were fighting against the Romans, discontent arose because their pay was not correctly disbursed, for which reason all

20,000 deserted, which would not, however, have mattered so much in itself had the consequences of that not been even worse.

Carthage, which was arrogant because of its power and wealth, acted tyranni-cally towards the other African nations. It consumed the produce of the toil of others and burdened them with a double tax, and among the leaders of the people those were most favoured by the government who could extract most revenue, for which reason the oppressed made common cause with the discontented sol-diers, renouncing Punic rule and with a force of 100,000 assaulting Carthage itself, which in its extreme distress had to plead for help from its hereditary enemies the Romans, who sought to assist them both with men and mediation, and the city was barely saved from destruction on that occasion through the courage and ingenuity of its loyal Hamilcar.[15] Carthage lost Spain largely for the same reason.

Thus, power is misused in free societies to the profit and prosperity of a few and the oppression of other citizens. The Carthaginian republic was free, for it was not subject to an autocrat but was governed by rulers who were appointed annually in accordance with the will of the people. But what kind of people was it? It consisted of the inhabitants of the immense commercial city, who regarded all other regions as swarms of bees and their own city as the hive to which they had to deliver all their honey.

Stübelius notes in this regard: *Such is the service*, he says, *that one gets from mercenary soldiers*;[16] but I would like to know if one should expect more from native-born ones who are not in anyone's pay.

§ 6

I referred just now to Romans. The very people! How did they rise to such a height of power and fame that they became a marvel to the whole world and then collapsed again into the ashes of their past? A people that thoroughly understood the correct uses and misuses of government, whose laws are still revered throughout Europe, who by their political revolutions and vicissitudes provide a mirror for all societies, in which a thoughtful person without any prophetic gifts can read their impending fall and recovery.

It was indubitably freedom that laid the first stone for the walls of Rome. Freedom filled it with people. Rome would never have existed had Amulius had his wish fulfilled of doing away with its founder and had tyranny not been fore-stalled by his death.[17]

But what would a city be without citizens and walls without a garrison? The founder therefore made Rome a sanctuary for all refugees, oppressed people and slaves. The freedom that he offered each of them was such a valuable and rare reward that there could be no lack of participants in such a noble enterprise, and that was the first step towards the power of the new city.

It was at first ruled by monarchs, though without having lost its freedom; the community was governed by the king, but in accordance with the wishes of the councillors and the people, so that historians regard it as a stain on the government of Lucius Tarquinius[18] that he obeyed neither. He tormented the common people in the workshops of the smiths and with other labour appropriate to slaves, and his son Sextus Tarquinius,[19] a prince brought up in effeminate company, was even more imprudent, causing the dynasty to lose both Crown and fatherland.

By his audacity, Lucius Junius Brutus,[20] inspired by a spirit of freedom more noble than conceited, removed the yoke of autocracy, the harshness of which had already turned the people against it, strengthened the laws and stripped the vices of their excuses, so that the nobles of that period (the cronies of Sextus Tarquinius) bitterly complained about it: *The king, they said, is a human being, from whom one can ask for justice or injustice, whichever one needs. There is scope there for mercy and kind deeds, anger and forgiveness. One can then distinguish between friend and foe. The laws, on the other hand, are a deaf and implacable thing, more propitious and favourable to a poor man than to a rich and powerful one, never offering any reduction or remission of a sentence as soon as one oversteps the mark, and it would be hazardous where human faults are so numerous to defend oneself by innocence alone,*[21] hoping by such weighty arguments to overturn freedom entirely; but Brutus made the consuls annual[22] and protected freedom in every respect.

During the whole period of its freedom Rome was indeed involved in bloody wars abroad and discord internally; but I can certainly see no other reason than freedom for the fact that the Republic nonetheless continued for so long to expand and that it was indeed servitude that brought about its downfall.

Every year many thousands of Romans usually died on the battlefield, but freedom compensated for that deficit many times over. Encouragements for marriage through freedom to settle and work and the means to feed a wife and children achieved a deal internally, but immigration from outside probably contributed most.

Tullus Hostilius[23] in his time already devised the scheme of receiving his enemies and giving them a place on the Aventine in which to build a house. May it not have been the victorious arms of the Romans that increasingly induced the surrounding nations to come over to their side on such favourable terms?

Continual dissensions between the people and the council, the court of the former (*tribunus plebis*)[24] and the consuls appeared to threaten the state with destruction, but remarkably enough it nevertheless continued to grow throughout all this. The people were then still aware of their power and strove for freedom. The council did indeed infringe it from time to time, but when it did so too blatantly, the common people champed at the bit and gave their riders a jolt; then the consuls had to moderate their behaviour. The group of ten men (*decemviri*) who were installed as rulers, on the model of Athenian laws, conducted themselves well the first year, so that the same individuals remained in power into the second year, but the third year the *decemviri* retained power without consulting the people at all. But as their power quickly exceeded its limits, the evil deed of the nefarious Appius soon brought that regime to an end.[25]

However, the Republic flourished, as I said, as long as the contest was between the council[26] and the people, for the latter were then still able to curb tyranny, and the nation was relatively satisfied with itself, although the seeds of ruin were already growing in its midst.

But when a different contest developed, between the councillors[27] themselves, matters took on a quite different complexion. Then the disputes were no longer about freedom but about which of them would have the honour of being its destroyer. The common people effectively lost their voice. The consuls, who were also commanders of the army, had already had time to acquire riches, which posed a threat to freedom. Caesar, Pompey, Antony, Sulla, Octavius and others[28] competed among themselves to gain support among the soldiers, for power often accompanies armed force, and when it could not be gained otherwise, it was bought for large sums, and the soldier soon began to believe that his arbitrary will represented the freedom of society as a whole, but when the common people had to be consulted, they were also made accustomed to respond to gilded arguments. Although unprecedented encroachments were thus now made, the heart of the republic languished in bondage under the tyranny of greed, voluptuousness and arrogance, so that when it was at its most impressive in the eyes of other nations, little more than the shell remained, for Tacitus says that *it was weakened by the mutual rivalry of the powerful and the greed of the government, therefore grew tired of the consuls and threw itself into the arms of autocracy.*[29]

Under the Empire, vanity, effeminacy and voluptuousness corrupted the rulers of Rome. The army was the supreme power; its extravagance became limitless; emperors were elevated and overthrown at its might; but the rest of the people already toiled under intolerable burdens; and that state would never have lasted so long if the illusion that Romans were happier than all other people in the world had not been imbibed for so many generations with their mothers' milk.

It may thus be possible for a time to maintain by illusions a state that has previously flourished and developed a positive view of its happiness, but one that has long suffered oppression cannot be restored and made content with flattery and shadow-play.

§ 7

But I have no more time to follow my Romans to their ultimate ruin. There are more recent events that provide evidence for my case.

Spain, which was populous in ancient times and in the time of Julius Caesar could reckon its population at 15 million but is now, on the contrary, a land destitute of people and commodities, should especially engage our attention.

Montesquieu lays the blame on the amalgamation of the many small polities into a single state, but in my opinion the union was not the cause of that but rather its consequence, and I believe that two things in particular are responsible for its present lack of population, namely a variety of constraints at home and the hope of making money hand over fist in America.

In extensive countries their main resources are generally concentrated in and around the capital, which often regards itself as constituting the country and views other provinces with disdain. It has most opportunity and the best chance of obtaining from the Sovereign Power legislation that will benefit it in particular, but as that is seldom possible without detriment to the more distant provinces, they generally languish in servitude, powerlessness and contempt, and there is then no way of saving such provinces from dereliction and its inhabitants from emigration.

The provinces of the Netherlands, wealthy and powerful thanks to their commerce, which fell to Spain by inheritance, were reasonably satisfied with the regime as long as they were allowed to retain their freedom under its rule, but that did not last for long. They were subjected to constraint in their administration: the Council of State[30] was abolished; commercial constraint: their commodities were charged with an impost of one-tenth of their overall value; constraint in their budget: several new bishops were imposed on them, who had to be paid for out of it; judicial oppression: for their cries went unheard, and the suppliants were brutally turned away with their petitions; religious oppression: none were allowed to profess themselves of the Protestant faith; oppression in what was most dear to them, namely life, for thousands of them had to lay their necks on the block erected for them by the Duke of Alba and submit to being murdered by the soldiers.[31]

Imagine how many thousands abandoned a wretched fatherland during that time, apart from those who died at home.

It was strange how these provinces endured for so long a bloodbath that continued for many years and, so to speak, offered to serve such a tyrannical regime if only they would be granted some relief; on the other hand, however, their vulnerability was the main reason for that.

Yet it was impossible for that to last very long. The Spaniards had to turn their weapons against those whose brethren they had previously slaughtered unopposed when they finally renounced their allegiance to Spain in 1581; and the strength possessed by a small province when it is fighting strenuously for its life and freedom is proved by Isabella Clara Eugenia's three-year-long siege in Ostend.[32]

Nor could Portugal, which at that time was likewise subject to Spain, endure it for long but in every continent simultaneously shook off the yoke that had become so intolerable. And Spain had to recognize the Netherlands as a free nation, having tried in vain to subdue it by force into renewed bondage.

The kingdom of Spain itself was scarcely less weakened by the harsh inquisitions which, apart from those who were murdered, led thousands to save their lives by flight and leave their native country in a miserable state of decay.

That is what oppression achieved on the one hand; but I maintain that the gold and silver mines of the New World, which dazzled this nation above all, ravaged their land no less.

Since the most ancient times, gold has acquired a peculiar ascendancy over the actions of human beings, though that has been due to their own folly. Hardly has any kinship ever been so close, any friendship so solid, any justice so established or any power so sovereign that they are not occasionally found to be bewitched by its attractions.

It devastated the Spanish lands in particular in two ways. The people thronged to America with their entire families and households, established new settlements there and preferred to dig for gold and silver in a foreign country rather than cultivate a meagre soil with spade and plough at home. The more people who emigrated to acquire treasures, the fewer who stayed behind to receive them, the more their stock of money grew. But a rapid increase in the stock of money in a country with a dwindling population has always promoted extravagance and indolence. It was thus a pity, in the first place, that Spain lost its inhabitants but an even greater pity that the riches corrupted the few who were left behind.

In that way the Spanish nation allowed itself to be seduced by the wealth of the New World, sold off its cultivated and populous homeland and, by means of what is regarded as the greatest wealth, impoverished itself.

They reckoned their highest temporal advantage to be an abundance of gold and silver, the lack of which must then necessarily appear to one and all as a constraint. And that imagined constraint or poverty was an incentive to such emigration.

§ 8

Constraints have always been harmful to societies. If they are maintained for long, they inevitably make the general public dissatisfied with their way of life and their fatherland. The Thuringian nobility treated their peasants badly: they were deprived of their freedom to elect their own parish priests, and such as could speak of nothing but masses and purgatory were imposed on them. Their livelihoods were also put in jeopardy; the commonalty therefore rebelled in 1525 under the leadership of Thomas Müntzer, and the matter erupted into open warfare in which more than 50,000 peasants died and the rest were again placed under the yoke, but the concealed effect of such things on emigration is something that writers have been unable to record in detail.[33]

When the Florentines formerly subjugated the Pisans, they adopted a perverse measure in order to ensure their submission. All trade and liberal arts were banned among them, with the aim of reducing them to ignorance, the principal promoter of servitude. But the Pisans were provoked by those constraints into secession and fought valiantly for their freedom before they could be subdued. That was a way of reducing people to slavery through ignorance, which will indeed never fail, though it should be pursued by gentler methods so that it is not noticed.[34]

King Godfred in Denmark no doubt thought he would increase the power of his kingdom by the use of oppression when the Frisians were tormented with an insufferable tax and were mocked by the laws themselves, for some record that they had to wear around their necks osier collars in place of ornaments. No one listened to their complaints, nor did anyone fear their threats. In that way the oppressed were finally driven to take up arms and thus expelled the Danish garrisons.[35]

The immediately adjacent nations, which then enjoyed freedom and prosperity, became much indebted to the Danish monarchy for that oppression; for intelligence, virtue and diligence always seek out the places where they are rewarded and are thus obliged to abandon their wretched native land.

Another thing occurs to me with regard to Denmark: how large would that kingdom not have been had its monarchs not by oppression induced whole countries to desert it? During the period of the Kalmar Union[36] our dear fatherland was stripped bare by Danish rulers, and when Christian II[37] thought he had drained every drop of noble blood from Swedish hearts, he was soon made to realize how coercion and slavery imposed on an enlightened nation will never strengthen a regime, for if it is ever to succeed, ignorance must necessarily precede it, but that has to be introduced so gradually that the nation does not become aware of the underlying aim. Only then did Christian realize that royal authority is constituted only by the number of those who are willing to obey, and when there are none, a king is equivalent to a crofter and a beggar.

Cunning neighbours always know how to exploit the oppression of others, for nothing in the world is as able in a short time to increase a population so much as freedom. A prolific people is obliged to devote one-third of its labour to children who do nothing yet but consume, but freedom brings in people who are at their most productive. If the oppression is exercised among a prolific people, it cannot be pitied enough. Every year they invest millions in their children, but a dangerous neighbour will absorb 100 per cent of that.

The example of all rapidly growing powers provides tangible evidence of this. Prussia, which was so insignificant at the beginning of this century, has in this way within a short period grown into a marvel and terror to the whole of Europe. Its rulers have followed the example of Romulus, made their country into a haven for all refugees, among whom those from Salzburg were not the least significant.[38] The king constructed dwellings for the refugees and assisted others with building loans. He was reluctant to put pressure on anyone in matters of conscience and religion and only too willing to extend civic freedom to all, and the prosperity achieved by some induced an incredible number to move there. The laws were made effective, and successful efforts were made to curtail lawsuits, so that everyone would be able to enjoy his rights with the minimum waste of time and money.

An assemblage of many kinds of people, of whom a large part are not constrained by either conscience or religion, tends to be regarded as impossible to turn into useful citizens, but the King has shown that it is not only morality that can make a person law-abiding; the laws and the administration of them should produce civic virtue.

§ 9

It is now time to consider the main issue more closely. From what has been adduced it has thus been proven that oppression alone is and remains the true cause of all emigration. Dear reader, who have patiently followed me to other countries, do not now grow tired before we see how things stand at home.

We have before us the writings of learned men who have sought to persuade us that Sweden is in a state of perfect prosperity, while others of equal renown would lead us to believe the opposite. But we must not rely on authorities, for evidence alone must now decide the matter.

That complaints and dissatisfaction are voiced in every social gathering none of us would deny. Complaints are always based on some supposed constraint: whether the constraint is real or imaginary, it inevitably causes emigration. If it is the latter, the nation must be informed, so that the people will be aware of their well-being, though experience soon tends to correct such perceptions; but should the former be the case, the wounds should be uncovered and examined by caring and honest individuals, so that the remedies may be prepared and adapted to the causes and symptoms of the disease.

That it is by no means mere dreams that make our nation so unhappy about its fatherland but real disadvantages that are plain to everyone, we should be able to conclude with complete certainty from what follows.

Wherever we turn our attention the constraints are apparent to us. We see that some disadvantages affect a larger or smaller portion of the country's inhabitants, while others are more general.

The members of a nation are either *producers* or *consumers*. Each of these face their own difficulties. The former constitute its real strength; the latter enable that to be utilized in a country. There are many economic pursuits and each one of them has its own constraints, just as every plant on earth has its specific worm and pest. Among the economic pursuits *agriculture* is the principal one, the foremost and the most crucial, and although nature has by no means left us badly off in that respect, it does labour under almost innumerable difficulties, so that the reason why it has not developed further among us cannot seem strange to a thoughtful person – rather, that person will wonder how it has been able to manage as well as it has under such severe and numerous constraints.

Its difficulties must relate either to the *soil*, its *products* or its *cultivators*.

§ 10

The first obstacle facing Swedish agriculture is that of *small and unredistributed holdings*.[39] Communally owned forests are openly plundered by their owners at the expense of their co-owners to produce excessive amounts of ship-timber, saw-timber, tar-wood, firewood, for charcoal burning, slash-and-burn farming and superfluous fencing and house-building. Unredistributed and collectively utilized pasture land is the worst maintained and more like woodland and moss-grown, while small plots cause a great deal of trouble, produce poor crops and prevent the improvement of agriculture that is achieved by turning arable land into meadow and meadows into arable land.

But unless a more expeditious way is found of dividing and redistributing holdings, or it is pursued more energetically and with better supervision than hitherto, that improvement will indisputably come too late in most places, and half a century will barely suffice to redistribute the land in an extensive county even with the maximum number of staff. For even if a parish has been surveyed previously, it will nevertheless be difficult in practice, if the slightest error has been committed, to make sure that the measurements made by many individuals at different times and then joined together will be accurate at the stage of general redistribution, so that a large part is likely to need to be re-surveyed, which must then be done at an additional cost to the rural population and the Crown. This leads me directly to the second constraint that afflicts our Swedish land, namely when the surveying is not carried out with due dispatch and accuracy.

When the Survey Commission was first established there was much talk of the energy and orderliness of this work and how the far-flung Finland would within a few years be surveyed and undergo a general redistribution of land holdings. The honourable Estates of the Realm were themselves regaled with such promises and, in order to expedite such a useful project, notably enlarged the establishment by adding a new Survey Commission. But whether those promises have been or can be kept, the present and still more the coming period will bear witness – especially if the survey is begun simultaneously in every region, the work of many different individuals is amalgamated, surveyors are transferred from one parish to another, from one county to another, before they have completed their work, and sometimes before they have even begun, and are granted leave with their tasks unfinished.

Could that be regarded as one of the lesser obstacles for agriculture? Or are these secrets that must not be discussed?

§ 11

As a third constraint *on our cultivable land* I regard the fact *that it may not be owned by those who have both the inclination and strength to work it with their own hands*. There are large Crown domains, officers' estates and taxed freehold farms, most of them owned by absentee landlords or else looked after by subordinates who do not possess the interest, knowledge or energy to improve the land, or else they are let on short leases.

In any case, an excessively large proportion of Swedish arable and pasture land forms part of such farms. Few of their proprietors derive the wealth and utility from them that they could and should provide, causing a substantial loss to the country. Managers, farm bailiffs and foremen are generally in charge of them. They look after other people's business without close and strict supervision. Their indolence, extravagance and fraudulence may year by year reduce the incomes that could otherwise be substantially increased.

In order to forestall that evil, others lease out their land for a certain number of years, but the leaseholder, who then knows when he is due to leave, is constantly aware of that when he is to undertake anything; he always seeks to gain the greatest profit for himself and cares least of all about what he will leave to his successor. In that way many thousands of acres of arable and pasture land are neglected, and the country people, who are both able and willing to improve the land, are not even allowed to turn their hands to doing so, although they would gladly pay the owner if only the land were left in the permanent possession of its cultivators.

§ 12

The produce of the land is no less encumbered in various ways. I do not have the time to deal with lesser obstacles. One of the chief ones in this connection I hold to be the *lack of serviceable communications between the rural regions.*

If the people who are exhausted and die because of onerous transport work and long military campaigns were to be urged, each in their own locality, to labour on the opening up of river and land routes, what a blessed benefit would that not be to agriculture?

I really ought not to say any more about this, since the caring attention of the honourable Estates of the Realm has so recently and seriously been extended to this part of our general economy, if one thing did not still concern me in this regard, namely that a larger part of the funds allocated for this blessed project is absorbed by salaries for the senior officials than for the labourers, whereby the work costs the Crown much but benefits the country less. Could the civil establishment not be substantially reduced in this case by appointing fewer officials for such a peaceful purpose?

In many localities, agriculture is also seriously hampered by restrictions on the trade in grain and provisions, so that the countryman is not allowed to sell the produce of his land and labour where the profit is greatest. That includes the regulations concerning prescribed trading areas and prohibitions on the export of grain and provisions.

Mr Montesquieu presents this entertainingly in the form of an African legend regarding the two reasons for the decline of their former agriculture.[40] The second measure, he says, was intended to prevent famine in the country, for which purpose the export abroad of all foodstuffs was prohibited. One province was not even allowed to move them to another one without special permits, which must necessarily give rise to monopolies. In that way the stock and produce of the country went to waste during good years, and as all incentives for the countryman ceased, both arable farming and meadowing were neglected and the good years were followed by hard years which still prevail.

The excise duties[41] are also a considerable burden on agricultural production, as others have clearly shown. If one adds up all the days of labour of which the inhabitants throughout the country are annually deprived because of them; if as many individuals as constitute the excise service in Sweden and are now engaged in superfluous work are regarded as working unproductively year on year, or that almost 300 days have been squandered in each; if the many thousand *daler* that are now spent every year on their salaries are added to that and if, moreover, the many barrels of gold that the excise contractors by that means collect from the trades are included; if the many trades and workshops that could be carried on by their employees are now reckoned as lost; and if, finally, the ill will that is provoked between the Crown and the subjects by the excise duties is laid on top of that and all this is gathered in one scale of the balance and in the other the advantages of those who by the abolition of the excise duties might lose a goldmine, as well as the complaints of some indolent officials about their loss of employment, it should not be difficult for a people that boasts of its liberty to conclude which of these should outweigh the other.

The yield of the land is no less diminished *by the heavy or even unbearable taxes* that are a necessary consequence of the enlargement of the civil establishments.

Had the internal strength of the kingdom increased at the same rate as the number of its public officials in recent years, it would be terrifying to our neighbours. But if we examine this closely, we observe that half the former number of Sweden's inhabitants is now governed by twice as many senior officials as before, or, what amounts to the same thing, every productive citizen now has to feed four times as many consumers as his forefathers.

I shall pass over entirely all the previous increases in the size of the Swedish bureaucracy. In recent years we have acquired as many officials as we now have time to enumerate. The number of appeal courts has been doubled; jurisdictions have been divided; ombudsmen, public prosecutors, secretaries, deputies, notaries, amanuenses, assistants, etc. etc. have increased in almost all departments and other government bodies, and in addition to these a number of quite new ones have been established, such as the Banking, Law, Statistical, Education, Health, Economic Affairs, Survey and other Commissions and Diet Committees.

The amount of business is blamed for this. That may be so. Promises are made that it will be reduced thereby, but only time will tell whether that is the case. No one should believe, however, that people in our time, generally speaking, work too hard, although there may indeed still be some hard-working officials among the rest. For I have not noticed the absence of honourable participants from our festivities any more than in the old days, although they have become far more extensive and more numerous than formerly. Plays, dances, banquets, ceremonies, concerts, promenades are still attended by respectable people. One also sees worn-out card tables in aristocratic milieux, and taverns and coffee houses are busy and not frequented only by the mob.

I am therefore inclined to think that there is no lack of recreations in our day or of time to devote to them. I would at least maintain that the people as a whole are in no way responsible for this increase in official business, either in the legal or the public finance sector. Can anyone say that our countrymen are by nature more quarrelsome or unmanageable than before? Or have the Crown rents now increased so abnormally that they cannot be collected and are therefore accounted for by the ordinary tax collectors? Our currency is neither confusing to count nor difficult to transport.

§ 13

But however severe these constraints may be for agriculture, none of them has such a direct impact on the emigration of people as those that affect *the cultivators of the land.*

Who can look back without emotion to the regulation whereby all increase in the numbers of people on a farm was prevented when *the country people were not allowed to employ on their holdings more than a certain number of labourers* in proportion to the tax they pay, and the rest were confined to annual labour contracts, military service or saltpetre-boiling duties?

To prevent the increase in the number of people on a farm is actually to prevent all land reclamation. But to think of developing of the country without an expansion of farmland would, without positive evidence, seem to be unreasonable. When the young people were thus denied the chance of being useful to their own fatherland, they sought out another that appreciated their services more.

Another constraint on the cultivators of the land was that *a large part of the working population was enticed by means of privileges and rewards away from the plough into our factories* when they were established. Sweden's agriculture was not capable of providing the towns with bread while the factory workers were still countrymen; but when they moved to the towns their plots of land were left fallow and neglected. Thus, bread must become scarcer but its consumers in the towns more numerous.

The factory workers gradually became accustomed to extravagance and indolence. Once the government subsidies had been used up, an accidental fire or the bankruptcy of investors would often put an end to the whole enterprise, and a number of people were thrown out of work and consequently pauperized who could never again be persuaded to care for or cultivate the land, their primeval mother. They had by then already changed their way of dressing, habits and names to show how far they had risen above their perceived lowly origins. Distress and pride made them disillusioned with their former abodes, and the accounts of fools regarding other people's happiness became so enticing to them that they deliberately took their leave of Sweden and transferred their allegiance to another Crown.

That is lamentable evidence of the problems caused by excessive freedom in less important trades as compared with the most essential ones, which correspond exactly to the problem that a free country should expect from constraints on its productive members and the self-indulgent freedom of a few consumers.

For farmers it is also a considerable constraint *that colonists, crofters, dependent lodgers and cottars are not tolerated.*

The freedom to which human beings are born is desired by all. The servants eventually grow tired of working for others, wishing to do something for themselves; if they cannot do so at home, they will gradually be drawn to places where freedom is to be found. The aim of this prohibition was to overcome the difficulty of obtaining servants engaged by the year, but at the same time it drove the labourers from farming into exile and, what matters more in the long run, prevented farmhands and maids from marrying and the increase in population that flows from that.

A few years ago a royal ordinance was indeed issued which allows proprietors the freedom to accept colonists and crofters on their holdings,[42] but as long as their land is communally owned or intermixed with that of their neighbours, it is not able to produce its blessed effect everywhere.

The fourth constraint on farmers is *that they do not have complete security of tenure for the land that they possess*. I do not wish to mention the expedients and devious means by which farmers paying land tax can be removed from their land. Suffice it to say that holdings on Crown land are taken away from their tenants without reason, when they are fulfilling their obligations.

When a simple countryman who has put his trust in the promises made at the time of the original settlement and whose family has had the holding in undisputed possession for generations finds himself with his wife and children driven onto the public highway, while the results of his forefathers' and his own toil are handed over to undeserving people, then the security of the general public must suffer considerably thereby. Their leave-taking is pitiful to all who hear it: *Farewell our native soil! We have often before watered you with our sweat but now finally with the tears of our wives and children.*

I leave the public to judge *whether the insecurity suffered by tenant-farmers and crofters on manorial estates* may be regarded as the fifth constraint on our farmers. Not only do they not enjoy secure possession of their holdings and crofts but they are also in the dark about how much may be demanded of them.

Where, dear reader! do you think these fugitives should go? What interest will such people have in marriage? Or what desire will their children have to remain in Sweden?

§ 14

I will finally mention the impediment that may possibly be the worst of all, namely *the contempt for farmers and people in other trades*. In all societies we observe how powerful is the role played by honour. Rulers therefore wisely tend to bestow honour on each individual according to his achievements. That is also the real origin of the orders of knighthood that exist in Europe. They do not in themselves constitute anything real; their worth depends only on the ruler's command that they shall be held in a certain regard.

Most, however, are still oblivious of the need to reward the greatest achievements in the world with adequate honour. The purple is worn with great responsibility and much anxiety, but it has its moments of pleasure, seeing itself revered, displaying its luxurious living, being entertained by pastimes. Countries are occupied and defended at the cost of blood and often of lives, but victors are compensated for that with honour, spoils and an easier life in times of peace. Academic studies are pursued with great toil, but they also lead to an honoured, peaceful and comfortable old age. Yet individuals in all of these categories have to obtain their food and clothing from the soil, although none of them lift a finger to work it, and the soil does not supply a single need of theirs of its own accord.

It has to be attacked, and although it is not invincible, it never concedes total victory, but as the needs are daily ones, it must also be confronted every day. The land makes a mockery of blunt weapons in indolent hands; the victories do not actually have to be paid for in blood, for the encounters are fought hand-to-hand, but the sweat flows all the more copiously and thus not without some attrition of the blood.

Heroes of that kind are recognized by their inward-turned feet, trembling knees, bent back, rough hands, stiff fingers, thin limbs, bowed head and wrinkled faces, all bearing witness as to whether they have won laurels by playing or gained merits while they slept.

If, next to God, we have our companions of Mars[43] to thank for the protection of our national borders, the credit for most of the things that are found within them is due to the labour of these people.

Should such individuals then not also be honoured? For what inducement will one of them or his children have to sacrifice themselves utterly in the service of the general public if, in return for all that, he sees himself held in contempt by those who live from his sweat?

At this point I recall what I read some time ago in Livy about an old Roman knight who had unwittingly incurred some debt and whom his creditors, having on that account taken possession of his ancestral estates, had confined in a place of correction and torment.

He appeared in public on one occasion in a pitiable condition, with all his ancestors' heraldic insignia. His clothes were all dirty, his face pale and thin, with a long beard and his hair hanging down over his eyes and an emaciated body. And while he could show the scars on his chest that he had incurred for the fatherland, his bloody back bore witness to how he had been rewarded for that in his old age. During his sufferings in prison he had lost his health and succumbed to an incurable consumption.

The Roman people resented this deeply. *It is futile*, they said, *to fight for our liberty and our country abroad when we are oppressed by fellow-citizens at home. Our liberty is less endangered in external wars than in times of peace, among enemies rather than fellow-citizens.*[44]

§ 15

We now move quickly away from agriculture to consider the disadvantages that constrain our *handicrafts*. Among these, with good reason, I place the simultaneous pursuit of various crafts first.[45]

It is amazing how this circumstance alone holds back our workshops and makes them incapable of ever developing our manufactures to the same level as other nations or to sell their products at the same prices as they do. Our masters need to keep learning throughout life and sometimes only have the opportunity once or twice in their lifetime to do certain things that are now regarded as forming part of their profession. It thus requires an uncommon skill to be able to adapt themselves to such specific cases and circumstances if the work is to be satisfactory, but the dexterity, which can never be achieved without thousands of repetitions, is still lacking. The less skilful ones are not even able to make ends meet; the workshops are therefore not profitable among us, and the workers have to look around somewhere else, where they can make a better living with less knowledge.

Second, our crafts are held back by *slack inspection*. The government and the country have not been sparing with investments to provide support for newly established industries, but how these are then used demands careful supervision; they can be spent on extravagance and high living, and people always believe they will find a way, if challenged, to excuse themselves somehow. A little entertainment, some cash in hand can soon make inspectors amenable, attribute minor errors to accidents, turn a mediocre establishment into an incomparable one and turn craft items assembled from everywhere into products of their own workshop on the day of inspection.

Personal profit should indeed encourage every investor to be proactive, but excessive hopes should not be entertained on that basis. Not all those who obtain investments are accustomed from childhood to work and supervision; they may sometimes fall into the hands of those who have squandered their money, learned and done nothing and now wish for nothing more than to be supported on any grounds whatsoever. With such people the risk is excessive and the capital virtually lost. But if they are able to dodge responsibility by any possible means, then others of mediocre diligence are lulled into security: they think they can always use the same expedients to avoid being called to account that have served the former and then share their idleness. Eventually hunger and poverty intervene, and when the fatherland at last grows tired of providing support to idle hands, they often take it into their heads to seek it abroad. We have seen useless citizens among us become industrious and hard-working ones elsewhere when they have been closely supervised. The generosity and indulgence that is thus shown to slackers in that way contributes little to the improvement of the fatherland.

Third, our handicrafts are forced *by excessive measures for small factories*. Such a grand building plan is often conceived among us for the construction of a factory that half or a whole generation is spent in completing it before the work can even begin. As the investment hardly suffices for the former, the latter comes to nothing.

Extravagance and the aim of achieving fame due to one's projects have hitherto been the main incentives among private individuals, but if such factories are to be established at public expense, another and more dangerous one arises, when the funding becomes the main attraction and one looks more to how long a means of livelihood may last than to when and how well it may recover the capital invested in it.

Fourth, and last, our crafts are quite considerably hampered *by compelling the workers to submit to guild rules and other regulations*. That unskilled people and interlopers should not be permitted, especially in towns, to impede experienced craftsmen in their lawful occupation is quite reasonable, but that those who have learned some craft should still live under constraint will never do the country much good.

Restricting the number of craftsmen turns them into monopolists. That power of theirs becomes intolerable for the people who need their services, but even more so for their employees. They are then able to set such a value on their work as will support their high living and extravagance. And their workers must be content with the wages that they think fit to pay.

We had pitiful evidence of this a few years ago in the Tailors' Guild in Stockholm. Its members had come to an internal agreement on what should be provided in payment in kind and weekly wages to journeymen in their employ, which the latter regarded as impossible to live on. The journeymen requested an increase but were not heeded: despair, hunger and resentment drove them to obtain by coercion what they could not gain by persuasion. The measures taken by the authorities did indeed reduce them to obedience again, but what love that awakened in them for their fatherland and how long they may all have remained in Sweden is easy to judge.

§ 16

Our mining industry is under no less constraint than other branches of the economy.

In this regard, those principally constrained are impoverished owners of metalworks who do not themselves have the funds with which to conduct the enterprise. The honourable Estates of the Realm took their distress to heart, and in order to assist them the Ironmasters' Association[46] was established. But when that regulation was implemented, a certain measure was adopted against the protests of clear-sighted and upright individuals.

By means of that the wealthy, with easy loans from the Bank, were enabled to purchase iron-working estates as the highest bidders and to become suppliers of credit to the others. And because they were the same men who by unacceptable borrowing conditions influenced the exchange rate, that caused something even more deplorable to happen.

These creditors, who were at the same time exporters and financiers, stipulated by written contracts, at a reasonable exchange rate, a certain level of production and payment of so many *daler* for every *skeppund* of iron, which was to apply for ten years or more. But as soon as that had been done, they let the exchange rate rise to more than 100 *mark* per *riksdaler*, whereby one *daler*, which at a reasonable exchange rate was one-twelfth of a *riksdaler*, now amounted to only a twenty-fourth of one. The impoverished owner of the metalworks was thus obliged to sell his iron for half of the agreed value, although he received the same number of *daler*.

When the owner, due to such a contract, was within a few years facing financial ruin, a sincere friend could hardly have given him better advice than to abandon everything to the wealthier men and look to his security elsewhere.

Second, *the smiths and labourers at the metalworks are constrained by inadequate wages.*

It is in effect they who do the work, and they should therefore be provided with suitable and nourishing food and a living wage, for otherwise they will become dissatisfied and turn into idlers, thieves and, as a consolation in their poverty, the most debauched drunkards. No skilled workers can be obtained from outside. Industrious men who notice that their diligence is not generally highly valued here regard their life as one of servitude. Some of their lamentations may be read in our *Riksdags-Tidningar*,[47] but agreements and contracts have to be maintained even if things themselves have changed. If they do not accept that, they have to look for better conditions elsewhere, a consolation, however, that does not appear to mean very much once they have a wife and children and somewhere to live, especially since all the Swedish mines have been concentrated in the hands of so few men.

The cold winters of the North that conceal the food from our summer birds drive them in flocks to enjoy the pleasures of the southern lands. Hunger and poverty without relief often indicate the same road to the workers at our metalworks.

Third, our mines are encumbered by another constraint, which especially *affects the surrounding rural population*, and although it does not appear to harm the iron-working estates directly, it is nonetheless obvious that no mining industry in a well-ordered society can be based on the ruin of the countryman.

How these matters stand among us cannot be unknown to anyone who cares in the slightest for his native country. There is no need of guesswork here. It is unnecessary to corroborate anything with old events or one-sided complaints: obvious truths will decide the question. I know of an iron-working estate that pays no more than 3 *daler kmt* for a *stig* of charcoal along the coast, although it costs 10 or 12 *daler kmt* a few *mil* from there. But nothing has so completely convinced me of this constraint as the story inserted in no. 96 of the *Riksdags-Tidningar* during the last Diet concerning the eight years of servitude, courageous resistance and meagre victory of some farmers paying land tax; it is worth keeping in mind.

They were obliged on pains of a fine of 20 *daler smt* to sell the *stig* of charcoal for 5 or 6 *daler kmt* less than its market price; they were convicted in the wrong court; when they appealed against that, they were fined; their notice of appeal was nullified by the execution of the original judgment, as ordered; they then claimed that all the plaintiffs should be heard, but that was rejected; they appealed but were again fined for that. And when the honourable Estates of the Realm declared the judgments and actions of the officials and the Royal Board to be wholly *unlawful and contrary to manifest law*, they finally had their fines repaid but received nothing for their protracted lawsuit nor any compensation for having lost 5 or 6 *daler* on every *stig* of charcoal that they had been obliged to sell over a period of eight years.

§ 17

Among the branches of economy, Sweden's commerce is still under the yoke and contributes disproportionately to our emigration.

Great trading nations have by free and unrestricted trade and navigation made their flags respected throughout the world. Sweden has had the same objective as them but has used quite different means to that end.

We have been convinced that restrictions, exclusive privileges and secrets would be most effective. For that purpose a commercial ordinance was issued on 10 February 1614, but as it still did not have the desired effect, another one was issued in 1617,[48] which concentrated the commerce in fewer hands: it specified certain towns that were to be solely permitted to engage in overseas navigation, others were allowed to engage in shipping between themselves within the country but some only to Stockholm and Turku. All rural trading was banned and a long list of contraband goods enabled any inspector to accost a merchant whenever he so wished.

These regulations are already so old that they have had ample time to demonstrate their effectiveness. The English are now able to deploy more than 300 sail in their navy, but Sweden does not even reach a third of that number, with regulations like these.

Medicines that fail cause a sick person to resort all the sooner to one that has helped others. Yet our merchants assert as eagerly as ever that the old constraint is the only remedy for our flagging commerce and regard any changes in it as matters of conscience *in politicis*.[49] Even if someone could therefore show with mathematical precision that the old ordinances no longer even suit the condition of our commerce, that a free trade increases the quantity of commodities and that the resulting quantity of commodities employs and retains more citizens, they still stand by their assertion as firmly as ever.

I am obliged on this occasion to be briefer on a subject that demands more extensive treatment than I had intended. The matter has been dealt with by several writers elsewhere,[50] and the arguments adduced against freedom of trade have already been addressed and clearly refuted. But if authority buttressed by arguments is more impressive, the proceedings of the honourable Estate of Nobility on this subject recorded during the last Diet, and in particular those of 24 April 1762, deserve to be read with due attention.[51]

§ 18

Here are the reasons why thousands of productive citizens have to leave their native land. Remote regions languish for want of industries; workers flee such grim dwelling-places. They flock to the coast, where there is more enterprise and activity, but they soon realize, under our present conditions, that neither town nor country will provide them with a plot of land on which to settle down, marry and maintain themselves.

To toil like a slave for others as long as they have the strength, to be cast aside in poverty in old age and to die in misery are the laurels that are to induce the labouring multitude to love their fatherland. They unfailingly sense that Sweden is not yet Plato's happy country; they yearn for freedom; they hear our mariners talk much about the splendour of the southern lands; they are unable to resist such enticing pleasures; they become seamen; they write their farewells; they do not stop until they reach some foreign ports where freedom is available. "They would rather settle among a people whom they barely understand, where enterprise is untrammelled, than among their own brethren, where everything is decayed and dead, and in all their actions one reads this maxim: *A fatherland without freedom and livelihood is a big word that signifies little!*"[52]

Thus, our noble labouring multitude leaves us; does that not signify anything? It is that multitude that puts every piece of bread in our mouths. With their taxes and from their crafts we clothe and adorn our bodies, which, without those things, could not even be distinguished from those of the workers, by either our ancestral honour or aristocratic descent. Our elevated status dissolves into mist when there is no one to serve us, and our supremacy is at an end when there are no longer any subordinates.

§ 19

Enough on this subject. A number of constraints still oppress our beloved Sweden. Nor are the consuming citizens free of these; our officials, both higher and lower, have their own burdens to bear.

Learning, experience and *virtue* are the best qualities of officials; where they exist, the people are refreshed like a withered plant by cool evening rain. Happy are those regions which that rain reaches! Those who apply for vacancies always pay most heed to that which is primarily taken into account in filling them. If these three chief qualities are the government's main touchstone when confirming appointments, none of them will be lacking in our nation, with its love of honour. But if the main consideration is for something else, they will be rarer. Ignorance, misguided legal measures, self-interest and violence will soon emerge everywhere. Book-learning will then become a dearly bought extravagance, merits dispensable and piety an object of ridicule.

Never have the Estates of the Realm laboured harder for a time to bring order into the relations between the officials in the service of the kingdom than during the recent Diets, but nor have the Estates ever been more disturbed by the most deplorable complaints about legal bias.

Much of their precious time is taken up by the Estates in correcting such matters themselves. An impartial observer would conclude from this either that the decisions of the Estates on these matters are so obscure that they cannot be fathomed by anyone but the Estates themselves or that they can be infringed with impunity by subjects.

That learning, experience and virtue are taken for granted in officials once they have obtained a royal appointment and have not been legally convicted of anything to the contrary seems a reasonable assumption, since objective evidence is so hard to obtain. But virtue that a society does not reward, it also has less right to demand; and gifted men whose intelligence and diligence are never rewarded will move away.

What should I say about officials who only have a cash salary based on the pay scale of 1696? Either their duties must be discharged as a spare-time occupation or else they must steal or flee or starve to death.

§ 20

Such are the disadvantages that individually oppress productive and consuming citizens, but there are still others that affect all subjects generally, which have no less of an impact on emigration than those hitherto adduced.

Among these I count, first, *obstacles to marriage*. That the population is the basis of the actual strength of a state no one is likely to deny, while everyone knows that marriage is the true source of any increase in the population and that the inclination to marry is a natural one, as the Almighty included it in the Creation. Obstacles to it are therefore a constraint on nature that makes people dissatisfied and obstructs the growth of population and the strength of the state that flows from that.

We no longer live in those dismal times when the marriage of priests and monks was regarded as a sin; we no longer make a burnt offering of the property of the unmarried before the throne of his Roman Holiness; the monastic life is not now seen as an obligation or pious duty. Our law allows everyone to marry. Nor am I sure that the ban on the marriage of juveniles should be included here; it may be useful, for mature parents are able to produce sturdy infants, and from them we in time expect steady and cheerful workers.

There is thus no legal constraint. A large part of the citizens are in a situation, both at higher and lower levels, where they do not regard themselves as able to support a wife and children during the years when they would be most suited to marriage, and when they finally are able to, it is often too late.

Inevitably, thousands of children are every year in this way left unborn in the kingdom of Sweden who under the system ordained by the Almighty and by nature ought to be of benefit to our underpopulated society.

The children of persons of rank must tread the road to learning for a long time before they reach the academic heights. The laurels are an honour but not a source of food, nor does a livelihood very quickly follow on from them. A man still has to wait for ten, 15 or 20 years and possess great patience before he can be sure of the most meagre living based on his merits. Should he marry before then and his household increase, he has to feed and clothe wife and children with his honour, which amounts to nothing but empty hopes, but as they will not be content with that for long, he has to promptly sell his place on the waiting-list,[53] which has left him deeply in debt, and take up the beggar's staff. He has learned no craft and he can hardly gain employment once he has been forgotten by his superiors. Who would be so oblivious of his well-being as even to think of marriage under those circumstances? If a farmer has one or at most two sons, he can marry them off at home, to take over from him eventually, but if there are more, he regards them under our present conditions as a burden, does not believe that they can support themselves from his land, still less a wife and children, and therefore strongly advises them against marriage.

But this constraint is felt most harshly by our servants. For them to get married means immediately becoming paupers. The husband may eventually find a position, if he is prepared to leave his wife and children, but he will then get no food for them. His wages scarcely suffice for clothes for himself, so who is to feed and take care of his poor family, who are homeless?

They have nonetheless decided to devote all their bodily strength to taking care of their fatherland, are also willing in their poverty to provide it with workers for the future and are thus the most useful citizens one could wish for, yet, for all that, no reward is more certain for them than the beggar's staff and pouch and reproaches from everyone as to how foolish it was for them to get married. Are these encouragements to marriage? No. Before one of them engages in that, he will adopt any other solutions that may be possible.

He first looks around for some farm that is hampered by a shortage of people in order to become a son-in-law there. If that succeeds, he is preserved for the country, but otherwise he will do something ill-advised, often wallowing in the most wicked vices, which bring about either no increase in population or one that is illegitimate. He spends his days in despair and anxiety, and when he imagines how burdensome his grey hairs will be to him in poverty and scorn, and how long the days of his old age, when no one will any longer take care of him, he often cuts short such worries with a decision to escape in good time from his misfortune.

Thus, they emigrate and their labour is lost to the crafts of the country. If we also bear in mind the families and households that could arise from them by marriages under the blessing of the Most High but are now lacking in Sweden, the loss will be many times greater.

Maids face the same disadvantages as those mentioned above, and involving even greater hardship, as they cannot easily save themselves by flight. Their arduous work is rewarded in the same way in old age as that of the above-mentioned ones, with the addition that they have to suffer more stinging taunts because of their age and unmarried status, which is no fault of theirs, which they would dearly have liked to be able to change and which is an inevitable consequence of constraints on marriage and the resulting emigration of the farmhands. Their honesty is placed under the severest strain, and their groans are in no way beneficial to our native land. If farmhands and female servants were sexless, like the bee and the worker-ant, born merely to be slaves, they would not need to be pitied, but, as things are otherwise, the constraint ought to be alleviated with the greatest sympathy. If it is truly said that *patria est ubi bene est*,[54] would one not then be justified in saying that these have no fatherland?

§ 21

Swedish citizens as a whole suffer, second, from *constraint in lawsuits*. The administration of justice in a society is a matter of the greatest importance. Every subject, as long as he fulfils his obligations, is entitled to benefit from it; all are indeed in need of it, or else they will be oppressed by each other. That is the reason why they have sworn obeisance to a society, pay tax and obey orders.

When justice is upheld, virtue is rewarded, excess is controlled, injustice is curbed, arrogance is chastised, innocence is protected and the vices are punished without mercy and regard to persons, but above all those who disturb that peace which the King has sworn to his subjects to uphold. If the opposite is the case, then constraints are present in the judicial system, which cause discontent and complaints and also have an effect on emigration.

On this occasion I will refrain from examining whether such things arise from faults in our legislation, from limited accountability on the part of our officials, from their complicity with the legislative authority, from feeble supervision or from a decline in our morals, but if any constraints in our judicial system really do exist among us, then regardless of how they have arisen, their effects are certainly relevant here.

I do not wish to refer to the general grievances and discontents of the common people, although they constitute strong evidence. I do not have the space to include the numerous grievances from town and country that are submitted daily with regard to injustices suffered. I will merely touch upon three events of which the truth has already become so apparent to the Sovereign Power that no one can deny it and it is on record for posterity.

An upright citizen of rank, to which no regard should, however, be paid, as everyone in society has the same rights, was by order of an officer with a few privates seized at night in his bed, his papers taken from him and he, untried and unconvicted, fettered, thrown into a dungeon and darkness for a year and a half, in cold and wretched conditions, separated from his wife and children, without being allowed to prove his innocence or be informed of the identity of his accuser. I shudder to speak of this. He lost his health there, and when his case was finally examined, he was found to be without the slightest stain. The Estates themselves declared him innocent and wronged, but his persecutors were completely forgotten. For him in his misery it was enough that his innocence was made clear, but the breach of the peace is in no way redeemed thereby, nor the security of the general public restored. Such things cry out for vengeance. Let us not forget them; our children will in any case disinter them and present them to posterity, to the shame of our epoch.

A drawn-out property dispute is dealt with by Mr Nordencrantz[55] and his critic, in which a purchaser was exhausted at every level by a 20-year-long process and was finally forced to accept a compromise settlement, with the loss of 300,000 *daler*, in order to save the remainder of his property from the same fate. The case has been so carefully analysed with all its circumstances, though without naming individuals, that it does not need to be recounted here.

In order to save time, the third event may be represented by the protracted lawsuit mentioned above in § 16 between some farmers paying land tax and some owners of metalworks, in which wrongs suffered over many years, the loss of several thousand *daler*, an expensive lawsuit and judgments clearly contrary to law by both higher and lower courts are rectified, with the repayment of the 60 *daler smt* that they had been wrongly judged liable to pay.

Tell me how many persons of rank there are who are able to conduct their case to a definitive conclusion with such honesty, disregard of expense and unflagging patience? Not one in a hundred. How can it then be expected from one in a thousand of the country people? Most are bound to succumb before then, which may indeed often be just as well. Can one demand that such wretches should love their fatherland? My heart bleeds. But let us hasten from these lamentable scenes to something different.

§ 22

We then come to the third general constraint, *which relates to property*. The intention here is not to adduce the many possible and customary ways in which one may be deprived of one's legitimate property.

The King and the Estates have assured every subject undisputed possession of their property. It is least of all fitting for the latter to throw any doubt on such hallowed vows. Nor have subjects therefore hesitated to deposit their property in government institutions and funds, which are insured. The Bank[56] has received most of this. Old accumulations of capital in ready money are on deposit there. When the representative coinage was introduced, the entire circulating currency of the country was allocated to it and the Bank issued assurances not only that it was safe there but also that it could be withdrawn at the request of the owner. Those assurances are equivalent to what are now designated banknotes and which function as currency in all our commercial transactions but are in themselves nothing but the Bank's payment orders to itself, which, as long as they are honoured by the Bank with payment in cash, will preserve their value.

Now almost every single subject of the kingdom has, in the course of trading, converted some part of his property into these payment orders and must therefore be entitled, according to the Bank's plain statements, the Royal Accession Charter and the guarantee of the Estates of the Realm, to retrieve his property intact from the Bank whenever he so wishes, not only by the name and number of *daler* on paper but in actual ready money or its equivalent value.

The matter is in itself quite simple and can be understood by everyone. But the concealed though latterly quite apparent fall of the Swedish *daler*, which has dropped since 1734 from a ninth to one twenty-seventh of a *riksdaler*, has made the matter more complicated, for of the designation *daler* we have formed a fixed notion that does not tally with our new *daler* in relation to any ready money.

Mr Christiernin[57] believes that this change in the value of the *daler* has not harmed the country and is now of the opinion that it should at present amount to one-eighteenth rather than one-ninth of a *riksdaler*, provided that it is stabilized at that level. He asserts that it is not possible to lower the exchange rate without changing and increasing the value of the standard coin. He asserts that the latter consists of nothing else than *slantar* that correspond to an exchange rate of 72 *mark*. Now these *slantar* have been the standard coin for ten years, yet during the same period the exchange rate has risen to 30 or 40 *mark* above the standard coin and has, without any change in *slantar*, fallen by as much as 20 or 25 *mark*. In what way has it then accommodated itself to the standard coin? Or what standard coin did we use as a basis when the exchange rate was at its highest level? If it has now been able to fall by 20 or 30 *mark* without any change in the standard coin, why could it not fall still lower if the reasons for its present level were to be removed? Might not then *plåtar, caroliner*, etc. regain the honour of being reckoned as the standard coin, without any drastic reduction?

To have an unstable value for the *daler* and yet to use that term in one's business transactions is the same as using alternating steelyards every month, each showing 20 *mark* for every *lispund*, though the *lispund* of one never equals that of another, and then buying and selling with these thousands of times a day without knowing whether and how much they differ in weight. And yet that is prohibited on pains of a severe penalty. If the seller now regards all the *lispund* as shown on his altered steelyards as the same, while the purchaser always measures them by his own unaltered one, the latter will sometimes have to pay more than usual for the seller's *lispund* and will still make a significant profit. The seller who regards all his *lispund* as the same and all those who use the same kind of steelyard as he does that month will sell off all their goods during that period, because they believe them to command such a high price, and the purchaser accepts them just as eagerly, as he fleeces the seller of a few *mark* per *pund*.

Ignorance about the decline in value of our *daler* in outlying border regions has in that way deprived us of millions, for it has not been possible to blind our neighbours with the term *daler*. The profit has induced those who are ignorant of this to collect as much gold, silver and copper coin as they can gather within a radius of 30 to 40 *mil* and to take it across the border, as they received more *daler* in banknotes there than they had cost at home in old *daler*, without realizing that the country nonetheless lost a few thousand through them.

You are already becoming tired of accompanying me any further. I have to leave out much that ought to be said. Worries and anxiety depress you; you want to escape, to banish your unease in more amusing company. Dear reader! just wait a moment. I only wish to mention one single thing, and then we can proceed together to more cheering subjects.

§ 23

There are constraints on reasoning, writing and printing, which I, fourthly, still have to say something about, not because enough has not already been written on this subject but because it must not be passed over at this point.

As pleasant as day is compared to night, light compared to darkness, sunshine compared to thunder and lightning, so exciting to citizens is knowledge of their well-being and distress. For that reason, learned subjects are pursued, writers are roused to compete with each other and the printing press exhibits their thoughts. Free societies in particular need such information. They have to manage their welfare by themselves. If they are benighted and leaderless, they will fail to reach the goal of felicity, will hit the rocks and plunge their entire native country into an unfathomable abyss, just when they thought they were about to drop anchor off the shore of happiness. They will then learn how hazardous it is to be a pilot in unknown waters and a leading seaman with no knowledge of the compass.

Sweden has indeed experienced this to its own detriment. Scarcely had a pale aurora borealis appeared in our sky than we thought that it heralded the delightful red light of dawn; a small signal fire, a shining meteor that burns for a few minutes has often captivated us so much that, before we knew where we were, we had strayed from the correct fairway. We have believed them to be sparkling rays from the island of the blessed, but after admiring these quickly extinguished flares for a while, we have found ourselves surrounded by breakers and high cliffs. Most people were completely at a loss, abandoning both sails and rudder, others said that we would soon be able to anchor in a desired haven, but those who were clear-sighted said that the vessel would perish unless we changed course.

It is not enough in free states for a few to have fathomed this. It is the majority that will decide matters. Those who have advanced that far are too elevated above the common people: they are individuals who, once they have gained the confidence of the country through their zeal, are soon led astray from the right path by an insidious self-interest; they should therefore be honoured, but not worshipped, and be followed, but not blindly.

If that is to happen, the nation itself must be enlightened, but that requires reasoning. That is best developed when we put our thoughts down on paper. But there is little encouragement for that unless the printing press makes it public. That provides a noble defence for truth and innocence. Virtue is not sullied by the black stain of slander; it is purified from dross and shines twice as brightly. It is unafraid of daylight, never suspicious of enlightenment and least of all fears any setbacks when that is allowed to prevail.

But there are also others who prefer to stand behind a screen when they are to do something and only occasionally emerge in front of the public and then perform wonderful tricks, but with a proviso similar to that of a conjuror, that no one may come close to them or look behind the screen. Dr Ernst Schubert appears to be referring to such people when he says in his *Heilige Reden*:[58] "Do not be surprised, my friends, that truth provokes such deep and implacable hostility from the world. There have never been two such diametrically opposed things as truth and the opinions and aims of the children of the world. The latter look for nothing but a vain glory, perishable treasures and reprehensible carnal desires. Their intention is to give these godless desires some appearance of virtue, deceive the simple-minded and gain an opportunity to indulge their sensual pleasures. But as soon as truth emerges, the evil of their hearts is exposed and they are deprived of many opportunities to achieve their evil aims. Imagine the difficult situation of a person who seeks his highest bliss in his desires! He thinks he will lose everything when truth prevails and can lodge itself in people's hearts. And that single thought is enough to rouse him to fury, cruelty, vengeance and persecution against those who publicly and fearlessly profess the truth." And in another place: "Piety often prevents us from agreeing with the aims of those who hold power. The love for our neighbour often obliges

us to take up the cause of the poor and wretched, who are oppressed and persecuted by others. Justice often forces us to reveal the wickedness of those who
have gained great renown in the world. And this circumstance, which in every
way conflicts with that of the world, cannot possibly leave us in peace for long.
People become infuriated with us. They seek to get rid of us. Lies and imputa-
tions are concocted and deprive us of our good name. We are charged with all
kinds of vices and crimes. They shun neither cunning nor force in order to
destroy us."

Baron Rudolph of Hollenburg[59] says: "There are three methods in particular
that rulers tend to use to promote individual gain to the detriment of the public
interest, namely: *To deprive the general public of any ability to harm them*, by
getting rid either by cunning or force of all those who have from childhood
learned to think and have the enterprise to carry that into effect for the common
good, who act on the sanctity of promises and can never be seduced by flattering
words, without whom, he says, the rest of the people are a body without a soul,
an army without a commander, a ship without a crew and are soundly asleep. *To
impoverish all the noble-minded by coercion*, through confiscating the possessions of the wealthy, collecting intolerable ground rents, using them for private
advantage, overwhelming the citizens with work and seeking to involve them in
foreign wars. *To use discord to set the citizens against each other*, by banning all
meetings, promoting stupid people over the competent ones, depriving some of
their properties and allocating them to others."

"To be a republican," says another author, "and not to understand the external
and internal interests of one's fatherland due to prevailing secrecy and constraints on thought, is a contradiction in terms. Ignorance is fitting for barbarism
but not for a free republican spirit."

§ 24

Thus, we have now wandered through foreign lands as well as our own country,
through earlier and more recent times, sought and presumably also found the
cause of emigration from our beloved fatherland; here we are confronted by the
second question: *By what measures may it best be prevented?*

It can be answered either briefly or at length. Briefly: when its cause is
removed, its effect will necessarily cease. At length, by discovering the proxi-
mate and more remote mainsprings of constraint, seeing them all in their context
and indicating how one may be removed by persuasion, another by effective
action, one immediately, the other gradually.

The former is likely to be inadequate in this case, the latter on the other hand
excessive.

— — — *medium tenuere beati.*[60]

I will try to keep to the middle way. At another time and in another place that
will have to be achieved which is now inadequately dealt with.

Our countrymen are of different opinions as to the feasibility and the means of improving Sweden. Despair has seized the minds of most to such an extent that they no longer believe that it can be improved by any other measures than that of first overthrowing everything. The edifice of the state, they think, has in our time already become so distorted everywhere that even the best master builder is unable to restore its correct shape and appearance unless it is completely demolished and rebuilt again from its foundations according to the best rules of architecture. Others again praise the blessed liberty in which we live and believe that little is wanting before Sweden will reach the pinnacle of its felicity. Have not both gone too far?

If everyone is bewildered, who is then to improve our native land? The means still exist; the country still has the ability to get back on its feet, if only it understands how to use it correctly. To overthrow everything is a violent cure. It is also uncertain how expeditious and conscientious the master builders will be that may then be available, and apart from that, a large amount of building materials tends to be wasted in such situations.

It is not enough, however, to place a few small plasters here and there on the wounds of the country with the intention of curing its illness entirely. A corrosive sourness in the blood demands powerful internal drugs if all is not soon to be consumed.

§ 25

Freedom is the real antidote to oppression, but it is a term with too wide a meaning; it can be both used and misused in innumerable ways and must therefore be applied with great care if it is not to be of more harm than benefit. For the freedom of a few individuals has been the ruin of all states and could also become ours unless it is curbed in time.

We need not dwell upon the freedom in our actual constitution. It is a valuable possession that we never want to lose as long as we and our descendants are called Swedes.

By freedom, as I use the term, I understand the advantage that every citizen ought to possess through a country's laws and regulations in order to promote his own happiness, as long as he in no way offends against that of his fellow-citizens or society as a whole.

We are all human beings, all tainted by evil desires; all of us therefore need each other's help and all of us careful supervision. As long as we stand outside society, each one of us deals with his own affairs as he wishes but then also has to face the consequences alone, without protection from anyone, and that freedom is natural. But as soon as we seek the protection of a society, its best interests are also our fundamental law.

We have all voluntarily sworn loyalty to the Swedish Crown, a Crown that is all the dearer to us as it rests on pillars of freedom. No one should therefore lord it over another, no one be another's slave: all possess the same right, all the same advantage. When that is the case, a citizen possesses everything that he can reasonably wish for or can ever obtain in a well-ordered society; nor will there then be any reason for him to emigrate, but a hundred that will keep him here.

The country is in this respect just like a set of scales. Should the freedom of one or more individuals rise too high in one scale, that is only ever possible by depressing that of the others too far into servitude.

§ 26

Whether entrepreneurs or civil servants enjoy greater freedom among us is something on which not everyone agrees. If a farmer pays his taxes and debts in full, it is said, no one can be better off than him, but an official must live in constant anxiety of having to account for his actions. Our leading poets have composed a great deal about the blissfulness of a farmer and the tranquillity and innocent pleasures of shepherds and the advantages they possess as compared with those who are shaken by all the winds of fate. I recently accompanied one of them to observe and experience these rural pleasures. There we caught sight of a countryman ploughing. "Oh! What a pleasure", he said, "to be so far from the din of the town as he is in his innocent tranquillity!" We walked some way across the ploughed field to get a closer view of his pastime, but when we got there my companion said, in a fair sweat: "We have done well to get here, I almost gave up earlier." "What about him, then," I said, "who has to do this all day long and at the same time use all his strength to control the plough and the oxen?" A while later we fell in with some shepherds. "This sort of life", said my companion, "is an earthly paradise" etc. We stopped to observe their innocence, but at that moment one of them came running out of the woods shouting: "Ah! The best sheep in my flock is lost. I have looked for it in vain all day. I am so worn out I am ready to drop, and though I know I am in no way responsible for this misfortune, I am bound to have to pay for it this evening with the skin on my back and at the end of the year with my wages." We pitied him and asked if he had such an unfair master. "No," he replied, "he is not unfair, but if we did not have to fear such things, we would not care whether half the flock were lost. I have seen how those behave who have indulgent masters: they spend their days aimlessly, and by the evening they scarcely know where a single sheep is."

All of a sudden a terrible thunderstorm broke above our heads with darkness, rain and lightning; it was impossible to find shelter. We had to endure it. "What bad luck we have had", said my companion, "to be caught in such foul weather." "No worse luck", I said, "than that of the shepherds, who have to be prepared for such things all the time." "I would give a ducat", he continued, "to be back in town now." "It is harder for the shepherds to do so," I said, "as they do not have one." "See the shepherds", I added, "moving on with their flocks now; let us go along with them until the evening." "No," he replied, "even if I were given all the flocks that are moving along there, I would not do so. I want to go back. I fear, as it is, that we will become exhausted along the way."

"Precisely," I said, "then sing no more so sweetly of the pleasures of countrymen and shepherds." To spend a moment watching the farmer working in a field and shepherds driving their flocks may be a pleasure, but to hold the plough oneself and to step altogether into the shoes of the shepherds are unpleasant and strenuous experiences that all refuse to let anyone else impose on them. But decent handicrafts, you say, are less arduous. Try them, go into the workshops, do not judge their wages until you have experienced their work. Wield the hammer for a day in the forge and then share the day's wages with the smith; handle the carpenter's plane for a while; move the spool energetically in a loom, et cetera; I am sure that before evening you will give me the same response as my companion.

§ 27

Freedom never exists without causing us to desire it once we know of it: our desires guide us in all our actions. If freedom is greatest in the productive occupations, why are we not especially drawn to them? But when we see that they are short of people and our bureaucracy is overstaffed, it seems undeniable that freedom is too limited in them and too great in the latter.

That is the reason why there are so many on the unattached lists and understudies in every department, so many unemployed clergymen, so many supernumeraries and curates; that is why the number of official posts has to be increased in order to provide them with status and earnings and everyone yearns for promotion. The farmer wants to become a burgher, the burgher a councillor, the councillor a burgomaster, the burgomaster a district magistrate, the district magistrate an assessor, and so on. The farmer and the burgher want their son to be a clergyman, the clergyman his to be a bishop, the bishop his to be a nobleman.

This eventually distorts the shape of society. It becomes large and unwieldy at the top; but the roots and the lower branches languish and rot away, whereby the tree is soon at risk of being blown down by the slightest puff of wind.

If the matter is to be resolved, therefore, and the ruin of the country to be averted in time, the sap must eventually be led back into the root. All disfiguring secondary twigs, which absorb nutrition and never bear fruit, should be broken off, others be lopped and adjusted, but the soil around the roots must be carefully dug over, manured and watered, and one will soon observe that the root becomes stronger and the lower trunk begins to put out new live shoots, which promise to change its appearance within a few years.

§ 28

From the preceding I therefore derive the following general rule: *The trades ought to be held in higher respect than other things, and that in accordance with their utility and necessity to society, that respect being increased until consuming individuals become inclined to abandon less advantageous official posts and engage in trades.*

Such respect does not consist of some pretty phrases about farming and the handicrafts. Our age takes pride in having developed a greater interest in the economy than our forefathers; but as economic activity is an art of acquiring and preserving possessions, I really do not know any era in Sweden's history that has made as bad use of it as we have.

For 40 years now we have lived in relative peace, with heavy expenditure, but never have the public funds been in such a profound state of debt as they are now, not even during the lamentable 20-year-long war that was brought to an end by the death of Charles XII.[61] With the Bank a rich source of money was unexpectedly opened up for our age, which in a short space of time made us suddenly affluent but had the same disadvantage as the Portuguese diamond trade, namely that, owing to the excessive increase in the supply, the price of the commodity collapsed, and it is still uncertain how far it may fall. Unless the honourable Estates of the Realm remedy this, we could end up making ourselves poor in everything except paper.

That respect involves, in the first place, *that the productive citizens enjoy every possible freedom and are treated very considerately,* as if they were the most precious possessions of the country; that their rights are first safeguarded; the constraints on them are actively opposed and the injustice suffered by a single farmer is punished *exemplariter* and speedily. They should not be oppressed by threats, inducements or pressure; burdensome general redistributions of landholdings, detailed land surveys and tax assessments should not be imposed on them, but they should be encouraged by examples, representations and the personal advantages that accrue to them from that, and the way in which it may all be brought about with the least cost should be carefully monitored and adjusted.

The Sovereign Power has already, with the best of intentions, for a long time past taken great pains by means of laws and regulations to control all the actions of the subjects, which has given rise to so many laws, regulations and ordinances that they cannot keep up to date with what their obligations are, much less fulfil them. When it comes to their observance, insuperable difficulties have moreover arisen, which have forced the government to issue so many new elucidations and counter-regulations concerning them that even the court clerk is unable to apply all of them in his court, still less the subjects to observe them, which has caused the latter to see themselves cut off from their natural liberty on every side and obliged to live in constant fear of becoming entangled in the law.

The Creator, who has made everything in nature perfect and human beings sociable, having also made their inclinations such that the more freedom they are allowed, apart from practising those vices that should be checked by the laws, the more do they add strength and well-being to society and each individual, and vice versa, and experience shows that whenever human devices have, after the most careful deliberation, been set up in contradiction to that, they have sooner or later provided evidence that all human reason forms a mere drop in that sea of wisdom that is required to ensure the continuance of countries and societies in the world and that the ruin of the state will sooner or later arise from these. As proof of that, I could refer in our case to the once so highly praised Copper and Tar Companies and the Salt Office.[62] I am not sure whether I ought to include even more among these before they have reached the end of their terms. The harm caused by a whole number of lesser artifices is less obvious, so that they may indeed be defended with total conviction for several centuries. It is wonderful how statecraft has increased in our time in Europe and especially among us; the only thing I miss is an acknowledgement of the fact that we do not yet understand any state thoroughly. We are not satisfied with viewing a state in the simple form that the Almighty wished to present to humanity but want to set the masterpiece of the Almighty in regular motion with our clumsy fingers and turn all the wheels according to our own preference, although we are obliged, with little credit, to hand it on in a more faltering condition than when we received it.

Perhaps excise duties, guild and currency regulations, rural trade, commodity ordinances, staple towns, privileges, societies, companies and so on would need to be examined more closely, so that a Swede would be able to learn about his obligations and would in other respects be freed from unreasonable constraints and the tyranny of self-interest. It may be feared that, with such a free rein, the whole of society would utterly collapse, but experience shows on the contrary that the more a people has made use of that freedom, the more considerable has its growth also been in terms of wealth and citizens, but the greater the restrictions on it, the poorer will the people be. The Chinese may serve as an example of the former and we ourselves of the latter. Nor did freedom really have any distorting effect on the trades, but caused them all to be more active and vigorous.

If that does not happen but the constraints continue in the trades, all encouragement for enterprise is destroyed; the workers are fettered and burdened by the institutions themselves. Lawsuits, administrators of the law and the daily consumption of paper, under the closest supervision, increase markedly at the expense of the trades until the officials finally, for lack of further nourishment from the trades, shed their feathers and fade away, having been driven by hunger to consume their mother.

I wish with all my heart that this prediction of mine may never come true; but I also believe that in our present situation nothing different could happen, if it has not already happened. In this regard I no more apprehend a verdict of disgrace from posterity than Cicero did when he hoped for the immortality of the soul. Here is the key to helping our native land and the true remedy for emigration. For either a citizen must be induced to believe that he is free although he has bolts on his legs, or they must be loosened, so that a Swede may boast: "When I fear my God and obey authority, no one can trouble me. No one may imprison me on suspicion alone; no one take me to court without my knowing my accuser; no one may force me by torture into a confession before I am convicted; no one touch the slightest part of my property or take a piece of land away from me; no one prevent me from making a living in a blameless manner, whenever and wherever I can." These were actually the rights of a Roman citizen, which aliens had purchased so dearly during the period of liberty but which, on the contrary, were no longer worth a groat by the third century when the nation lost its liberty.[63]

Our multitude of vagabonds reminds me of long-hunted deer, who scarcely hear the snap of a twig before they rush off in flight, crying: "*vestigia nos terrent*".[64] Here traps and snares have been set for them everywhere. If they have suffered the fate of being born to a farmhand, crofter or dependent lodger or had the misfortune of being the third, fourth or fifth surviving child of a farmer, they are born to be slaves, no less than aristocrats are born with noble blood.

They are hunted under the designation of vagabonds; they are condemned to become soldiers; they are recruited, bought, sold, enlisted, exercised, beaten, suffer agonies and finally die. Each county, moreover, sets nets all around its borders so that, though it cannot itself provide them with food, work or an income, they are nonetheless prevented from being useful to others. What happens? *Nitimur in vetitum*.[65] The same happens to them as to a child; it happily dances in the ring among its playmates half the day, but if you tell it that the ring is maintained to prevent it escaping from there, it will rush away between their hands.

The poor fugitive is pursued like an escaped prisoner, is caught, tied up and bound, although he has done nothing but seek a place in his fatherland where he can best serve both it and himself. How is it possible that such a hunted group will spend any more nights within the borders of Sweden than it needs to succeed in escaping from it?

How is it possible to remedy this unless one offers general and permanent immunity to such wretched individuals? One often whistles at a hare in mid-leap to make it stop, but only in order to be able to take better aim at it. The *fides publica*[66] must first be fully restored and all hunting banned, so that those who have become frightened and lost may slow down and gain a respite in which to gradually seek a living.

The ordinance of 18 February[67] on the establishment of crofts and new settlements on the land of freehold farms may have brought a little calm, so that one or two were already choosing a pleasant location where they intended to settle down, marry their girl and propagate their family. But the gracious royal ordinance of 3 July 1759 ordering unemployed men in rural regions without delay to take up farmsteading, although that was not possible for them, or some other lawful occupation, or else to enter military service, gave rise to new anxieties, and before those who were then driven from their homes will dare to settle down again there will have to be a period of calm.

Care should be taken in particular that food should not run short for the labouring multitude. Distinguished and respected men, who have many lofty matters to consider, regard food and clothing as vulgar things to worry about and seek to raise their thoughts to higher and nobler matters. That is possible for those whose needs are met from the Treasury, bake their bread with the sweat of others and clothe themselves from the looms of others, but to wish to implant an equally elevated taste in every citizen is senseless. Life is the dearest thing of all; it is lost within a few days when food runs out, and without firewood and clothes one freezes to death within a few hours. The worker has no one else to rely on, and a short postponement of these needs will soon place him beyond all temporal needs. To be complacent about all this is thus for him to be a fool, and of all material things, next to life itself, to value the means by which it is sustained is the most sensible thing that can be expected from human beings. We wonder at this attitude of the general public, or as the proverb goes: *He who fills a mouth is good*, but it is more curious that we do not realize what a vital necessity this is or fail to consider how much sweat a loaf of bread costs a labourer. Nothing appeals more to the minds of the people than never to lack the necessities of life. The fiercest lions and bears restrain their fury towards those who feed them; they show their affection and pleasure towards those who provide them with their necessities. Nor is there any measure that sooner subdues the grumbling and discontent of the public than when the Sovereign Power concerns itself with the needs of the very poorest.

Vespasian[68] personally sat outside every day feeding the people and let nothing prevent him from doing so. In his letters, King Charles XII warned his generals of nothing so often as that his troops should receive adequate pay and provisions, as the principal means by which he could keep a handful of people together in a foreign land and imbue the soldiers with the courage to risk their lives for their fatherland.

They demand no more than to escape a severe tutelage and be permitted to live undisturbed in their cabins, to moisten their bread with their sweat during the day, be able to put it in their children's mouths and tell them: "Bless your God and our freedom, which has allowed us to go out and get your food", and to send their small children to sleep in the evening with such a lullaby and rest their own heads on a stone placed by nature in their abode, to await there the moment when the purple in the starry vault promises them a new day and the celestial torch emerges between the mountain crags and they can again begin to rival the worker-ant in gathering in something as winter food for their families and in making smocks for the children, so that they do not freeze to death in their cabins.

§ 29

As the human mind is always most avid for respect, however, the second measure is *to accord respect to producers, not only as between themselves but also in relation to consumers*. Who, you may say, is so thoughtless as not to respect a good-natured farmer, an industrious craftsman, a diligent shopkeeper; but of such respect I take the same view as Montesquieu did of the general pardon granted by Julius Caesar once he had utterly abolished the freedom of the Roman Republic: *The compliancy*, he says, *that one shows after having crushed everything is not worth much praise.*[69] We do indeed allow them some respect, but never such as could be compared to our own; it may cause a little mutual rivalry between them, yet all the same they yearn for greater respect than they receive.

As long as rank is observed outside the official sphere, and the position of a producer remains one that no consumer any longer wishes to occupy, it will be impossible to supply people for agriculture and crafts and to reduce the number of applicants for administrative posts. The contempt among a large proportion goes so deep that not only are they disregarded because they cannot carry themselves, dress or speak in accordance with our elevated taste but, even if that were in no way an impediment, the contempt would still be there merely because they earn a living by their own labour.

If the respect is to be capable of achieving anything, it must be such that they will regard themselves as gaining in esteem thereby. There can be no more exact measure of this freedom than that the Sovereign Power should continue to extend it until the emigration of the labouring multitude ceases and consumers reckon themselves fortunate to be able to become productive citizens; only after that, but not before, should moderation in that regard be considered.

§ 30

That constraints also oppress our officials has been demonstrated in § 19, but that these are not caused by the body of workers should be deducible from the immediately preceding one.

It is a perilous situation for the country when honest officials, seeking promotion through merit, begin to complain of injustice. The general public, which has a good opinion of them, is disturbed by such things, and their example makes a deep impression on it.

To forestall this in good time, the Sovereign Power must be circumspect in every regard; moreover, measures are required *that stimulate a competition in competence and virtue.*

Our constitution expressly states that education shall be encouraged and that with regard to official posts those should be particularly considered who have achieved exemplary qualifications in that respect, so that deserving men will be supported and no foreigners, or still less, people without religion, gain promotion among us. No whippersnappers should be permitted to take precedence, trampling sense and scholarship underfoot and making a mockery of learning; it has cost its possessors many a late hour and much care, while the others have satisfied their desires in indolence, pastimes and sensual pleasures, and without it our native land will within a short time sink into the obscurity of dreadful ignorance.

Men who have served honestly, with care and conscientiousness, should be promoted, not because they have money, for that is indeed the weakest proof of their probity in their previous duties, but rather because they need more of it for their subsistence, as they have not been willing to obtain anything by unjust means, and to become wealthy in any other way than by inheritance is scarcely possible in our time.

If he is therefore to advance himself by means of money, he must in his earlier post make justice venal and ensure delays, so that the price of the commodity will have time to rise, and finally decide the matter in favour of the one who makes the highest bid, so that an office can soon be transformed into an auction room, with the difference that at auctions only the highest bidder pays but here the lower bidders sometimes also have to acknowledge their bids.

May it then be time to become honest again when he has advanced to a higher position by means of money acquired in such manner?

In the words of one of our peerless poets:[70]

But should he change his mind,
too far by then he's gone,
For having crossed the line,
he has to keep right on.

In former times our leaders stood out above the rest by their pious example, and it was not regarded as admirable to promote atheism and moral laxity, and for that reason religion was held in high respect. Those who then felt obliged to engage in religious exercises were given encouragement and licence to do so by the example of their social superiors. But how do things stand now? Religion is either directly associated with one's office, or else it will be non-existent in most people.

Knowledge of divine matters is required for that, and it also requires practice. Where does one now find a trace of either? The education of most people is arranged from childhood in such a way that they cannot learn much about piety. The parents are delighted if their children can amuse them with long memorized passages from fables and novels, but the fact that they have never seen or read anything of the catechism, the Bible or other pious books causes them little concern.

It is deplorable to see in what spiritual darkness a large proportion of the high-born in particular grow up, without any care taken in that respect. When they are to assume official positions, to what extent is it then investigated whether they possess genuine piety and whether they have taken the Lord's Holy Communion and other matters relating to devoutness? Many may rather believe it to be a merit to be a mocker of religion, and once that kind of people occupy seats of power, those of a different view are not likely to extol their fate.

How does this come about, you say? Why is supervision in this respect so feeble? Or could it not be improved? Not, in my opinion, unless the Sovereign Power banishes godlessness, stupidity and self-interest, for it is impossible for the vices to be their own prosecutors or judges.

§ 31

I have just made some reference to the ranking of professions; I must again repeat that here, as well as in its proper place. Its serious consequences have been fully demonstrated in several publications.[71] Unless this matter is dealt with seriously and the Estates themselves, without regard to the complaints of the officials, after mature consideration, adopt measures regarding it, it will not be possible to remove the constraints either between consumers and producers or between the consumers themselves.

When agriculture and crafts have been accorded concern and respect, as proposed above, and the authority of officials, outside their official sphere, has been limited in that manner, the number of applicants for offices has been reduced and the number and motivation of working people have been increased, only then will it be the right time to make appointments to certain offices for periods of one, two or at most three years. Then no office will any longer be something to compete for, but a duty that one cannot evade when called upon to perform it. And then, but not before, we will be able to rejoice at the victory of freedom.

When Rome threw off the yoke of autocracy, Brutus made the consuls annual,[72] on which Livy comments: "Believe me, freedom owed its origin more to the fact that the consuls were annual than that the royal power was in any way reduced."[73]

Certain appointments for life are not very encouraging, least of all on the basis on which they exist among us, but annual ones, on the contrary, cause us to engage in a perfectly honest competition to excel others in integrity and virtue during the brief time that we hold an office and thus make ourselves more deserving of confidence from the nation. Then everyone is also inclined to become familiar with the laws of the fatherland and to understand what the rights of a Swedish man involve; then the official will not be ashamed of work; then we shall be able like the English to sit in judgment on our sacks of grain and wool, and a general, like the earliest Roman ones, will be called from the plough to lead an army, conduct successful wars and, when his command terminates, return to the plough.[74]

§ 32

Let us see what effect these measures may have on *marriages*. When agriculture, commerce and handicrafts are accorded the respect they deserve, then a significant number of unemployed men waiting for official appointments would enter the trades, set up households, make a living through work and soon be able to marry, beget children and bring them up to be useful citizens; if their work were to provide them with a better living, respect and reward than before, they would within a short time be followed by others.

As soon as more enlightenment, more freedom and educated sense begin to appear in the productive occupations, the farmer will lack neither examples nor a conviction that the earth produces necessities for us not according to its extent but to the number of those who work on it. He would no longer need to be perplexed as to what he should do with his many children once they have grown to adulthood, either with other people or at home, but would give each of them a plot of land on which to live and work in perpetuity.

When farmhands develop a wish to become seamen, we ought to realize that it is a desire born of their natural yearning for freedom. Honourable compatriots should then counter that by offering freedoms at home, show them the places where they may establish new settlements, crofts and cabins, promise them and their descendants undisputed possession of the land that they clear, support them and in particular persuade them to marry. Nor should wages be restricted as long as we are short of workers; that would be to covet a few *öre* today and thereby lose an entire *plåt* tomorrow.

§ 33

But if constraints in lawsuits are ever to be prevented among us, it is necessary *to make officials more answerable and punishable than is generally the case,* so that someone who regards himself as having been wronged by them can at least receive satisfaction from them as easily as from any other citizens. Is it not said that the law is sufficiently strict in that respect, regarding misdemeanours by officials? The law would indeed suffice to keep the officials within bounds, but it is a dead letter that in itself can never affect anyone; the question here is not what could or ought to happen under the law but what actually does happen.

It is not unusual for one and the same official to pronounce two completely contradictory judgments in two identical cases. How many officials can be shown to take responsibility for their actions? Or what is the level of that responsibility? Does it correspond to what the others have suffered from their actions? The events referred to in § 21, with many others that could be adduced, will bear witness to that.

Could it not be ameliorated, as some have imagined, first, by not allowing any official who is accountable to the Estates to be eligible to represent any estate during the Diets; second, by ensuring, when cases are revised and appeals are dealt with, that those officials who have acted deliberately, that is, contrary to manifest law, and have departed from the truth should promptly and without any protracted process be punished by the rigours of the law as a warning to others, including the higher officials, not only for their own actions but also for what they have connived at with regard to their subordinates?

It is by no means enough for the Estates to establish good laws; they should also be the first to put them into execution. Imagine if we were to hear three times a year that the legal penalty had been increased for thieves yet were nonetheless to see one after another being allowed to keep their stolen goods, with a warning; how would such a law protect our property? Would such humanity towards malefactors not be to turn the law into a shadow and put the lives and property of the other citizens at risk of being arbitrarily plundered by them?

The officials of the kingdom really ought to be the ones who attend to the execution of the laws among the people, but how is that possible if they do not themselves apply them in their official capacity? They have other officials above them, it is said, who order them to do so. But I ascend as many stairs as I can and finally ask who should be giving orders to those at the top. None but the Sovereign Power itself, for the law never touches anyone unless it is first fully applied by the Estates themselves, without the slightest respect of persons, to those who are to give it force and effect among the other subjects of the kingdom.

And precisely here is the actual point of leverage for law-abidingness throughout society. As the honourable Estates of the Realm set this wheel in motion, such will also be its motion throughout the body of the realm. But if that is left undone, even if one were then to manipulate other ones as much as one likes and attach more weights to get the clockwork moving, it will fall apart before it can be brought into any regular motion.

This is the real helm by which the whole ship is to be steered. What is the use of equipping it in the best possible way unless the Sovereign Power itself holds the tiller and sets the ship on the right tack?

For impartial legislation it is also, third, necessary to have complete reciprocity between the judge and the one who is judged; for the greatest joy of a Swedish man ought to consist in his right to proceed boldly, secure in his innocence, from the magistrates' court all the way to the royal throne, without risking anything, and to smile at the frenzy of evil, as long as the law protects his back, extending its branches and sheltering him from the storm-winds of superior power.

These would be such splendid undertakings that Swedish subjects would for ever celebrate festivals of rejoicing on the days when these wheels were set in motion, and, even before the Estates of the Realm could conclude such blessed deliberations, these remedies would already be bringing freedom to the most distant subjects of the kingdom. A few years would reward by 100 per cent such a blessed labour; many citizens who have been exhausted by libel cases and have emigrated would listen to our joy and again begin to love the fatherland that had formerly been so hateful in their eyes, and Swedish men would never flee a native region where they are treated with such consideration.

Constraints in lawsuits should also be inhibited by shortening them. Everyone knows how much legal petitioners are burdened by the many and lengthy byways with which our judicial process is encumbered. No one can deny that some curtailment would be possible: the kingdom has indeed invested considerable sums in this matter alone and has encouraged legal experts to present proposals; a number have actually been submitted, but of all this the general public has seen nothing except that the number of officials and Crown servants increases year by year, that lower courts, government departments, appeal courts and chanceries are drowning in paper and that many petitioners do not outlive the conclusion of their cases.

I revere everything that our lawyers have formerly written and thought about this subject, but I have seen some conscientious, efficient and legally expert judges, despite their best efforts, being overwhelmed with so many and such complex court cases that one's mind reels at the thought of it, and if all demonstrable breaches of the law had been submitted to the court, three would quite certainly have been as fully engaged as one is now. I can also testify that it has not become more common to increase the volume of court records for the sake of perquisites, nor to misdirect cases, and yet the same courts are overwhelmed with such a number of cases that there is not enough time to resolve them.

Either some curtailment should now be possible or it is not. If it is possible in other countries to decide a case with less waste of money, paper and time, then why not among us? A Swedish man is in no way more unruly than a Prussian or an Englishman; nor can he imagine that he could be dealt with more conscientiously.

I do not deny that self-interested judges and troublesome parties may often be responsible for prolonging cases, but when neither of these are present and the lawsuits nonetheless increase daily, whom are we then to blame for that?

No more than three alternatives are possible here. The fault must either lie with the judge or the parties or else in the legislation. However, apart from the fact that judges and parties must generally be such as the laws and regulations in a country have made them, it may be observed, even when neither side breaks the rules, that the lawsuits cannot be curtailed to any significant degree. I therefore ask for permission to look at the third one.

Least of all do I wish to touch upon the constitution of our government; I revere our solemnly confirmed fundamental laws; I do not wish to criticize those that concern our moral actions under divine and natural law, nor those that by the dispensation of nature distinguish between mine and yours; and finally I hold sacred that which has been found necessary in order to maintain a society and must therefore remain invariable in all societies and every epoch. But if we suppose all of these in their simplicity to be quite unalterable, there remain an incredible number of economic and political laws and regulations in Sweden that I, as a free Swedish man, may venture to discuss with the best of intentions, not with the aim of finding fault with them, still less of overturning them, but merely in order to give those who hold power some reason to consider this important subject, as to whether they could be reduced or completely repealed.

On this globe there are societies that possess very few or no such laws at all, having left all this in the hands of nature, and we realize with astonishment that they have reached the height of blessedness that may in temporal terms be desired for any country. We find on the contrary that we have by legislation sought to determine almost every step that a subject has to take, defined every branch of industry with great ingenuity, divided them into separate categories, sometimes given support to one and sometimes another, set values on commodities, and, among other things, on pains of heavy fines persuaded ourselves to believe that five *mark* of copper in tiny bits is equivalent to nine in larger pieces and have by all such means woven so many and such fine threads through society that the inhabitants in their movements have become trapped in them to such an extent that no human being would be able to unravel them except in the way that the Gordian knot was undone, namely by cutting through the whole bundle of bonds. It then happened that some trade that was released in that manner wished to distance itself from the others that were still entangled, which led to a spate of new concerns to get this one woven in again as soon as possible, on a different pattern, before it brought the whole of society tumbling down.

What has been the result of all this? Well, our trades are to a large extent in monopolistic fetters, which in some promote extravagance and indolence, in others stifle enterprise and drive people to desperation, making some suicidal. We infringe the law of the state and consequently that of God, wounding consciences by breaches of the law. We have been provided with so many economic regulations that a lifetime does not suffice to absorb them. Perhaps we have so many lawsuits so that they will never cease – a good source of income for public prosecutors, ombudsmen, judges and lawyers. There would be busy hands in every government department, even if they were twice as numerous as they are now. An ardent desire, indeed a proficiency in making laws for almost every *casus specialis*.

But what else? Well, we have become underpopulated without war and plague, hungry without years of bad harvests and destitute with the most productive mines. And that which is most lamentable of all, while we have thus entangled ourselves, the foreigners have, by the leave of a few wealthy citizens, emptied our traps and fished with an innocent air in murky waters long enough to become rich and have obtained *ius patronatus*[75] over a large part of our most valuable manufactures, while others have pocketed the money of their fellow citizens. What a wretched situation!

§ 34

In § 22 we showed the risks and real losses that Swedes have to face with regard to their property. Did we not combine into a society in order to enjoy security for our lives and property and entrust the protection of them to the Sovereign Power?

To achieve such a great aim it is necessary, first, to stabilize the exchange rate appropriately.[76] It may not respond to any instruction as long as its causes are left to operate freely and no one does anything about them. Such were the earlier attempts to reduce it, which could not possibly have succeeded, but if the mainsprings are slackened in careful stages, the exchange rate will eventually relax of itself, without any decrees regarding the actual rate.

All this was clearly and circumstantially presented to the honourable Estates of the Realm at the last Diet, including a draft of the actual regulation by which it might be brought about, but little has been done about it, so that the effect of that has been minimal. If this is rejected, then Mr Christiernin's proposal for a 72-*mark* exchange rate may be adopted, though on condition that he stands surety for the kingdom against all indemnities should the proposal not succeed or not endure longer than the stabilization of the exchange rate that a few years ago cost the kingdom more than 60 *tunnor guld*. For we certainly have no more money to squander, when the kingdom is already riddled with debts.

Second, once that has been done, the general public should be informed of the rate at which all our currency – *dukat, riksdaler, carolin, sexstyver-stycke, plåt, slant*, etc. – will be reckoned in *daler* according to its intrinsic value in the stabilized exchange rate, so that neither natives nor foreigners may fleece us by means of it, for otherwise there will never be a lack of expedients by which to enrich oneself at the expense of the general public.

In short, Sweden has long been shrouded in obscurity by the exchange rate. It is already high time to pay for the goods and labour of the inhabitants in coin of genuine value and not merely a stamped denomination.

§ 35

From everything that has been described here I have not found a single remedy for the emigration of people that could be applied without the most forceful action by the honourable Estates of the Realm. At every turn such a strong opposition will be met with, of power and of specious reasoning, that a more than common constancy is required if anything is to be achieved.

Three things are thus required for a successful outcome of the matter. First, *an exact and detailed knowledge of all matters pertaining to this*, with all the reasons for and against them, from which one may conclude to what extent the truth lies on one side or the other. These are things that every enlightened citizen should thoroughly familiarize himself with so that, in the event that he were elected to be a delegate of his estate at a session of the Diet, he would then be equipped with the knowledge that his important task demands of him.

But where, you say, should such things be learned? From all kinds of published polemical tracts for and against on issues that concern the welfare of our fatherland, for then the truth is most effectively revealed. For that reason a lawful freedom of writing and printing is one of the most powerful defences of our freedom that can be imagined. But if nothing but one-sided arguments and proposals are allowed to see the light of day, the high authorities themselves are likely to remain in the dark. It thus befits the Sovereign Power to keep a concerned and watchful eye on this aspect of our freedom as well.

Such things are unnecessary, you think? The members of the Diet ought to be able to learn such things during the actual Diets. But is it not too late to begin to study the legal code when one has taken one's seat in a court of law? I at least would not wish to bring a complicated case before a judge who was obliged every now and then during the trial to ask my adversary: what does the law say on the matter? Or how should that section of the law be understood? I on my part could not but suspect him of receiving one-sided explanations from his instructor; or is it not possible that by hearing such secret advice during one's time of tutelage one might be led to adopt the same approaches?

It is therefore necessary for the Estates to look at everything from their own and not a borrowed perspective and to already have an a priori conception of the use and misuse of all the measures adopted.

To what end and how far this freedom should extend has already been examined above.

Second, *integrity* is required for this purpose. Opportunities and occasions for cajoling, pleas, friendship, entertainment, gifts, the return of favours and mortal threats place the most genuine virtue in extreme peril of being shipwrecked here. Hypocrisy, vainglory, overbearing behaviour, conceitedness and other things which generally conceal themselves under the cloak of uprightness heel over at the first puff of wind, and although they then right themselves again, they still mostly remain waterlogged during the rest of the voyage. The voters should therefore focus their attention on integrity.

Even if a member of the Diet, especially during protracted Diets, who participates in the legislative power for a long time and in successive sessions of the Diet may have the opportunity to rise too high above his fellow citizens, one would hardly expect him to forget the divine law and not remember from whom he derives his authority.

Third, *frankness* is necessary for the implementation of the proposed remedies, so that, once mature consideration and integrity have established the equity of something, it is then unhesitatingly and without a moment's waste put into effect by the Sovereign Power. The welfare of the whole country rests on its shoulders. It should not be intimidated by powerful opposition when it has truth and the best interests of the country on its side. What is easy today, when justice has prevailed in people's consciences, may tomorrow, when it has been forgotten, become more difficult, but the day after tomorrow, when self-interest has had time to muster its forces, it will be impossible. If a soldier, when he has nerved himself, is allowed to attack his enemy at once, he has the courage to defeat him, but once he retreats, in order to await a better opportunity, he often loses what he had, the other side's courage growing while his own diminishes, and then it is best in the end to capitulate.

Finally, as these are not always general qualities, it is better if a free people entrusts its affairs to many rather than to a few individuals. The more numerous they are, the better do they represent their society; the less easily can they be swayed by particular interests; the less can they be silenced by threats and the harder it is to corrupt them. If they are few, and such individuals as most of whom most hope to have a share in power during further Diets, regulations to restrict their number and simultaneously increase their authority and free them from all accountability will be a natural consequence. But who is unaware that it is the freedom not only of the delegates but also of their constituents that constitutes a free and happy society?

§ 36

More could and perhaps should have been said, but on a subject of this scope the choice has been difficult. To be able to present the matters in proper order, to be brief but not cryptic, to demonstrate something though without indelicacy, is not given to every man. I have done what I could. Perhaps I have gone further in my treatise than the Royal Academy intended, though not beyond the prescribed subject.

Uninhibited accounts do not appeal to everyone, but our misfortunes will never be brought to an end until the vices are laid bare.

The matters that are dealt with here are mostly old ones, but truth is always appealing to its lovers. That on which our epoch tramples will be taken up by posterity. And what is now called audacious will then be honoured with the name of truth.

Eternally merciful God! We have trampled on Your mercy and made ourselves unworthy of the freedom that You have granted us. You have a right to afflict us and our children in Your wrath, but we know Your disposition towards us. You cannot yet allow all Your mercy towards us to be exhausted. In Your counsel there are means enough to assist us. Do not tarry, then, Lord, or we shall perish!

Notes

1 "*Quid liceat nescimus adhuc..*": The quotation is a travesty of a passage in Ovid's *Metamorphoses* IX:554f. "*Quid liceat nescimus adhuc et cuncta licere credimus*" ("What is allowed we have not yet discovered, and we believe all things allowed"). Chydenius has replaced "et cuncta" with "sed aequa" and the passage can be read "We do not yet know what is allowed, but we believe that justice is allowed."

2 Johan Fredrik Kryger (1707–77) was an economic writer and a leading administrator (*andra kommissarie*) at the Manufactures Office in Stockholm. In 1770 he was appointed Board of Trade Councellor (*kommerseråd*) and since 1755 he had been a member of the Royal Swedish Academy of Sciences. He was one of the leading proponents of the Hats' policy concerning manufactures, which implied heavy subsidies and regulations to support the industry. He was the author of several pamphlets and books published from the 1750s onwards dealing with economic issues and he especially pointed to the positive role of manufactures. Kryger's essay won first prize in the competition and was published in 1765.

3 Anders Schönberg (1737–1811) had been the Swedish historiographer royal (*rikshistoriograf*) since 1761 and in 1777 became Chancery Councillor (*kansliråd*), a high administrative position in the state. He was also a versatile and productive writer on historical issues; especially well known is his *Historiska bref om det svenska regeringssättet i äldre och nyare tider* (published later, in 1849–51). Chydenius met Schönberg at the Diet of 1765–6 and afterwards regarded him as a friend. They exchanged many letters over the coming decades. Chydenius here refers to Schönberg's own essay on the causes of emigration from Sweden, which he entered in the competition in 1763.

4 The "*anonymous author*" is Pehr Adrian Gadd (1727–97), professor of chemistry at the Academy in Turku, who also published his essay in 1765.

5 "*... won the codille and the forfeit as well*": here Chydenius uses two terms from card games to describe a situation where the opponent, or the enemy, takes it all.

6 "*... as Seneca believed*": Chydenius presumably makes a mistake here: it was Tacitus, not Seneca, who wrote about the northern peoples. This passage seems to refer to Tacitus's *Germania*, ch. 4. If it really is a reference to Seneca, it could be to his *Naturales Quaestiones*, part V, dealing with the winds and climate in various parts of the world.

7 "*... record statistics for the entire population*": refers to the activities of the Swedish Office of Tables (*Tabellverket*). See the following Commentary, note 9.

8 The citation is from the chapter "Qvaestio IV. Quare patria prae aliis terris gratissima?", written by Johann Reinhard Storck (1592–1654), in M. Berneggerus, *Ex C. Cornelii Taciti Germania et Agricola questiones miscellaneae, olim moderante Mathia Berneggero, academicis exercitationibus sparsim disputatae, unum in corpus certumque ordinem... / edidit Jo. Freinshemius*. Argentorati [Strasbourg], 1640. A similar passage can be found in Justus Lipsius's *De Constantia*, I:10, 1584.

9 Chydenius has here added the word 'properties'. No corresponding word can be found either in Storck or in Lipsius.

10 "*Nothing is dearer than one's fatherland*": this is a reference to *The Odyssey*, book IX (v. 34ff.). Odysseus, telling the Phaeacians his story, explains why neither Calypso nor Circe (both of them beautiful goddesses) was able to keep him: "for there is nothing dearer to a man than his own country and his parents, and however splendid a home he may have in a foreign country, if it be far from father or mother, he does not care about it" (from the translation by Samuel Butler, revised by Timothy Power and Gregory Nagy).

11 "*Sweet it is...*": the citation is from Horace's *Odes*, 3.2.13: "Dulce et decorum est pro patria mori."

12 St Laurence's Fair was an important yearly fair in Sweden up to the nineteenth

century, held on 10 August. It signalled the end of the period starting on 29 July, under which either the master or the servant was allowed to give notice to the other party. During the following seven weeks the servant was obliged to seek new employment and the master could look for a replacement. The yearly employment period ended on 29 September, which was followed by a week of leave during which those who had changed their place of employment were to look up their new masters.

13 "*... the time was very hard in the land*": the citation is from Genesis 12:10.

14 "*Suffetes*" were the highest officials in many Phoenician cities. In Carthage, two *suffetes* were elected every year; their position resembled that of the Roman consuls.

15 Hamilcar Barca (*c*.275–228 or 229 BC) was a Carthaginian general and statesman, father of Hannibal and Hasdrubal.

16 "*Stübelius notes..*": this refers to Andreas Stübel (also: Stiefel), (1653–1725), a German theologian, pedagogue and philosopher. The citation "Hi sunt fructus militum externorum" is from *Cornelius Nepos De excellentibus viris in usum locupletissimum notis perpetuis ad modum Joh. Minellii illustratus a M. Andr. Stübelio, adjunctis fragmentis schottianis & adjecto indice rerum, vocum, & phrasium accuratissimo.* Editio nova revisa. Lipsiae: M. G. Weidmann, 1733, p. 294, note 1. There are also several other editions.

17 "*Rome would never have existed had Amulius...*": Refers to Amulius, who according to Roman mythology was the son of Procas and the unfriendly uncle of Romulus's and Remus's (the founders of Rome) mother. Amulius tried to drown his nephews, but they were famously saved by a she-wolf and eventually overthrew their great-uncle.

18 Lucius Tarquinius Superbus (535–496 BC) was the seventh and last king of Rome until the revolt in 509 BC, which led to the establishment of the Republic. He was remembered as a despot.

19 Sextus Tarquinius was the son of Lucius Tarquinius Superbus and is said to have instigated the revolt by raping the noblewoman Lucretia.

20 Lucius Junius Brutus was the leader of the revolt that led to the founding of the Roman Republic in 509 BC and served as one of its first consuls.

21 "*The king is a human being...*": cited from Livy's *Ab urbe condita* 2.3.

22 "*... made the consuls annual*": the two consuls were the highest officials in the Roman Republic and were elected by the people for a one-year term.

23 Tullus Hostilius was, according to the annalistic tradition, the third king of Rome. His traditional regnal dates are 673–641 BC, though it must be noted that the chronology of early Roman history is problematic.

24 "*... tribunus plebis*": In republican Rome, the tribunes of the plebs, ten inviolable officials who were charged with protecting the plebeians against the patricians, were elected annually in the plebeian assembly (*concilium plebis*). The tribunes, who had authority to intercede against any Roman magistrate, had to be plebeians themselves.

25 "*Decemviri*" is Latin for "ten men". In ancient Rome the designation is most often used in reference to the *decemviri legibus scribundis*, a board of ten charged with writing down the laws. Demands for the codification of the customary laws had long been raised by the tribunes in their struggle to improve the legal security of plebeian citizens. Two separate boards of *decemviri* were elected, for one year each, and during all of this time the regular government was suspended. The first board of *decemviri* ruled with moderation and prepared ten tables of law in 451 BC, and the second one completed the *Law of the Twelve Tables* (*Lex Duodecim Tabularum*), but when the *decemviri* refused to resign and their rule turned violent, an uprising broke out, in 449 BC, and the ordinary administration was restored. Chydenius makes a mistake here: in fact, only Appius Claudius Crassus was member of both boards, which was controversial, because re-election was against traditions. According to Livy (*Ab urbe condita* 3.44–58), Appius was attracted to the plebeian girl Verginia, daughter of Lucius Verginius, who as a consequence of a conflict had to murder her in order to preserve her innocence. See also note 3, p. 137.

26 *"the council"*: i.e. senate.

27 *"the councillors"*: i.e. senators.

28 *"Caesar, Pompey, Antony, Sulla, Octavius and others"*: this is a reference to the power struggles and the strong men of the last century BC.

29 *"... for Tacitus says that it was weakened"*: Chydenius is probably referring to Tacitus's *Annales* 1.2.

30 The Council of State (*Raad van State*), the highest advisory council in the Netherlands, was established in 1531. In 1578, King Philip II dissolved the council.

31 *"Duke of Alba"* refers to Fernando Álvarez de Toledo, the third duke of Alba (1507–82), often referred to as the "the butcher of Flanders". He was responsible for Philip II's repressive policies in the Netherlands and among other things – which Chydenius refers to here – carried out a massacre of thousands of men, women and children, considering it better to lay waste an entire country than to leave it in the hands of heretics.

32 Isabella Clara Eugenia of Spain (1566–1633) was infanta of Spain and Portugal, archduchess of Austria and the joint sovereign of Spanish Netherlands. The Siege of Ostend was a three-year siege (1601–4) during the Eighty Years War between Spain and the republic of the Seven United Netherlands that resulted in a Spanish victory in 1604.

33 *"... under the leadership of Thomas Müntzer"*: Thomas Müntzer (*c.*1488–1525) was an early Reformation-era German theologian and leader of a peasant revolt in Thüringen in 1525.

34 *"When the Florentines had formerly subjugated the Pisans"*: Pisa was conquered by Florence in 1406, but was able to regain its independence in 1494. In 1509 Pisa was, however, reconquered by Florentine troops.

35 *"King Godfred in Denmark"* refers to Godfred, king of Denmark at the beginning of the ninth century. In 810 he plundered the Frisian coast and forced the merchants and peasants in the area to pay heavy taxes. Godfred was killed the same year.

36 The Kalmar Union was a series of personal unions (originally created by Queen Margaret I of Denmark) that joined Denmark, Sweden and Norway during the years 1397–1523.

37 Christian II (1481–1559) was king of Denmark, Norway (1513–23) and Sweden (1520–1). In Denmark he was called Christian "the Good", but in Sweden "the Tyrant" – the latter because he instigated the so-called Stockholm Bloodbath in 1520, when a large part of the Swedish higher nobility was executed.

38 *"... followed the example of Romulus"*: as is mentioned in § 6 of this text, the mythic founder of Rome is said to have invited slaves and outlaws to come to Rome to live and develop the city. According to the legend, he also captured the women of the Sabines and let his men marry them. Religious refugees from Salzburg were welcomed to Prussia by King Frederick William in 1731.

39 *"small and unredistributed holdings"*: in § 10 Chydenius deals with the question of redistribution of landholdings and forests. During the eighteenth century, before the landholdings and forests had been redistributed, property was often scattered and divided into small strips. The forests were to a large degree communally owned and could therefore be used – and misused – by everyone. Everyone had the right to take the amount of timber and firewood he needed, but many were wasteful and careless in their usage. As a solution to the problem the idea of a complete redistribution of landholdings and forests was introduced. One of the strongest advocates was the chief land surveyor, Jacob Faggot. In 1757 the General Redistribution Act was put forward by the government, which stated that farms should not have more than four fields each. The old system had been based upon a principle of justice, which implied that each farm in a village should have access to fields of different qualities. The implementation of this act was uneven, so it was followed by even more radical acts in 1807 (*enskifte*) and 1827 (*laga skifte*). See also the Introduction, p. 12.

40 *"Mr Montesquieu presents this entertainingly...":* Chydenius refers rather often to Montesquieu in his writings published in 1765–6, although it is possible that he had not read *Persian Letters* or *The Spirit of the Laws* in original. Instead, he seems to have based his views on Montesquieu mainly on second-hand sources. However, Chydenius was probably familiar with Montesquieu's theory that the world's population had once been ten times as large as it was in modern times. In his texts, Chydenius frequently mentions that the population of Sweden had once been much larger.

41 Between 1622 and 1810, anybody who wished to bring his wares to the town for sale had to pay a customs duty known as *landtullen* or *lilla tullen.*

42 The royal ordinance referred to is that of 18 February 1757, which admitted the free establishment of crofts on taxed freehold farms (*skattehemman*).

43 *"companions of Mars":* soldiers; Mars was the Roman god of war.

44 *"It is futile...":* The passage refers to Livy's *Ab urbe condita* 2.23.

45 *"... the simultaneous pursuit of various crafts":* Chydenius here presents a notion that was fairly common during the Age of Liberty: since the craftsmen did not specialize enough and pursued several crafts simultaneously, their professional skills were poor and hence the quality of their products low.

46 See the Introduction, p. 24, concerning the Ironmasters' Association.

47 *Riksdags-Tidningar* were periodicals that were issued during most of the Diets during the Age of Liberty and reported the discussions and decisions taken in the different Estates.

48 *"... a commercial ordinance was issued on 10 February 1614; but as it still did not have the desired effect, another one was issued in 1617":* this refers to two commercial ordinances that circumscribed the rights of the lesser towns to engage in foreign trade (the so-called staple system).

49 *"in politicis":* in or on politics.

50 *"... by several writers elsewhere":* especially referring to Per (Petter) Stenhagen's tract *Tankar om nödwändigheten af stapel-städers anläggande i Sweriges norra orter och i synnerhet i Öster- och Wästerbottn* (Stockholm, 1762). It is possible that Chydenius also means his own tract on this subject, *Wederläggning af de skäl, hwarmed man söker bestrida öster- och wästerbotniska samt wäster-norrländske städerne fri seglation,* which was published two months earlier than his piece on emigration. See the Introduction, pp. 21–2.

51 *"the proceedings of the honourable Estate of the Nobility":* Chydenius is probably referring to discussions concerning the staple ordinance. At the very end of the Diet of 1761–2 the Estate of Nobility decided to approve of the establishment of three new staple towns in Ostrobothnia and two in Norrland. However, on this particular day the minutes contain hardly anything that coincides with Chydenius's description.

52 *"They would rather settle among a people whom they barely understand...":* a citation from the end of § 30 in another text by Chydenius, namely *Wederläggning af de skäl, hwarmed man söker bestrida öster- och wästerbotniska samt wäster-norrländske städerne fri seglation.* (1765). The orthography is somewhat modified.

53 *"... sell his place on the waiting-list":* The official system of promotion allowed buying and selling of official posts within both the state administration and the armed forces. Chydenius here refers to the possibility of selling one's place on the "waiting-list" to someone willing to pay for a more advantageous position higher up on the list.

54 *"patria est ubi bene est":* 'the fatherland is where it is good', a citation from Cicero's *Disputationes Tusculanae* 5.37, where he refers to the tragedy *Teucer* by Pacuvius. A similar passage is found in *Plutus,* a comedy by Aristophanes.

55 Anders Nordencrantz (1697–1772) was an economic and political writer and one of Chydenius's most important intellectual and political influences. See the Introduction, pp. 19–20.

56 Regarding the Bank of the Estates, see the Introduction, pp. 23–4.

57 Per Niclas Christiernin (1725–99) was an economist and philosopher at Uppsala

University. The pamphlet Chydenius refers to is his *Utdrag af föreläsningar angående den i Swea Rike upstigne wexel-coursen* (Stockholm, 1761). See also the Introduction, p. 39.

58 Johann Ernst Schubert (1717–74) was professor of theology in Greifswald and published among other works *Heilige Reden* in two volumes (1743–7).

59 Rudolf von Dietrichstein-Hollenburg (1603–49). The citation is from Matthias Bernegger, *Ex C. Cornelii Taciti Germania et Agricola questiones miscellaneae, olim moderante Mathia Berneggero, academicis exercitationibus sparsim disputatae, unum in corpus certumque ordinem...*/edidit Jo. Freinshemius. Argentorati [Strasbourg], 1640.

60 "*... medium tenuere beati*": Latin for "the happy ones have kept to the middle way". A citation from *Summa de arte praedicatoria*, ch. 1, by Alanus ab Insulis (Alain de Lille) (*c.*1128–1202).

61 Charles XII (1682–1718) was king of Sweden from 1697 to 1718.

62 "*Copper and Tar Companies and the Salt Office*": a copper company with an exclusive right to sell Swedish copper abroad was inaugurated by the Swedish king Gustavus II Adolphus in 1619 and lasted until 1639. The tar company referred to is probably *Norrländska Tjärkompaniet* (1648–1712), which had a monopoly on all tar distilled north of Stockholm. The Salt Office controlling the Swedish salt trade was in operation between 1750 and 1762.

63 "*... the nation lost its liberty*": the military anarchy of the third century AD is the part of the period of soldier-emperors (AD 235–284), when the Roman Empire nearly collapsed. Twenty-five different emperors ruled the empire during this time and the empire went through a series of military, political and economic crises. Frontier defence was neglected and barbarian invasions followed. At the same time, the emperors kept minting more and more coins in order to cover their expenses, which resulted in hyperinflation. The period ended with the accession of Diocletian and his reforms in AD 284–305.

64 "*... vestigia nos terrent*": Latin for "the footprints frighten us". Refers to Horace's *Epistles* 1.1.74, where he in turn refers to Aesop's fable on the fox and the lion. There were many footprints leading to the lion's den, but no footprints could be seen leading away from it.

65 "*Nitimur in vetitum*": Latin for "we strive for the forbidden". A sentence from Ovid's *Amores* 3.4.17.

66 "*fides publica*": Latin for "the public or common trust".

67 "*The ordinance of 18 February*": see note 42 above.

68 Titus Flavius Vespasianus (AD 9–79), Roman emperor who reigned from AD 69 until his death.

69 "*The compliancy, he says, ...*": this is from *Considerations on the Causes of the Grandeur and Decadence of the Romans* (*Considérations sur les causes de la grandeur des Romains et de leur décadence*, 1734), ch. 11. In the original text, Chydenius cites the Swedish translation (1755).

70 "*one of our peerless poets*": the citation is from the poem "The Despiser of the World" ("Wärldsföraktaren") by Gustaf Fredrik Gyllenborg (1731–1808). The poem was published in 1762 in a collection of contemporary poetry, *Witterhets arbeten II*.

71 "*in several publications*": Chydenius is most probably referring here to Anders Nordencrantz, who in a number of contemporary pamphlets and texts directed an angry critique against the growth of the state bureaucracy.

72 "*Brutus made the magistracy annual*": see notes 22 and 24 above.

73 "*Believe me, freedom...*": cited from Livy's *Ab urbe condita* 2.1.

74 "*a general, like the earliest Roman ones*": refers to Lucius Quinctius Cincinnatus (519–438 BC), a politician in the Roman Republic who served as consul in 460 BC and dictator in 458 BC and 439 BC. Cincinnatus was appreciated for his modesty and high civic virtue. He was ploughing his field when he received a group of senators, who

informed him that he had been named dictator. He immediately left for Rome and conquered the enemy, after which he resigned as dictator and returned to his estate, only 16 days later. See Livy, *Ab urbe condita* 3.26–30.

75 "*ius patronatus*": Latin for "the right of patronage".

76 "*... to stabilize the exchange rate*": note here Chydenius's standpoint, which is widely different from what he later held in *A Remedy for the Country by Means of a Natural System of Finance*. See p. 170f and the Introduction, p. 25, 38–9.

Commentary

Lars Magnusson

This essay was sent in as a response to a prize essay competition launched by the Royal Swedish Academy of Sciences in 1763. The Academy had put the following question to potential responders: "What may be the cause of so many people annually emigrating from this country?" It is probable that Chydenius first read about the essay competition in *Lärda Tidningar*.[1] He sent his response to the Academy in Stockholm at the end of the year 1763, but it remained unpublished until 1765, when it was printed by a printer in Stockholm, Peter Hesselberg. As no original seems to exist, we do not know whether the printed version is exactly identical to the one sent in to the Academy; as Virrankoski has noted, it is likely that Chydenius did make some changes and corrections before printing it.[2]

To launch competitions of this kind was very common at this time. Most likely the inspiration came from foreign academies such as the Prussian Academy in Berlin as well as the Académie française in Paris. In general, the prize essay competitions put up in Sweden must be looked upon as typical manifestations of the kind of "utilism" during the Age of Liberty which emphasized the spread of new useful knowledge in order to help the economy – agriculture as well as manufacturing industry. The Royal Academy, which was inaugurated in 1739, had held prize essay competitions with regard to economic and medical subjects at least since 1761 – made possible by a private donation by the noble family Sparre. Such launchings continued also after the Gustavus III's *coup d'état* in 1772, when the wealthy director of the Swedish East India Company, Niclas Sahlgren from Gothenburg, donated a quite considerable sum to the Royal Academy to be used to remunerate persons active in carrying out agricultural innovations, including both landlords and peasants. With regard to the so-called Sparre prize questions, the reward for the best essay was a gold medal, and the fact that the Academy undertook to publish the winning essay.[3]

In this case as many as 30 entrants responded to the call, and it seems that the jury had great difficulty selecting a winner. Several of the contributions raised critical points against the government. As the majority of the Academy members belonged to the ruling Hat party, including for example the Uppsala professor Anders Berch, this caused some consternation. In the end, Chydenius did not receive a prize for his essay, and because of this it was not published until two years later, when he arrived in Stockholm to take part in the Diet of 1765–6.

The winner was instead the Commissioner of Manufactories (*Manufakturcommissarien*), Johan Fredrik Kryger,[4] who, incidentally, was also a member of the Academy and a steadfast Hat. However, his piece too seems to have been excessively critical of the government. Like Chydenius's essay, it was never published by the Academy, and as a protest Kryger refused to accept the gold medal.[5]

Chydenius's text was without doubt the most radical. Moreover, it was the most extensive and probably also the best-written text. In particular, it stood in stark contrast – according to Ulric Rudenschöld (1704–65), who was a member of the jury – to some other contributions, which were so "simple-minded that they could not be published at all".[6] It is clear that Chydenius was quite upset by the fact that the jury did not mention his contribution at all, and that it regarded it as seditious. In a letter to the Academy's secretary, Pehr Wargentin, in 1764, he complained that he had not received recognition either for his essay on emigration or for his piece on carts, which he had sent as a response to another prize essay competition the same year. The fact that the first price in the cart essay competition had gone to a member of the Academy, J.F. Faggot, clearly showed that the Academy was biased, he complained. He pointed out that its turning down of the emigration piece showed that the political establishment was afraid of critical thinking.[7]

As earlier biographers have noticed, the essay on emigration was written in a specific political context. The general background was, as we have seen in the Introduction (pp. 21–2), the general grievances that the representatives from Ostrobothnia had had since at least the 1730s against the so-called staple policy, which prevented the towns in the north from receiving staple rights.[8] It was the campaigning for the establishment of new staple towns that stimulated Chydenius to write the essay prize contribution concerning emigration from Sweden in 1763. The text is full of references to the issue of free navigation as a means to increase the population and wealth of these remote areas of the Swedish realm. Moreover, the lack of possibilities for starting enterprises, developing proto-industrial production and carrying out trade in the countryside is depicted as the most pertinent reason behind the alleged emigration out of Sweden. In hindsight, it seems clear that his allegation was somewhat exaggerated; emigration out of Sweden in the middle of the eighteenth century was most probably minuscule. However, the fear of depopulation was a mantra often expressed in public discourse during this period.[9] Here, as in many other texts by Chydenius, it is proposed that the Swedish realm (most certainly Ostrobothnia) was grossly underpopulated. It would be able to support a much bigger population, he believed. Like many others during this period, Chydenius held the opinion that the country had been much more heavily populated earlier, but that a decline had set in as a consequence of the many wars Sweden had taken part in. In his view, the many regulations and prohibitions regarding trade also had a detrimental effect on a much-needed growth of the population.

Notes

1 P. Virrankoski, *Anders Chydenius: Demokratisk politiker i upplysningens tid*, Stockholm: Timbro, 1995, p. 107. *Lärda Tidningar* was a literary journal published 1745–8 and 1751–73 containing among other things poetry, essays and information on new books.

2 Ibid., p. 107.

3 S. Lindroth, *Svensk lärdomshistoria: Frihetstiden*, Stockholm: Norstedts 1978, p. 58.

4 About Kryger, see note p. 2, p. 115.

5 Kryger later published the essay at his own expense. Virrankoski, op. cit., p. 107; G. Schauman, *Biografiska undersökningar rörande Anders Chydenius*, Skrifter utgifna af Svenska Litteratursällskapet i Finland 84, Helsinki: Svenska Litteratursällskapet i Finland, 1908, p. 49.

6 Schauman, op. cit., p. 48.

7 Letter from Chydenius to Wargentin, 3 August 1764. Cited in Schauman, op. cit., p. 51f.

8 G. Sundberg, *Partipolitik och regionala intressen 1755–66: Studier kring det bottniska handelstvångets hävande*, Studia Historica Upsaliensia 104, Uppsala: Uppsala universitet, 1978, p. 32f; Virrankoski, op. cit., p. 102f.

9 The conception that Sweden was grossly underpopulated derived from the Great Northern War (1700–21), during which hundreds of thousands of people had died or fled their homes, and the period following it. But as no reliable information on the number of inhabitants existed, the estimates varied. The Swedish Office of Tables (*Tabellverket*) was established in 1749 and it started to gather information on the population in the Swedish realm. Rectors were ordered to send in information on the annual number of births and deaths and the distribution of age and sex among the members of their congregation.

2   *The Source of Our Country's Weakness*

Stockholm, Printed by Director Lars Salvius, 1765.
Imprimatur Niclas von Oelreich.

Human beings are by nature so constituted that they need the help of others and must therefore gather together in larger or smaller societies, but as soon as that happens, the society is promptly beset by enemies, both external and internal. History also shows that nowhere near as many societies have been overthrown by external enemies as by internal ones who have concealed themselves in the garb of fellow citizens. Yet it is a curious fact that most states keep a watchful eye on those who are outside that society but often leave those within it well armed, since we ought to know that human beings are similar wherever they are and are always more easily able to do harm under the cloak of patriotism than in the guise of an enemy, and under cover of a spurious faithfulness than in open hostility.

Free nations have indeed eventually realized this, though rarely with due attentiveness until they have felt the arrow in their breast and grown faint, their heart mortally wounded and liberty on the verge of destruction.

It was lamentable to see the Plebeian Tribunes[1] in Rome lie slain in their blood,[2] honourable men surrounded by ruffians, and the dart in his child's breast[3] being a father's only means to protect its innocence. But it was too late to curb a licentiousness that had initially been left unchecked. The abuse of the laws regarding redistribution of land placed such large properties in the hands of certain people that they could at once put all of liberty at stake, at which point it was bound to be lost. After that, it hardly mattered to whom these events were attributed.

It was thus no longer a mystery among the Romans that extensive amounts of property in private hands constituted a danger to liberty, but no one was any longer able to strike a blow against self-interest unless he wished to receive two in return.

Every free state that fails to pay careful and studious attention to this internal enemy is as certain to collapse, even without war, pestilence and years of bad harvests, as is a clock bound to stop when the mainspring has broken, no matter how often one sets the pendulum in motion. One can see from this how it is possible

Figure 16 The title page of *The Source of Our Country's Weakness* (1765). Kokkola
University Consortium Chydenius.

for the greatest national profit in trade and commerce, if it is concentrated in a
few hands, to be far more harmful to the country than if it loses an entire province as a result of war. As desirable as it is for a nation to preserve its liberty, so
too must it pay equal attention to the wealth that accumulates in certain places.
The community at large may have no right to the property of private individuals

when it has been legally acquired, but on the other hand it also contributes to the ruin of the country if it does not promptly open those dams that have gathered wealth together in a few places and impoverished the rest.

The closer a nation has remained to nature, the wealthier and more populous has it become, the more evenly is its wealth distributed and the more felicitous is its government. Likewise, the more anyone has interfered with commerce and industries, the worse and the more wretched is the state.

China,[4] the wealthiest country in the whole world, provides incontrovertible proof of this. There, towns have no privileges, and there is no difference between urban and rural industries, so that the entire country is like a town and all the towns are like the most attractive countryside. There are no tollgates or custom-houses there, so that Crown and subjects alike have sufficient wealth. There is never any difference between non-staple and staple towns, so that business runs smoothly and briskly; there the crafts are free and the workers therefore inexhaustibly diligent, and jacks of all trades go into voluntary exile without being legally obliged to do so. There is no commodity ordinance or prohibition against ships that do not carry their own commodities; instead, they are eager for anyone to take the trouble to distribute their products; and for that reason they are in control of commerce, and the prices of their own commodities increase all the more. There are no coins there, but everything is exchanged commodity for commodity; metals are weighed out according to their intrinsic quality, so that there is no monetary standard or financial system over which many Europeans have racked their brains, although they have plenty of gold and silver. Imagine if Sweden had been allowed to enjoy such freedom for the past 400 years; it would then be, if not a China, at least a Holland, a Switzerland, an England, or the like. Where would then all the disputes about urban privileges and rural trade be? Where would the many customs regulations and burdensome tollgates then be, or the expensive matters of staple towns, guild regulations, commodity ordinances and retorsion acts, monetary regulations, finances, exchange rates, and a hundred other things? Where then would all the lawsuits be that these have brought about? Where all the prosecutors who have initiated them, all the lawyers who have pursued them, all the judges who have presided over them, and, finally, all the salaries, food and paper that all of these have consumed in the process, all of it a drain on the economy?

Holland is, next to China, the state that has freed its commerce and crafts the most, and after that England, and for that very reason they are the most stable societies in Europe. Yet they have left nature nowhere near as unchanged as have the Chinese, and I therefore believe that the latter are right when they say that other nations are blind, the Dutch and the English seeing only with one eye but they themselves with two, for the matter speaks for itself.

In contrast to that, Sweden has believed that financial and commercial secrets, exclusive privileges, bounties, constraints, and a variety of prohibitions would bring us prosperity. We have now struggled with all this for a long time and have finally come to the point that, without pestilence and war, we have become underpopulated; without commercial liberties, the commissioning agents of foreigners; without bad harvests, hungry; and with the greatest of mines, destitute of coin.

I beg to be allowed to lay before the reader, with the most sincere conviction, one fundamental reason for this misfortune of ours.

On 10 November 1724 a prohibition was secured against foreigners importing anything but the products of their own country, which was declared on 28 February 1726 to mean that neither were foreign ships permitted to carry freight between Swedish towns nor could Swedish subjects who were engaged in commerce import anything on a foreign ship apart from the products of the country from which it came, on pain of confiscation of both ship and commodities.

The manner in which this Commodity Ordinance was secured and the extent to which it was done in a legal fashion ought not to be hidden from any Swede. During the Diet of 1723 the Royal Boards of Chancery, of Mining and of Trade submitted a report to the most Reverend Estates of the Realm on 10 April of that year in which they recommended the promulgation of the Commodity Ordinance by the Estates. The matter was discussed by the Joint Committee on Trade and was thoroughly examined, in particular by the members of the Estate of Burghers, and communicated to the other respective Estates in the form of a memorial dated 10 May, in which the impossibility of carrying out this proposal was presented to the Estates of the Realm, with irrefutable reasons, together with the unfortunate consequences that would inevitably result from such a statute. In consequence of this, the Estates of the Realm indicated to His Royal Majesty by a communication of 27 July that "*as the Kingdom is not yet provided with as many ships and vessels as are required for the full operation of commerce, the Estates of the Realm therefore regard it as inadvisable that such a prohibition* (namely, against the importation of foreign commodities on the ships of other nations) *be introduced at this time but would rely for that on the ability and enterprise of the subjects themselves*". On the 31st of that month, His Royal Majesty conveyed this to the Board of Trade with the explicit warning "*to ensure in advance, in order to avoid further accountability, that there rather be a surplus than a shortage of the requisite Swedish ships, so that no dearness of commodities might be caused if the Board, in reporting to His Royal Majesty on the number and draught of Swedish ships, were to be over-hasty*".

Be attentive, dear Reader, and you will now be furnished with the key to the promulgation of the Commodity Ordinance. It was of course the Royal Boards that urged the Estates on in this matter; but the Estate of Burghers protested against it (apart from the members from Stockholm, who, be it noted, agreed with the Boards), and as they were not able to entangle commerce in this net straight away, the matter was submitted to the decision of His Royal Majesty, which appeared to recognize the nature of the game when he prohibited the Board of Trade, under the threat of being held to account, from being over-hasty. What happened? The said Board, despite all that, submitted its report the following year, asserting the adequacy of the number of our ships, although the Estates a year earlier had regarded them as insufficient to export one-third of our commodities and to import what we require, whereupon the Ordinance was promulgated without further delay.

Had the Estate of Burghers not correctly figured out its purpose? Take the trouble to read its whole report, which is attached below,[5] as it is well worth the effort. But who could fear anything when the matter was placed, with a warning of that kind, in such eminent and impeccable hands? The delegates from the towns were indeed aware that it would restrict commerce to a few individuals and that it would lead to speculations in particular in the prices of salt and grain, but it was of no use: *vana sine viribus ira.*[6] The case was greatly embellished. It was said: we ought to obtain salt directly from the producers and boost our shipping companies and shipyards.

The consequences were as consistent with the statute as they were deplorable for our national interest, for:

1　the Dutch and the English were immediately excluded from maritime trade with Sweden unless they were prepared to use sand and stones as ballast. The result of that was

2　that the Dutch and the English were obliged to sell their commodities more dearly in order to cover their freight by the dearness, as they were prevented from recuperating it by the bulk carried; for the salt that was previously used as ballast no longer formed part of their cargoes; as a consequence of which

3　the Dutch through their Retorsion Act of 1725 excluded all Swedish ships from the lucrative carrying trade to their colonies, something which other naval powers would have been equally entitled to do with reference to the Swedish Commodity Ordinance.

4　Foreigners were thereby prevented from visiting our ports in the same numbers as before, as they were not allowed to bring with them an assortment of commodities in demand in Sweden aside from the products of their own country. At the Diet of 1723 the Estates found the number of Swedish ships to be inadequate for such a system, as may be observed from His Royal Majesty's letter to the Board of Trade of 31 July that year and the royal letter of 17 August 1725. This unexpected change of policy inflicted a damaging blow to our commerce, owing to our cold climate and the difficulties of our export trade. Because our winter lasts for six or seven months, we are unable to make more than one voyage to Holland in the summer with our own vessels, which must then by that single run support the crew for a whole year; but the Dutch are able to use their ships during the remaining time in other waters and earn an income almost continually and therefore sail here at lower freight charges than we ourselves can. The reduced number of exporters and the disadvantages of the climate itself therefore naturally increased the freight costs, expensive freight made the commodities dearer, the dearness of the commodities reduced sales, and reduced sales diminished production itself, or, in other words, our products decreased and import prices rose.

5　The lesser staple towns, which lacked commodities that they could export to Spain and Portugal, now had to request all their salt from the few exporters that are to be found in some larger towns. They had to pay for it at a rate at which the salt could cover its freight by itself and thus rather dearly, where they had previously obtained it from the Dutch for half or a quarter of the freight charge and consequently at a more favourable price.

6   When both exports and imports were thus concentrated in a few hands, it was not only the natural dearness that then began to afflict our nation but also the obvious monopolies that were associated with that. Salt was our most indispensable foreign commodity; but the price of it rose so much that pitiful complaints were ever afterwards heard during each Diet concerning both its scarcity and dearness, which neither King nor Estates were able to remedy. Specific evidence of that is the petition of the rural population of the Finnish archipelago during the Diet of 1731 for liberty for foreigners, when they came to collect Finnish commodities, to arrive there with a ballast of salt, which was rejected by the Royal Resolution on the General Grievances of the Rural Population of 28 June, § 45. During the following Diet in 1734 the dearness increased and the people submitted a bitter complaint, which His Royal Majesty in § 51 of the Royal Resolution on the General Grievances of the Rural Population of 17 December that year promised to remedy most assiduously, in part by abundant supply and in part also by other appropriate measures, although that was in fact quite impossible, as § 56 of the Royal Resolution on the General Grievances of the Towns of 12 December had rejected its import. During the Diet of 1739 the same complaint was submitted by Swedish towns, as may be seen from the Royal Resolution on the General Grievances of the Towns of 12 April.

During the Diet of 1741 the entire rural population was compelled to complain, and His Majesty regarded the matter as resolved by his letter of 1 October, addressed to the Governor of Stockholm and the county governors, regarding the submission of inventories of salt received and other matters, so that the Royal Resolution on the General Grievances of the Rural Population of 1 September, § 14, declares that salt would thenceforward be available both in sufficient quantity and at a fair price. In this context it is also worth noting that although His Royal Majesty promised, in the above-mentioned letter of 1 October, that if the matter were still not resolved thereby, the same measures would be taken with regard to the salt trade as had previously been applied to the grain trade, namely, to exclude it from the terms of the Commodity Ordinance, that move was obstructed, despite the continual increase in dearness and complaints, no doubt through pressure from the monopolists. On 29 May 1742 an order was issued to deposit one-eighth of all salt cargoes in bonded warehouses; despite that, however, the price of the commodity rose, for it was controlled by a few individuals, and the distress became so great that His Royal Majesty, in §§ 55 and 56 of his Resolution on the General Grievances of the Rural Population of 10 September 1743, had to concede that the rural population had fallen into a destitute condition (and could therefore not be helped without some infringement of the Commodity Ordinance) and that the dearness had subsequently increased unnaturally, which must be regarded as all the more incontrovertible evidence of the

Die Quelle
von
Schwedens
Unvermögen.

Aus dem Schwedischen.

Stockholm 1765.

Figure 17 The Source of Our Country's Weakness (1765) was printed in German by an unknown publisher the same year. The National Library of Finland.

pernicious monopolies that prevailed in the salt trade as the exchange rate had by then not yet markedly lowered the value of our *daler* and thus conflated the apparent and the real dearness. During each Diet since then, the King and the Estates have acted to assist commerce, among other things by establishing a Salt Office and a fixed price for salt, but to so little effect that the most Reverend Estate of Nobility during the last Diet, in its Extract of Proceedings for 24 April 1762, conveyed its deep dismay to the other respective Estates *"that the more distant regions have been unable even for banknotes, and scarcely indeed for cash, to obtain a few* mark *of salt, and that the shortage has increased at the very time when the Estates have long endeavoured to avert it and those at home have eagerly awaited forceful action from the Estates of the Realm on this matter"*. It was indeed pitiful that the most Reverend Estates of the Realm had to conclude such a long meeting of the Diet without being able to remedy this matter, for salt, which was worth 30 *daler* a barrel in the summer of 1762, was sold the following winter at 50 *daler kmt* even in the city of Stockholm, providing evidence that the words neither of contracts nor of statutes are powerful enough to curb self-interest when it in any way enjoys the protection of the laws.

With regard to the trade in grain and provisions, on the other hand, the Commodity Ordinance had an equally deplorable effect, and it would soon have caused the death of many a Swede had His Royal Majesty not, from a fatherly concern for his subjects, felt obliged, in the case of grain, to suspend it on 12 February 1741 until the end of June, a liberty that was prolonged on 14 April to the end of August but extended on 10 June, on the recommendation of the Secret Committee, to the end of that year and then successively, owing to the need to import these commodities, until the following June, from there to the end of the year, further to July 1743, and finally to January 1747.

His Royal Majesty's statement on this matter on 11 June 1746, in his warning against unreasonable increases in the price of grain, is noteworthy, namely that "the cost of grain and flour has, on arrival in Stockholm, been quite excessively increased, so that their prices, to the great oppression of the suffering poor, have risen to almost twice as much as they cost the previous winter in Finland, from where they came; whereby the poor were given cause to groan and complain". The merchants were warned to lower their prices, or else His Royal Majesty promised to resort to such expedients as would certainly suffice to restrain an injurious self-interest and release his loyal subjects from an arbitrary constraint in this trade.

Whatever measures His Royal Majesty may have taken for that purpose, it is clear that they were inadequate to remedy either the constraint or the dearness. For, the following year the Estates of the Realm presented yet another general complaint concerning them and therefore directed their concern in the Resolutions of the Diet of 14 December 1747, § 10, towards the improvement of agriculture, by which little could be achieved, however, as manufactories, established at all costs in a country devastated by war and pestilence, had drawn some thousands of people away from farming and increased the number of mouths to be fed in the towns. Moreover, the Commodity Ordinance had turned a large portion of the farmhands into sailors on the new vessels and others into carpenters at home to supply the shipping companies with more vessels and, most damaging of all, had held back the fisheries and the provision trade by the shortage and dearness of salt. Should anyone take the trouble to consider the other foreign goods required by our country, he will soon discover how many difficulties the observance of the Commodity Ordinance has imposed on us with regard to them as well. I do not have the time to deal with that on this occasion. I merely wish to say this: is it more advantageous for the country to collect commodities in great quantities from Lübeck and Danzig, where the Dutch have their emporia, than to allow the latter to bring them straight here? Which will more assuredly bring in contraband, foreign ships or our own mariners, who have friends everywhere and know all the byways intimately? During which era has Swedish commerce flourished more? During that of Gustavus Vasa,[7] when a *skeppund* of pig iron was exchanged in Lübeck for a few barrels of carrots? Or in our own time, when a *skeppund* of finished bar iron is exchanged for a *lispund* of coffee beans in Danzig and Lübeck?

But let us also see what effect this has had on our exports. What happened to the iron trade, Sweden's most important gold mine? When the Commodity Ordinance was promulgated, iron was worth 9 or 10 *riksdaler* per *skeppund* in England, but immediately afterwards it dropped during the first three years to 8 and then to 6 or 7 *riksdaler* per *skeppund*, which lasted for about 20 years. Our other exports have had to suffer the same fate proportionately. But what is the cause of that?

It is so obvious that it can be understood by the most simple-minded person, yet at the same time so contrary to the nation's outlook, indeed I would almost venture to say that of the whole of Europe, that I cannot expect assent except from those who come fresh to the subject and from intellects unclouded by preconceived ideas and self-interest.

I rest my argument on two axioms concerning commerce. The first is that the more buyers turn up in a market, the higher the price that the seller receives for his commodity, and vice versa. The other is that a commodity never costs as much when I am compelled to offer it for sale as when the buyer is obliged to search for it.

The merchants in our larger staple towns realized quite clearly that the English and the Dutch were obstructing their designs in the major ports of the country: they undersold them in the salt trade or obliged them to offer their fellow citizens bargains; they coveted our iron and other exports and engaged in competitive bidding with our own merchants, so that it was not possible to establish monopolies among us. They realized equally well, on the one hand, that neither the Portuguese nor the Spaniards, lacking such exportable commodities as were allowed to be imported into Sweden, ever sailed here, in relation to which the Commodity Ordinance was needed, and, on the other hand, that neither the Dutch nor the English found it profitable to send a significant number of ships here, as they were not allowed to bring salt as ballast or to carry an assortment of various kinds of general cargo.

Our Stockholm merchants saw that not only the non-staple towns and the entire countryside but also the smaller staple towns would have to come to terms with them regarding all their requirements from abroad, as they themselves had no commodities to ship that were in demand in the salt-exporting ports and the foreigners were prevented from helping them out. What happened? The Commodity Ordinance was promulgated; the buyers of our export products were reduced to a few; the prices of our most important exports were therefore bound to decline in value, until most of the ironworking estates fell into the hands of those very exporters, so that even our citizens had to buy the iron from them, and that at a steep enough price.

As few foreigners were able to enter the country, our exporters themselves had to export most of our iron, and for the little that the foreigners were able to take, they were obliged to pay all the less as their voyages here in ballast cost them dearly. When the Commodity Ordinance made it unprofitable for the English and the Dutch to come and get the iron, we were at the same time prevented from charging them a fair price for it unless it was agreed in advance, for we then had to offer it for sale and sell it below cost rather than risk a new and expensive voyage without being certain of a better reception somewhere else; we were thus rendered quite incapable of conducting a steady overseas trade in our iron. This statute is also the basic reason why iron is stored in special weighing-houses in the staple towns and why the Ironmasters' Association[8] has been established at such great expense for that purpose.

What else? Who has benefited from all this? The common response is: our *shipping companies* and *merchants* and along with them the entire country. Even if I were to admit that it has increased the number of Swedish ships, it has been shown above that this has been achieved, in an underpopulated country, at the expense of the general public and has knocked the feet from under agriculture. But when we consider the weak state into which Swedish shipping fell during the most recent 20-year war and from which it by itself began to recover during our first and consequently most innocent period of peace, it remains uncertain whether the Commodity Ordinance may reasonably be regarded as having played a part in that. We are astonished to see in the report of the Royal Board of Trade of 22 May 1697 to King Charles XII[9] *concerning the state of commercial affairs at that time* that the merchant fleet had grown considerably in 12 to 14 years, so that Stockholm alone had 79 larger or fully equipped ships[10] and 150 semi-exempt ones,[11] 229 in all, which were employed in overseas navigation. The shipping companies earned 500,000 *riksdaler* annually from overseas freight alone, and there were more than 4,000 seamen on the merchant vessels. The customs revenue grew over ten years to a level that exceeded that of the preceding ten years by 19 *tunnor guld*, and the maritime customs from Livonia, Estonia and Ingria grew during the same period to 11 *tunnor guld* reckoned in *riksdaler*. Would we be able to say any more about our shipping companies over an equivalent period? The Royal Resolution on the General Grievances of the Towns in 1734, § 5, does indeed state that the number of Swedish ships in the Baltic ports had increased; but the same could not be said to have happened in the Mediterranean. And what was most certain was the fact that we were entirely excluded from the lucrative carrying trade to the Dutch colonies by the Retorsion Act of 1725. As far as our merchants are concerned, however, it may be conceded that they have gained by this, at least at first glance, but at whose expense is a more sensitive question. Not at that of the foreigners, for while some of our exports have to be sold below cost, others have to remain in the weighing-houses in our own staple towns, at our expense, owing to the lack of buyers. The salt that we were to obtain directly from the producers under this system cost so much in freight, owing to the fact that the ships, being unable to carry an assortment of other more profitable commodities, had to sail with salt alone, that it became almost twice as expensive as that which we could buy from the Dutch, who used it as ballast. We find further objective evidence for that in the remarkable difference between the prices of salt in Stockholm and Gothenburg, which ranges from 25 to 50 per cent, so that the latter town sometimes finds it preferable to obtain it from Stockholm rather than from Spain, and that chiefly due to the lack of profitable export commodities to carry to the salt-exporting ports. Nonetheless, the exporters did well out of this. They were few, and fully engaged in marketing our commodities and ordering foreign ones from abroad. They were thus in a position to set the prices of each at a level that best suited their interests. But the country and the general public have gained no benefit from all this.

The lesser branches of trade were neglected, for the exporters had their hands full with the sale of iron, copper and brass sheeting, brass wire, iron and timber; thus, the other manufactures were bound to decline and die away. Owing to the small number and almost cartel-like character of the buyers, not only were the non-staple towns subjected to greater hardship, but even the lesser staple towns, which did not themselves have enough export commodities, were deprived of their foreign trade, as the English and the Dutch were prevented from visiting them. Previously, not only could more native men but also foreign ones draw bills of exchange, and the remitter could search out the best price, so that it was not feasible to let the exchange rate rise freely; but when the constraints on trade concentrated everything in a few hands, it resembled an autocratic rule, the like of which in exercising financial tyranny the world has never seen. The shortage of salt and grain brought workshops to a standstill, taxed the farmer to the very bones; hampered the fisheries and provision trade; raised the prices of all our manufactured goods; impoverished the Crown and private individuals who were forced to buy them; and made the products (short of providing large bounties, which became a new way of draining the resources, first of the Crown and then of the workers) unsaleable to foreigners. In a word, it has drowned the country in misery.

But is this not an exaggeration? Whoever attentively and impartially observes the fortunes of commerce throughout the world will soon discover that the freer commerce has been in a nation, the more commodities, the more workers and the greater industriousness there are, and vice versa; and that such causes must of necessity produce such an effect.

We see the whole of our present fate represented in miniature at the time of Gustavus Vasa. In 1527 he banned the Lübeckers from sailing to most of our ports, with the intention of improving the commerce of the realm, and thus took the first step towards establishing the remarkable difference, otherwise unknown among all trading nations, between staple and non-staple towns. The non-staple towns then lost the lively trade in all kinds of commodities that they had previously conducted in their own harbours; some of the producers then had to become seamen, as a consequence of which the quantity of commodities diminished; then prices were bound to drop, for the commodities had to pass through the hands of the merchants in the staple towns to the foreigners, and the recently revived weaker branches of trade were bound to wither away completely. Nothing was then more inevitable than that the country would soon lose out in the balance of trade with the foreigners, which was the very evil that was to be prevented by this. When the quantity of export commodities diminished, the deficit had to be made good with money, so that the silver currency began to flow out. The King together with the Council of the Realm and the Estates expressed serious complaints about that in the Resolutions of the Diet in Örebro on 24 January 1540, clause 6. *"It is likewise also a severe and intolerable injury to the whole country that almost all the merchants in this kingdom have now, be it noted, for many years* (and not, therefore, since time immemorial) *dealt most unwarrantably with the coinage of the Crown, which almost all of them have carried out of the kingdom and to Denmark, the German towns, Riga, Reval,*[12] *Danzig, Lübeck, and elsewhere."* – – His Majesty then strictly prohibited anyone from that day forward, on pain of the loss of life, estates and property, from doing so, although it was impossible to prevent it in a nation involved in overseas commerce that was losing out in the balance of trade as long as the constraint lasted, though it would have ceased of itself had the trade been left free.

Trade cannot bear the slightest constraint without being harmed by it. The same thing happened to us more than 400 years ago that Montesquieu describes as the cause of the decline of agriculture in Africa,[13] namely that the grain, which was previously available for sale in abundance, was banned from being exported in 1303, which impeded agriculture and prepared the way for the famine that afflicted the kingdom 12 years later.[14] The same question has long been debated in France, though now at last decided by a victory for liberty.[15]

The English were forced to import grain until they allowed and encouraged the export of it. As long as foreigners were themselves allowed to visit Skåne to buy oxen, they were paid for incomparably well in solid *riksdaler*. Now we ourselves hazard them at sea and transport them to foreign countries but have to be satisfied with much less; for the seller cannot without loss to himself sail with them from one port to another and even less return home with them. The English have banned all exports of wool; but were that to be strictly obeyed, and if the so-called smugglers were not driven by their own avarice to avert the fate that thereby threatens, that alone would be capable of ruining their expensive sheep farms.

The Chinese never desire to export their commodities to Europe themselves, even if they were able to do so. How easily they can see that their goods would then soon fall in value. We regard that as folly in them, but they possess an abundance of people, commodities and money under their system, whereas the Africans, due to their restrictions, inhabit a wilderness and we with our many ships are lacking in everything. Poland, Prussia, Courland[16] and Livonia[17] regard it as far better to allow Dutch vessels to visit their ports and collect their grain, linen, hemp, wool, etc. than to keep them out by means of navigation acts and commercial ordinances; for now they can be persuaded to pay higher prices for the commodities than if they were available to them in their own ports, unless they wish to return with empty vessels.

But what need is there to provide further examples? Or who can be persuaded by them to believe anything other than what he has heard since childhood? It offends against the fashion and outlook of our time, just as it never enters a seaman's head that the earth moves and the sun stands still. Regulations, ordinances, exclusive privileges, all kinds of prohibitions, even extending to manifest envy between states and citizens, are the steps by which Sweden has decided to attain the pinnacle of its fortune. What pointless complication and vain exertions! In no way would the great Master of Societies open the way for humanity to a glorious prosperity by such blind and dubious ventures. Nature itself opposes it and demonstrates that nothing but liberty and love of humanity are the appropriate building materials to endow societies with power and prestige. I am no enemy either of shipping or of manufacturing establishments, but I also see how limited all human reason is compared to the depth of wisdom that is required to make a state happy.

It is reasonable, some may think, to allow freedom of trade in a populous, flourishing and morally unspoiled nation; but among us, where none of those predicates really applies, that would be to place the overall good of the society in jeopardy. We have been frightened by that bogey for long enough. Let us see what reasons underlie this. Is it not constraint of trades and enterprise that inhibits the multiplication of our workers, chains that no populous nation in the world either bears or could bear without becoming as underpopulated as we are within half a century? What else prevents us from flourishing than that very constraint, which kills the desire for gain and helps one citizen to climb on the shoulders of another? When one person in a state is able to skim off the cream of another's toil, he must become extravagant, and extravagance infallibly offends morality. Is there not here a clear *argumentatio in circulum*,[18] i.e. that we must not allow free enterprise because we are underpopulated and corrupt, and that we are so because we have not had liberty? If constraints are the true source of our misfortune, we cannot be helped in any way except by liberty, and as long as that does not happen, it is vain to hope for any relief.

Dear reader! the subject is worth pondering; put aside all preconceived ideas; do not imagine liberty in one branch of industry alone, for then you will not get far before you meet with resistance and confusion; in your mind, free the state at once from all the fetters and regulations that confine it; let the example of others convince you of its feasibility, and allow yourself time to consider the matter properly; then you will soon see how free enterprise abroad and at home revives the smallest branch of trade, prevents foreigners from fleecing the country and one citizen from enriching himself at the expense of another; how security for the farmer in the possession of his land and freedom to exercise a craft and make a living as he wishes leads him imperceptibly and without legal regulation to the livelihood that brings him and the country the greatest reward: how crafts and manufactures, when free, inspire the worker to diligence and moderation, when he is not dependent on the inferior work of some badly paid journeymen and is busy getting ahead of others by industriousness and good workmanship; how all the trades combined, when free, move people to the right places, where they are most useful to themselves and the whole country: and finally how no political laws in the world have been able to correctly regulate this, which nature achieves so easily and effortlessly.

Should the gentle Reader find that I have taken truth as my guide on this subject, he will presumably not refuse to agree with me; but if, despite my best intentions, I have overstepped the mark, it behoves him to convince me of that with reasoned arguments.

Notes

1 *"the Plebeian Tribunes"*: In 494 BC the Plebeians in the Roman Republic were given the right to elect their own officials, the Plebeian Tribunes (*tribuni plebis*). Originally there were two such officials but their number was later increased to ten.

2 *"... slain in their blood"*: refers to the fate of the Gracchi brothers, Tiberius and Gaius, who served as Plebeian Tribunes. Both Tiberius (elected to the office in 133 BC) and Gaius (elected ten years later, in 123 BC) pushed for a land reform programme, including redistribution of landholdings. The reforms led to conflicts, as many people feared their lands would be confiscated. The Gracchi brothers faced violent deaths and were clubbed to death or otherwise slain, together with their supporters.

3 *"the dart in his child's breast"*: refers to the story of Verginia, related in Livy's *Ab urbe condita* 3.44–58. See note 25, p. 116.

4 Like most of his contemporaries, Chydenius was fascinated by China and believed its civilization to be far higher than the one prevailing in Europe at the time. A great inspiration here for Chydenius and others was Jean Baptiste Du Halde's *Description de la Chine* (1735). Du Halde (1674–1734) was a Jesuit historian and professor at the Collège de Paris. Although he seems never to have left Paris, at least according to Voltaire's *Le Siècle de Louis XIV* (1754), Du Halde's four-volume book compiles information collected by Jesuit missionaries in China since the middle of the seventeenth century. The Enlightenment was extremely fascinated by China, and to make comparisons with great civilizations outside Europe, especially the empires of Asia, became even more fashionable after the publication of Montesquieu's *The Spirit of the Laws* in 1748. It is clear that many eighteenth-century writers idealized the conditions in China. This was something that had begun with Leibnitz in the seventeenth century, and Voltaire looked upon China as the homeland of tolerance and reason. Even in 1776, Adam Smith was still hailing China as perhaps the best-developed and most prosperous country in the world. Certainly this mighty and populous nation was ruled by an omnipotent emperor, but he was said to rule by law and constitution, allowing a great number of freedoms to ordinary people. Chydenius's intellectual father-figure Anders Nordencrantz also referred to China as an example to follow. In his *Oförgripelige tankar, om frihet i bruk af förnuft, pennor och tryck* (1756)

("Indefeasible thoughts on freedom in the use of reason, pens and print"; see the Introduction, p. 26) he explicitly cited Du Halde in order to show how freedom of speech and printing was held in high esteem in China, even more so than in England. Chydenius in fact published a text based on information from Du Halde, *Berättelse om chinesiska skrif-friheten* (1766) ("Account of the Chinese Freedom to Write"), which was a translation from Danish made by Chydenius of part of an essay that had appeared in Fredrik Lütken's *Oeconomiske tanker til høiere efter-tanke* (1759).

5 The report described as being "*attached below*" is not published in this volume as it is not a text written by Chydenius. In the original tract it was included in the overall pagination and covered pages 22–6.

6 "*vana sine viribus ira*": a sentence often attributed to Livy, which can be translated as "an anger not supported by strength is in vain".

7 Gustavus Vasa (1496–1560) was king of Sweden from 1523 until his death.

8 The Ironmasters' Association, the so-called *Järnkontoret*, was inaugurated by King Frederic I in 1747 and is still in existence today. Its main task during its first hundred years was to keep up the export price of Swedish iron and steel. See the Introduction, p. 24.

9 Charles XII (1682–1718) was king of Sweden from 1697 until his death.

10 "*79 larger or fully equipped ships*": refers to the size of the ships and their suitability to be mounted with a certain number of cannons in wartime. In peacetime, such vessels were used as ordinary merchant ships and exempted from one-third of the customs duties on the goods they transported.

11 "*150 semi-exempt ones*": refers to smaller merchant vessels, which in wartime could be mounted with fewer cannons than the so-called fully equipped ships. In peacetime the vessels were used as ordinary merchant ships and exempted from one-sixth of the customs duties on the goods they transported.

12 The city of Reval is today known as Tallinn, the capital of Estonia.

13 "*Montesquieu describes … Africa*": see note 40, p. 118.

14 "*… the famine … 12 years later*": The Great Famine of 1315–17 hit a large number of European countries, possibly including Sweden, and is explained by modern historians as a consequence of a number of wet and cold summers leading up to 1315.

15 "*a victory for liberty*": several countries in Europe, including France and Tuscany, lifted the ban on the export on grain during the 1760s and 1770s, anticipating the great reform by Turgot in 1774, liberalizing the market for grain.

16 Courland was a historical and cultural region of present-day Latvia, situated south of the Gulf of Riga.

17 Livonia was a historical region located along the eastern shores of the Baltic Sea, today split between Estonia and Latvia.

18 "*argumentatio in circulum*": circular argument or reasoning, a logical fallacy.

Commentary

Lars Magnusson

Among the pamphlets published during Chydenius's stay in Stockholm as a delegate of the Diet in 1765–6, *The Source of Our Country's Weakness*, printed by Lars Salvius in April 1765, aroused most interest among the public. According to Chydenius's autobiography, a new edition was printed after only two weeks. Later the same year it was even translated into German and published under the title *Die Quelle von Schwedens Unvermögen*.[1] Although *The Source* was published anonymously, the name of the actual author must have leaked out gradually. This made him a famous man in the heated discussions that were held during this Diet – which has been described as something of a showcase trial castigating the former Hat government.[2] At least nine small pamphlets were published criticizing the anonymous writer, who undoubtedly here presents his views in such a clear and condensed manner that it was easy to read and comment upon them. These critical comments too were published anonymously, but it has been supposed that the well-known economic writer Edvard Fredric Runeberg was among the authors with a piece called *Water Tests Conducted at the Source of Our Country's* Weakness,[3] published in the summer of 1765.[4] Chydenius wrote at least two rejoinders to his commentators. The first rejoinder, *A Circumstantial Response to the Refutation of the Treatise Entitled: The Source of Our Country's Weakness, and Remarks on the Water Tests Conducted at the Same Source*,[5] was written as a direct response – as well as a response to Runeberg's piece – to a small tract published during the summer of 1765. This tract was probably written by Bengt Junggren, a secretary to the Board of War.[6] The second rejoinder was called *Advice as an Answer to the 14 Questions Presented to Chydenius, M.A., regarding The Source of Our Country's Weakness*,[7] which was a response to a list of critical points that had been raised against his original text.

Runeberg and Junggren to a large extent approve of the existence of the staple system as well as the ordinance of 1724, which Eli Heckscher called the "fundamental law" of the old Swedish mercantile shipping system, the Commodity Ordinance (*produktplakatet*).[8] As we have seen, the Staple Ordinance allowed direct export trade only from certain ports in Sweden and Finland: the ones that were granted staple rights. The Commodity Ordinance prohibited foreign merchants from transporting to Sweden goods that did not originate from their own country, and from this it followed that their contribution to Swedish exports also diminished. The general argument behind both the staple system and the Ordinance was that they would stimulate the development of Sweden's own shipping industry so that Sweden would not have to rely on Dutch or English ships, for example, for its import and export trade. Not always explicitly put was also the argument that a great commercial fleet of one's own was necessary for naval strength and military omnipotence during times of war. Chydenius's argument was instead that regulations of this kind made imports much more expensive, as foreign ships had no cargo to take back, and that the demand for Swedish exports would diminish. Perhaps even more important from Chydenius's point of view was that a small number of big merchants in Stockholm and other staple towns would monopolize exports. According to him, the prohibition on "selling directly to the foreigner" would imply that Swedish growers and producers would receive a diminished price for their goods.

Later on in life, when Chydenius in his autobiography discusses *The Source* and how it came about, he notes that "[t]he subject was at first quite alien to me". Lars Salvius, the printer of some of Chydenius's tracts and in whose library he seems to have spent much time, acquainted the young member of the Diet with the subject, however. As a consequence of this, his arguments cannot be said to be particularly original. They had been repeated over and over again in pleas at several Diets. One particular authority that Chydenius follows rather closely is a text published by the Academy of Sciences in 1761 and written by a professor of chemistry at the Academy in Turku, Pehr Adrian Gadd, *A Speech concerning the Finnish Climate and Its Consequences for the Country's Economy.*[9] Moreover, Christopher Polhem, Christian König, Anders Nordencratz and of course Lars Salvius had earlier published works criticizing the Commodity Ordinance.

However, Chydenius seems to have picked up one new source when, as a member of the Fisheries Joint Committee, he was able to study the otherwise secret archives of the Board of Trade. What he found was a small memorandum dating from 1723 written by Emanuel Swedenborg, then assessor at the Board of Mining, in which Swedenborg forcefully criticized the Commodity Ordinance for causing a rise in the price of salt, which, he argued, would have detrimental effects on the Swedish economy.[10] In *A Circumstantial Response* this text is mentioned without naming the author.

On the whole, the general result of Chydenius's campaigning was mixed. As we have seen, the battle for staple rights for Ostrobothnian ports was crowned with success in 1765. However, to what extent Chydenius played an important role when the Estate of Burghers at last agreed to comply with the other estates in reforming the system we cannot know. With regard to the Commodity Ordinance, the campaign was a failure, as the ordinance was not lifted until the 1820s. However, through the publication of *The Source*, and the debate that ensued, the chaplain from Alaveteli had made a name of himself as a radical opponent of the prevailing protective system.

Notes

1 P. Virrankoski, *Anders Chydenius: Demokratisk politiker i upplysningens tid*, Stockholm: Timbro, 1995, p. 127. The German translation was published in Stockholm, but it is not known who had it translated or who did the translation.

2 See the Introduction, p. 25.

3 E.F. Runeberg, *Wattu-prof wid Källan til rikets wanmagt*, Stockholm, 1765.

4 Virrankoski, op. cit., p. 130.

5 *Omständeligt swar, på den genom trycket utkomne wederläggning af skriften, kallad: Källan til rikets wanmagt, jämte anmärkningar öfwer de wid samma källa anstälda wattu-prof*, Stockholm, 1765.

6 Junggren's tract was called *Circumstantial Refutation of the Treatise Called The Source of Our Country's Weakness* (*Omständelig wederläggning af skriften, kallad: Källan til rikets wanmagt*, Stockholm, 1765.)

7 *Anwisning til swar, på de magist. Chydenius föreständte 14 frågor, rörande Källan til rikets wanmagt*, Stockholm, 1766.

8 E.F. Heckscher, "Produktplakatet: Den gamla svenska sjöfartspolitikens grundlag", in E.F. Heckscher, *Ekonomi och historia*, Stockholm: Albert Bonniers förlag, 1922, p. 164f.

9 P.A. Gadd, *Tal om finska climatet och dess följgder, i landets hushållning*, Stockholm, 1761.

10 G. Schauman, *Biografiska undersökningar om Anders Chydenius*, Helsinki: Svenska Litteratursällskapet i Finland, 1908, p. 175f.

3 *The National Gain*

Respectfully presented to
The Honourable Estates of the Realm

By one of Their Members

Stockholm, published by Director Lars Salvius, 1765.
Imprimatur Niclas von Oelreich

§ 1

That every individual nation pursues profit as the chief aim of its economic and political regulations is incontrovertible, but if we consider the means that each has adopted to achieve that, we observe an incredible variety.

All compete with each other to be first, but they shape different courses and carry quite different sets of sails, although they are all subject to virtually the same wind.

They fight each other for the windward position and use particular nautical tactics to run foul of each other, even though they have enough room and depth to sail abreast. It looks as if sometimes one ship and sometimes another were sailing without pilot or helmsman.

They are undeniably depending on different factors here. Either their compasses are misleading or else their charts are faulty.

A new indicator is presented to the reader here. It is quite small, so that anyone can carry it in his pocket. It is also new, I would say, for it scarcely agrees with any other in Europe. I also believe that it is accurate, as I have tried to construct it on the basis of reason and experience. Let us first agree on our terms.

§ 2

A nation is a multitude of people who have combined in order, under the protection of the Sovereign Power and with the aid of officials, to pursue their own well-being and that of their descendants.

Human beings feel well when they possess their necessities and comforts, which are referred to in common parlance as goods. It is nature that generates these, but they never become useful to us without labour.

Den Nationnale

Winsten,

Wördsamast öfwerlemnad

Til

Riksens Höglofliga Ständer,

Af

En Deras Ledamot.

Anders Chydenius
kyrkoh: i Gamla Carleby

STOCKHOLM,

Tryckt hos Directeuren LARS SALVIUS, 1765.

Figure 18 The title page of *The National Gain* (1765). Kokkola University Consortium
  Chydenius.

The needs are manifold, and no one has ever been able, without the help of
others, to acquire the minimum of necessities, while there is hardly a nation that
has no need of another. The Almighty Himself has made our species such that
we ought to cooperate. Should such mutual assistance be obstructed within or
beyond a nation, it is contrary to nature.

When we exchange these commodities among ourselves it is termed commerce, and the kinds of commodities that are generally desired and received are gold and silver, of which larger or smaller stamped portions are called money, which becomes the measure of the value of other commodities.

No commodity is such that it cannot be converted through trade into these metals, nor can any be obtained without them in the absence of other commodities desired by the vendor; and the amount of money that must be paid for the commodity is called its value.

The amount by which the value of exported commodities exceeds that of imported ones is rightly called the profit of the nation, and the amount by which the value of the imported ones surpasses that of those that are exported always constitutes its loss. But a smaller loss compared with a larger one is, relatively speaking, called its profit, and in the same way a lesser profit obtained when a larger one is possible is termed a loss.

§ 3

If the statement were in all respects true that Sweden during the past year of 1764 exported commodities for approximately 72 million *daler kmt* but the imported ones amounted to no more than 66 million, then our national profit for that year would be six million *daler*.

Of the total sum of our exports, the value of iron constitutes almost two-thirds, but let us suppose that within a century the export of iron will have been reduced by half, owing to a reduction in forest or for some other reasons, and would thus constitute no more than one-third of our exports, while others, such as grain, provisions and timber, were exported in place of the one-third lost in the iron trade. My question, assuming all other exported and imported commodities to be of the same value as now, is whether the national profit would not then remain at the same level? Or, should the iron exports at a certain time be reduced in value by six million *daler* but the ten million paid to foreigners for grain last year instead be retained in the kingdom, would the nation not after all have gained four million by that change?

If we imagine a state that possessed neither agriculture nor a mining industry, neither cattle-raising nor shipping, but only produced a large quantity of earthen or clay vessels that were in demand throughout Europe and would thereby not only be supplied with all its necessities but also annually receive two million in gold and silver, would those two million then not undeniably constitute a profit for that nation?

However, if one-third of the same nation, following the example of others, were to abandon this industry of theirs and become farmers, with the intention of obtaining bread for themselves and their fellow citizens by that means, in the belief that they would gain more thereby, but the grain were to be worth 1 million less than the former output of that third, then it is clear that it has earned the nation 1 million less in profit, or, in other words, incurred a loss of the same magnitude.

This makes it obvious that a nation does not gain by being employed in many kinds of trades but by engaging in those industries that are most profitable, that is, where the smallest number of people can produce commodities of the highest value.

§ 4

The wealth of a people thus consists of the quantity of its products, or rather in their value, but the quantity of products depends on two main factors, namely, the *number* of workers and their *diligence*. Nature will produce both if it is allowed to operate without artificial constraints.

Should the great Master, who adorns the vale with flowers and clothes the very mountain peak in grass and moss, expose such a great flaw in human beings, His masterpiece, as that they should be unable to populate the globe with as many inhabitants as it can feed? It would be base of a pagan to think so but godless of a Christian, in view of the command of the Almighty: *"Be ye fruitful, and multiply; bring forth abundantly in the earth, and multiply therein."*

For fallen humanity it was a punishment that they should live by the sweat of their brows, yet it was so arranged that nature itself imposed it, as they were obliged by necessity to do so, having nothing to rely on for their needs but their own hands; and the toil was lightened by covetousness, as they realized that they could acquire what they needed thereby.

Should either of these be lacking, the fault ought to be looked for in the laws of the nation, though not actually in any defect in those, but in the obstacles that are placed in nature's way.

If these laws render citizens incapable of feeding themselves and their children, they and their offspring must either die or abandon their native country. The more opportunities that the laws provide for some to live on the toil of others and the more obstacles that are placed in the way of others' ability to support themselves by their labour, the more will industriousness be stifled, and the nation cannot but reflect the mould in which it is cast.

§ 5

If that is the case, I intend to base the following hypothesis on it, namely, *that each individual will of his own accord gravitate towards the locality and the enterprise where he will most effectively increase the national profit*, provided that the laws do not prevent him from doing so.

Each individual pursues his own advantage. That inclination is so natural and necessary that every society in the world is based on it: otherwise laws, penalties and rewards would not even exist and the whole human race would perish completely within a short space of time. That work is always best rewarded that is of the greatest value and that most sought after that is best rewarded.

As long as I can produce commodities for 6 *daler* each day in one industry, I am most unwilling to engage in one that brings in 4. In the former the profit both to the nation and to myself is one-third larger than in the latter.

When anyone is thus either obliged or induced by public subsidies to work in some other industry than where he earns the highest reward – for it will not happen otherwise, any more than a merchant will sell his commodity below its current price – that will inevitably incur a loss to the nation.

If the person whose work someone else is obliged to perform earns as much as the worker has lost, it is not profitable to the nation; but should he earn more, only the difference will constitute a profit to the nation, although obtained by the oppression of citizens.

It thus becomes obvious that when someone conducts an enterprise with the labour of others but neither pays nor, without suffering a loss, is able to pay as much as the workers can earn in some other line of business, the deficit in their daily wages must constitute a loss to the nation.

§ 6

For example, if an ironworks producing 2,000 *skeppund* of wrought iron per year should have a hundred farmers subordinate to it, each contracted to perform 50 days of labour annually for the works but for 1 *daler kmt* less than they could earn working either for themselves or elsewhere, in order that the export commodity could be sold abroad with some advantage, it is clear that each farmer thus loses 50 *daler kmt* a year or, in other words, produces goods to a value of 50 *daler* less than by other work, which will constitute a loss to the nation of 5,000 *daler*.

If the same ironworks should also have a few hundred farmers subordinate to it who were obliged to supply it with the charcoal required for its operations, for example 3,500 *stigar*, either for a sum of *daler* agreed to at some earlier time or else for whatever the proprietor of the works is willing to pay, for example 6 *daler kmt* less for each *stig* than they could have earned in other ways during the same time – even granted that the proprietor of the works is unable to pay more for this commodity if he is to be able to sell the iron abroad at some profit – but the farmers had nevertheless been able, during the time that they have spent producing the charcoal, to make up the loss that they incur on every *stig* of charcoal, namely by producing goods for 21,000 *daler kmt* more in farming, crafts and weaving or some other line of business, it will be obvious that the loss to the nation will thereby be increased by the same amount. If, in addition, we add the almost irreplaceable loss of the best forests in the kingdom, which after some time could have supplied us with all kinds of woodworking materials and timber, allowing ten loads of fire-logs for every large *stig* of charcoal, then 35,000 loads of wood are required for these 2,000 *skeppund* of bar iron from when the ore is extracted from the mine until the iron is hammered out into bars, which, reckoned at only 16 *öre* per load, will increase the loss by 17,500 *daler*, thus creating an overall loss of 43,500 *daler kmt*.

If those 2,000 *skeppund* were to be sold at an average price of 6 *riksdaler banco* per *skeppund*, excluding freight, and, at an 80-*mark* exchange rate, brought in 240,000 copper *daler*, then it is clear that rather more than a fifth of that sum will constitute a loss to the nation, even if the entire amount is sold to foreigners.

§ 7

Gold and silver are indeed the most precious metals but do not therefore by any means always increase the national profit, as they have to be extracted from the ground. All mercantile goods can be exchanged for the amount of these metals that corresponds to their value. Nor is a ducat ever so red that it cannot buy some bread, as our forefathers used to say.

Would it not perhaps be necessary to consider whether the 38 *marker* and 4 *lod* of gold and 5,464 *marker* and ½ *lod* of silver that have been produced between the beginning of 1760 and the end of 1764 equal the expenditure and labour employed for that, together with the land-rent of several parishes allocated to it and other things, or whether many times more gold and silver could not have been imported at the highest exchange rate, whether such patriotism and love for Swedish gold and silver really has increased the national profit, or whether they only have to be subsidized in the hope of a higher yield in the future?

May it not also be that the discontents and the poverty of the workers and the country people living at and around the ironworks, when they are forced to work there, are evidence of a loss to the nation and of their wish to use their time and energies on what would be more useful to themselves and to the kingdom?

I am not referring here to those ironworks that exist without creating any problems for the country people and the workers; they are assets just as valuable to the kingdom as its agriculture, commerce and manufactures.

§ 8

It follows from this as a matter of course that it will be unnecessary for the Sovereign Power to use legislation to transfer workers from one occupation to another.

How many politicians have nonetheless occupied themselves with this? Almost the whole of Europe is engaged in removing people from their former occupations by compulsion or inducements and transferring them to others. They take credit for producing a profit to the nation equivalent to the value of the new production and usually forget that the workers employed for that purpose would, had they been free, have produced commodities of equal or greater value in their former occupation, so that in the first case there was no gain and in the other an actual loss to the nation.

If ten men in one trade produce commodities to a value of 100 *daler* a day but in another to no more than 80, it is clear that the work of the ten men in the latter causes the nation a loss of 20 *daler* every day. Whether these ten men are allowed to sell their products freely or else without compulsion hire themselves out for a daily wage to those who conduct that trade, the difference in their daily wage will always be proportionately the same, and they will then infallibly enter the former, as being more profitable both to themselves and to the nation.

But if the same workers are compelled to remain in the other trade for 20 per cent less, then that 20 per cent is a loss to the nation and to themselves. How unnecessary do the laws then not seem to be in such cases?

§ 9

Neither production bounties nor premiums for exports stand the test that they increase or promote the national profit in any way.

These are widely used throughout most of Europe but especially in England, yet everywhere they infallibly increase their actual loss. The production bounties are harmful in a straightforward way but those for exports in two ways.

If there are enough workers in a trade and production bounties are nevertheless provided, too many people will be drawn from other trades, it will become less profitable, owing to a surplus of commodities, and the bounties will cause a shortage of workers in other profitable branches of business, and the state is burdened by enriching particular citizens. If people will not engage in an established trade without subsidies, it is obvious that it is less profitable than the others where there is no shortage of workers.

If the state compensates for the losses caused to the workers and the nation in that trade by providing subsidies, there will of course be those who will engage in it, but their labour will be wanting in a more profitable trade. The amount by which the values of the respective products differ will unquestionably constitute a loss to the nation.

§ 10

Export bounties have not only the above-mentioned disadvantages, however, but also far more serious ones: citizens are here taxed twice the amount of the bounty that is paid and hand over a large proportion of that to foreigners, which cannot but concern anyone who has any sense of patriotism.

The vendor always seeks the highest price for his commodity. The owner agrees to sell it to a foreigner at 6 *riksdaler*, for instance, but receives 2 *riksdaler* as a subsidy for it and thus earns 8 *riksdaler* for his commodity.

If a Swede should wish to purchase the same commodity, he will indubitably have to pay the vendor the same that he earns from what he has sold to a foreigner, namely 8 *riksdaler*, or else the vendor will regard himself as having lost on the transaction.

The foreigner thus enjoys a purchase price that is 2 *riksdaler* lower due to the export bounties, while a local man is doubly taxed, namely 2 *riksdaler* to the fund to reduce the cost of purchase to the foreigner and 2 *riksdaler* to indemnify the vendor.

This must also enable the foreigner to conduct a very advantageous trade in our products among ourselves. I shall extend the simple example above: The Swedish manufactures that were sold to the foreigner for 6 *riksdaler* can immediately be sold by him, at a profit of 25 per cent, for 7½ *riksdaler* to a Swede, who will then be able to buy them for ½ a *riksdaler*, or 8⅓ per cent less[1] than from the manufacturer's retail shop, so that there will never be a lack of buyers.

If one then adds the 33⅓ per cent advantage on the foreigner's purchase price to the 25 per cent gained on his sales, it will produce a profit of 58⅓ per cent for him,[2] due merely to the export bounties, which would never otherwise have arisen or been possible. Nor is that simply a theoretically demonstrated truth, as it has also been proved in practice many times over.

I would be able to reveal a little business plan that could earn Sweden several thousand from some foreign export bounties if I did not fear to awaken others from their slumbers, when they might seek to close some of the loopholes that at present, without showing up in the trade figures, actually reduce our deficit.

I therefore hope quite sincerely that the English and other nations will not only retain their export bounties but also that they may be significantly increased on all those commodities that can be sold to us, while our own country will, on the contrary, get rid of them, together with the fetters that prevent us from freely and actively exploiting our neighbours.

§ 11

I now dare go further and assert that regulations that direct people into particular occupations are harmful to the nation and to its profit: I feel obliged to do so for what in my view are four supremely important reasons.

In the whole of Europe there is not as yet any fixed principle to follow in this matter of distributing workers, for such regulations are sometimes adopted in order to promote a new craft or technology, sometimes in order to provide employment for more of the population and sometimes to give the owner of some manufacturing works a higher income by means of lower wages.

In one case it is done in order to make our products exportable, in another case to fulfil one or other of our requirements within the kingdom. At times the purpose of such a measure is that local shipowners should gain from carrying our commodities and native workers from their wages, at other times to obtain gold and silver within the country. Sometimes they are designed to prevent people from emigrating, sometimes in order to curtail luxury. On one occasion it is deemed to be necessary to maintain proper order among the trades, on another it is required to prevent craftsmen from working in more than one art, with innumerable other reasons.

Is there not a lack of a proper system in all this? And must not a house that is constructed from so many blueprints acquire a strange appearance and lack the necessary stability?

§ 12

The second reason is this: that no politician is yet in a position to state positively which industry can produce the greatest national profit for us, so that the legislator is bound to remain in a quandary as to where he is to direct our workers by regulatory means.

Who, some might think, is so ignorant as not to know that? I assure you that it is not as simple as people think. Many who have thought seriously about these matters have indeed created their own system and ranked each industry in a certain order, but if we compare their ranking with those of others, we are struck by the differences that exist between them.

I believe that my system is the best, but when I realize that everyone has the same faith in his own system, I must as a rational being remain in doubt about the entire matter until it has been fully examined.

M. maintains that agriculture is best, E.S. that handicrafts deserve that honour; O.R. proves that it is commerce, A.G. that the kingdom must be sustained by our mining industry as the source of the main exports of the kingdom, etc.[3] Who of all these is right?

All of them are enlightened and conscientious men and, moreover, enjoy the confidence of their fellow citizens, and it will be a long time before this controversy is resolved. In the meanwhile, which of these industries should the Sovereign Power regard as being of the greatest utility, and to which of them should it attract more people to the profit of the kingdom? And how can mistakes be avoided under these circumstances?

Even if this controversy were to be fully settled, however, and a system be based on it that would direct the mass of people to the most profitable industry, would the legislator be able to say how many thousand people should then work in it to the profit of the nation as well as that such a regulation would have the desired effect within so and so many years? It might all too easily happen that people would be drawn away from other industries and produce a surplus of commodities in this one, which would thus lose their value abroad, causing a significant loss to the nation.

§ 13

Even if they were capable of possessing all the knowledge required for that, however, which is quite impossible, it could nonetheless happen that those who deal with this matter might not have good intentions, which I regard as the third reason.

It might easily be the case that they could have a personal interest in moving the people into one particular branch of industry or another and would therefore argue in favour of that. What else would then happen but that a most useful industry would be drained of people, to the irreparable loss of the kingdom?

§ 14

Lastly, if we imagine that we have overcome all these obstacles and adopted regulations that are ideally suited to the purpose, some unexpected events could undermine the whole of this elaborate system and turn the most useful regulations into thoroughly harmful ones for the nation, which appears to constitute the fourth of the reasons against them.

What changes in commodities, what fluctuations in value do we not experience daily? Providence quite unexpectedly opens up a source of wealth for a nation that lasts for a time but then abruptly ceases and is soon replaced by a second or third one on which the national profit chiefly depends. The law, even if optimal, will therefore, among the thousand possible eventualities, not be suited to more than a single context, namely the one for which it was designed, and be prejudicial in all others.

And these are the real reasons why our regulations, although themselves good (as regards their intention), have had such a deleterious effect.

§ 15

The time may now have come to examine more closely what kind of regulations transfer people from one occupation to another.

Among them are all those that directly or indirectly offer certain advantages in one occupation rather than another. That is done directly when the terms of the regulation expressly include them but indirectly when it becomes a necessary consequence of carrying the regulation into effect.

They thus include all economic privileges, not only the exclusive ones but also any others that offer some specific advantage to a tradesman, namely, all classifications of occupations that are established by law; for nature produces its own classification, which is the most reliable one, but as soon as anything is legally added to or subtracted from it, distortions arise that favour certain people but hinder others in the conduct of their business. Also included among them are all bounties on production and exports as well as all limitations on the freedom of residence and trade in the towns and rural regions.

What else are these but dams that concentrate the people in certain places, removing them from one place and moving them to another, without it being possible to say in which place they will be most useful and increase or reduce the national profit, as has been demonstrated above?

When the stream is allowed to run evenly, every drop of water is in motion. When there are no obstacles in the way, every worker competes for his livelihood and thereby increases the profit to the nation. By means of regulations, people are concentrated in certain groups, the opportunities to move into industry are reduced and a small number of people within each group rise above the majority, whose well-being is presented as evidence of the prosperity of the whole kingdom.

§ 16

These are the same dams that prevent the increase in the number of Swedish workers, although, as was shown in § 4, that is the main foundation of a national profit.

In a dam, the weight of the upper layers of water rests on that which lies closest to the bottom, so that the structure must be many times stronger and more watertight furthest down; for it is known from experience that the lower water gushes out through the slightest aperture at a faster rate than the other.

The same applies to our own population. We may consider any given occupation and the number of people employed in it.

If we consider farmers, we shall scarcely find a single example of anyone possessing a large manor who wishes to flee the country, although those who expect to inherit that estate from him would willingly pay for his travel; but can one be equally sure about the crofters on that estate or their children?

I have often asked them where their children are but have received a pitiful answer from most of them: what are we to do with them now at home? We can only feed ourselves in this place with the greatest difficulty as long as the Lord permits. Our eldest son sailed on the Holland route for a few years but then stayed there and is said to be doing well now. Our second son sails between here and England, but when we last saw him he took farewell for ever, intending to settle down there. Our third son went with the army to Pomerania; he was captured by the King of Prussia, but when God gave us peace he was unwilling to come back; he is now in Prussian service and has married there. Our fourth son is still a child, and God knows where he will go or what may become of him.

Why does a yeoman farmer[4] in our kingdom not run away? Because he has a right of residence. But why is a labourer more likely to do so? The answer is obvious: because the regulations have not allowed him to settle down anywhere.

§ 17

If we consider our craft associations and the number of our people who belong to them, we observe a small number of prosperous masters who no longer need to personally sit in their workshops but live a life of leisure, dress themselves and their families according to the latest fashion, keep a decent table during the week, make and receive visits much of the time, and have ten or 12 workers in their workshop, of whom six work for their food and the rest for a few *daler* a week. My question is whether such a man would abscond from the country. As long as the guild is able to provide him with workers and ensure that the number of masters does not become excessively large, so that he will inevitably be approached for work and is thus able to set his own price, it will certainly not happen.

But how his journeymen and apprentices are faring is a more sensitive question. I have sometimes heard their swansong, and a general complaint in the kingdom that they go abroad to Prussia and Russia, for there everyone who wishes to can become a master straight away.

Just think how helpful our guilds are, which do not debar a poor man's children from filling some of the vacancies thus created for no pay!

§ 18

If we look at our mining industry we will soon see that not many of the owners of our metalworks wish to abandon Sweden; but the complaints of a number of poor owners of metalworks about the lack of capital with which to run the enterprise, sluggish sales and fixed prices, as well as the poverty that threatens them, are quite a different matter.

What do smiths and foundry workers complain about? Why do those who are brought in from abroad not remain for long, while those who are born locally seldom marry and generally end up as paupers? And how does it happen that trading in grain and provisions becomes hardly less profitable for the foundry proprietor than the production of iron itself? And why is it that the farmers subordinate to the estate get cinders on their fields* and tell the same sort of personal stories about their children as the crofter mentioned above.

The manufacturer certainly goes as well clothed in his own products as anyone else, but the workers in the spinning-mill often sit half-naked and others go badly dressed on the street and beg, saying that they are foreigners brought in from abroad who now wish they were back home again instead of standing outside other people's doors in Sweden, ultimately dying in poverty.

Among those who move away from the towns, the desire to escape rarely affects the affluent and the magistrates but very often the poor and the humbler townspeople.

I believe it is almost unheard of for sea captains and mates to abscond, unless for offences committed in a foreign port, but I dare not assert the same of a sailor or the cook's boy.

Dear reader! do you not now see why our labour force cannot increase, and with it our national profit? It will never, in my opinion, be possible to prevent this attrition unless the dams are opened.

The less the pressure, the more easily is the water retained, but the shorter the column of water, the less the pressure, and it will always be lowest when the sluice-gate is opened.

§ 19

The second mainstay of the national profit is the industriousness of the workers, that is, when the smallest number of people produce commodities of the greatest possible value.

Many who look only at our nation might easily get the impression that it lacks nothing in industriousness, but I have to admit that I have been hurt to hear the

---

* A farmer subordinate to an estate is said to get cinders on his field when he is working so hard at the metalworks that he neglects his own fields and cultivation, which leads to a failure of the crops.

reproach made against us by foreigners that the Swedish nation is lazy compared to the others.

A merchant in Holland sits in his office every morning from 5 or 6 o'clock managing all his business affairs; he dresses simply and his table is not over-loaded with sumptuous meals, he makes good use of every hour of the day to accomplish something; and he ridicules French fops and haughty airs.

An Englishman is hardened and indefatigable in his work. A carpenter in an English shipyard works with such energy and speed that one can barely see the mallet in his hand while he works, and he completes a warship in as many days as the state shipyards in Sweden tend to take weeks.

§ 20

What is the cause of all this? The wilfulness of our workers, some may opine, as they are not strictly supervised. Vagrants, it is said, are living in indolence everywhere in our rural regions. Journeymen and apprentices are not what they used to be. Farmhands and maids will not lift a hand unless the master himself accompanies them.

I do not know whether there are more overseers anywhere than among us, but who is to exercise supervision when they themselves sleep until 10 o'clock in the morning? I have heard a number of proposals to the effect that if a tenant farmer will not work hard on his holding, he should be flogged, or at least evicted from the holding. It has indeed already happened that some have been punished because they could not immediately abandon an ancient livelihood, without which they would at first have been at least half-starving.

Such people will infallibly recognize our form of liberty. Flogging and liberty combined: what a strange notion!

Let us not blame our nation and its particular character for its inertia; let us not lay the blame on corrupted manners. That would indeed be the easiest thing to do, but it is of little use to the country. The source of this evil is to be found elsewhere.

The more opportunities there are in a society for some to live on the toil of others and the less others are allowed to enjoy the fruits of their labour, the more will industriousness be destroyed; the former become overweening and the latter desperate, while both become neglectful.

That basic proposition is so well founded and so thoroughly confirmed by knowledge of human nature and daily experience that I challenge anyone to rationally disprove it.

Industriousness and diligence require a cheerful disposition and constant competition if they are not soon to slacken off. They never exist under oppression, but when they are encouraged by liberty, a rapid turnover of products and individual profit, that natural sluggishness will be overcome which can never be permanently removed by violent means.

§ 21

Commodities are never produced unless they are needed and in demand. The needs reveal themselves; they are manifold and thus automatically bring into being occupations and products that are then sold to those who require them. If those who need to buy a commodity are prevented from doing so, it remains in the hands of its producer, becomes a burden to him, and is branded with a black stamp that reads: *Wasted sweat and toil*.

That deals a blow to industriousness. This is the cord that ties the worker's hands behind his back and the potion that produces bad and somnolent citizens.

No nation can be industrious as long as that stamp remains on its products, and it can never be removed until the commodity may be produced by whomever so wishes and be sold to whomever needs it.

I will not cite as proof of this the example of other states: my own fatherland is an irrefutable witness to it, which I invoke all the more boldly as its condition is most familiar and no one is likely to be able to consider it without lamenting its misfortunes.

Swedish industriousness resembles a crop on a badly tended field. Here and there a few lush stands grow, but most of it has withered away and will barely replace the seedcorn.

§ 22

In Västergötland,[5] handicrafts and weaving are diligently pursued: there an old man is not ashamed to sit at a spinning-wheel; knives, bowls, plates, ribbons, bells, scissors and other wares are available there at more favourable prices than elsewhere. What is the cause of that? Inhabitants of that province have the right to travel wherever they wish to sell their wares. There the town of Borås has for a long time past been permitted to practise peddling throughout the kingdom. That means freedom to go from farm to farm, buying goods and selling one's own to others.

As no other province in the kingdom has possessed such a liberty, I also doubt that any other can display such industriousness as exists among its inhabitants. It is thus clear that here either industriousness has created liberty or liberty industriousness.

A few years ago, large quantities of chairs and spinning-wheels were produced in Västerbotten, Hälsingland and Västernorrland,[6] of which the former were sold for between 9 and 12 *daler* a dozen, the latter for between 6 and 9 *daler* each. Now these manufactures have largely ceased, owing to certain prohibitions against their sale, and it looks as if the inhabitants will soon have to buy them from others.

Along the coast of Ostrobothnia, people are active during both winter and summer; but 30 or 40 *mil* inland, where there are no towns, the occupation of the majority during the winter is to sleep and to cut as many splinter torches as they need for lighting. As there are no buyers for those wares, none are made for sale.

Around Pori (Björneborg), Rauma (Raumo) and Uusikaupunki, the country people are almost indefatigable in woodworking. The worker is already hard at work by one or two in the morning producing all kinds of wooden vessels throughout the winter and is therefore able to dispose of them at a more reasonable price than anyone else in Finland, although many others have not only better access to forests along the coast but also workers skilled in this craft. Let us establish the reason for this. It is quite impossible that such industriousness could have arisen and been maintained without the freedom to export.

The above-mentioned towns have for a long time past enjoyed the right to sail round the Baltic Sea with spars, laths and wooden vessels. The staple towns have often sought to deprive them of that privilege of theirs, although they have not succeeded so far; these towns now supply not only several foreign places with such goods at a moderate price but even to a degree Stockholm itself, and in such a manner that they undercut almost everyone else.

Had the ban succeeded, however, sales would inevitably have been reduced, and consequently, to the same extent, production. Reduced production inevitably produces unemployment and dear commodities, and should it ever become possible for other towns to prevent those sales or for these towns[7] to deprive workers of the freedom to produce, it is as certain as that two and two make four that Stockholm would have to pay more for wooden vessels than before, that these towns would reduce their business and the country its population and income, and that the kingdom would be deprived of its profit.

§ 23

Look! Here is the key to industriousness and profit. If the door to profit is opened by free enterprise and sales, every man will be fully employed within a few years; if that does not happen, however, the nation will inevitably, regardless of all other measures, become as drowsy as it was before and inclined to be sleepy in broad daylight.

Certainly there should be freedom, the reader will think, but not without order. One must carefully distinguish between urban and rural trades and not allow farmers to engage in other activities, thus causing agriculture to be neglected. Well said, truly in the fashion of our age! I would only, with the greatest respect, stipulate one thing, namely, that whoever assumes this despotic guardianship of the farmer and ties him exclusively to the soil will also, like a true father, take paternal care to see that he does not perish from hunger when agriculture fails to feed him and his children. If that is not feasible, I think it is more advisable to put the beast of burden out to pasture to seek its own food than to tie it to a post and leave it standing there unattended for a few weeks, for it is too late to learn a handicraft when there is no more food.

To restrain trades in the countryside is to prevent the growth of the population and all rural improvement, and to ban handicrafts and commerce is to inhibit the enterprise of old towns and the development of new ones.

A skilled tanner settled in the country many *mil* from the nearest town and served the country people and persons of rank by expert leather-dressing; he was banned by the nearest market town from practising that handicraft there and was therefore ordered to move to the town. The system was fine, but he who was doing well in the country became a pauper in the town, and more than a thousand hides must therefore now be spoiled every year by bad treatment. That is hardly the way to increase the national profit.

§ 24

That part of our laws that concerns rural trade deserves our special attention.[8] A merchant is not allowed to travel around the country and sell his wares, nor the farmer to buy up anything from his neighbours and take it to market in town or to provide them with any goods from the town in return.

Unless a neighbour is willing to become his agent, he must personally undertake a journey of two or three days to the town, often for a lighting flint or a twist of tobacco, perhaps during the busiest period of harvest time. Who, then, is to pay for his journey? Had his neighbour been allowed to conduct a little trade in the most necessary wares, he would have avoided this waste of time, but, as that has been banned, I can only attribute this waste to the regulation itself.

I must regret that it has not been scrupulously obeyed, but I also believe, out of deepest conviction, that such law-breaking has saved at least a quarter of the nation from a wasted existence.

To discuss such an important matter fully is not possible here. I simply wish to encourage the reader to give some thought to it.

The whole of Savo (Savolax), Häme (Tavastland) and Karelia[9] lie far from any towns. Grain and provisions are their products, in exchange for which they obtain salt and other necessities from the towns. The more affluent buy them up from their neighbours, who do not have horses or cannot take these goods to the town themselves, and in return provide them with their necessities.

No one undertakes to act as an agent for poor people, nor is anyone able to deal with 50 or 60 individuals. If this rural trade had not been conducted, the country would therefore be deprived of their products and the poor would waste their lives in hunger and idleness. If there is no demand for the commodity, production will come to a complete standstill, and what happens then to the national profit?

§ 25

I know a farmer who lives some 5 *mil* from the nearest market town and who, among other kinds of rural trade that he conducts, purchases fatstock in the autumn within a radius of many *mil* around him and annually drives three or four herds of cattle to the town, each with 20 or 30 animals.

By law, no other townsmen than the butcher is permitted to travel around the country to buy them up, but every individual is obliged to drive his animals to town himself. Few of them have more than one or two to dispose of, which have to be driven by two or three persons, as many as the rural trader needs for his entire drove.

These two or three persons lose four or five days each on this journey to town during a busy threshing time, so that the trek to the town costs eight to ten days' work, often for the sake of a single small head of beef cattle, thus reducing the profit by 4 or 5 *plåtar* and causing essential work on the farms to be neglected. Nothing could therefore be more certain than that a farmer would rather eat his own ox than consume half its worth in travel costs.

If the regulations concerning rural trade were obeyed, the town would thus also lose 50 or 60 fat cattle a year from this rural trader alone, and hardly ten oxen out of his several droves would arrive in the town, nor would his neighbours be inclined to increase their stock. Who knows whether these and other such regulations, which are regarded by most people as trivial, are the basic cause of the shortage of grain and provisions complained of in the kingdom?

I am certainly not advocating that a farmer should be kept from his farm work by trading. I would prefer to see that the burghers, who in most places have plenty of time to do so, especially during the winters, would themselves undertake the task of serving the countryside around the towns, at the same time benefiting themselves.

As our towns do not do so, however, it seems to me that they wish to be regarded as the fathers of the country who tell all the children to gather round their chairs to put food in their mouths one by one. O hard times! when the offspring has begun to order its mother about and the child wishes to take its father's place.

§ 26

A merchant who enjoys freedom of trade extends his concerns far and wide; he is continually occupied in marketing his commodities advantageously. If one should attempt to make excessive gains, he will attract competitors who will take a share of the profit and protect citizens from arbitrary extortion. Each one must then be content with a smaller profit on each commodity and instead depend for his livelihood on turning them over all the more rapidly.

Interest rates will then fall; people will then also engage in the minor trades that cannot be considered or pursued when interest rates are high, as they are less profitable. In a word, monopolies, bill-jobbery and a national deficit can never arise unless they are protected by the laws but may well be maintained once they have been established.

Owing to a peculiar distinction between staple and non-staple towns, foreigners are prevented from obtaining commodities and paying for them in cash in a large number of ports. These have to be offered to the inhabitants of the staple towns; if they will not pay for them, there is no market for them. Industriousness loses much of its incentives, production is reduced and the money begins to flow out. A great profit for the nation!

§ 27

The Commodity Ordinance prevented foreigners from obtaining any advantage by visiting the smaller staple towns, as they could not dispose of whole cargoes of their own products in them and were not allowed to carry assortments of other goods. Few of these towns were able to freight an entire ship with their own exports, so that they had to be sold in the larger staple towns. The Dutch and the English were no longer permitted to supply them with salt, nor was it worth sailing in ballast to Portugal for that, but it, too, had to be purchased from the larger staple towns.

Is it not remarkable how commerce retreated to a few localities from the rest of the kingdom? The name staple towns was indeed retained, but for most of them the advantage had really been lost.

Our commerce would nevertheless have prospered reasonably well if the foreigners had been allowed to conduct trade freely in the largest towns and to challenge the vested interests in the country through competition. But they have not profited much from that since they were totally excluded from the salt trade, which was then concentrated in the hands of a few citizens who were able to decide whether or not to supply the kingdom with that commodity and at whatever price they wished.

The number of purchasers of our exports was thus reduced. The products remained in the hands of the producers or were sold to the exporters at a loss. The loss forced many owners from their properties, which inevitably fell into the hands of the exporters or made the former tributary to the latter.

In order to redress that evil, the Ironmasters' Association was founded, which was to advance loans to poor owners of ironworks when the price of iron fell; but as to whether this benefited the poorer or the more affluent ones is common knowledge.

When bank transfer notes began to be issued, ready money began to pour into the Bank. Imports could not then be paid for in money nor any ready money be exported to pay for them, but everything had to be done by means of bills of exchange in return for exports that, to cover the entire commerce of the Crown and the kingdom, were only available from a few individuals, who therefore had complete control over the bills of exchange. Freedom of trade was thus stifled, and I am not sure that one should simply blame individuals for that. Matters were so arranged that freedom would be lost.[10]

"If Caesar and Pompey", says Montesquieu, "had thought like Cato, others would no doubt on the contrary have thought like Caesar and Pompey." And elsewhere he says: "[W]hen one grants titles of honour one knows exactly what one is giving away; but if one also adds power to that, one never knows how far it may be extended."[11]

§ 28

Laws, prohibitions, regulations and classifications could then be procured to ratify that power. The attention of other traders would be limited to certain commodities, certain localities and certain times, and otherwise impoverish them and deprive them of their livelihood, and they the countryside around them.

It is strange that one should wish to disassociate the Commodity Ordinance from such inevitable consequences. Did the Estate of Burghers not predict that it would lead to shortages and high prices? The prediction was fulfilled, and when general distress arose, the remedy was seen to lie in suspending it; and yet it is said: the nation profits from the Commodity Ordinance.

We wish to develop a water-powered process; we have seen that it begins to operate when the dam is opened, yet we assert that it works best when it is closed. Is not the destruction of industry and immiseration of the citizens a hard way to earn a profit for the nation?

§ 29

We moan about the consequences but will not go to the source from which they flow. As soon as anyone mentions free trade, the response is: we must not confuse such private matters with the general and national ones. I am not sure what to say: either we read nothing or we think very little.

Is not our unhealthy obsession with bills of exchange the greatest restraint of trade that could possibly exist? Is there, then, any other conceivable remedy than to establish free trade?

There are two major means, in particular, towards that end: the first is to break the power of those who have exercised the tyranny of the bills of exchange, without respect of persons, so as to render them incapable of doing anything more. If it is too late to do so, it is obvious that the state has given away too much and is obliged to tremble before the weapons that it has itself placed in their hands. Once power has been lost, one is obliged to behave submissively.

The second is to repeal those regulations that in any way inhibit trade and destroy industry. If everyone had the right and opportunity to trade personally with foreigners, not so many would need to pay tribute to the exporters in order to purchase bills of exchange; and to oblige them by laws and oaths to charge a reasonable price in the hope of thereby bringing relief to the country is, in my view, to build castles in the air.

Both of these measures are indispensable. The latter will be useless unless it is preceded by the former, and the former will be of no avail if the regulations remain in force, for others will then inevitably take the place of the previous ones, and it will scarcely make any difference to the nation whether the man exercising arbitrary power is named Caesar or Octavius. It will be bad enough once liberty has been lost!

As simple as these remedies for an unstable exchange rate may seem, they are the sole and only effective ones, without which no relief may be expected.

All agree that increasing the country's exports and increasing the amount of currency in circulation serves to lower the rate of exchange. The former can never be done without freedom of trade and I know of no other method of creating wealth than by foreign trade. If that is in the hands of a few individuals, they will necessarily continue to maintain the same kind of Exchange Bill Offices,[12] though under different names from the former ones, which is bound to have the same effect on the rate of exchange.

All domestic transactions and even the most subtle financial operations that do not also expand foreign trade are, in my view, as useless as abstract theories about a *perpetuum mobile* or a water-powered contraption that is to keep itself in motion inside a well.

The inventor of these may develop them as far as he wishes. They must nevertheless eventually come to a stop. And even he who has made the most subtle calculations will finally see, when his proposal is carried into effect, that the entire operation amounts to nothing more than transferring something from one hand to another.

§ 30

Whenever a new industry has been established in which people can be employed, it is believed that their output constitutes a profit for the nation, irrespective of whether that industry pays its workers adequately.

We consider that the people who are recruited to work there have not previously earned or been able to earn anything, even if someone who unfailingly made a living for himself and his family in his previous occupation, without begging or stealing, earned more than he does in the new one, where his income is barely sufficient for him alone, while his wife and children must roam the streets and live on the earnings of others.

It is quite advantageous for a people to conceive of new industries, as there may by chance be one among them that is more profitable than any of the earlier ones and that consequently increases the profit to the nation. But to keep an enterprise afloat by means of bounties or constraints on other citizens will always infallibly produce a loss to the nation.

The argument that more people can be supported if the trades multiply is quite inapplicable here, for it is in no way their number that increases the profit to the nation but solely the value of their output, even if it were only in a single trade. As long as land lies fallow, the ironworks lack workers and our workshops stand empty, efforts to establish even more trades are, in my view, superfluous.

This reminds me of the moral of Aesop's fable[13] about the dog that saw the reflection of a piece of meat in the water while it swam and lurched towards it, only to immediately lose the piece it had found in the butcher's shop. By gaping to excess, he implies, one ends up with less.

Nor do I regard it as a valid argument that the work is often undertaken by people recruited from abroad. For if they have been attracted at a heavy public cost to work in a less profitable occupation, thousands of them would have come without the slightest expense to the state had they simply been freely allowed to support themselves as best they could, that is, to pursue the trade in which they would most increase the real profit to the nation.

Once foreigners have arrived, a sound polity demands that the best possible use should be made of their labour, and that infallibly happens in the trade that provides the greatest rewards for its practitioners but certainly not in those places where they have to be fed at the expense of the state and of the public. They spontaneously seek out the former but do not voluntarily remain in the latter except under coercion, and in the end their reward for immigrating will be poverty.

§ 31

This concept of the national profit, as critical as it may seem of our new arrangements, is really in itself the most innocuous and simple one.

It provides freedom for all lawful occupations, though not at the expense of others. It protects the very weakest trade against oppression and promotes industriousness and unhampered enterprise.

It weighs them all in the same scales, making profit the true yardstick for deciding which of them should be preferred.

It spares the Sovereign Power a thousand bothersome concerns, regulations and supervisory duties when private and national profit merge into a single interest, and the injurious self-interest, which always tries to conceal itself behind one regulation or another, can then most effectively be controlled by mutual competition.

It guarantees a Swede the enjoyment of his most precious and greatest natural right, granted to him as a human being by the Almighty, namely, to earn his living by the sweat of his brow in the best way he can.

It removes the bolster of indolence from those who are now, because of their privileges, able to sleep away two-thirds of their time. All means of living without working are blocked, and none but the diligent is able to prosper.

It will effect a desirable reduction in our lawsuits. The many regulations, their expositions, exemptions and applications, which in any way inhibit trades, will then become pointless and fade away, and once a law has been repealed it can no longer be infringed.

§ 32

I know that these novelties will appeal to only a minority of my readers. However, they have entertained me so much that I feel it is also my duty to offer them to the public, among whom I have no doubt that there will be some who will honestly share in this pleasure of mine.

Uncertainty about how best to help our country has led me to think about this subject, and as a free Swedish citizen it was my obligation to understand the laws of my fatherland. I compared them with each other but failed to find in them the aspect that tends to emerge from the instructions of a prudent master, namely that they should have a purpose.

I hear complaints about emigration and also observe many measures that bring it about. We may wish to promote industry, yet we place obstacles in the way of the industrious man being able to support himself. While asserting that the prosperity of the country needs to be promoted, we forbid a whole province to buy bread for itself, merely on the pretext of preventing smuggling. Obedience to the government's orders is demanded, yet there are so many of them given during the past several centuries that even lawyers are able to find them only with great difficulty, and they include some that could hardly be observed without causing misery.

We complain about a trade deficit yet prevent each other as far as possible from selling our commodities to foreigners. We wish to expand trade yet attempt to restrict it to 15 or 20 individuals. We are squeezed dry by a high rate of exchange yet seek by all means to restrict buyers of bills of exchange to the fewest possible sellers of bills, who already exercise absolute control over the exchange rate.

We strive to increase the national profit, yet we employ our people in work that can barely earn them bread and water from day to day. We plan to shorten lawsuits and increase compliance with the law, yet we daily multiply our laws, so that even a judge can only with great difficulty find them in the register, and barely one in a hundred is aware of his obligations. Tell me, then, benevolent reader, what will all of this ultimately lead to?

For my part I can only echo the cynic Lisidor:[14]

From everything I hear, my thoughts are in a jumble:
Despite so many lights, along the road I stumble.
The noise and arguments but make me more confused;
And though I Swedish know, it leaves me now bemused.

§ 33

I have tried in every way to analyse a single small branch of industry and mentally draft the regulations that ought to be applied to it, but everywhere I have met with insuperable obstacles, when I have not been misled by personal bias, and have thus been unable to make headway, in particular for the reasons outlined in § 11 and the following paragraphs.

On consulting historical precedents, I soon observed that the greater the amount of freedom that has been allowed to exist in any trade, the more rapid has its growth always been and vice versa, and the more equitably that freedom has been distributed, the more naturally have the trades achieved a mutual equilibrium.

The manner in which other states deal with the trades likewise taught me that freedom always turned out to be the measure of their level of development. Wherever I looked, however, I saw self-interest so entrenched in the regulations that it was everywhere difficult and in most places quite impossible to eradicate it.

The more closely I began to measure our trades by the amount of liberty they enjoy, the more I seemed to see the possibility of reviving them; I was liberated from my anxious perplexity about the relative advantages of the trades and the many regulations governing them, a problem, I am quite convinced, that far surpasses the wit of man yet which nature itself so easily resolves.

A single measure, namely that of being able to reduce the number of our regulations, has ever since then become an absorbing subject of research for me, which I would most highly recommend as the principal and most significant one to consider before any new ones are now promulgated.

To find a few collaborators in this effort is the essential purpose of this little treatise. Adversaries worry me not in the slightest. The truth that I have sought is so agreeable that I am pleased merely to have been able to describe it to my fellow citizens: it is immutable and fearless even when the waves drench it in their spray. It can withstand being buried by self-interest in the gravel with which the angry breakers cover it, yet despite all that it remains unshakeable and unalterable.

> Truth, O truth, your bright rays shining
> Penetrate the hardest stone:
> Virtue pure is thine alone;
> Man's duplicity declining,
> All defining,
> Each of us you grant his own.[15]

A *Circumstantial Response* to the *Circumstantial Refutation of the Treatise called The Source of Our Country's Weakness*, published by the Royal Printing-Press, will appear at the earliest opportunity.[16]

Notes

1 "*8⅓ per cent less*": Chydenius made a mistake in calculating the percentages. It ought to be 6.25 per cent.

2 " *profit of 58⅓ per cent for him*": Chydenius here makes another mistake when he adds 25 per cent to 33⅓ per cent. Percentages cannot be added in this way.

3 "*M. maintains that agriculture is best, E.S. that ...*": M. is believed to stand for the French Physiocrat Mirabeau (1715–89). E.S. is likely the Swedish author Eric Salander (1699–1764). O.R. is perhaps the Swedish author Ephraim Otto Runeberg (1722–70). The initials A.G. are so common that no identification is attempted here. They could stand for a number of authors in Sweden and elsewhere at this time.

4 "*a yeoman farmer*": the Swedish *odalbönder* were freeholders cultivating their own land.

5 Västergötland is a county in south-west Sweden known for its tradition in textile-making.

6 Västerbotten, Hälsingland and Västernorrland are three counties in the north of today's Sweden.

7 "*these towns*": i.e. Pori, Rauma and Uusikaupunki.

8 "*... that part of our laws that concerns rural trade*": so-called *landsköp* or *landthandel* (buying up in the countryside) or farmers trading with each other was in principle forbidden, and had been at least since 1538. Instead, farmers were obliged to transport wares to cities in order for them to be put to market. This also included the provision

that farmers had to pay a duty when entering the city (the so-called little toll). The latter existed until 1810. The last restrictions on rural trade were lifted in 1846 and 1864 in Sweden and in 1859 in Finland (see also the Commentary to "Answer to the question on rural trade", pp. 277–80).

9   Savo, Häme and Karelia are three counties in Finland.

10 *"When bank transfer notes began to be issued..."*: note here Chydenius's interpretation; see the Introduction, pp. 23–5.

11 *"If Caesar and Pompey..."*: citations are from *Considerations on the Causes of the Grandeur and Decadence of the Romans* (*Considérations sur les causes de la grandeur des Romains et de leur décadence*, 1734), ch. 11. Chydenius here quotes the Swedish translation *Herr Montesquieus Tankar öfwer orsakerne til de romares wälde och fall*, Stockholm, 1755.

12 *"Exchange Bill Offices"* refers to a group of influential merchants, who during the years 1747–56 and 1758–61 were commissioned by the state and with financial aid from the same to try to improve the value of Swedish money. In practice this was done by taking up foreign loans and using the money to draw bills abroad. The operations of the *wäxel-contoir* in 1758–61 failed completely and contributed to the defeat of the Hat party in the Diet elections of 1765. Many held the persons who had taken part in the operations of the Exchange Bill Offices responsible for the deplorable economic state of the Swedish realm. Initially Anders Chydenius also held this view, being under the strong influence of his intellectual father-figure Anders Nordencrantz at the time. See the Introduction, p. 25.

13 *"Aesop's fable"*: Aesop was most probably a slave and storyteller who lived in Greece between *c*.620 and 560 BC.

14 *"Lisidor"*: refers to the poem "The Despiser of the World" ("Wärldsföraktaren") by Gustaf Fredrik Gyllenborg (1731–1808) and its main character, Lisidor. The poem was published in 1762 in a collection of contemporary poetry, *Witterhets arbeten, utgifne af et samhälle i Stockholm*, vol. 2, Stockholm, 1762.

15 *Truth, O truth, your bright rays shining...*: the verse is from the poem "The Power of Truth" ("Sanningens styrka") by Olof von Dalin (1708–63), originally included in Dalin's play *The Jealous One* (*Den afwundsiuke, Comedie i tre öpningar*, Stockholm, 1739), and published posthumously in *Olof von Dalins Witterhetsarbeten, i bunden och obunden skrifart*, vol. 3, Stockholm, 1767.

16 As is noted in the Commentary to *The Source of Our Country's Weakness* (*Källan til rikets wan-magt*), this pamphlet gave rise to the publication of several refutations, and *A Circumstantial Response* was Chydenius's response to these. See p. 139.

Commentary

Lars Magnusson

It is mainly *The National Gain*, printed and published by Lars Salvius in July 1765, that has caused Chydenius to be viewed as a Finnish "predecessor to Adam Smith". However, as we saw in the Introduction, judgments of this kind can be misleading. No doubt this short pamphlet written during Chydenius's extremely busy year 1765 vividly illustrates his extraordinary talent and vision. Chydenius belongs to a group of economic writers common in both France and England during the first half of the eighteenth century, who denounced economic regulation of a kind that in the first of those countries was labelled "Colbertism". In general, such writers were critical of towns and preferred the countryside. On the other hand, they seldom went as far as the sect around François Quesnay, the Physiocrats, which denounced all forms of work outside the agricultural sector as unfruitful. In particular, they regarded the prevailing state support for manufactories – indeed, *dirigisme* in its essence – as a partisan policy detrimental to the rest of the economy. Generally they found support for their views in the moral philosophy of natural liberty: regulations most often distorted the natural order of things. On the other hand, they differed strongly concerning the issue of whether luxury consumption was beneficial or evil. They were at best uninterested in the idea that economic growth of a nation could be enhanced with the help of aggressive export policies and a strategy of import substitution; some others were outright critical of foreign trade and regarded that too as an unfruitful activity. The "national gain" did not hinge upon any form of export surplus that a country would be able to catch, but rather upon the number of poor people that could be employed and supported. Hence, they instead favoured agricultural reforms and the establishment of a free market of corn and other agricultural products. No doubt it is within this broad group of economic writers that Chydenius belongs.

Against this background it is perhaps peculiar that Chydenius right at the beginning of his tract states that "the profit of the nation" is determined by the amount "by which the value of exported commodities exceeds that of the imported ones", especially as § 4 defines the "wealth of a people" as consisting of the quantity of its products, and the quantity of products in its turn depends on the number of workers and their diligence. Is he here still fettered to an old mercantilist prejudice? Be that as it may, Chydenius's main argument here is by no means to propose that a country should attempt to export for more value than it receives in import. Instead, he argues that a country ought to *specialize* in what it is best at and can produce with the highest value. If the country's workers are better at producing agricultural products than iron, it is best that they bring exports of the former to foreign markets as this will create greater incomes and support more people at home. His principal argument is that artificial support for some trades (read: the manufactories) should be denounced, as such support is always detrimental to trades where "the smallest number of people produce commodities of the greatest possible value".

To a greater degree than the previous tracts, *The National Gain* seems to have been directly stimulated by Chydenius's work in the four different committees to which he was appointed by the Estate of Clergy: the General Appeals Committee (9 February), the Fisheries Joint Committee (26 February), the Grand Joint Committee (29 March) and lastly the Appropriations Committee (8 June). To be a member of the Grand Joint Committee was especially prestigious; this body was in fact an extension of the Secret Committee where the most sensitive political issues of the day were discussed. It was perhaps the mundane work of reforming the regulations on fishing that provided him with arguments against regulations on industry in a more general sense. At the start, he was confronted with an almost endless list of regulative measures that had been taken over the years in order to promote fishing. A special state fund was in existence with the aim to support fishing through a complicated system of export premiums and bounties. To make it more complicated, this financial support varied between different sorts of fish; the export of herring to Mediterranean ports seems to have been especially cherished, as well as whale hunting (of which very little catch was exported from Sweden!). This complex system must have been extremely confusing, and not only in Chydenius's eyes – and quite often contradictory: export premiums were speedily instigated and withdrawn without much thought, it seems. Without doubt he here made a great contribution to reforming the system, as Schauman argues. Eventually his work was crowned with the establishment of a more liberal Fishing Ordinance in 1766.[1]

The experience Chydenius gained in his work towards reform of the fishing industry can be clearly detected in *The National Gain*. As a general feature of economic policy, export premiums and production support are condemned by the author for leading to what we today would describe as the opposite of an optimal allocation of resources: premiums for a certain trade drew away hands from such activities as would have been more gainful. Moreover, wares that were in less demand were produced while the production of those in higher esteem was abandoned. Without doubt, this critique could have been directed at most of the trade regulations of the time, including for example the prohibitions that hindered the development of rural proto-industry in south-west Västergötland or Ostrobothnia. Subsidizing manufactories in the cities, by forcing peasants to travel to towns in order to sell their produce and by prohibiting free competition by means of guild regulations, means that the nation will be unable to prosper and increase its population – this is the general conclusion that he draws.

However, such critical remarks on the prevailing system of regulation had also been propounded by other Swedish reform-mercantilists such as Salvius, and perhaps especially by Carl Leuhusen (see the Introduction, pp. 34–7). But more forcefully than anybody else at the time, Chydenius argues that freedom of trade and enterprise is the main propelling force to guarantee that each individual is employed in the most gainful way. It is clear from what he says at the end of the text that he believes that on this point he is saying something novel that has not previously been clearly spelled out. From his work in the Fisheries Joint Committee he drew the conclusion that the discussion should not ultimately be focused on which of various trades is superior – he suggests – but on allowing trades to be free so that every individual can enhance his own private gain as much as possible. This goes beyond what the Physiocrats were saying at the same time: insisting that agriculture was more productive than other trades. On the other hand, without doubt they too argued that allowing individual gain was the best way to enhance production in a country, as also did Turgot; this is obvious, for example, in the discussion concerning the liberation of the corn trade.

The National Gain was most likely written during the period when the readers' reactions to *The Source of Our Country's Weakness* had begun to pour in. As has already been explained, Chydenius responded to his critics with two small tracts, one published in 1765 and the other in 1766. In the first of these, *A Circumstantial Response to the Refutation of the Treatise Entitled: The Source of Our Country's Weakness*, he returns to the issue that he presents as novel in *The National Gain* (which it was not, if we take into account the contemporary French and British literature), namely that the country profits the most if individual gain is foregrounded. How can a stable order be built upon such a seemingly unstable ground? he asks. Contrary to the majority of "mercantilistic" economic writers at the time – even some of the reform-mercantilists – he points out that there is basically no contradiction between the public and individual interest. He points out the similarities between humankind and the ocean, "where one column of water with immense power every moment puts pressure on another, but an equally powerful counteracting pressure nevertheless keeps the surface even and horizontal". Anyone who tries to make one of the columns higher than the other will surely fail, he adds.[2] Although his "liberal" attitudes here seems to point forward to modern equilibrium analysis, one must acknowledge that such statements were not unknown in the pre-Smithian liberal economics propounded by the French *économistes* as well as by some British writers (e.g. Josiah Tucker and David Hume) in the mid-eighteenth century. Despite Smith's high reputation as an economic thinker, he is more often portrayed as a synthesizer of ideas than as an innovator.[3] He picked up ideas that were circulating at the time and created his own synthesis. Hence, ideas like the ones Chydenius presents in the *The National Gain* contributed to the new system of political economy of which Smith is held to be the father. The fact that Smith knew nothing about our chaplain from Alaveteli is of course another matter.

Notes

1 G. Schauman, *Biografiska undersökningar om Anders Chydenius*, Skrifter utgifna af Svenska Litteratursällskapet i Finland 84, Helsinki: Svenska Litteratursällskapet i Finland, 1908, p. 193f.
2 A. Chydenius, *Omständeligt swar, på den genom trycket utkomne wederläggning af skriften, kallad: Källan til rikets wanmagt, jämte anmärkningar öfwer de wid samma källa anstälda wattu-prof*, Stockholm, 1765, § 99.
3 The classical reference here is J.A. Schumpeter, *A History of Economic Analysis* [1954], London: George Allen and Unwin, 1968, p. 181f.

4   *A Remedy for the Country by Means of a Natural System of Finance*

Presented by Anders Chydenius, Member of the Diet.

Iactabatur temporibus illis nummus sic, ut nemo posset scire, quid haberet. Cicero, *De officiis*, book III.[1]

Stockholm, printed at the expense of Director Lars Salvius, 1766.

Delivered before the Estate of Clergy on 11 June 1766, when it was resolved that the Estate should permit this paper to be printed.
Witness, J. Brander.

§ 1

So many learned works have been published recently about the decline of our finances and the means of restoring them that it would at first glance seem superfluous to publish anything further on this topic.

However, as our situation has unfortunately not yet improved, although the salvation or ruin of the entire country chiefly depends on it, I assume that my worthy fellow countrymen will not refuse to give their attention to this publication.

I may indeed have had one or two things printed previously, but until now I have never acted as a project-maker[2] and have certainly not taken up the pen on my own behalf, but for the sake of the distress of the community at large.

Whether the proposal is appropriate or not, of that I will let you, dear reader, be the first and then posterity to provide the most impartial verdict.

One always finds faults in proposals made by others but not so easily in one's own. Those of others appear to us sometimes to be costly, sometimes unfeasible, occasionally self-interested and at other times difficult to understand and rather strange.

The more simply one can present a matter, the better. I shall try to make the truth visible without glasses and therefore *first* describe the correct and simple basis for a system of finance, *next* show the source from which the confusion among us arises, *then* briefly examine the main proposals offered by others and, finally and *fourth*, present my own proposal to the reader.

48.

Rikets Hjelp,

Genom en

Naturlig

FINANCE-SYSTEM.

Föreståld
Af
ANDERS CHYDENIUS,
Riksdagsman.

*Jactabatur temporibus illis nummus sic, ut nemo posset
scire, quid haberet.* Cic. de Officis, Libr. III.

STOCKHOLM,

Tryckt på Direct. LARS SALVII kostnad, 1766.

Figure 19 The title page of *A Remedy for the Country by Means of a Natural System of
Finance* (1766). Kokkola University Consortium Chydenius.

§ 2

By a system of finance I do not mean the finances of the Crown, which consist in distributing among the citizens and utilizing those charges that are indispensable for the maintenance of the Crown and the state with the greatest security, the least confusion and the most equitable sharing of the burden, but the finances of the country, which should be carefully distinguished from the former and consist in the manner of *establishing the coinage of the realm on such a footing as will best promote security and enterprise in all productive occupations, from which the country as a whole and each individual subject derive their proper increase and strength.*[3]

As long as I myself produce all that I require to meet my needs, I have little or nothing to do with this financial system of the country, but as there is not a single one among us, of whatever rank and condition he may be, who can subsist in this way on his own, it becomes indispensable for each one of us to obtain from others what he needs in exchange for such things that he can more easily do without.

§ 3

As long as no one knows my needs better than I do myself, and since no one is prepared to provide me with my necessities, I should have the right, according to the laws of nature and of Sweden, to obtain them through commerce.

Commerce is thus nothing but an exchange of commodities in amity and with the consent of buyer and seller, by which people provide each other with what they need. All commodities are produced by toil and labour, but their quantity and supply and the demand for them establish their natural value in relation to other commodities.

Such an amicably arranged exchange of commodities, whether among citizens domestically or with foreigners, should be conducted on both sides without deceit and trickery, unless we wish to trample openly on the very foundations of all natural law.

The more precious metals, such as gold and silver, have gained such general popularity throughout the world due to their attractiveness, durability, rarity and easy mobility that they, more than all other commodities, are willingly received and exchanged for others and have on that account become a universal measure in commerce.

These more precious metals nonetheless have an unstable value, firstly among themselves and secondly in relation to other commodities, according to whether the supply of and demand for the latter are lower or higher.

When one considers that coins are nothing but larger or smaller stamped portions of these metals that the seller receives in exchange for his commodity, he ought to be aware how much of these metals those coins contain; if he does not know that, he is acting blindly. If he believes that they contain more than they do and bases his purchase on that understanding, he will be deceived.

No one can justify such commerce unless he is willing to assert that injustice and deception are permissible means by which to enrich oneself, and such a deed is in no way made better even if it is authorized by rulers through monetary regulations, and least of all ought one to hope that such things, being contrary to the laws of God and nature, are able to produce lasting wealth for any society.

As these more precious metals can be mixed in innumerable ways with inferior ones and yet preserve their former appearance, and as their actual intrinsic worth cannot be ascertained without great difficulty through the art of assaying, one is very liable to be mistaken about them, and that all the more easily the more frequently the standard of coinage is changed and the more secret that alteration can be kept.

§ 4

Rulers have nevertheless believed themselves entitled, with more or less deleterious intentions, not only to change the composition of these metals but also, by means of laws and decrees, to impose values on the coins that differ from their weight and quality, which must necessarily lead to the seller receiving a varying amount of these metals for one and the same commodity, according to whether he is paid for it in coin with a greater or a smaller precious metal content.

These changes in the value of the coinage have sometimes gone so far that one has assumed it to be in the power of rulers to order the seller to accept 1 *lod* of copper for a commodity for which he would otherwise be entitled to receive the same quantity of silver or, which amounts to the same thing, to believe the copper to be silver, or at least that both of these metals are of equal value.[4] And as in commerce 1 *lod* of fine silver relates in value to 1 *lod* of copper approximately as 100 *lod* to 1 *lod*, that command has also obliged me to believe that 100 shall equal 1, which cannot but be one of the most difficult articles of faith that may be imposed upon a subject.

Can there be any greater abuse? But in what does this crime consist? It consists in the fact that the seller does not receive the quantity of these metals that corresponds to the value of his commodity but has to be content with the stamped or tale-value that the Sovereign Power has allocated to them.

Even if it differs in degree, the crime can never thereby change its nature, and it can never become more lawful to dispossess my neighbour of 1 *riksdaler* than it is to take 100. It is for this reason that Board of Trade Counsellor Polhem[5] states in a postscript to a letter dated 14 February 1715 and submitted to the Board of Trade, "*Such devices in the monetary system are either childish follies or merely cunning tricks,*" and, he adds, "*it is a wonder that Sweden has been able to remain prosperous for so long!*"

§ 5

This simple demonstration undermines most of the current maxims of minting in Europe, which themselves are nothing but subtle frauds and make enterprise everywhere difficult, complicated and uncertain.

He who personally wishes to use his reason and does not let himself be blindly led by others must therefore accept as incontrovertible the fundamental truth that human beings, according to their right derived from nature, ought to receive for a negotiable commodity a cash payment corresponding to it in value and that the Sovereign Power, in that regard, when minting metals, does not have the right, in order to ease circulation thereby, to establish by law any other value of a coin than that which the same amount of metal will command as a traded commodity and contains in terms of precious metals.

This fundamental principle invalidates the opinion accepted in most countries that a country's small coins should be of a lower quality than its standard coin, which situation now causes such great confusion.

Some would object that it would be hazardous for Sweden to adopt such a straightforward standard of coinage when other nations have established their coinage on some other basis, but that means nothing, for foreigners never receive our coin except as a commodity, while a Swede likewise sets a price on his commodity according to the intrinsic worth of the coin with which it is to be purchased by the foreigner.

The argument for a low-quality coinage in a country also tends to be put forward that it makes no difference to the inhabitants of the country whether they receive inferior or better coin for their commodities as long as they will receive for it from others the same quantity of commodities as that which they had exchanged for it. But the response to this is that the more strictly an agio[6] for the inferior coin is prohibited and the more closely such a monetary system is observed within the country, the more must the inferior coin drive out the better.[7] For it is obvious that when 1 *mark* of fine silver minted into *riksdaler specie* is, according to the monetary system, worth 7 or 8 per cent more inside the country than 1 *mark* of fine silver minted into *caroliner*, then the foreigners through their agents will be actively looking for the *caroliner*, and while it is all the same to a Swede whether he pays the foreigners in *caroliner* or *riksdaler*, as they are worth the same according to the monetary system, Sweden has thus been deprived of millions of *caroliner*, all at a loss of 7 per cent to the country. If the *carolin* or any other coin is minted as inferior to a *riksdaler*, it will be the turn of the *riksdaler* to disappear. In the same way, *slantar* have driven out *plåtar*, which is indisputable. People denounce the stealthy exporting of the better coin as smuggling, but it is simply the fault of rulers who have set such different values on the metals, and it can never be prevented under such circumstances.

If, on the other hand, one wished to debase all the coinage of the realm generally in the same proportion, or, which amounts to the same thing, raise its tale-value, nothing would be gained thereby, as the commodity prices inevitably rise to the same extent, but on the other hand the inferior metal and higher minting charge represent a loss and the more precious metal is itself reduced in price by the amount it costs to smelt and purify it.

§ 6

Having laid such a foundation, we shall examine more closely the causes of the present confusion in our financial system.

Almost everywhere throughout Europe the monetary system rests on such fraudulent and artificial foundations that it causes a greater or lesser uncertainty in the value of commodities and to the same extent inhibits enterprise in the world of commerce.

Such confusion infallibly stems from a certain kind of governmental self-interest, which has then been adopted everywhere and has in recent times been regarded as one of the most secret maxims of state by means of which either rulers or certain individuals in the state have sought to gain possession of the property of their fellow men.

The artful measures of one state in this respect have served as a model for others, and things have already gone so far in this regard that one has begun to regard them as indispensable for the very existence of the state.

§ 7

He who would wish to absolve our ancestors, several centuries ago, from numerous and grave mistakes in the regulation of our monetary system would be inadequately informed about the financial history of the kingdom, while he, on the other hand, who would deny that we ourselves have contributed the most to this situation would be too blind and conceited.

Nine hundred and sixty years ago there were 16 *lod* of fine silver in one coined *mark* – that is, 1 *mark* in coin really did weigh 1 *mark* of silver – although in 1762, at an exchange rate of 108 *mark*, it corresponded to 864 *mark* in coin, each of which weighed about the same as a peppercorn, or 1/864 of a *mark* of silver.

Throughout these 900 years the tale-value has always gradually risen, and the commodity prices have risen accordingly, and if one takes the trouble to examine the causes of this development, one will always find them in the debasing of the intrinsic worth and weight of the coinage itself under the denominations of *öre*, *mark* and *daler*, which the rulers wanted to be regarded as larger proportions of a full-weighted *mark* than those in which they actually struck them for their own purposes.

By as much, therefore, as the coined *mark* was short of 16 *lod* of fine silver, so much was it at once debased.

In 1170 the coined *mark* had already been debased by 100 per cent, in 1422 by 800 per cent; that is to say, 1 *riksdaler specie* was then equivalent to 1 coined *mark*. During the reign of Gustavus Vasa[8] it was found to be so weak that 2 *mark* or more were reckoned as equal to a *riksdaler*. This state of disorder was perpetuated to such an extent that 100 years later, 120 *mark* were minted from 1 *mark* of silver, and in 1716 240 *mark*, or 36 coined *mark* per *riksdaler*.

It is upsetting to read in old documents how the changes in our coinage have always been brought about, the deplorable disorders that have arisen from that in

commerce and enterprise, and how the subjects have barely extricated themselves from one chaotic situation before they have been led into another by the
rulers.

The denominations in *daler* and *mark* have thus not denoted any specific
quantity of fine silver, but as soon as the rulers have noticed that the subjects had
been able to ascertain the intrinsic worth of the minted *daler, mark, öre* and
örtug coins in pure silver and to adjust the value of their commodities and bills
of exchange accordingly, they have been ready to mint coins of an even lower
intrinsic worth with the same *daler* and *mark* denominations, which initially, and
as long as their intrinsic worth could be kept secret, retained the value of the
better ones, but once that became known and the old currency had been melted
down and disappeared, the *daler* and *mark* denominations that were either
stamped on the silver coins or prescribed by monetary regulations did indeed
remain but represented less silver than before; that is to say, the new *daler* had a
smaller ratio to a *mark* of pure, 16-*lod* silver than the previous one, which gave
rise to new disorders.

I therefore fully concur with Board of Trade Counsellor Polhem when, in his
memorial to the Board of Trade of 14 February 1715, he says that *"the many
mintings, one time after another, have amounted to the same as granting elevated titles to lowly and common people, when the individuals are not made any
better or nobler thereby but the title is debased and demeaned." "For that
reason,"* he says, *"there is no basis on which to value anything by a coined
mark unless it can be done against a mark of fine silver, or its parts, and in so
far as 4 mark constitute a daler, the daler has the same status as the mark."*

On the other hand, it is clear that if such a change in the metal standard of
common denominations had never been allowed or one could have used other
impressions than those that have denoted the quantity of fine silver that the coins
contained, and if everyone had possessed the right to weigh, test and assess
them, as is still done in China, such a debasement would never have occurred,
nor could the tale-value have been raised or any financial disorders arisen.

§ 8

It is unnecessary, however, to dwell long on the damage caused to our finances
in a past era. Our own age has particularly distinguished itself in this regard. Let
us look at the situation in our time.

One still hears some people praise the Bank loans and lobby for the reopening
of the Bank,[9] but even more who wish to lay all the blame on them and believe
that our monetary regulations are unparalleled and would absolve them from
playing any part in our tragedy. But if the reader simply wishes to pursue the
truth, I hope he will not fail to observe how over-hasty such opinions are on both
sides. Unless the matter is understood in its context, it will be impossible to cure
the malady correctly.

The evil described above, namely that the denominations *daler* and *mark* have
not denoted a definite quantity of any metal, has continued in our time, so that

the *daler* has within a few years undergone erratic changes of from 100 to 200 per cent, during which time the same denomination has nevertheless been used in all commercial transactions as a measure of the value of commodities.

One and the same amount of silver, for example 2 *lod* of silver of a purity of 14/16 or 1 *riksdaler specie* corresponded in 1735 to 36 coined *mark* but in 1762 to 108 *mark*, and has passed through every degree in between both before and since then. As certain and incontrovertible as it is that 2 *lod* of fine silver is and remains the same, so, too, does 1/36, or the *mark* of 1735, also relate to 1/108, that is the *mark* of 1762, as 3 does to 1, and as there are 8 *öre* to each *mark* and 32 to each *daler*, it is also obvious that the value of the *öre* as against any metal has undergone the same change.

Throughout all this, as also long before, the silver *mark* and *daler* coins have, under the monetary regulations, retained their ratio to the copper *mark* and *daler* coins unchanged at 3 to 1 and have thus been debased in exactly the same way.

Now in order to grasp the chaotic nature of all of this directly and in a few words, let us just imagine that it were to become permissible in a retail shop to use a different ell every week, which within a few years might become two-thirds shorter than the one used previously, and to use these in part to lend, in part to sell thousands of ells of all kinds of fabrics without comparing them to any standard measure, and add to that a ruling that one may not call in the loans by the same ell-measure with which they were measured out or pay for the ell that was two-thirds shorter with less money than for the longer one, simply because both are called ells, then I ask: What commerce? What security, dear reader, do you think such a procedure would achieve? Or how easily might it not happen that many a simple person, unaware that the ell was being whittled down a little every week, could quite innocently trade away all his property, which would fall prey to the cunning rogue.

But it would seem even more peculiar to me if, in order to correct such a thing and to establish a standard ell-measure, one were to assert that it was indispensable to add a small piece at a time to the shortened ell over several years.

§ 9

That is now the simple state of the matter. But there are two reasons for it. I want, *first*, to prove that our own monetary regulations have given rise to it.

As the commodities never possess a stable value against each other but change every day according to the lesser or greater supply of and demand for them, two kinds of metal likewise cannot be used with any certainty as currency of the same tale-value. For as uncertain as it is that 2 *aln* of *Ras de Sicile*[10] should always be exchanged equally for 1 *aln* of fine broadcloth is it also that 2 *lod* of fine silver should always be worth the same as 200 *lod* of copper, for it might easily happen that the demand for copper were to be high in Europe but the supplies of it so far diminished that foreigners would willingly offer 2½ *lod* of fine silver for every 200 *lod* of it. If both of these metals were now to be struck into coins, which would relate to each other in weight as 1 to 100, with the same *daler* denomination and an injunction that they should be of equal value in all commercial transactions, foreigners would be able to purchase our small copper coins or *plåtar* with silver, to the detriment of the realm of 25 per cent, which could not happen if the copper coins were allowed to freely increase in value within the country.

In like manner, when the price of copper for the opposite reasons falls by 10 per cent, but yet, under the monetary regulations, 200 *lod* must be regarded as equal in value to 2 *lod* of silver, then foreigners will seek out the silver coin, causing a 10 per cent loss to the realm. Ever since copper was adopted as a metal to be coined along with silver, experience has provided the most deplorable evidence of this fact, and it can never be prevented as long as the relative value of copper to silver is determined by law.

This, however, is by no means the only cause for the deterioration of our finances to be found in our monetary regulations. There is another, even more important one, namely that all specimens of a coinage, taken together, have not been allowed to correspond to the whole. That is to say, 2 *lod* of silver of a purity of 14/16 is worth less when minted into *caroliner* and more when struck into *sexstyver* pieces than if the same 2 *lod* were minted into a *riksdaler*. That is to say, 1 *mark* of fine silver, which never is nor can become anything more nor less, corresponds by our monetary standard to 7 to 8 per cent more *daler kmt* if minted as *riksdaler* than if struck into *caroliner* but to 3⅛ per cent more *daler* when it is struck into *sexstyver* pieces rather than into *riksdaler*, somewhat more than 2 per cent fewer *daler* when it is struck into *fyrastyver* pieces, but 16⅔ per cent more *daler* when it is struck into *vit styver* pieces than when it is struck into *riksdaler*.

The *daler*, which, on the grounds outlined above, ought to represent a certain quantity of fine silver, is thus, according to our monetary regulations, worth most in *caroliner*, 7 per cent less in *riksdaler*, and more than 10 per cent less in *sexstyver* pieces than in *caroliner*.

However great the difference may thus be between *daler* of the same metal, our regulations have nonetheless not allowed for any such difference but have instead most severely prohibited any undervaluing of the coin of the realm. Yet, as it must concern buyers and sellers no less differently whether they receive or pay 24 per cent more or less silver for a commodity, a preference for certain kinds of coin, whether among natives or foreigners, can hardly be avoided, and that will also determine that the *daler* denomination will lack a stable value in any of the silver coins.

The natural difference between our *daler* coins will turn out to be even greater when we turn our attention to the minting of copper coinage.

Mathematical axioms tend not to be denied or disputed, but it is certain that under our monetary system, when a *skeppund* of copper is minted into 540 *daler* in *plåtar* but 900 *daler* in *slantar*, one is urged to believe that 1 whole equals 5/9ths or that 64 *slantar* equal one 6-*daler plåt*, but what is to make up the rest here, or 4/9ths, is incomprehensible, unless it is the generally accepted prejudice that small change should be inferior to the standard coin, though I am well aware that it is precisely that view that has taken our *plåtar* out of the country by the ship-, boat- and cartload, for little return.

When one thus looks at the differential minting into *daler kmt* that our copper has undergone, which varies by 66 per cent, I then ask with good reason how many *lod* of copper represent 1 *daler*; the answer I receive is 1/6th of a 6-*daler plåt*, but should I not be allowed by law to add 10 *styver* and 2 *öre* to that and assert that the *daler* would then be complete? Does anyone have the right to undervalue the coin of the realm?

I ask further what security he has who sells a commodity when he is uncertain whether he is being paid for it with 1 or 5/9ths of a *skeppund* of copper for one and the same agreed-upon amount of *daler*?

§ 10

Such is the difference between the *daler* of each separate kind of metal, but it may, with regard to what was previously said about the comparison between different metals, become considerably greater and be as high as 80 or 100 per cent, and no one is then likely to be surprised if the productive occupations become insecure and are devastated, and that not by accident but as an inevitable consequence of the regulations, whether or not bank loans had ever been permitted.

Let us now proceed and see how all of this has affected paper money. In order to understand the matter more clearly, we must make a distinction here between the bank transfer notes that have been issued by the Bank against ready money in order to ease circulation and long before bank loans were permitted,[11] and those that have been issued more recently as loans against property, real estate, etc.

Before the loans were made, no deposit-receipts were in circulation for which the holder of the receipt had not deposited an equal amount of ready money in the Bank. All receipts were made out in *daler kmt*. If the monetary regulations of the realm were to be respected by the Bank, the depositor should receive a deposit-receipt for 900 *daler* whether he deposited the sum in *slantar* or *plåtar*, that is to say, whether he deposited 1 or 1 4/9ths of a *skeppund* of copper or in whatever sort of current silver coin, without the Bank's promissory note indicating what kind of currency had been paid into the Bank or containing any assurance that the receipt-holder would be able to withdraw his capital against that receipt in the same kind of coin that had been deposited when it was issued.

When such receipts were being cashed in, it was thus in the power of the Bank to honour its receipt either in *caroliner*, *pjäsar*, *plåtar* or *slantar*, that is, whether it wished to pay for one and the same sum 60 to 70 or up to 100 per cent more or less, without the receipt-holder being aware of having lost any of his *daler*.

Thus, the *daler* number on the receipt did not denote a specific quantity of silver or copper but only what the Bank was willing to pay for it; but the more inferior the coin with which the receipts were honoured, the less the quantity of silver or copper the *daler* number on the receipt represented and the less value did the receipt have; that is, commodities must be paid for with many more *daler* in receipts than in *caroliner* and *riksdaler*, so that if the Bank had exchanged the receipts for nothing but *slantar*, the value of the *daler* on the receipt would of course already have fallen against the former by 60 or 70 per cent and more, and all of this as a result of the monetary regulations.

When these different *daler* are compared to the *riksdaler specie*, which represents a certain quantity of silver, it is clear that it requires a different amount of the more valuable than of the less valuable *daler* to purchase *riksdaler*, which is precisely what has now come to be called a high exchange rate[12] and is nothing other than an agio between the better and inferior sorts of coin according to their intrinsic worth, and which neither can nor ought to be rejected, for anyone would certainly be a fool who would want to exchange 2 *lod* of silver for 1¾ *lod* of equal fineness and he an even greater one who would want to sell 2 *lod* of fine silver for 100 *lod* of copper, when he could otherwise get 200 *lod* for it.

§ 11

Such a confusion of high and low exchange rates thus already inevitably arises, even without any bank loans, simply from the kind of coin that the Bank is willing to pay out for the *daler* amount deposited in the Bank in exchange for the transfer notes.

Yet in all this there was nevertheless a measure in the value of the actual metal with which the receipt was honoured, above which the agio could not rise particularly far. But when bank loans were permitted against iron, houses, properties and shares, the loans were facilitated and increased; that is, when banknotes were issued for things that were not even coin and the Bank was not able to honour its notes on demand with coin, even though it held some property of the depositor as surety, only then did an inordinate fall in the exchange rate for bills begin, and these particular loans are the *second* cause of the ruin of our finances.

Had the Bank, when it thus refused to redeem notes, been liable, like all other banks in Europe, to be immediately sued by the note-holder and legally obliged to honour its notes, then the abuse in the issuing of notes would not have gone so far. This is the very thing on which the security of other banks depends, however great the secrecy of the Bank, but as the issuing of notes, as well as the secrecy, was governed by a power able to conduct matters without accountability and orderliness, all security was lost, which could not but lead us so far into confusion that there is scarcely a way of escaping from it any longer.

It is precisely this that constitutes the weakness of our banking institution.

For if, first, it does not lay down in what kind of coin or valuables – that is, with how much fine silver or copper – it must eventually redeem its notes;

Second, if its cash balance, income and expenditures, books and administration remain in future, as they have hitherto, a secret; but, third, if the note-holder is not advised in what court he may legally pursue his case against the Bank and benefit from the general law on claims, then not only will it be and remain impossible for the Bank to obtain any credit or for its notes to acquire any value, but also the subjects are put in danger, through the operations of the Bank and through no fault of their own, of losing house and home and all their property, as a sparrow is driven from the ear of grain.

Whether all that is to be regarded as equitable or not; whether it promotes or destroys the security of productive occupations and commerce; whether the Bank, established on such a basis, is of benefit or harm to the country; whether a Swede thereby retains the security pledged in § 2 of the constitution[13] or is forcibly deprived of his property – all that the reader himself may judge.

With regard to these last three listed points, however, it should be noted that if the first and third condition are observed, the middle one will be unnecessary, and the last one can similarly be dispensed with if the first two are put into effect. But without the first, reinforced by one of the others, the matter cannot possibly be remedied or any bank remain in existence for very long without ruining the country.

To issue banknotes at will on the basis of a fluctuating tale-value; to keep the administration secret and not be responsible to any court in the world for one's promissory notes, surely amounts to the greatest power of which it has hitherto been possible to conceive, which despots have been unable to exercise more extensively, and which has never lasted.

But if the exercise of such things is to be termed *liberty* among us, then each and every person can easily see what little significance that word has in Sweden.

§ 12

In view of this, it was not surprising that the Bank's promissory notes, despite all decrees and ordinances, came to have a fluctuating value, namely that which those who had commodities or bills of exchange to sell were prepared to set on them, to which the incredible number of banknotes that came into circulation within our country in that way also contributed all too much, for which I may well cite the remark of the late Board of Trade Counsellor Polhem: *"Where pearls are gathered by the shovelful, they cannot possibly be of the same value as when they are set in jewelry and necklaces."*

There are thus generally three causes of the debasement of the *daler* or the rise in the relative value of the *mark* against the *riksdaler*: first, our own monetary regulations; second, the measures adopted by the three respective Estates with regard to the Bank through their Secret Committee, banking committees and directors; and third, the speculation of merchants, in that they have either secured such regulations or at least made use of them to their own advantage, which, even if ten have avoided doing, the eleventh has nonetheless infallibly done, and if the first two of these causes are done away with, the third will lapse of itself. With regard to which, one should really not apportion all blame to exporters and issuers of bills of exchange.

Matters were arranged in such a way that the outcome would be that which we are now experiencing.

All this caused the *daler* denomination printed on the banknote not to have any defined value against the current coin, and this uncertainty in turn caused the current coin not to coexist easily in circulation with the paper currency, which made the value of the latter all the more unstable.

The paper *daler*, or the *daler* denomination shown on the banknotes, has thus fallen from 1/9 to 1/27 of a *riksdaler*, or, which amounts to the same: when someone has required cash payment for his commodity or a buyer ready money with which to order some commodities, he has been obliged to pay from 36 to 108 paper *mark* for a *riksdaler*, or from 9 to 27 *daler*, and as the *riksdaler* is now worth exactly the same as it has been for the past 30 or 40 years, it is clear that the paper *daler* and *mark* have been devalued by two-thirds, during which time commodity prices in *daler kmt* have risen to the same extent. And although the *riksdaler* has now fallen again to 70 *mark* or slightly above that, owing to the withdrawal of the circulating notes and other reasons, the commodity prices have not yet had time to adjust themselves to that but in the meantime cause complaints and distress in all economic pursuits and enterprises.

§ 13

It is not incumbent upon me on this occasion to describe all the confusion that has arisen from this situation, apart from which it is also contrary to the brevity for which I strive. It is in my opinion quite impossible to correct everything that has occurred in the past, or to compensate all those who have suffered as a result.

The only question is: "How may our financial system henceforth be regulated in such a manner as to cause the least harm to the Crown, the Bank and citizens in general and change the productive occupations the least and be constructed on a natural and firm foundation, so that the country may in future be secure from all kinds of harmful revaluations of the currency?"

To fulfil the promise I made at the beginning, I must therefore first address the remedies suggested by others before I may put forward my own.

§ 14

Among the many proposals presented on this subject, two in particular are so general that almost all the rest can be subsumed under one or the other of them.[14] One is to keep banknotes in constant circulation in the same quantity as at present, accept them in the Bank and put them into circulation again at an exchange rate of 72 *mark*, without actually withdrawing any. The second is to undertake the largest possible withdrawals of banknotes and each year force the exchange rate down by a few *mark*, until the *daler* and *mark* denominations on the notes reach the parities laid down in 1715, i.e. 36 *mark* or 9 *daler kmt* per *riksdaler*.

With regard to the first proposal, it is completely contrary to the natural security in commerce of receiving a cash payment for a negotiable commodity and not having to be fobbed off with symbols and illusions, which, although it is customary in a number of countries, can nonetheless never become lawful, still less useful for any society, though indeed advantageous for certain purposes and persons within it.

That is to sustain a state of inebriation by means of opiates or strong drinks in someone who has already over-imbibed in order to avoid the pain of the headache that he can expect should he sober up. In that way, *materia peccans*[15] is maintained in the body politic, which in the course of time may again break out in the form of various unexpected ailments. It is asserted that the remedies for them are too harsh, and the patient is advised against using them in order to preserve the honour of previous physicians who have prepared the ground for the evil by their quackery. I need probably not linger on this proposal, as it is hardly likely to be defended by others than those who are accustomed to jobbing by turns in currency, exports and securities or else by someone who looks no further into the finances of the realm than that he believes them to be best when such activities flourish, even if everything else should fail.

§ 15

The second proposal for reducing the exchange rate of the banknote against *riksdaler*, on the other hand, has gained more support and the most powerful advocates, concerning which I must, before I comment on it, sincerely declare that I possess capital neither in cash nor in banknotes, am neither significantly in debt nor a creditor for any sum and moreover occupy such a humble position in our community that my affairs and consumption are comparatively modest and that I am, in a word, in such a situation that, whatever financial proposals may be adopted, I will become neither rich nor poor thereby.[16]

I bring this up deliberately in order that the reader may judge from this to what extent I may or may not be regarded as impartial in this matter, for even people with the best intentions and the most honest hearts tend to depart somewhat, often to their own advantage, from the truth and the true interest of the country. I have also refrained as long as possible from writing anything on this subject and have left that problem to those more directly involved in business. After I have carefully reflected on the consequences, however, the instinct of restraint has no longer been able to prevent me from laying the matter before the public.

In order that the reader may now obtain a clear grasp of the main question, I undertake to prove four things, namely that reducing the exchange rate to 36 *mark* or, what amounts to the same thing, increasing the value of the paper *daler* by 100 per cent is first *impossible*, second *unfair*, third *unnecessary* and, fourth and finally, in several respects *harmful*.

§ 16

The *first thing* to be examined now is therefore whether such a devaluation[17] is *impossible to implement*. For that purpose I must first point out something that can scarcely be gainsaid by anyone, namely that banknotes are nowadays almost the only available currency in all domestic commerce or enterprise, apart from a few *slant* and *pjäs* coins used as small change, and that therefore any changes made in regard to the banknotes would apply immediately to almost all the currency of the realm, from which it also follows that if any arrangements were adopted by which the banknotes could not be profitably used in productive occupations and enterprises, the country would at once be entirely deprived of money.

In the next place, I hope people may agree with me that the tale-value of the paper currency has now been raised by 100 per cent compared to what the numerical value of the *daler* stood for in 1735 and the time before then or, what amounts to the same thing, the value of the *daler* number on the banknote has been debased.

I spoke too soon, dear reader! This is precisely what is likely to be disputed first. I must therefore prove my proposition. The tale-value is said to be raised when the impression on the coin shows a higher figure than that formerly used to express its intrinsic value.

For example, when copper first began to be struck into *plåtar* during the last century, it was minted at 187½ *daler* per *skeppund*, but from 1661 to 1665 the same amount of copper was used to strike 225, then 270 and in 1675 300 *daler* and finally, at the beginning of this century, 540 *daler* per *skeppund*, during which time, or within one century, the tale-value was raised, or the copper *daler* fell, by almost 200 per cent. That is to say, if one wished to purchase a *skeppund* of copper, which at the beginning of the last century was worth 187½ *daler*, one had to pay 540 *daler* for it in this century. It is exactly the same with the paper currency; when it first began to be issued, each *daler* represented one-ninth of a *riksdaler*, but when the Bank began to honour its promissory notes in inferior coin and finally only with new promissory notes, it was inevitable that the *daler* denomination on the note must be debased; that is, that a larger number of paper *daler* and *mark* than of the original *daler* were necessarily required to purchase a *riksdaler* or a *skeppund* of copper and all other commodities. And because of the nature of commerce, it must be just as impossible to make the original *daler* and the present paper *daler* equal to each other, simply because they all bear the same denomination in *daler kmt* that they had in the last century, as it is for the same reason to make all copper *plåtar* and *daler* worth the same. To speak of an exchange rate of 70 or 80 *mark* or say that the *riksdaler* is sold at 18 *daler*, to debit the *Wäxel-Associerade*[18] many more paper *daler* than shown in the impression on the exported *plåtar* and yet to assert that a 6-*daler* note represents a 6-*daler plåt* and a nine-*daler* note one silver *riksdaler* is so incomprehensible that I cannot possibly fathom it. And still less to read an ordinance recently issued by the Sovereign Power, that the *riksdaler* is worth 70 *mark* or 17½ *daler* in banknotes, and yet deny that the tale-value of the paper *daler* has been raised.

§ 17

Since it has now been demonstrated that the tale-value of the paper *daler* has had to be raised by law, both because of the use made of it and from necessity, closer consideration should be given as to whether reducing it to its previous value would or would not be possible.

There is much to be read in the financial documents of former times about attempts of that kind, but not a single one of any significance turns out to have succeeded anywhere.

Rulers have on such occasions generally tipped their financial system from the frying-pan into the fire. Many such experiments have been carried out with the utmost rigour in Sweden, especially during the most recent periods.

King Charles IX[19] issued a proclamation in the severest terms, in which he ordered on pain of death that a Swedish *daler* or 4 *mark* should be worth 32 *öre*, while the *riksdaler* was worth 36 *öre*, but entirely in vain, as the *daler* was 50 per cent slighter in metal content and value. Futile efforts were likewise made during the minority of Queen Christina[20] in 1638 and by her herself in 1645, and the report of the Public Finance Board on the information called for by King Charles XI[21] regarding such devaluations of the currency, dated 13 March 1695, is especially remarkable. It states among other things: "It is absolutely incontestable that the better the coinage, the greater the advantage and value to him who possesses it, but whether it is feasible in the manner proposed, in this kingdom any more than elsewhere, to achieve stability, import silver and retain the good coin in the country while, on the other hand, we remain safe from the insidious introduction of false and worthless coin, one has good reason not only to doubt but to regard as absolutely impracticable. Past times have proved this, as when, in the time of King Charles IX, Swedish silver[22] was related to a *riksdaler* as 32 to 36, as well as in the time of Queen Christina in 1645, when 48 *öre* were to be worth the same as 1 *riksdaler*, or 3 *caroliner*, which could not be maintained for four years. What else could be expected now, if one were to undertake such a devaluation?"

Continual efforts were made to make 36 *öre* equal to 1 *riksdaler specie*, but when that was unsuccessful, the preference was for 48 *öre* to do so, and soon afterwards that 52 *öre* should correspond to 1 *riksdaler*, but nothing lasted until the currency was stabilized in its natural equivalence in 1681, making 1 *riksdaler specie* equivalent to a 6-*daler plåt*, or 64 *öre*, and in order most conveniently to escape from the whole muddle and not mix the various *daler* up with each other, the expedient of giving the inferior *daler* the name of *daler kmt* and the others *daler smt* was hit upon, which never meant, however, that the inferior *daler* was composed of copper and the better one of silver, for all *plåtar* are stamped *daler smt*, and the *daler* has often had as slight a content of silver as of copper, which shows that *daler kmt* in reality denotes neither silver nor copper but is a tale-value[23] that is applied in Sweden to the entire currency and is used in all commerce, although it is now asserted that it only denotes copper *plåtar*, as it is desired to have the banknotes exchanged for assets at the lowest tale-value, even if that were to cause the greatest harm to the country.

At the beginning of the seventeenth century there was thus as yet no more than one kind of *daler* in Sweden, but as the *daler* was increasingly debased in minting as against the *riksdaler*, it was found necessary to reckon with two kinds of *daler* and to call one "a copper coin" and the other "a silver coin". This *daler kmt* has now again been debased by 100 per cent, as has been demonstrated above; it must therefore become as impossible as then to make them equivalent, and the most natural remedy, to escape from the confusion into which we have fallen, will be either to entirely abandon the reckoning in *daler* or to differentiate between *daler* in copper coin and *daler* in banknotes.

At the beginning of our liberty,[24] much consideration was also given to lowering the tale-value, which had been raised in 1715, but an anonymous writer[25] showed in 1722, in an exhaustive essay entitled *Indefeasible Thoughts on Lowering and Raising the Value of the Swedish Coinage, Printed in Stockholm by Joh. Hind. Werner*,[26] how extremely hazardous any devaluation of the coinage would be. He expounds on the matter with such clarity and force that it can hardly be improved upon and simply needs to be applied to the crisis in which we now find ourselves.

He first of all shows how raising the value of the coinage had within six years increased the price of all commodities and trades in the kingdom by 100 or 150 per cent, demonstrates this with special reference to copper and iron, and says that *"since they have by now, through the raising of the value of the coinage, together with the paltry value of the token coins, deteriorated from their optimum and earlier condition and have been brought into a different one, they face risks and danger should a single further change be made in the coinage"*.

He deals with the metalworking industries, demonstrating how every branch thereof had been transformed along with the currency, how the cost of pig iron, ore, charcoal, haulage and freight, and the like had risen, and then says reflectively: "If changes were to be made in the currency, from the revaluation of which all this flows, then the very foundation of iron production will be affected. One could, for instance, imagine those works where iron cannot regularly be produced[27] for less than 35, 40, 45 *daler*, and where, by a devaluation of a currency, the price would fall to 30 or 35; will not works of that description then perish and the rest struggle on without making a profit until they eventually fall into decay?" "What concern", he continues, "do those have for the welfare of the kingdom who regard a devaluation of the currency as beneficial for the country despite the fact that the kingdom's most valuable treasure is thereby exposed to such a great risk?"

The alteration in the currency and in the value of commodities, he continues, "may arise from any cause whatsoever, yet it will become more and more enduring and by degrees irreversible. It is not so easy to alter what has been rising for so many years and because of so many circumstances.

"To reverse all the above-mentioned by law and compulsion is sooner said than done; in the case of a currency, all such things are easier to raise than to lower; those are more able to adapt themselves who are necessary to the operation of the works and who can with less injury leave the work undone or the materials unsold than the owner can on that account allow the whole works to come to a standstill."

He finally deals with all the disadvantages that follow from the raising of the value of the currency and shows how the major ones had already been removed and the remainder could also easily be remedied without exposing the welfare and survival of the kingdom and the citizens to extreme peril by a devaluation. But since commodity prices, purchases, productive occupations and metalworking industries have now adapted themselves to a level of *daler* that corresponds to the higher tale-value which the banknote has been shown to have, to attempt to lower it seems, to me at least, impossible and that too much is thereby set at risk on what may be an unreliable calculation.

§ 19[28]

In spite of all this, let us nonetheless for a moment accept the matter as feasible and briefly consider its implementation. There we may perhaps discover new evidence.

The honourable Estates of the Realm have brought to light how many thousand *skeppund* of *plåtar*, how many *riksdaler, caroliner, dukater*, and so forth have been withdrawn from the Bank, and how liberal the management of the Bank has been in other respects has also recently been publicized in print. Money has not dropped into the Bank from the sky, so it must belong to the subjects, and the funds of the Bank have inevitably been diminished to an incredible extent thereby.

As the value of the paper money depends on the amount of assets that the Bank is willing to exchange for it, and as the Bank is nowadays unwilling to consider a conversion rate of 70 *mark*, or 17½ *daler kmt*, per *riksdaler*, how strange must it not seem when it is said that banknotes will in a few years' time be converted at 36 *mark*, or that the Bank for every 9-*daler* banknote will then give the possessor of the note one *riksdaler specie* or a 9-*daler plåt*.

To my simple mind it seems that even if the Bank expected such a large income during these years by which it would be able to convert all banknotes at a rate of 36 *mark*, it would seem necessary, not least of all out of concern for the resources of the Bank when an annually falling conversion rate is being established, that it should redeem most of its notes now, at least from those who wish to remit bills of exchange, and do not receive the stipulated rate on the Stock Exchange, which would also, among other things, be the only way of implementing the royal ordinance that has been issued on this matter.

But to plan a conversion rate 100 per cent higher than the actual present value of the banknotes to which all economic enterprises have already adapted themselves, and to do so at a time when the resources of the Bank cannot sustain such a move, holding the Bank to its word appears to be such an audacious step that it could potentially endanger the capital of both the Bank and the realm itself and be a much too generous promise to the banknote capitalists.

Finally, in my view, there is an impracticality in the fact that such a plan of operation extends over such a long period of time, during which the inconvenience it causes may dissatisfy all producers, and thus the majority of people in the country, and there can hardly be any power that can guarantee its survival in the future, whereby all the effort invested in it could be wasted.

§ 20

The second thing that I have undertaken to prove is that such a reduction of the conversion rate or of the paper *daler* to 36 *mark is unfair*, first, because it is well known that only a small percentage of the notes have been issued by the Bank at a rate of 36 *mark* but most of them at 72 and 108 *mark*. Fairness, after all, requires that those who issue promissory notes and debentures should not be obliged to redeem them at a higher rate than that which they have actually been worth. That is, the possessor of a debenture is not entitled to demand from the issuing party a greater quantity of silver or copper than that for which it was made payable and which he could originally demand for it. Now, it is easy to calculate the quantity of silver at which a banknote issued at a rate of 72 *mark* was made payable, namely two 9-*daler* banknotes for one *riksdaler specie* and, at a rate of 108 *mark*, three 9-*daler* notes. If these banknotes are then redeemed by the Bank a few years later at the rate of one *riksdaler specie*, or its equivalent value, for each 9-*daler* note, then it is clear that the Bank will redeem its promissory notes with a quantity of silver two or three times larger than that for which they were actually made payable.

With regard to those banknotes that were issued at a lower or par rate,[29] however, fairness would require that they should likewise be redeemed in current coin. However, as they would now have passed from hand to hand over a long period of time, been mingled with the rest of the same *daler* denomination, and along with them declined in value, and as it likewise cannot be known in whose possession they now are, and if those who first drew them from the Bank had actually lost something on them or if they had lost a little of their value everywhere during their circulation among several hundred people, thus distributing the suffering almost evenly among the subjects, then the question is whether it is not far more equitable and more prudent for the survival of the Bank to redeem all banknotes on the basis on which the majority of them were issued than to establish another basis, whereby holders of banknote capital would be able to command two or three times the amount in silver capital that the banknotes had been worth when they came into their possession.

§ 21

When, second, one considers the manner in which our immense stock of banknotes has come into general circulation, namely by loans, partly to the Crown and partly also to private individuals, and as no one can say that either of them actually received larger loans from the Bank than what they could immediately have exchanged its notes for sums of *riksdaler* or valid bills of exchange, then it would also seem to be contrary to equity and common practice in all commerce and lending were they to be obliged, in the event that they did not possess promissory notes of the same Bank with which to repay the loan, which by the way they had not been obliged to do, and, against the laws of humankind or of nature, to repay their loans with a larger quantity of silver or commodities than they would have been able to obtain with those promissory notes of the Bank.

Third, if the Bank is held to be duty bound to apply such a level of redemption at a par rate, then the borrowers similarly are entitled to repay their loans at the same rate.

If that is denied, it is obvious that the funds of the Bank must become an innocent victim of the profit of a few, unless it is able to call its customers to account, in the same way as it is itself called to account by note-holders. But if that is conceded, then borrowers are likely to provide the clearest evidence to the general public of what kind of fairness they are dealt in this respect.

And as the Crown is the very greatest among them, having obtained most of the loans at a high rate for the war and having had to use them to purchase expensive bills of exchange on the Stock Exchange for the needs of the army, the nation itself should one day be entitled to ask how the Bank can demand in payment for the principal it has lent out more *riksdaler* than the Crown would have been able to purchase for its notes.

If the Estates have established an annually falling exchange rate – that is, an annual rise in the value of the circulating banknotes – then the borrower is entitled, in the same way as everyone else, to benefit from the rise in their value and can therefore in no way be obliged in the meantime to repay his loan in banknotes. It is only fair that the Bank should be content to receive payment in silver or *riksdaler* at the present high rate. For example, if my debt to the Bank were 10,000 *daler kmt* and I actually possessed such a large sum in banknotes, who could deny me the right, along with others, to wait for a par rate for these notes and instead repay my debt this year at a rate of 70 *mark* with 571 3/7 *riksdaler*? If I hold the banknotes until the rate reaches 36 *mark* a few years later, I shall be able to receive 1,111 1/9 *riksdaler* from the Bank for the same sum of banknotes for which I have paid it 571 3/7 *riksdaler*. The unfairness of this thus appears to be obvious.

§ 22

I now come to *the third thing* that was to be proved, namely that such a reduction of the increased tale-value of the banknotes is *unnecessary*. Once the reader and I are in agreement upon the simplest and most natural basis of finances, without which no financial system has been successful or able to endure, namely that everyone engaged in trade is entitled to receive for a negotiable commodity a cash payment corresponding to the value of that commodity, then everyone who is not in the grip of strange prejudices but exercises common sense will easily grasp that it is all the same to me whether the quantity of copper or silver that I am to receive for my commodity is described as 9 or 18 *daler smt* or *kmt* or in banknotes, as long as I know how much I will receive and actually ought to receive.

As far as banknotes as such are concerned, although they do not in themselves have any intrinsic value or contain any kind of metal that could constitute money, they do nonetheless acquire the value at which the Bank undertakes to redeem them, as long as the possessor is allowed, whenever he so wishes, to receive his property from the Bank in the same way as from a private individual, a right that every note-holder possesses in the case of all other European banks and without which neither a native nor a foreigner would feel that he had full security.

It would seem undeniable that the rise in the tale-value has caused the kingdom indescribable harm, owing to the fact that the prices of commodities were unsettled during the first few years and could not quickly adapt themselves to the rise but were paid, to the considerable harm of the productive occupations, in the old *daler* denomination, although it had in reality been debased.

In that way, all purchases and contracts incurred for a longer term were disrupted, the money-rents of the Crown were diminished and public officials lost part of their original salaries.

In this regard, however, one must distinguish carefully between what is *essentiale* and *accidentale* in a state. An inevitable part of the former is that people who live in societies must be able to support themselves by working and trading, without which the society cannot possibly be sustained. Reductions in the money-salaries of public officials and Crown rents are among the latter.

Both of these things need to be dealt with and attended to with care, though with the difference that we pay attention mainly to the former and in no way accept any financial proposals to remedy the latter that would at the same time upset the former.

§ 23

With regard to the productive enterprises, which constitute the soul of a society, it is common knowledge that wherever commerce and enterprise are at all free, not only have they in every respect adapted themselves to the present high tale-value but also, in view both of the even higher one to which the *daler* rose for a time and of the insecurity that every producer has experienced during the daily fluctuations between a higher and lower rate, the prices of most manufactures have risen far above that.

In this respect it is thus all the more uncalled for, with regard to the productive enterprises, to reduce the tale-value of the banknote still further, especially as they already suffer perceptibly from its present one.

And as far as the rights of the Crown to money are concerned, the shortfall that has arisen in that respect has probably already been met by appropriations or under other headings, or will, if urgently required, in a free state, be met in future by the subjects. In the same way, the public officials of the realm, who depend on money-salaries, are entitled to receive a remuneration corresponding to their original salaries but certainly not through the lowering of the tale-value, as that affects the productive occupations, which are the apple of the kingdom's eye.

I have tried to inform myself from older documents as to how such disadvantages were formerly remedied when the tale-value was raised.

To the same extent that the tale-value and the prices of commodities have been raised from time to time, the revenues of the Crown have also increased, sometimes under the same and sometimes under new headings, so that it has never been possible to regard that as a valid reason to lower the tale-value.

In 1695, King Charles XI asked this very question and requested a report thereon from the Public Finance Board, which on 13 March, among other things, stated the following with regard to it: "Nor is it really probable that His Majesty or the general public will suffer any loss in future even if also 1 *daler smt* will not be revalued at ⅔ of a *riksdaler*, as His Majesty will always have a free hand to increase taxes, customs duties, excise duties and other such things, when conditions and circumstances allow and permit it."

The same matter arose again in 1720 and the following years, on account of the raising of the tale-value that occurred in 1715.

The anonymous author whom I cited above says with particular reference to those who are on money-salaries: "Those who receive their remuneration in the form of grain etc. can benefit reasonably well from the increase, but not the others, as everything consumed as food and maintenance has to be paid for at the raised tale-value, for which it would be fair to compensate them by a salary increase proportionate to the raising of the tale-value. And while that disadvantage can be remedied, it would, on the other hand, be just as unfair to disregard the general and private welfare of the whole country in order to restore the value of the wages of the kingdom's officials, and no more fair than paying them the same wage in debased as in improved coin."

It has been proved above that when a financial system is simply based on realities, the matter is resolved, enterprise flourishes and neither native nor foreigner can make an undue profit from the other. It has also been proved that the tale-value of the paper *daler* is too high, as are, in accord therewith, the prices of all commodities. What, then, is the point of the hazardous measure of reducing the value[30] of this *daler*, disrupting the productive occupations and deliberately repeating all the disorders into which we happen, from carelessness, to have fallen?

§ 24

From what has already been said above, every thoughtful person will easily find how damaging such a basis for conversion or a falling rate must be to our public affairs.

I regard it as *harmful in the highest degree*, first, to *the Bank*, which has already extended its credit far beyond reason and would hereby fall victim to banknote capitalists who have exploited the state of the market, speculated in loans and properties, and increased their *daler* holdings many times over at the nation's expense. For example, if someone had bought himself a property worth 90,000 *daler kmt* in 1736 and had paid the purchase price at the then current rate with 10,000 *riksdaler specie* but had sold the same property in 1762, without any particular improvement, for 270,000 *daler* in banknotes, which at the then current rate of 108 *mark* corresponded exactly to the purchase price, a sum that he had made productive in the longer or shorter term by lending it against promissory notes in *daler kmt* but after the passage of six to eight years, when the rate would again be 36 *mark*, presented to the Bank for redemption, he must receive 30,000 *riksdaler specie* in exchange, or three times the original capital.

I then ask with good reason, first, is he entitled to such a large sum? and second, who in this case is making him wealthy? Is it not the Bank, whose banknotes in 1762 were not worth more than 10,000 *riksdaler* but when he has to redeem them will be worth 30,000 *riksdaler*, or three times as much?

Even if the Bank were as wealthy as water is deep, it is nevertheless the private money-capital of the subjects who have deposited it there in good faith that is plundered in this way, but when the Bank is moreover unable to redeem its promissory notes at a 70-*mark* rate, how hazardous must the harder rate of conversion then not become for the whole country?

Moreover, if I had borrowed from the Bank, say, 10,000 *daler*, and had reason to believe that the approved lowering of the rate could be implemented within a few years, it is obvious that I, as a rational person, although possessing this amount of capital in banknotes, would rather, at a rate of 70 *mark*, repay my debt in *riksdaler*, or, if there was no other solution, have the property I had put up as collateral sold at auction on behalf of the Bank and pay the Bank off in that way, as I would without fail be able to demand from the Bank 1,111 1/9 *riksdaler specie* for my banknotes after a few years, although I had paid 571 3/7 *riksdaler* for them this year, and I could likewise be sure that I would always be able to buy myself a better property for 1,111 1/9 *riksdaler* than for 571 3/7 *riksdaler*.

I now ask again: who is the loser here? The Bank.

I will probably be told: It is good when the Bank acquires valuables; it will be all the better able to convert its banknotes when they are one day presented for redemption. That is true, dear reader! but consider how much it will receive. Barely more than half of what it has to pay out. I therefore ask again: from where is the other half, or 540 *riksdaler*, to be taken? From the Bank's own funds; that is, from the properties of the citizens.

§ 25

Second, *I regard it as harmful to the Crown.*

As the Bank will thus one day have to redeem its banknotes in such a way for almost twice the sum in *riksdaler* as what they are now worth, and as the Crown is the greatest borrower of all from the Bank and is now quite unable to discharge its debt expeditiously either with banknotes or with valuables, the Bank will be compelled, when the time for repayment arrives, to pursue its claim on the Crown to the last farthing, at an undiminished number of *daler*.

The loss the Crown will have to bear from this can easily be understood. If the Crown had, in 1761, raised a loan from the Bank of 1 million *daler kmt* for the conduct of the Pomeranian war and used it to purchase, for the requirements of the army, valid bills in Hamburg *riksdaler* at a rate of 72 mark, the Crown would have received 55,555 5/9 *riksdaler* for it, but when the same million *daler* are to be repaid to the Bank at a 36-*mark* rate in six to eight years, it will require twice that amount in *riksdaler*, namely 111,111 1/9 Hamburg *riksdaler*, before the number of *daler* is reached that, by way of the Bank, will fall into the hands of banknote capitalists.

Some may say that there is no danger to the Crown. The Bank will surely forgive most of the debt, or at least not pursue repayment urgently. But consider, dear reader! The sums in banknotes that the Crown has borrowed from the Bank to the value of a few hundred *tunnor guld* are not now in the hands of the Crown but are dispersed within the country and abroad and must all be honoured by the Bank on exactly the same basis as all other banknotes. If that is to be done at a 36-*mark* rate, the Bank has to pay out 1 *riksdaler specie*, or the equivalent value, for each 9-*daler* note, but if the Bank releases its claim on the Crown in the manner indicated above, either in part or in its entirety, it will have received little or nothing in payment from the Crown in return for a few hundred *tunnor guld*, yet it must, in a destitute condition, pay twice the amount in cash for those notes to the note-holders compared with what the notes were previously worth in someone's possession.

§ 26

Third, *the lowering of the exchange rate is harmful to private individuals* who borrow from the Bank and creates significant inequality between one subject of the Realm and another.

For while everyone else who has holdings in banknotes sees them increased by almost 100 per cent by the fall in the rate, those who have borrowed from the Bank will lose if they are obliged to repay their loans with banknotes amounting to the same number of *daler* that they owe the Bank.

I willingly admit that some of them have in times past acquired large properties by speculation with the help of loans from the Bank and therefore need not be pitied at all, but one should also know that this sort of luck has not befallen all borrowers. I know of many who have mortgaged their sole, properly acquired property to the Bank and then used the capital thus acquired to purchase another property at a time when the prices for them were at their highest.

Few properties yield a rent higher than what is annually absorbed by interest on the loan; when the principal has to be paid back, for which purpose the borrower is obliged to sell his new property, although its price has according to the exchange rate fallen to less than half its value in *daler*, he is unable, with the value of the new property, to pay more than half of the sum that he had used to purchase it and must therefore use his old property instead, which, if it is of the same value as the new one, will be wholly used up in repaying his debt to the Bank in *daler*, and he who may have innocently and by consent of the Sovereign Power entered into this transaction is driven away from all of it, like the sparrow from the ear of grain, simply because of the lowering of the exchange rate.

The same lamentable fate also inevitably awaits all private debtors throughout the kingdom who happen to have taken loans or bought on credit when the exchange rate was high and have not yet been able to pay off their creditors. What lamentation will there not be on that account among our debt-burdened manufacturers, merchants, ironmasters, farmers, craftsmen and all poor people, whether they are in debt to a native or to a foreigner, when, apart from interest charges, they have to pay their creditors twice as much as they have actually borrowed. While the exchange rate was rising, it mostly affected the capitalists; but they also had the strength to absorb the blow, whereas on the contrary now, when the rate is to be forced down, it is the poor producer in the state that is affected, and with him the essential strength of the state. There can be few these days who are free from debt, so that when the pain begins to be felt generally, we shall undoubtedly hear the voice of the nation concerning the plan of operation that many at present, out of ignorance, either instinctively approve of or look upon with indifference.

It will never do to be insensitive to the misfortunes of fellow citizens.

§ 27

Fourth, *such a financial system must also be harmful to the subjects of the Realm in general.*

Under the second point it has already been shown how the Bank, in the light of this conversion, must inevitably call in its loans from the Crown and what the Crown will suffer thereby. Let us now consider from where all this is to be taken.

Is it not the subjects who are compelled to provide all this for their denuded and despoiled Crown by means of new taxes and appropriations? But as everything that the subjects are able to accumulate by sweat and toil in order to assist the Crown is drawn into the Bank and from the Bank into the hands of the bank-note capitalists, the willingness to make such contributions cannot but be diminished.

The future will one day persuade us, however, of that which few are yet likely to believe, namely that unless the siphons that extend between the Crown and the Bank and the Bank and private individuals are soon cut off, it will be a sheer impossibility for the Crown or the Bank to recover, even if one were to concentrate there everything that exists in the country, for there are always priests of Baal who come by secret passages at night to consume the sacrifice, and before you know where you are, the Crown and the Realm will fade away and succumb to an incurable consumptive illness, the Bank will flaunt beautiful rooms and a large staff, comprehensive accounts and empty vaults, and a few private individuals will walk away from there stuffed and wealthy.

§ 28

Former kings of Sweden, when the Crown had fallen deeply into debt, raised the tale-value in order to facilitate the payments of the Crown to its creditors and of the subjects to the Crown. With what reason, then, in the country's present state of destitution and when the debt of the Crown is many times larger than it has ever been, does one wish to strive to lower it? Or must such a contrary measure not also have a contrary effect? And how will subjects and Crown be able to survive it?

Fifth, *it is harmful for all productive occupations and enterprises.*

This affects the soul of a country, and if that is harmed, everything else will be overturned, and public officials will then have to chase the shadow of their original salaries for a good long while.

All productive occupations need loans, and how few are not those producers who can do without them? Some trades require a loan for a longer and others for a shorter term. I have been amazed to hear many well-disposed people assert that no one needs a loan for much longer than one year and am therefore obliged to convince my reader of the opposite.

How many a farmer, working a poor homestead, with many small children and disabled parents, is not obliged to take a loan from his creditor for as long as 12 to 20 years before he is able to acquit himself of his debt? When an impecunious man settles in a wilderness to clear a new farmstead, will he be able to repay his loan in a year? No! scarcely within 12 or 20 years.

Tar-distilling, which is also a rural industry, probably requires loans for six to seven years, shipbuilding for four to five years. If anyone wants to set up factories, a textile mill, dyeworks, tobacco factory or anything else, establish new ironworks, hammer-mills, foundries, manufacturing works or extend, relocate or improve any of the above, it is clear that it will take several years to set them in order with buildings, working materials, labourers, and so on, but far more before they yield so much that, apart from the necessary working capital of the establishment and the owner's own consumption, they will show a surplus equal to the initial loan, which does not happen to some enterprises for as long as 30 or 40 years.

The situation is the same with commerce.

What will enable a beginner to start up in commerce? Is it not a loan? Will he be able to repay it after the first year? Would he not even under the most favourable conditions need to make use of it for several years in order to use the profit to expand his enterprise? How often does it not happen that he is left with the commodity on his hands for several years? Or how far will one actually get in commerce unless one merchant can give another a loan, for longer or shorter periods?

Everyone is then likely to discover how indispensable loans are in all productive occupations, for longer or shorter periods, and that those who deny that fact have considered neither the multiple loans with which many manufacturing works have been established and are currently being run, nor those that at a future time, with money still scarcer, will be found even more indispensable.

We shall therefore now reflect further on how those who possess sums of banknotes will be able, with a falling exchange rate, to lend them profitably on this basis of conversion or producers be able to make use of their loans.

Let us therefore first suppose that the ordinance issued during this Diet on the recommendation of the Secret Committee regarding the concluding of iron contracts in *riksdaler* were also to extend to all other loans. What incentive could the lender then have to advance loans, when he knows that within a few years the exchange rate will be 36 *mark*?

For example: if a young trader should request a loan of 9,000 *daler kmt* for six years at the usual interest rate and for that reason wished to set his promissory note, according to the current exchange rate, at 514 2/7 *riksdaler*, would the capitalist then not be a fool if he laid out his money for a paltry interest, when he knows that at the end of six years, at a 36-*mark* exchange rate, he will be able for the same 9,000 *daler* to draw 1,000 *riksdaler* from the Bank?

If the borrower cannot obtain a loan on that basis, however, but is compelled to give the lender his promissory note for 9,000 *daler kmt* to be paid after six years, together with a lawful interest, it is clear that if he has used it for any purpose at all this year, for instance to purchase bills of exchange, he will not obtain in return for it more than the above-mentioned 514 2/7 *riksdaler*, nor commodities for more than the same amount of *riksdaler*. He may make whatever other use he likes of this loan of his, yet 514 2/7 *riksdaler* is the actual total of his loan. I pass over both the interest and everything else that might in any way obscure the matter. Six years have passed, the interest has been paid, there remains only to repay the principal or to redeem his bond for 9,000 *daler*, but in the meantime the rate has fallen to 36 *mark*; he offers his creditor the 514 2/7 *riksdaler* he has received from him, but the latter will not surrender the promissory note until he receives 1,000 *riksdaler*, and he is entitled to do so, as he could have insisted on receiving that from the Bank for this banknote capital of his. How commerce and productive occupations can pay their way in such a manner, however, when, in addition to the interest, after the passage of a few years I will have to pay my creditor twice the amount of *riksdaler* that I can at present receive in exchange for its notes, is impossible to comprehend. If the productive occupations can endure this, then I can certainly endure it. All those productive occupations that do not over a few years, together with the interest and the subsistence of the entrepreneur, make a profit of over 100 per cent must thus perish.

Whatever period one may select, within which the exchange rate is to be 36 *mark*, the argument is not changed in the least thereby, and if the loan were not made repayable for more than two years but the exchange rate were to move to 36 *mark* within eight years, the same losses will in the end be incurred in all productive occupations, though over a longer period, which would be too complicated to explain.

Dear reader! such things would necessarily happen if the methods of lowering the exchange rate could be sustained long enough to reach 36 *mark*, but as I regard that as impossible, as the productive occupations will be compelled to break out one way or another rather than let themselves all be instantly suffocated, such a chaos is likely to arise in the productive occupations and among the possessors of money as no one can foresee and which, at a certain turning-point, could harm both sides far more than the complete collapse of the exchange rate for bills.

§ 29

Sixth, *the lowering of the exchange rate impedes the negotiability of all ready coin as long as any banknotes are in circulation.*

Everyone is likely to agree that our financial measures have as their chief purpose to bring good coin back into circulation among us, as it is undeniable that while the rate has been unstable, good coin has completely disappeared. But whether such a purpose can ever be achieved by this means is something worth reflecting on.

If 1 *riksdaler specie* had moved directly from 9 to 27 *daler* and then remained there, the *riksdaler* could afterwards have circulated just as well as before, along with the banknotes, even if there had been a drastic reduction in the value of the banknotes. But while the rate was fluctuating, so that I could purchase one *riksdaler* for two 9-*daler* notes one year but for three the next year, and then back again to two, although the *riksdaler* is and remains the same, there was no possibility of using it or any other coin with an intrinsic value in circulation along with the banknotes, which were thrown up and down by the exchange rate.

The coins will be regarded by the enterprises partly as a yardstick by which the value of other commodities is measured, partly also as commodities with which the others are paid for. Whichever way one looks at them, they can never flourish alongside the banknotes if the value of the latter is unstable. The *riksdaler* is and remains a constant yardstick, as long as it contains a certain quantity of silver. The banknote, however, as has already been shown at the beginning, is, when subject to a falling exchange rate, like an ell-measure that is extended every year by a few inches yet is still called an ell. As absurd as it is to use two ell-measures in a retail shop, one constant and the other expanding, which must cause indescribable confusion, is it also to use a stable and at the same time a falling tale-value in commerce.

If we regard the coins as a commodity with which we obtain other commodities by exchange, as they really ought to be, in which regard the banknote also contains as much silver, copper or gold as the Bank or anyone else is willing to pay for it, though the Bank or bill-dealers are willing to pay for one and the same sum of 9,000 *daler* in banknotes 514 2/7 *riksdaler* this year and a few years later 1,000 *riksdaler*, then I ask with good reason what the true value of the banknotes is or how *riksdaler* and other assets can flourish alongside banknotes when the distrust among the general public regarding the successful outcome of the new measure cannot be dispelled.

When we now recall that several *tunnor guld* annually enter the Bank, that the stock of banknotes gives rise to speculation during a falling exchange rate and has to be withdrawn from productive occupations and enterprises, as was demonstrated above, and finally that sums of ready money, for the reasons just given, cannot relieve the shortage or be profitably employed in the enterprises as long as there are any banknotes, then it will be obvious to every sensible person what a shortage of money, without any genuine shortage, what stagnation in commerce and productive occupations, and, finally, what poverty and distress all that must give rise to in the country.

It is argued against such a stagnation in the productive occupations that, as long as the circulating stock of banknotes is much greater than it was five or six years ago and the commodity prices remain high, the productive occupations cannot possibly be stifled by any shortage of money, which would also be true if (N.B.) the money could be profitably circulated. As it is removed from circulation, however, by a financial measure such as lowering the exchange rate, such a hope, which is already refuted by actual experience, is soon likely to reveal its fragility even more.

§ 30

Seventh, *such a lowering of the exchange rate will eventually become dangerous, with regard to foreigners*, who now hold considerable amounts of our bank deposit-receipts, the debentures of the Paymaster General's Office, with the acceptances of the Bank, or the bonds of private individuals in *daler kmt*, all of which, after the passage of a certain number of years, will be paid for with twice the number of *riksdaler* when the rate has reached 36 *mark* compared to what they actually represented at the time of issue, whereby foreigners, apart from the interest, will claim 100 per cent of our assets in return for nothing, causing an irremediable loss to the country.

In addition, this opens the door to foreign merchants for a new form of speculation, during such a scarcity of money as must exist among us, that of investing considerable sums of *riksdaler* in our trading houses against bonds made payable in *daler kmt*, at the current exchange rate, as they will within a few years, in the same manner as described above, gather in twice the number of *riksdaler* for their promissory notes before the sum of *daler* is fully repaid.

That such speculation does occur is all the less to be doubted, as it has in fact already frequently been engaged in previously, although at great risk, when the exchange rate has suddenly shot up. Foreigners risk far less if the Government itself lays out such a road, and if the shortage of money compels us to seek loans, even if they were to be provided on the harshest terms.

§ 31

There has been much talk recently of the utility and necessity of loans of silver by the Bank for the conversion of the banknotes, so that before I present my own proposal for remedying our finances, I should also comment on this matter.

To purchase silver for the minting of *riksdaler* in exchange for the fund of *plåtar* deposited in the Bank or any other negotiable commodity that is held by or will in future be paid into the Bank would, in my opinion, be quite effective in getting the silver currency into circulation, provided (N.B.) that the banknotes are given a fixed value that will remain unchanged against silver, for otherwise it will be of no benefit, but to borrow silver is directly contrary to the aim, which is the *reduction and conversion of the stock of banknotes.*

The borrowing of silver can be carried out in three ways.

The first is to raise a foreign loan against the bonds of the Bank, to which annual interest has to be transferred; for example: if the Bank had raised a loan of 400,000 *riksdaler* from a foreign bank, at 4 per cent, for the conversion of the banknotes, that loan would cost our Bank 16,000 *riksdaler* in annual interest or, at a 72-*mark* rate, 288,000 *daler kmt*, that is, almost 1 *tunna guld*. Against that the Bank has issued its note or debenture to the same number of *riksdaler* that is regarded by the Bank as equivalent to the aforementioned sum of *riksdaler*.

Should that foreign loan remain unpaid for 12½ years, the interest will already amount to 200,000 *riksdaler*, or half the capital, but if the kingdom should be unable to pay it off until after 25 years, even if the loan in the meantime were to be moved from one bank to another, the foreigners will have doubled their amount of *riksdaler* by such a loan, at Sweden's expense.

Whether such things increase or reduce the stock of silver in Sweden, help or hinder conversion and consequently benefit or harm the finances of the country does not appear to require further proof. One may in other respects adduce whatever considerations one wishes and accuse those who dislike the loans of either ignorance or ill will, yet plain truths can never be disputed or change their nature, for they are immutable.

Note further, dear reader! What has the Bank in such a case given foreigners as a surety for this stock of silver? Nothing but its note or promissory note for a certain term of repayment, based on the credit of the Realm and the guarantee of the Estates of the Realm. What are our bank deposit-receipts other than the bonds of the Bank? If the Bank has now been able to provide some new bonds, which had not previously possessed any value, with a security equal to that of silver or *riksdaler*, then it is obvious that the Bank could by the same means far more easily have maintained its old bonds at the same value that they had already more or less possessed previously. What, then, is the advantage of such a measure?

First, the stock of banknotes is thereby increased by 400,000 *riksdaler*, that is, at a 72-*mark* rate, by 24 *tunnor guld*, until that can be converted into an equivalent sum of banknotes.

Second, the Bank and the finances of the Realm lose thereby annually quite unnecessarily 16,000 *riksdaler* in interest, which could have been entirely avoided if the Bank had stabilized the value of its old promissory notes in the same way as it has done with that of the new one; for whereas it has to pay for the new one, it annually receives interest from the borrowers of the old ones, in consequence of which it has had to use these 16,000 *riksdaler* every year to redeem more banknotes, which must now disappear.

Third, once the conversion of these 24 *tunnor guld* has taken place, the stock of banknotes is just as large, and the Bank is just as much at risk at the expiry date of its promissory note of being descended upon by foreigners as it otherwise would have had to fear being descended upon by Swedes.

Fourth, if the Bank expects by the expiry date of its large bond to be in possession of such a large amount of silver as needs to be paid out to redeem it, why are Swedish subjects not immediately assured of that? I am sure that they are not in any way more mistrustful than foreigners, as long as they are offered the same security.

The second way is that the silver loan can also be provided by native merchants or capitalists, if they are tempted by advantageous terms to accumulate silver and, in exchange for bonds, to make deposits of it in the Bank.

Exactly the same applies to this loan as to the former one, for what are these bonds other than new banknotes, which, whoever possesses them, always retain the same value against silver, provided that the Bank does not refuse payment at the prescribed time?

The loss to the Bank will in both cases be precisely the same, the only difference being that in the former a foreigner but in the latter a Swede draws assets from the Bank.

If these bonds have an equivalent value against silver, which they necessarily must have before anyone will risk his silver for them, then I ask again: why, then, can the other bonds of the Bank, for the redemption of which such a loan is regarded as necessary, not be given the same form and security as the new ones? Would it not then have been possible to dispense with the loan altogether and save the interest?

The third way to obtain silver for the Bank for the conversion of the banknotes is to buy up silver for the minting of *riksdaler* with the banknotes that come into the Bank.

When one knows what a banknote is, namely the Bank's bond for the sum that the possessor of the note can claim in the Bank, one will readily understand that when the Bank, in whatever manner, has redeemed its promissory note but immediately issues it again or a new one for an equivalent sum, that is in itself nothing but a new loan, with the difference from the two preceding methods of borrowing that the Bank in this case avoids paying the interest for the borrowed sum of silver, which in the two previous cases it has to acknowledge.

Nor is the stock of banknotes diminished in this case. Here the banknote loses its value; that is to say, the silver *lod* comes to represent a larger number of *daler* as soon as the Bank begins to purchase large amounts of silver with notes. In short: turn the matter over any way you like, it is still much ado about nothing.

§ 32

Having sought in this way to fulfil the first three parts of the promise I gave at the beginning, it is now incumbent upon me to finally lay my own simple proposal before the eyes of my attentive reader. In so doing I shall, no less than in the preceding, attempt to disentangle the matter from all the complex circumstances that would otherwise, on such a topic, make the proposal obscure or ambiguous.

For that purpose I will first refer to what was said at the outset concerning a natural financial system, namely that everyone should be entitled to receive for a negotiable commodity a cash payment corresponding to it in value and that no one should be importuned to be satisfied with a mere stamp or illusions.

As paper money is almost the only currency among us that does not in itself possess any intrinsic value and has now undergone such manifold changes for the reasons stated above, it is in my opinion necessary to clearly elucidate, first, *how large a quantity of fine silver will be calculated for each paper* daler; *that is, how many* mark *and* daler *of the paper money will be reckoned against 1* riksdaler specie, *which must (N.B.) be adjusted to the resources of the Bank but principally to the approximate value that the commodities currently represent and on which most productive occupations are based, which should be established once and for all and for which the Bank should undertake to sooner or later redeem its notes with silver or negotiable commodities.*

As for the monetary system during the last century, both on account of the instability of the copper coinage against the silver coinage and of the promissory notes of the Bank[31] that were already current at that time, which were even then inferior in value to all other coin and in the same way as now caused the exchange rate to rise because the Bank was not able to offer prompt payment for them, Count Gustaf Bonde[32] says in his *Indefeasible Thoughts on the Instability of the Coinage*[33] at that time, dated Stockholm, 28 October 1664: "That it was first of all necessary that the coinage should remain at a fixed price, so that as it is paid out by one person it will also be accepted by the other, and it causes less confusion and harm when it is reckoned at a fixed one (even if that exceeds its worth) than when one is unsure of its value." He then adds something concerning the *res nummaria*[34] in Rome and from that concludes the following: "From this and much more one can assess and deduce the necessity of the coinage in every kingdom having a fixed value and being maintained at that, if one wishes to avoid the ruin of one's subjects, the oppression of the pauper, who, due to his destitution and great distress, has to accept what he is given and spend it again, at whatever level the rich man will accept.

"It is for that reason necessary," he continues, "should one wish to avoid the punishment of God, that we enact such things in our dear fatherland, especially when one considers the petitions and laments concerning this confusion that were presented by the Estates to the Government during the last Diet, or else we risk God's vengeance for the sighs of the poor man and ultimately an upheaval in the kingdom, the suppression of which, once the fire were lit, would not only turn out to be difficult but also risky.

"Furthermore, to demonstrate its harmfulness in commerce and so forth is excessive and superfluous, as no one is likely to have any doubts about this any longer."

Towards the end of the same treatise he says further: "As all this", namely, what he had proposed for the maintenance of the Bank, "must be applied to everyone, on the authority and with the guarantee of the Government, it would not seem inadvisable for the Government to inform itself about the condition of the Bank in respect of debits and credits and then plan and appoint its administration as required, in order that such a salutary enterprise should not again fall into such a maze and hazard and then find itself in circumstances when public opinion may not be as tolerant as it is now."

How large this quantity of silver should really be, or how many *daler* and *mark* ought to be calculated for 1 *riksdaler specie*, I would not set out in detail, but I venture to assert that if the exchange rate is reduced below 70 *mark* per *riksdaler*, the productive occupations will suffer a terrible shock and the Bank be severely affected, and to now raise it slightly above 70 *mark* would be to unnecessarily raise the tale-value and reduce the real value of the sums of banknotes. I am therefore of the opinion that, in order to avoid fractional arithmetic, it would be best to establish the rate at 72 *mark*, as the net *mark* and *daler* denominations of 1715 would then be doubled, and the commodities will also be virtually in balance with that, or rather be based on a higher than a lower exchange rate.

§ 33

I said that the value of the banknotes should be determined once and for all against the *riksdaler* or the silver and therefore never be lowered or raised, as long as any notes are still in circulation, if productive occupations are to have any security with regard to banknotes, but many may regard such a stabilization of the value of the banknote as both unfair and impracticable.

With regard to the former, it has been made clear that they would never otherwise enter into circulation or serve as money, but concerning the latter I wish to reply here specifically to the objections used to show its impracticability.

It is said to be futile as long as the Bank cannot undertake to redeem all banknotes simultaneously, for in the meantime the drawer may increase the value of his bill of exchange and the merchant that of his commodity. Such things can be done when a stock of banknotes is increasing but not when it is decreasing. Experience all too clearly refutes that, for although the Bank has done nothing since the Diet of 1762 but prevent new loans and has accepted banknotes both as principal and interest, the exchange rate has nonetheless spontaneously, and in advance of the ordinance on a 70-*mark* rate, fallen from 108 to 73 or 75 *mark*; though whether that rapid fall has harmed or benefited the productive occupations there is no time to examine now.

If it was possible for that to occur spontaneously, and before the Bank had laid down how much silver or copper each *daler* should represent, would one be any more certain now, were that to happen, that they would remain stable?

If the above-mentioned loans of silver were going to be raised, I ask: what would the Bank then have provided as a surety for the silver? Nothing except the guarantee of the Estates of the Realm and the bonds issued by the Bank on the basis of it. If such loans could be procured, would not the bonds together with the guarantee have been as valid to the lender as the sums of silver he had provided, although he would not be able to convert them into cash for several years? Undoubtedly, for otherwise he would not have exchanged any silver for them.

If these bonds of the Bank can represent a fixed quantity of silver without any deductions, what then prevents its bank deposit-receipts, which are also nothing but bonds, from representing the same amount, provided that the Bank, on the basis of its calculations, lays down a certain period, or within how many years all banknotes should be converted, each *daler* for instance by one-eighteenth of a *riksdaler*, the Estates of the Realm again guarantee the security and convertibility of the banknotes, and possessors of the notes, whether native or foreign, are informed how, if the Bank does not voluntarily make payment before then, they are to look for their security in the Bank's mortgage funds by means of taking legal action?

Once that has been done, all banknotes will, despite being made payable in *daler kmt*, immediately be equivalent to *riksdaler* notes and enter into all domestic and foreign commerce as convertible sums of silver, with little or no agio; for it is all the same to a native or foreigner whether he has the silver in his possession or the banknote for which he can with certainty sooner or later demand silver.

But as long as they had not been made payable for a certain quantity of silver or copper, as was demonstrated above, no term had been set for their redemption in hard cash and still less any method been devised by which the note-holder could reclaim from the Bank the money that he had deposited there, it was less surprising that they had fallen so much in value than, on the contrary, that they have been able to preserve as much of it as still remains.

In order to implement this measure, which is the most essential one, the Bank, however low its resources may be, could soon give an undertaking to those who wish to have their banknotes converted and redeem them either with bar-silver[35] or *riksdaler*, *plåtar* or *slantar*, reckoning the copper (N.B.) not by its stamp but its weight, according to the value of copper against silver, as a commodity, for otherwise the whole scheme is doomed to fail.

In doing so, the Bank risks nothing. The current coin enters into circulation, and the banknotes gain general credit and are by degrees withdrawn.

In England we saw an example of this some time ago when the credit of the London Bank's[36] notes began to decline. Although the stock of current coin represented barely one-tenth of its notes, it was made subject to conversion by everyone, of which a number of people initially took advantage, but that soon ceased, as the banknotes circulated much more vigorously and the Bank regained its credit.

In the Swedish Bank, into which a considerable part of the stock of notes annually flows as principal and interest and the notes are readily used in circulation, as long as they possess complete security in the manner indicated above, the additional portion that could be presented for conversion will be of little significance. And even if the Bank were to be emptied and be obliged to periodically suspend conversion until new funds could be accumulated from import duties, taxes on copper and iron-forging, etc., none of that would make any difference as long as the basis of conversion remains permanently the same. But unless this happens, the finances of the country will in future be irremediable, the Bank devoid of security and the previously stated harmful consequences inescapable.

Once the Estates of the Realm have established this and the Joint Banking Committee has laid down the manner of its implementation, little else should remain to the Bank than the book-keeping required to administer it.

One would then also hope that the necessary secrets of the Bank would be few or none and directors more or less superfluous, or at least deprived of their ability to interfere in matters of state security in the kingdom.

A good thing never needs to be concealed, but if the matter is dubious, it is most easily recognized by its secrecy.

§ 34

Second, *all coinage struck from now on should consist of* riksdaler specie *or subdivisions of them, of the same fineness and weight as our Swedish* riksdaler, for not only is the copper lost in the inferior alloys but the fine silver contained in the inferior types of coin also loses some of its value thereby. The silver coins struck hitherto may nonetheless freely enter into general circulation, but they should be spent and accepted according to the proportion of fine silver they contain in relation to *riksdaler specie*, of which official notification could be given in a publication as well as in almanacs.

The copper coin may well, for lack of silver coin, be used in the same way as before in commerce and enterprise, though not according to its stamp but rather to its weight and the price of copper abroad in relation to silver, for which purpose the Bank, which is certainly best informed about the price of copper, could annually present to His Royal Majesty, on the basis of its trade in copper, a calculation of the relationship of copper to the *riksdaler*, that is, how many *slantar*, 6- to 9-*daler plåtar*, etc. will that year be recognized as equalling 1 *riksdaler specie*, according to which the Crown should accept them in all its tax-collecting activities, and no account should be taken in that regard of the minting tax or minting charges, as these always provide an opportunity for some new acts of fraud, but all such matters should for the benefit of the country be compensated for by the Crown or the Bank.

However, in order that the Bank's calculation should be verifiable by the subjects generally, not only should they be free to pay their land rents to the Crown in whatever coin they wish, but in all private trade an agio should also be allowed between copper and the silver coinage, according to whether the price of copper is rising or falling, which can never occur, however, if the calculation of the Bank is unbiased.

Should the Bank wish to redeem notes with *plåtar* or *slantar*, that should also be done on exactly the same basis, for only then, but by no other means, will the subjects enjoy security for their property, nor should the confusion that arises in the copper account in relation to silver be equated with security, which will never be achieved in any other way. I also believe that these small inconveniences would induce the subjects to individually exchange their copper for silver and thereby attract silver coin from abroad, for on the other hand I fear that the procurement of such large quantities from abroad, which the Bank will have to undertake in order to replace the copper with silver, is likely to raise the price of silver and cause the Bank a considerable loss.

Whatever happens in this respect, however, it is of the utmost importance *that the copper coinage should in no way be fixed against a certain number of* riksdaler, for then we will fall into the same chaos as we did in the seventeenth century.

§ 35

Third, *all loans, purchases, contracts or whatever transactions they may be that were initiated before 1757 and have not yet been settled, whether between the Bank and the Crown or either of these and private individuals, or else between private individuals themselves, ought to be examined and settled at a 36-*mark *rate*, though in such a way that no cases that have already been settled may on any pretext whatsoever be reopened and disputed. *But all later transactions which are still current should be honoured at the exchange rate that applied when they were entered into,* and in order that no dispute or lawsuit concerning these may arise, all the rates of subsequent years should be reduced to an average for each year and be notified by an ordinance and prescribed as a basis for settlements in future years, which should in particular be observed in the case of all contracts for labour and loans that are still in force.

This will almost inevitably meet with strong opposition from some, but the matter is based entirely on the nature of a correct financial system. For if all commerce ought to be based on hard cash and it is precisely the exchange rate that denotes how much real value the agreed sum of *daler* represented at the time, then nothing is fairer than that each individual may benefit from the exchange rate when settling a transaction.

It can hardly be denied that some variation will occur in the payments due to this, and all speculation in order to gain by a rising or falling rate will at once become impossible, but should one abandon the whole game for the sake of a few inconveniences? The harm has been done. To remedy everything is impossible, but to leave it in its former disorder will be fatal to the body of the kingdom and to liberty. To fear some complications and thereby lose the security that is vital to all enterprises would be like allowing a ship that has sprung a leak to founder rather than face the trouble of pumping and attempting to save the passengers and crew.

In order to avoid many small payments, transactions entered into since 1757 amounting to less than 10,000 *daler kmt* could all be settled at an exchange rate established in the manner suggested under the first point.

§ 36

Fourth, *the payments into the Bank should as far as possible be proportioned to the period within which the Bank undertakes to convert all its notes and should be accepted in any kind of coin, gold, silver, copper or notes that may be most convenient to borrowers, but (N.B.) all on the bases outlined under the first and second points,* whereby the Bank will more quickly obtain valuables with which to redeem its notes from others and can thus with greater certainty maintain its credit.

§ 37

Fifth, because our high exchange rate has also inevitably arisen from the presence of many remitters and few drawers, and the reason for that is clearly to be found in our recent commercial regulations, it would be necessary to reduce the number of the former and increase that of the latter.

For that reason, all retail traders, grocers, manufacturers and craftsmen who need to import some commodities and raw materials, as well as noblemen and other persons of rank, ought to be permitted, under the Commercial Ordinance of 22 March 1673, § 5, to export and import commodities, either wholesale, individually or in companies and on commission and a few also to trade in bills of exchange, fit out ships and so forth.

These are the few and simple means that will undoubtedly, without artificial and expensive measures and great trouble, improve the decayed financial system of the country. Their equity can hardly be disputed, and their execution is as simple as the proposals themselves.

§ 38

In case the reader should hear this scheme denounced as threatening a bankruptcy that would unsettle the kingdom's credit and be dishonourable for a country, he should not allow himself to be intimidated by that but quietly reflect on the matter. I merely wish to state with regard to this:

First, that it has already been demonstrated above, with arguments, that the denominations *daler*, *mark* and *öre* have not for several centuries past, either for copper or silver coins, denoted any specific quantity of silver or copper that one would now fully accept as finite, but have undergone the very greatest transformations, to the harm of the nation.

There cannot thus be any demonstrable danger of a bankruptcy here, as the *daler* in *slantar* and the paper *daler* will, at a 72-*mark* rate, remain virtually identical, unless one wishes to similarly describe the minting of *slantar* as a four-ninths bankruptcy, which is nonetheless authorized by our monetary regulations.

Second, if this were a case of bankruptcy, then it has already been shown that it is by no means the first one in Sweden but that such cases have occurred from as far back as the ninth century to the present time, when a *mark* in coin has been devalued from 16 *lod* of fine silver, at the exchange rate now stabilized at 70 *mark*, to approximately 1/35th of a *lod*, and the *daler* in the same proportion. If bankruptcy is to be avoided and the credit of the country to be maintained by lowering the tale-value, the question will be when one ought to begin: in the year 800, 1600, 1670, 1715 or 1760? Unless we start with the first-mentioned year, I shall, with precisely the same arguments that are used now, prove the bankruptcy. People may respond to me: we are not responsible for what happened before, as long as we take care that it does not happen in our time; and I intend to give the same reply to those who would accuse us of causing a bankruptcy, because that is something for which the Estates of the Realm now assembled are not responsible and have no part in, for already long ago and before the Diet of 1761 the tale-value had been raised in all commerce, while *riksdaler specie* were not purchased for less than 18 *daler* but well above that during the following years.

For whatever reason this may have happened, in accordance with or against the law, owing to the Government's own regulations, as was shown above, or to usurers, it is nonetheless known throughout Europe that it really did happen and that all commodity prices have already adjusted themselves to it and, if that were disturbed, would fall into a similar but more painful confusion than that in which they had been during the rising exchange rate, when a high *daler* denomination encouraged producers to work hard, whereas its fall will on the contrary have a stifling effect on every kind of trade.

The nation undoubtedly desires to escape from the chaos once and for all by means of the prudent and well-judged measure of the Government, with the least possible impact on the country, but by no means necessarily to restore the financial system, by a long and hazardous process, to the same condition in which it was established in 1715, as it has not been determined whether that particular change was the best one or whether lowering the tale-value, which had often been attempted before but had always upset the productive occupations and never before proved feasible, could now be implemented.

Third, no one will now suffer more from this except those who have for 20-odd years allowed their holdings of banknotes to lie idle. He who has saved some assets of value retains their full value, and those who now hold the largest sums of banknotes are certainly those least entitled to have them converted at 36 *mark*, as they themselves have after all obtained them for half or a third of their value from others when the rate was high, and I do not understand by what kind of patriotism one can defend the practice of paying foreigners, after the passage of a few years, for all banknotes, debentures of the Paymaster General's Office and all promissory notes of private individuals, which were issued at a high rate of exchange and made payable in *daler kmt*, two or three times as many *riksdaler* as those foreigners had obtained them for, all of which would largely be avoided if the banknote were once and for all made payable by a certain quantity of silver.

Fourth, borrowers are presumably more numerous in this country than lenders, or at least it is essentially the productive occupations that make use of loans but capitalists and usurers who provide them. Which of these does the reader think deserve more sympathy?

During a falling exchange rate the indigent borrower will lose all he has, but at a stabilized rate neither of them, and if capitalists have indeed lost something, that has happened before and they are also those best able to bear it. How can such manifest truths be denied?

Fifth, if the Bank, due to this bankruptcy, if one is to call it that, should gain some additional strength as the loans are repaid, that would by no means be a bad thing; the Crown owes a debt to the Bank of several hundred *tunnor guld*, and the nation is weighed down merely by the payment of interest on it. The more wealthy the Bank were to become, therefore, the sooner would it be able on that basis to redeem its notes and its credit be restored, and the more easily could the Bank rescind its claim on the Crown, to the relief of all subjects, which will otherwise exhaust us and our children and always make matters related to our votes of supply awkward for the Sovereign Power and odious to the nation.

Sixth, such kinds of bankruptcy and far larger and more far-reaching ones are not uncommon in Sweden or other countries, without their losing credit on that account. I merely wish to cite two examples.

The token coins[37] that were stamped as 1 *daler smt* did lose a considerable amount of their stamped value in trading, so that the commodities purchased with token coins rose in price by 200 or 300 per cent, but the Government itself forced them down in one year by more than 1,000 per cent and at a stroke turned many capitalists into beggars. But at the same time and by so doing, the kingdom recovered its credit.

But nothing is now said about lowering or in the slightest debasing the value of the banknote but only about maintaining the value that it already in fact possesses, as almost the only currency in the country now acceptable in commerce and among producers. At that time the token coins were instantly reduced to one ninety-sixth of their stamped value but the banknote, even in comparison to our best *daler* in the monetary table of 1715, to no more than half of what it originally represented, although it has been demonstrated above that it had not at the outset possessed any specific fixed value, and yet such things are said to be unprecedented.

The Bank in France[38] closed down its operations at about the same time as Sweden devalued its token coins, but in what manner? Well, with a bankruptcy of 3,000 million *livres* or, by the Swedish method of reckoning, 20,000 *tunnor guld*, which amounts to about 50 times the amount of our entire stock of banknotes, whereby the Crown at once escaped from its debt.

Did France after this bankruptcy not have more solid credit than before? Or why does one decry the safest means of restoring a true credit, based on solid assets, as being the most dangerous to it?

The Swedish paper currency loses nothing of its present value by this arrangement; all its losses were incurred earlier. And those of us must be excessively naive and gullible who allow themselves to be persuaded that a foreigner or native who at present possesses sums of banknotes has actually given one *riksdaler specie* or a 9-*daler plåt* for each 9-*daler* banknote, or commodities to their value, and yet they are not ashamed to demand that of the Bank.

It is by no means only the rights of those who now possess banknotes that are taken away by a settled exchange rate, but those of the whole nation. To restore the nation's rights now by lowering the exchange rate and thereby discouraging the productive occupations will, in my view, be the most hazardous measure of all.

§ 39

This is how matters stand, as I see it, when viewed in their true light. Far be it from me to wish to blame or criticize the arrangements that have been or could be made, but as these matters, for the reasons adduced, seem to me to be of the highest importance, in which the welfare of the whole country appears to balance as if on the point of a needle, I could not have satisfied my conscience, as a citizen of a free country, until I had been able to submit my arguments to the scrutiny of the general public, and if they are well founded it should be possible for the proposal to be adopted by the Sovereign Power and be still further improved by those who possess the knowledge that I lack.

Otherwise, however, and if I should be going astray, the reader may find that at least the arguments deserve a thorough refutation among a people that ought to know its own rights, at a time when many others from the best of intentions personally worry about these problems.

In regulating a financial system to strengthen the country, a Bank man, *qua talis*,[39] even if he were the most competent and honest one, is not suitable, for he is only accustomed to look to the interest of the Bank; nor a merchant, for he aims at his own immediate advantage; nor a financial official, who only wants to increase the revenue of the Crown; nor a salaried man, who would prefer to see a rate of 24 *mark* even if that were to cause the ruin of all productive occupations; nor a borrower or lender, for each has his own personal interest in it; and least of all a banknote capitalist, who dreams each night of the transmutation of his banknotes into *riksdaler* and *dukater*.

Here a far greater and more extensive aim than any of those is to be achieved, namely the revival and security of all productive occupations.

If this is now yet again neglected, as has unfortunately tended to happen hitherto when regulating finances, and the productive occupations are depressed, whatever we wish to do to assist the Bank, commerce, the Crown, public officials, employees or banknote capitalists will be wasted effort.

All of these derive their sustenance from the productive occupations and cannot even exist without them.

It is an easy task to give the Bank and the Crown their due when there are a large number of wage-earners among whom to distribute the charges. The reason why this is so difficult for us now, however, is precisely the fact that the burden is large and there are few shoulders to bear it. Unless we now labour assiduously to obtain security even for the most vulnerable productive occupations and thereby increase the population, but rather increase the advantages of a few by means of artificial measures and by driving workers abroad, it must eventually happen that the load will become too heavy for the rest, so that they are either weighed down by it or throw it off, and we shall then see what the Bank and the Crown have gained by that.

When we thus have to deal with the finances of the country and wish to achieve a great aim, we must set aside all others, lest we lose the main one for the sake of inessential matters.

It is not my view, however, that the rights of the Crown and of public officials should be disregarded. Such matters, however, form part of the finances of the Crown. They are each in themselves important topics and should be resolved by the Committees of Finance and Trade, Budget and Appropriations, and they have no connection with the financial system of the country except that they cannot be accurately assessed and defined before that is stabilized, unless our measures are in future as hitherto to be makeshift ones that do not fit into the great chain, with the linking together of which the honourable Estates of the Realm are presently occupied, which is *the genuine well-being and happiness of the country*.

In the elaboration of this subject, a number of more or less complicated circumstances have emerged in its actual application, but as my aim has been to make myself understood to at least the majority of my readers, I have been obliged to pass over these and concentrate solely on the fundamental truths themselves, which I have endeavoured to explain with simple examples.

If the simplicity is regarded as a fault of mine, that is the very thing that I have sought to achieve. Should my treatise nonetheless still be obscure in certain places, it has not been in my power to explain it any better.

Were I to be honoured with some criticism, I would wish that it first dealt with that on which we agree, for then the truth will most effectively emerge, and I shall fulfil my purpose, which is the enlightenment of the general public and of myself.

Notes

1 *"Iactabatur temporibus illis…*: "at that time the value of money was so fluctuating that no one could tell how much he was worth".

2 *"a project-maker"*: Chydenius uses the Swedish term *project-makare*, often used disparagingly of persons making proposals for new laws, which shows that he was well aware of how delicate the issue was. See the Commentary, pp. 213–15.

3 Chydenius here defines the concept *finance-system*, which can be understood as "monetary system". In the original text he uses *penning-system* ("coin system") as a synonym for *finance-system*. Chydenius is, however, somewhat inconsistent in his usage of these concepts and we have therefore decided to use "system of finance" or "financial system" in the translation.

4 *"These changes in the value…"*: to debase money by clipping or filing silver and gold coins seems to have been a common practice among European rulers since the medieval period (and probably even long before that). During the Thirty Years War (1618–48) this practice was so common that this period has often been called the "Kipper und Wipperzeit". Chydenius most particularly refers to the so-called *nödmynt* (crisis coins) made of copper, which were issued by Charles XII in Sweden in 1715–18 in order to finance his extensive wars. A guarantee was issued which granted a certain value in regular silver and copper for the "crisis coins". The person responsible for the issue of such coins of inferior value was the king's adviser Baron Georg Heinrich Görtz. When it became obvious after Charles XII's death on 18 November

1718 that the "crisis coins" would not be exchanged for "real" money, they lost all their value. Görtz was subsequently executed in 1719.

5 Christopher Polhem (1661–1751) was a Swedish inventor, owner of iron manufactories, industrialist and economic writer. He wrote a great number of economic texts (most of them unpublished). Like Lars Salvius and other writers later on, Polhem was in general critical of trade regulations, which he believed especially harmed the iron industry.

6 An agio is the percentage of charge made for the exchange of paper money into cash, or for the exchange of a less valuable metallic currency into one more valuable.

7 "... the inferior coin drive out the better": this principle is often referred to as Gresham's law, which states that "bad money drives out good" when there are two accepted legal tender in circulation under protection of the state. It is named after Sir Thomas Gresham (1519–79), an English financier and adviser to the Tudor dynasty.

8 Gustavus Vasa (1496–1560) was king of Sweden from 1523 until his death.

9 "One still hears some people praise the Bank loans...": regarding the practices of the Bank of the Estates, see the Introduction, pp. 23–4.

10 Ras de Sicile was a patterned silk cloth in two colours, a specialty originating from Tours in France.

11 "... long before bank loans were permitted": at the beginning of the Age of Liberty, Ständernas bank in practice was forbidden to give out loans to private persons. This ban was lifted in 1731 by the decision made by the Diet to allow the loaning out of what the bank had gained in interest. In 1734 it also became possible for the bank to provide loans with iron as security. This right was in 1738–9 – with the inauguration of the Hat government – turned into a more general right to loan out money on the private market. In 1760 this right was abolished as a consequence of inflation, the fall of the Swedish exchange rate and the overwhelming economic problems.

12 "high exchange rate": During the eighteenth century the concepts of falling and rising exchange rates were reversed compared to how we see matters today. The modern expression would be "low exchange rate".

13 "... the security pledged in § 2 of the constitution": refers to the paragraph in the constitution that guarantees the ownership of all real and private property.

14 "Among the many proposals presented on this subject, two in particular...": this refers on the one hand to P.N. Christiernin's suggestion to accept the lowered exchange rate of the mark, and on the other to the decision taken by the Diet to inaugurate a scheme of gradual revaluation.

15 "materia peccans": Latin for "the cause or ground for sickness".

16 "... sincerely declare that I possess capital neither in cash": In 1766, Chydenius was indeed a man with only small means, so he is without doubt sincere here. His situation improved in 1769 when he became the heir to his father-in-law, the merchant Olof Mellberg.

17 "devaluation": during the eighteenth century the concepts of falling and rising exchange rates were reversed compared to how we see matters today. Chydenius here means that the exchange rate was lowered. Today we would speak of a revaluation, since the value of money increased.

18 "the Wäxel-Associerade": refers to the so-called Exchange Bill Offices (Wäxel-contoir). See note 12, p. 165.

19 Charles IX was king of Sweden from 1604 to 1611.

20 "the minority of Queen Christina": After the death of Christina's father, Gustavus II Adolphus, in 1632, there was a government led by Chancellor of the Realm Axel Oxenstierna until Christina came of age, in 1644. She then ruled Sweden until 1654, when she abdicated and left for Rome.

21 Charles XI (1655–97) was king of Sweden from 1660 (or 1672, when he attained his majority) until his death.

22 "Swedish silver": i.e. Swedish daler or 4 mark.

23 "*a tale-value*": here *räknevärde* could also be translated as "unit of account".
24 "... *the beginning of our liberty*": the so-called Age of Liberty in Swedish history lasted from 1719 to 1772.
25 "*anonymous writer*": the author was Emmanuel Swedenborg (1688–1772), scientist, writer, assessor in the Board of Mining and religious mystic.
26 "*Indefeasible Thoughts...*": *Oförgripelige tanckar om swenska myntetz förnedring och förhögning*, Stockholm, 1722.
27 "... *where iron cannot regularly be produced*": in the original text by Chydenius, the negation has been left out by mistake. In the cited work by Swedenborg the phrase is in the negative.
28 § 18 is missing, owing to a mistake in the original numbering.
29 "*par rate*": at the face value.
30 "*the value*": Chydenius here probably means "the tale-value".
31 "*the promissory notes of the Bank*": this refers to *Stockholm Banco*, which was started in 1656 and was the first bank in Sweden. It is also called *Palmstruchska banken*, after its founder, Johan Palmstruch. In 1661–4 it issued the first banknotes in Europe. As a consequence of its issuing too many banknotes, their value fell and there was a classic bank run that ended with the bank having to close down. After some years (1668) the Bank of the Estates (*Ständernas bank*) was inaugurated.
32 Carl Gustaf Bonde (1620–67) was a great landowner, and finance minister (*riksskattemästare*) from 1660 to his death.
33 "*Indefeasible Thoughts*": the memorial "Mine oförgripelige tankar öfwer närwarande Myntetz ostadigheet..." was attached to the minutes of the Council of the Realm of 28 October 1664.
34 "*res nummaria*": Latin for "money business" or "financial operations".
35 "*bar-silver*": the Swedish word *verksilver* refers to a silver alloy with the fineness of c.83 per cent (Scandinavian silver).
36 "*London Bank's*": the Bank of England was founded in 1694 and began to issue banknotes (the first printed ones appeared in 1725).
37 "*token coins*": Chydenius here refers to the issue of *nödmynt* between 1715 and 1718 and the crisis that followed; see note 4 above.
38 "*The bank in France*": refers to John Law's Banque Générale, which started its operations in 1716. The bank was private but three-quarters of the capital consisted of government bills and government-accepted notes. In practice it was the first central bank in France. Finance minister John Law was responsible for the Mississippi Bubble and the chaotic economic collapse in France in 1718.
39 "*qua talis*": as such.

Commentary

Lars Magnusson

As we saw in the Introduction, this publication was the ultimate reason why Chydenius had to leave the Diet after the decision in the Estate of Clergy on 3 July 1766. The text had been written in April the same year and the printing began at Lars Salvius's shop during the following month. In his autobiography, Chydenius explains some of the circumstances around this text, which he at first intended to publish anonymously.[1] Originally he was given permission to publish it by the censor, Niclas von Oelreich. However, soon after the printing process had begun, the censor was ordered by Thure Gustaf Rudbeck – the Speaker of the Nobles and in practice the head of the Cap party – to fetch the manuscript from Salvius's shop. After reading it, Rudbeck forbade any further printing of the text in its present form. This was certainly not according to the rules, but shows exemplarily how the political system worked during the Age of Liberty. Chydenius was ordered to cut out some of the paragraphs which seemed most offensive to the Cap government. It is most probable also that he was offered a tidy sum of money to keep quiet about the whole thing.[2] Chydenius then informs us that some time after these events he went to his superiors in his estate, who decided that three of its members should read the text and suggest a solution to the matter. After having done so, they returned to the estate and at a meeting on 11 June they argued that the text could very well be published as it stood. It should be added that the three readers, the *rectores* Pehr Högström, Carl Kröger and Per Niklas Mathesius, belonged to the radical wing of the Cap party and in general held political views close to Chydenius's. Hence, when Chydenius at the next meeting of the estate on 14 June asked whether the manuscript could now be published, no one spoke against it. As a consequence, the printing of the text continued and it was published on 26 June. According to one eyewitness present at the Diet, Daniel Tilas, the tract immediately caught the interest of the public; during the two days immediately following publication, it sold as many as 600 copies.[3]

However, the reaction from the political establishment was swift and harsh. Two days after the tract had been published, one of the leading Caps, Fredric Ulric von Essen, was able to unite his estate (the Nobility) in putting pressure on the Estate of Clergy, asking to what extent it as a whole stood behind Chydenius's pamphlet. At this point many of its members wavered. The estate officially claimed that it had "no knowledge" of the text and that it as a body did not support the text's conclusions. This made it easier for von Essen and his like-minded friends to act: on 1 July the matter was discussed in the Secret Committee and it was decided that Chydenius should be called to appear before the Committee. An inquiry was held the same day; the haste reveals the heated character of this issue. Harshly attacked by his opponents (at least, this was Chydenius's own view), he responded in a rather deferential manner. We must remember that it was still forbidden to openly criticize decisions once they had been taken by the Diet; such practices as severely hurt the authority of the Diet were condemned as "English ideas" at the time.[4] Hence, Chydenius defended himself by claiming that he by no means had wanted to criticize the decision to establish a new system of finance. Instead, he had only spoken his own mind freely, as he, like anybody else, was entitled to do "in a free nation".[5] Moreover, he agreed that perhaps some of his views were somewhat drastically formulated, but pointed out that he had been allowed to print the text by the censor and by his own estate. After having dismissed Chydenius, the Secret Committee discussed the matter. Some of the members present openly felt that Chydenius should be prosecuted. When he returned to the meeting, the interrogation continued. The question was even put whether he in fact was not an agent of the Hat party, or secretly siding with the party of the Royal Court (*Hovpartiet*).[6] However, the result of the heated discussions was that the matter was passed over to the Estate of Clergy for it to decide what to do with the author and his tract. At a meeting on 3 July, Chydenius presented a humble memorial in which he pleaded that he had acted in good faith and that he hoped that the estate would speak favourably in his defence in relation to the other estates. He also asked for forgiveness if he – against his intentions – had offended anybody.[7] After a long discussion and a vote, it was nevertheless decided that Chydenius should be expelled from further proceedings of the ongoing Diet, and banned from taking part in the next. The estate was split over the decision, however. What seems to have decided the case was that some of those in favour of him voted for expulsion, as they were afraid that otherwise, more severe measures would be taken. This fear may not have been totally without foundation: in other estates, as we saw, there were voices speaking in favour of prosecution and a severe sentence.

Hence, the official reason for sending Chydenius back to Alaveteli was that he had offended the Diet and the constitution by his harsh critique of the new Cap government's monetary and finance policy. We have already seen in the Introduction what the discussion was all about (see p. 25). The Diet of 1765–6 saw the downfall of the former Hat government, and condemned the leaders of the Bank of the Estates (*Ständernas bank*) in harsh terms. The latter were accused of being swindlers and jobbers who had artificially created a process of inflation basically in order to enrich themselves. The effect had been that the rate of exchange of Swedish copper money in circulation had fallen drastically in relation to foreign money. This view had been forcefully put by the new government made up by the Caps, and was based upon such intellectual authorities as the economic writer Anders Nordencrantz. Moreover, Chydenius seems initially to have agreed with this analysis; and, as we have seen, he was also one of the angriest critics of the "evil practices" of the Bank authorities. However, at some point he seems to have changed his mind. While we cannot know for sure, it is most probable that during his work in the General Appeals Committee (*allmänna besvärsdeputation*) he became convinced that the Caps' new system of finance, which ordained a gradual increase in the value of of the copper *mark* by reducing the amount of circulating money (mainly in the form of banknotes), would lead to a catastrophe that would severely hurt small traders and farmers, but also the economically very important iron industry. He seems to have received food for thought for revision through reading the critique of Anders Nordencrantz by Pehr Niclas Christiernin, adjunct professor of economics at Uppsala (see the Introduction, pp. 38–40), as well as a memorial written by the nobleman Christer Horn concerning the administration of the Bank of the Estates, which was published in April 1766. In his text, Chydenius refers openly to Horn, and many of the arguments he presents are very similar. Hence, when defending himself from accusations made against him, he naturally referred to Horn. He asked his critics why he should be so harshly condemned and his tract withdrawn when nothing of the sort had happened to Horn: "I am not the only one who enjoying the privilege to be part of the Honourable Diet has pondered on this matter and written about it in a similar fashion," he writes in an early version of his memorial from 3 July.[8]

Even more imperative was when Chydenius – perhaps in October 1765 – came across a secret memorial from 1722 hidden in the archives and possibly written by the same Emanuel Swedenborg who had inspired him when he was formulating his critique against the Commodity Ordinance (see p. 140). In any case, the anonymous writer of the memorial depicts in dark colours the effects of the deflation, especially for the iron industry in the early 1720s after the downfall of absolutism. Without doubt it only strengthened Chydenius's feeling that Christiernin must have been on the right track and that the present plan to increase the value of the *mark* would eventuate in a drastic fall of prices. Instead, he argues along the same lines as Christiernin – as we can see in the text – that the present (low) value of the circulating money should be preserved. Of course, in changing his mind he had not also changed his views concerning the "criminal" activities of Kierman *et al.* or the Bank of the Estates. However, the risk attached to the remedy suggested by the Cap government was that such a "cure" would make the patient much more ill than he already was.

Notes

1 G. Schauman, *Biografiska undersökningar om Anders Chydenius*, Skrifter utgifna af Svenska Litteratursällskapet i Finland 84, Helsinki: Svenska Litteratursällskapet i Finland, 1908, p. 213.
2 P. Virrankoski, *Anders Chydenius: Demokratisk politiker i upplysningens tid*, Stockholm: Timbro, 1995, p. 223.
3 D. Tilas, *Anteckningar och brev från Riksdagen 1765–1766*, del II, Stockholm: Norstedt, 1974, p. 313f.

4 Virrankoski, op. cit., p. 232.
5 Ibid., p. 227.
6 The king of Sweden, Adolphus Frederic, and in particular Queen Lovisa Ulrika made several attempts to extend their political power during the 1750s. They had some support within the circles closest to the royal court, a group mostly consisting of high nobility. The group was called *Hovpartiet*, the party of the Royal Court, although it cannot be compared to the Hats and Caps. The conflict between Queen Lovisa Ulrika and the ruling Hat party reached an acute stage in 1756, and the attempted royal coup that followed was a complete failure. The defeat was humiliating for the royal couple, and many of their supporters were either executed or banished. In the 1760s the party of the Royal Court slowly regained its position, and its importance and influence gradually grew. The *coup d'état* of 1772 eventually restored the political power of the king.
7 For the memorial, see Schauman, op. cit., p. 217f.
8 Schauman, op. cit., p. 220.

Part II
Pioneering freedom of information

5 *Memorial on the Freedom of Printing*

Humble memorial

Copy presented before the Third Committee of the Grand Joint Committee on 12 November 1765.

It requires no proof that an equitable freedom of writing and printing is one of the firmest pillars on which a free government may rest; for otherwise the Estates can never possess the requisite knowledge to institute good laws, administrators of the law will be subject to no control in the performance of their offices and those under its jurisdiction have little knowledge of the requirements of the law, the limits of official power and their own obligations; learning and good sense will be repressed, coarseness of thought, expression and manners gain acceptance and within a few years a horrific darkness will settle over the entire firmament of our liberty. But on what basis that freedom should rightly be established, so that on the one hand it cannot be suppressed by any one individual nor on the other hand decline into an arbitrary frenzy, is something that requires more careful consideration.

This subject divides into two main questions, namely: on whose responsibility should the printing occur, and under what laws?

Three alternatives in particular appear to deserve examination in this regard, namely whether the censorship shall be entrusted to a specific individual or to the author or else be entrusted to several individuals.

I can only conclude that it would be most hazardous for liberty to entrust this matter to a single man and thus set him up as a judge of the thoughts and the reason of the whole nation; even if he were a paragon, it would impose an incredible burden on book learning, for neither would he have the time to deal with everything nor could the opening thus created for self-interest be in any way closed off under such a form of autocracy. Certainly nothing would then be allowed to appear that in any way touched the personal interest of the censor himself, even if public interest might demand it. The censor would then be able to deprive those of their livelihood who have acquired nothing but scholarly knowledge and wish to make a living from their writings, he could withhold much useful information from the general public merely out of a personal hatred for certain individuals or certain truths, and by promoting publications that appeal to him and obstructing the rest, which seems to me to be the most sensitive issue, he

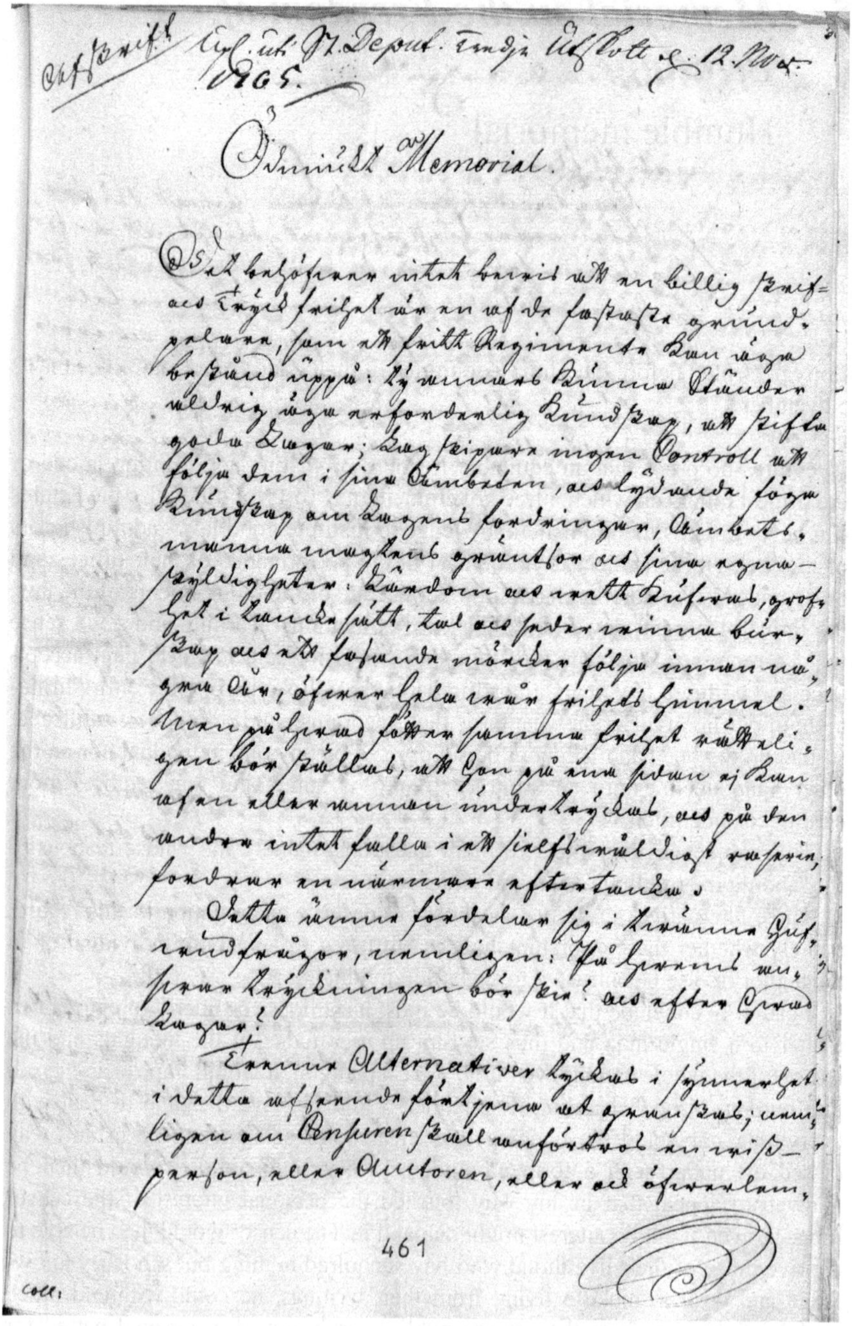

Figure 20 The first page of *Memorial on the Freedom of Printing* (1765). The National Archives of Sweden.

could within a few years recast the nation in his own mould as far as modes of thought, writing and expression and indeed our laws are concerned.

Daily experience teaches us that we cannot rely on the wording of instructions or on any laws unless the matter is self-regulating. Nothing can be written about politics so carefully that it may not by a governing power or by the prevailing opinion be considered as contrary to fundamental laws etc. when it conflicts with their interests and aims, and therefore be suppressed. Nor is anything needed for that purpose other than simply a delay in the censoring of such writings, in order to exhaust the authors, which will in a few years transform a whole nation.

The liberty of a nation is preserved not only by the laws but by public information and knowledge as to how they are being administered.

As regards the second alternative, making authors themselves responsible, I see three problems in particular with that. First, neither anonymous nor pseudonymous writers will then be able to have anything printed, although they often provide the best information and can be more impartially read and examined. *Non quaeritur quis, sed quid.*[1] In the next place it seems disconcerting to me that the nation could not trust most authors should a calumniator wish to disseminate libels and some ignorant or petty author not have the ability to avoid his own misfortune. Finally, most individuals also lack the impartiality and discrimination required to set a true value on their own writings and activities.

What humble, poor and defenceless author would then be safe to write the slightest thing against a superior power, if he saw that he could easily become sacrificed for the truth and for the liberty of his fellow citizens?

I therefore have no hesitation in agreeing with the third option: where censorship will be placed in the hands of several individuals, and emulation among them will encourage rather than inhibit reflective talents. That form of censorship could in its turn be implemented in two ways, for either certain censors should be appointed for each branch of knowledge or else the matter should simply be entrusted to the printers. Let us see which of these would benefit the nation more.

Excessive disadvantages are associated with the first alternative. First, a jealous squabble will then arise among them about the demarcations between the disciplines, which are in fact interconnected in innumerable ways. Then, secondly, our impoverished national treasury will be encumbered with a greatly increased salary bill. Third, a new burden will be imposed on the sciences and scholarship, either of paying them in accordance with the law or else of promoting some works by bribing the censor. Fourth, the political aspect of our freedom of printing, which is the most priceless possession of liberty, will remain in the same manner under a *censor politicus*, who will then exercise the same autocracy over that aspect as before.

Again, if anyone should wish to direct literature down the academic road and allocate all newly published writings to their appropriate faculties and from the faculties to particular professors within them for perusal and supervision, the burden on literature will thereby be increased rather than alleviated. It will, first, be a lengthy diversion for those who do not live close to the universities to send all their works there; second, a further expense in sending them there and back and paying the agent, as well as remunerating the censor; third, a great waste of time, so that both author and printer would grow tired before any work could be prepared for the press in this way; fourth, just as much autocracy over thoughts and reason as ever before; fifth, a monopoly in fees for the censorship; sixth, one and the same piece of writing would occasionally be subjected to censorship in all four faculties, as something purely theological, juridical, medical and philosophical may appear in it; and seventh, the professors could never be instructed to deal promptly with such writings, as they are usually able to find an excuse in their lectures, disputations and other time-consuming duties.

Nothing else thus remains than to leave it to the printers, after everything that relates to the foundations of our religion has been excluded, to print, strictly on their own responsibility, according to clear instructions, whatever they can turn to good account.

The advantages that will hereby be gained for literature are, I am convinced, quite extensive. An author will then, first, avoid the strenuous inconvenience of attending for several months on a censor who is buried in paper. Second, he saves around 10 per cent of the entire advance for printing the book, which is now spent on the censorship. Third, writers will be encouraged to compete with each other, whereby the printing houses will be able to select the best from a larger number of works that will be heaped upon them and to print them. Fourth, there will be even greater emulation between the printing houses to win a reputation in the nation for learned, elegantly written and useful works that emanate from their presses. Fifth, the state and the government would have an assured resort to the printing houses, should anything contrary to the instruction be found to have been published, far exceeding the redress that the nation could ever demand or expect from an offending censor and author. For printers possess almost the most valuable workshops that exist in the country, their equipment alone amounting to a capital of 60,000 or 70,000 *daler kmt*, being difficult to move and impossible to escape abroad with, apart from which printers are involved in so much business over and above that and are for all these reasons, by the nature of their own trade, far less likely to wish to abscond than both censor and author might be when under close surveillance. They can afford an imposed fine of several thousand *daler* and pay it to the Crown, but an author often scarcely a *styver*. If anyone abuses his freedom as a printer, the fine is capable of ruining his credit and weakening him, while his case will be a clear mirror to others in which to see the cost of self-indulgence and a warning not to kick over the traces, and all that without causing any inconvenience to literature. Sixth, by this arrangement our printing houses would also gain a reputation commensurate with such hard and responsible work, as learned men would enjoy conducting such a free and important enterprise.

That the majority of the printers in the country do not at present possess the requisite understanding for that should by no means deter us from immediately implementing this proposal. How often does it not happen that simple-minded

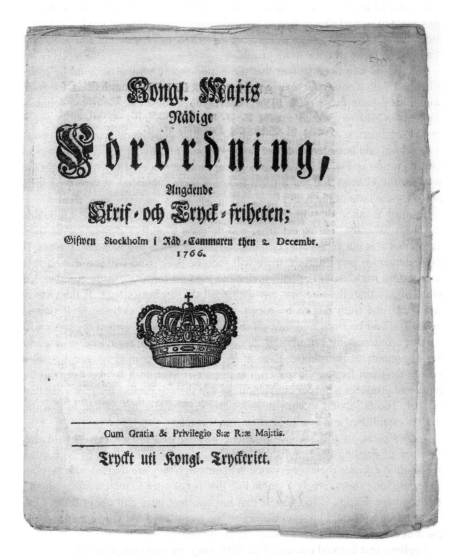

Figure 21 Chydenius considered the Ordinance on Freedom of Writing and Printing (1766) as one of his greatest achievements at the Diet of 1765–6. Kokkola University Consortium Chydenius.

people are convicted under a law of which they have been unaware? But if the law is concise and clear, printers should be able to learn to observe it, and it will be a question of the carefulness and responsibility of those who do not themselves understand the issue to engage to look through the manuscripts that are received, on whatever terms they think fit, men so learned, steady and upright that they could entrust to them a significant part of their welfare, which almost all officials are frequently obliged to do in their work, as they do not personally have time to deal with everything. Nor would that cost printers very much, if they were to restrict themselves to learned and honest people, of modest achievement, among whom there is often more diligence, understanding and judgment than among those who are more brilliant.

Nor would one need to fear that the nation would on that account be overwhelmed with a multitude of worthless publications. For competition for sales would keep them busy trying to please everyone. For the needs of the scholars no texts would be printed except those that are the most excellent in every branch of learning. Printers would then conduct correspondence about books both within and outside the country. They would endeavour to serve those who love literature and would therefore only print masterpieces. They would light the way for the citizens and teach them to know their fatherland, revere their king and obey the laws of the realm.

Printing is, after all, nothing but a method of communicating one's thoughts to others absently. To expect from people such a perfect expression of their views that it is not subject to contradiction and modification is utterly in vain. If the statement is preposterous, there will soon be those who will refute it. If it is founded on truth, it will remain invincible, and no fortress can be commended more highly than the one that has withstood the severest sieges. If the case is equivocal, the truth has to be ascertained by published exchanges. If that is refused, it can be from no other cause than fear of the day when the truth will emerge. And nothing can honour innocence more than allowing her to present her arguments to the public. Even if the evil that is printed is read by more people than can listen to a speech, the response given to it is likewise read by more and produces a deeper conviction, so that there is perfect reciprocity in that respect. The falsehood shames its originator but benefits the nation, in that the truth is established and is able to grow firmer roots.

I now come to the second question: that is, under what law should this freedom of printing be established? I know many Swedish laws of which the scope often exceeds their observance, and although they are drafted with all possible care, one sees scarcely a single line that is not open to misconstruction and infringement. Happy is the people that has succinct laws and obeys them. One could never wish the bitterest enemies of the realm anything worse than numerous and diverse laws.

I believe that it could consist of the following few and concise points.

First, everything that concerns the foundations of religion and theology should be supervised by a theological faculty or, in the absence of one, by a generally approved and learned theologian and be printed on his responsibility.

Second, it shall be forbidden to print anything that offends against our form of government, in so far as it promotes the abjured sovereignty[2] and deleterious aristocracy, on pain of a fine of 4,000 *daler smt*.

Should several individuals consult together and print matter designed to overthrow liberty, they shall all be punished under ch. 4, par. 8 of the criminal code.

Third, everything that libellously attacks individuals and offends against virtue and good morals shall likewise be banned, on pain of a fine of 1,000 *daler smt*, in addition to what the law prescribes. Whosoever offends against this shall be charged and judged at the next session of the appropriate court, for which purpose the printer should first be charged. If he is able to legally deflect the case from himself to the author, then both shall remain liable, though neither of these may be brought to trial unless an *actor publicus*[3] assists them and conducts their case, nor shall any verdict be executed that affects livelihood, life and honour before the Estates themselves have given their verdict on the case. All such cases shall immediately be admitted and decided by the judge, on pain of accountability.

Stockholm, 12 June 1765

Anders Kraftman

Notes

1 "*Non quaeritur quis, sed quid*": "What matters is not who says it but what he says."
2 "*the abjured sovereignty*": the new forms of government of 1719 and 1720 strongly turned against the sovereign rule of the former autocratic system of government. During the Age of Liberty, all officials, for example, had to take an oath binding them to oppose all attempts to reinforce autocratic rule in the state. A similar oath was included in the Royal Accession Charter.
3 "*actor publicus*": In ancient Rome the *actor publicus* was an officer who had the super-intendence or care of slaves belonging to the state. Since then, more generally an *actor publicus* is supposed to be the representative of the community (*res publica*), for example in lawsuits against the state or other authorities. He is often also called *notarious publicus*.

Commentary

Lars Magnusson

This memorial, presented on 12 June 1765 to the Estates, was signed by Anders Kraftman, a schoolmaster from Porvoo (Borgå) in Finland and member of the Estate of Clergy. Its real author, however, was Anders Chydenius.[1] In his autobiography (see p. 344) he describes the background in some detail: how he had written the memorial and then discussed it with Bishop Jacob Serenius, a leading member of the Estate of Clergy as well as of the Cap party, and also with the Court Councillor, Johan Arckenholtz. Serenius then suggested some changes and abridgements, some of them which Chydenius disliked.

This memorial was the first of the texts that Chydenius would write on the issue of freedom of printing and information, which became an important issue at the Diet and was crowned with the decision on 2 December 1766, which provided the Swedish realm with the most liberal Act on freedom of printing in Europe at the time, except for Great Britain. In his autobiography, Chydenius proudly declared that he had worked hard to achieve the goal to abolish the previous censorship and to make state documents and minutes available for the general public. Later on, in 1774, the law on freedom of printing was made much more restrictive by Gustavus III (although the monarch claimed that the changes were very minor), but it was re-established again in 1809 with the new constitution after the downfall of Gustavus IV Adolphus and the loss of Finland to Russia. Hence, in historical overviews the year of 1766 is most often remembered as the year when Sweden received its freedom of printing and saw a breakthrough for freedom of information (*offentlighetsprincipen*), which granted the general public access to most official documents.

We have already in the Introduction discussed the steps taken to introduce a more liberal freedom of printing and information policy before the Diet of 1765–6 (see p. 26). To argue for the freedom of printing and information was most certainly by no means a sudden impulse on the part of Chydenius.[2] We have seen already in his piece on emigration (pp. 96–8, 113) that he regarded freedom of printing as extremely important. However, it is clear that his proposal for freedom of printing and information to a large extent must be placed within the political context of the time. In favour of a more radical reform along the lines of what became law in 1766 stood the radical *falange* of the Caps, while the noble members of the Caps as well as of the Hats stood in opposition.

As Stridsberg and others have shown, the issue of freedom of printing is an example where differences of opinion did not follow party lines, but was instead based on which estate one belonged to.[3] Moreover, it was particularly the Caps of lower social standing in the Estate of Clergy who were most radical in their campaigning for more freedom of printing. Most probably also it was *not* the abolition of censorship (at least as long as it did not include religious literature) that was the most controversial part of the kind of reform which Chydenius and others proposed. Instead, it was the suggestion that documents and minutes (including those of the discussions in the different estates) should be allowed to be printed, i.e. freedom of information, that was the more problematic. Even radical persons, in principle in favour of the freedom to print, felt that freedom of information might lead to their not being able to openly speak their mind in committees or at meetings. Even more dangerous, it seemed that this might imply that a politician was to be regarded as a representative of his constituency. As we have seen, such a view, the so-called doctrine of principalship (*principalatsläran*), was regarded as unconstitutional during the Age of Liberty and strictly forbidden by law (see the Introduction, p. 7).

In the commentaries to the subsequent chapters, we will follow the story of the establishment of the Freedom of Printing and Information Act at the Diet of 1765–6, and Chydenius's role in how it unfolded.

Notes

1 P. Virrankoski, *Anders Chydenius: Demokratisk politiker i upplysningens tid*, Stockholm: Timbro 1995, p. 179; G. Schauman, *Biografiska undersökningar rörande Anders Chydenius*, Skrifter utgifna af Svenska Litteratursällskapet i Finland 84, Helsinki: Svenska Litteratursällskapet i Finland, 1908, p. 158f. Cf. also J. Manninen, "Anders Chydenius and the Origins of World's First Freedom of Information Act", in J. Mustonen (ed.), *The World's First Freedom of Information Act*, Kokkola: Anders Chydenius Foundation 2006, pp. 41–2.
2 See the discussion in Virrankoski, op. cit., p. 194f., arguing against Hilding Eek's proposition that Chydenius's standpoint against censorship was initially based on practical arguments, and only later, in 1766, primarily on arguments of principle. However, while it is easy to agree with Virrankoski on Chydenius's general standpoint, it is clear that he often – and perhaps also in this case – changed his views regarding exactly how such a principle should be formulated.
3 O. Stridsberg, "Hattarnas och mössornas ställningstaganden till tryckfrihetsfrågan på riksdagarna 1760–62 och 1765–66", *Historisk Tidskrift*, 1953:2, pp. 158–66.

6 Report on the freedom of writing and printing

*Report of the Third Committee of the
Grand Joint Committee of the
Honourable Estates of the Realm on
the Freedom of Writing and Printing,
submitted at the Diet in Stockholm on
18 December 1765*

While it has been considering this rather important matter with the utmost care, the Committee has not failed to perceive how obscurantism and ignorance, in all those particulars on which in a number of respects human felicity or misfortune depend, are our most inescapable inheritance at birth.

If that deficiency of nature is to be remedied and a nation be brought to knowledge and sincere adoration of the true God, as well as to a thorough instruction in those duties that each individual is obliged to observe towards himself and his neighbour as well as to the sciences by means of which reason is perfected in so far as credulity and prejudices are removed, then the insights of some and their mutual exchange of experience and information must eventually produce the understanding, clarity and knowledge that will create a happier refuge in an uncertain world than nature alone appears to have prepared for us as we first enter it.

The Committee doubts that there can be any more certain means than the free use of pens and print for this important purpose, for where no innate ideas are present, so to speak, they can be inspired if those members of a society who, by superior education and assiduous efforts, have achieved some particular knowledge in various subjects, are able to freely enlighten and guide others in these and also to clear away the false knowledge or the harmful delusions that have arisen either from a lack of rational thought or by contrived manipulation.

A considerable power also resides in the fact that a free nation governed by the law, whose birthright it is to freely enjoy the kind of rights that under despotic, absolutist, aristocratic and democratic governments[1] may only be desired but never possessed, is aware of its rights and of the security that is enshrined in the innermost purpose of the form of government but likewise also how far it may, with the vicissitudes of time, have become separated from these and what expedient and timely remedy is most urgent in such a case; and in that respect the Committee also regards the freedom of writing and printing as the most effective and reliable means.

The fundamental advantage of such a freedom has been thoroughly experienced by every state, while England, whose freedom of printing was obtained at the cost of blood,[2] regards it as one of the strongest bulwarks of its constitution.

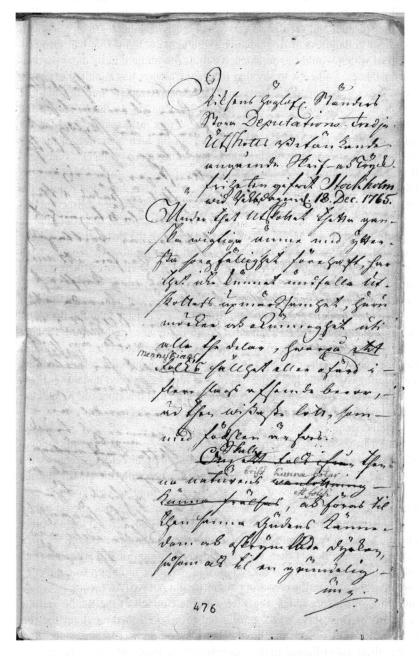

476

Figure 22 The first page of *Report of the Third Committee of the Grand Joint Committee of the Honourable Estates of the Realm on the Freedom of Writing and Printing, submitted at the Diet in Stockholm on 18 December 1765*. The National Archives of Sweden.

On the other hand, one finds in the histories of every epoch deplorable examples of the severity with which communities and societies have been controlled by both the spiritual and secular powers when these have been effective enough to keep them in darkness or to gradually extinguish the lights that had formerly shone, all of which would be too extensive to deal with here in its more particular circumstances. Suffice it to say that ignorance always has a malign effect on manners, poses a danger to the survival of a free government, impedes the true improvement of regulations and branches of the economy to the benefit of the state that is indispensable in every epoch, and offers little security against the audacity or arbitrariness of judges and officials in the administration of the law and of the national economy, with innumerable other inconveniences, both generally and for each and every individual in particular.

All this has led the Committee to seek to ascertain from the oldest records the nature of the freedom of writing and printing when it was first established in this country, to enable it to then make a proper comparison with the condition in which it now finds itself and by what kind of measure the difference may have been caused, in order that the Committee shall then be able to propose what appears to require such improvement in that regard as will strengthen general and individual welfare and security.

When the craft of printing was introduced in this kingdom, some form of supervision was presumably established from the very outset, although the Committee, in the absence of documents that could really shed light on this, cannot report anything definite on the matter. The earliest information that the Committee has been able to gather about it is that censorship acquired a certain stability during the minority of the late King Charles XI[3] and was placed under the supervision of the Royal Board of Chancery, a regulation that the aforesaid King, after his accession to the throne, further confirmed by new decrees and extended to cover various circumstances.

In the instruction on 11 separate points that was issued for the above-mentioned Board on 7 July 1688, the acting censor is directed to report what occurs to the Board and to receive his orders from it, while the Board and the censor are given all the more freedom to reject the kind of writings that they have not thought fit to approve, as the nature of such writings that should not, in terms of this instruction, be allowed to be published is not defined therein other than by the words *harmful and vexatious*, or if they did not possess *any merit*, a characterization and defect that, with no closer definition of these having been provided, could easily apply to every text that, whether in regard to content or the person of the author, the censoring authority did not wish to favour.

The office of censor, which, together with the Council of the Realm and the entire Board of Chancery, was subordinated to absolutism throughout the following period until the change in the constitution in 1719,[4] has since then become entirely subordinated to the Council and the Board of Chancery, and the Chancery Ordinance of 14 June 1720, in its § 20, has also used the similarly undefined terms *objectionable* or *indecent* to characterize those writings that ought to be regarded as worthy of rejection and has again instructed the censor not, without a previously submitted report and the subsequent approval of the Board, to permit any writings and books to be printed, whereby the censor's examination was not only on several occasions virtually nullified but the Board was on the contrary given a free hand, by the application of such terms of exception, to condemn such treatises, information and truths to eternal silence that did not accord with the opinions and intentions of the period.

Evidence of how far this unlimited scrutiny could be extended is already found in a letter that the Board of Chancery humbly communicated to His Majesty on 16 February 1735, in which the said Board sought to place obstacles in the way of a most innocent work that had been registered for publication under the title of *Then Swenska Patrioten.*[5] The Board states in that humble address that it had found this work "*abounding in errors* and so contrived that one would certainly be of the opinion that it could be of very little utility and edification for the general public in view of a number of *objectionable and alarming expressions* in its judgments, while the Board also feared that such things, were they to be so rashly granted permission to be printed, would in future give mischievous people occasion by such means to disseminate lampoons among the people with impunity", with other arguments for rejecting this work. However, this attempt to abrogate the freedom of writing and printing was not approved on this occasion, but His Majesty ordered in his gracious reply of the 28th of the same month that this work should not be refused permission to be freely printed nor be subject in any other respect to censorship except in so far as it might contain anything contrary to religion, the state or good customs.

On 20 March in the same year of 1735, His Majesty's gracious permission was also granted to print court records together with the verdict given by the judge, but the Committee finds no reasons to be adduced, or fundamentally valid, in support of the fact that the individual opinions of the judges were excepted therefrom, especially as a judge who cares for uprightness has no need to fear people when he has a clear conscience, and his honour lies in his impartiality in the administration of justice becoming manifest, whereas, on the contrary, there is too great a risk that much injustice and trickery may be practised under cover of the secrecy of voting.

Although freedom of printing appeared to have been allowed some scope on these occasions, it nonetheless happened that when, among other publications that appeared in 1745 regarding the high exchange rate and the balance of trade, one was also to be published under the title of *Supplement to the High Exchange Rate and Low Balance of Trade as Well as the High Cost of Living,*[6] His Majesty himself, in an extract of minutes for 1 April, expressed the opinion that it was found to be written in *objectionable terms* against the regulations that His Majesty had issued with regard to the economy and thrift, for which reason the Board of Chancery was graciously ordered to immediately take appropriate measures to ban the said publication and confiscate the copies that had already been printed as well as to summon the *censor librorum* and intimate to him that "similar writings submitted to him hereafter, which in any way touch upon or are contrary to the regulations with regard to the economy and thrift that have already been or shall hereafter be issued by His Majesty and the Estates of the Realm, should not be allowed to be printed", and so forth.

With that, the freedom of writing and printing was again placed within the narrowest limits, which subsequently also led the Board of Chancery on its own initiative, without any previous inquiry, to ban the late Superintendent Baron Hårleman's diary,[7] simply because it referred to the danger facing the battle fleet at Karlskrona due to the ships lying right in the middle of a group of timber buildings and wooden warehouses, although the Board, on closer consideration, eventually revoked that ban.

Following the repression that was thus increasing, another era finally commenced when greater latitude was allowed for the freedom of writing and printing, which had been repressed long enough; that happened as a result of the recommendation of the Estates of the Realm, through His Majesty's gracious letter to the Board of Chancery of 9 February 1748, which explained "how useful inventions, observations and information are often held back, if not completely stifled, so that many a person imagines himself subject to some form of liability and prosecution should he publish any propositions on some matter or other that, although innocent enough, are contrary to prevailing practice; and His Majesty has thus found it most necessary to draw the distinction that, however *criminal* and *seditious* it may be to throw doubt by means of printed publications on the power and authority of the fundamental laws of the kingdom, the King and the Government and the Estates of the Realm, as great may also be the utility that it can provide if, on other matters, as with regard (N.B.) *to the financial administration, the economy, commerce, agriculture* and other *trades* and *institutions*, various *thoughts* and *observations* become widely known, as in all sciences the truth is most certainly discovered when one has the opportunity to carefully compare the arguments that may exist both for and against; in regard to all of which His Majesty has graciously decreed that, should anyone be inclined to publish his observations and remarks on the above-mentioned innocuous and useful topics, that should not only, after a preceding appropriate censorship, be permitted but also redound to his credit for the zeal and perspicuity manifested on such an occasion".

But this freedom, however sparingly and cautiously it was still applied at that time, was not for long left unaffected and unchanged, in that the Board of Chancery, without a reason for its existing in any royal decree, chose to declare by means of a rescript that "although anyone was permitted in the manner just stated to write *in oeconomicis*[8] and to have his thoughts printed, that freedom should nonetheless hereafter be circumscribed in so far as whatever is strictly the outcome of executive action by the Government or else examines and judges the regulations that have already been adopted by it should be excluded therefrom."

It would take too long to reiterate all the many further expositions and qualifications that have from time to time been issued by the Board of Chancery and by means of which a number of writings and works have been denied publication; they all have in common that they make freedom of writing and printing increasingly so precarious that its status at present is such that whenever the Board of

Chancery has wished to deny the right of any text to be published, it has needed to do nothing else in that respect than to characterize it as *useless, harmful, vexatious, futile, indecent, worthless, unfit, objectionable* or *doubtful* and other such things, without showing in what respects all this was actually the case.

At both the Diet of 1761 and at the present one, the honourable Estates of the Realm have again, with the uttermost zeal and enlightenment, realized what significant and harmful consequences this constraint on the freedom of the pen and printing has already had and is capable of causing in the future.

The noble intention of the honourable Estates of the Realm to loosen the bonds by which freeborn Swedish talents have hitherto been fettered and that have prevented them from collaborating for the development and improvement of one another as well as of the public sphere will probably be recognized by all future ages with all the more gratitude as a more enlightened posterity will most clearly be able to see the value of it.

The Committee regards it as no less a matter for rejoicing than a duty to promote such a splendid objective with the greatest energy.

And as an often regrettable experience shows that a multiplicity of laws, regulations, rescripts and declarations regarding a matter serve more to obscure and inhibit than to actually promote the chief aim of the legislator and, on the contrary, most commonly provide the less competent or more contentious legal officials with scope, by comparing so many laws and all kinds of declarations, directly contrary to the intention of the legislator, for enveloping the clearest matter in obscurity and ambiguities, the Committee is of the opinion that the worthy objective of the honourable Estates of the Realm in this most important matter would most surely be attained and strengthened by revoking all previously promulgated laws, orders, resolutions and regulations regarding publications, censorship and printing, and now presents to the honourable Grand Joint Committee for its further mature consideration a revised ordinance to replace them, which at once comprises all that the Committee on its part believes should henceforth usefully and necessarily constitute the law.

To achieve greater clarity and order therein, the opinion of the Committee is that this ordinance should be divided into three articles, of which the first and most important concerning the freedom of writing and printing itself is now initially enclosed herewith, while the Committee's drafts of the other articles on censorship and so forth will follow without delay as soon as a firm principle has been adopted by the honourable Estates of the Realm with regard to this first part, on which those other aspects principally depend.

Year and day as above.

On behalf of the Third Committee of the Grand Joint Committee of the honourable Estates of the Realm.

Gustaf Reuterholm, Carl Fredrik Mennander
Erik I. Miltopæus and Henrik Paldanius

Notes

1 "... *under despotic, absolutist, aristocratic and democratic governments*": this is apparently the only passage in which Chydenius uses the word "democratic". During the Age of Liberty, "democratic" or "democracy" were sometimes used in a modern sense, but often, "democratic" or "democracy" referred to a "bad" form of democracy, a chaotic anarchy or mob rule, more in accordance with the original definition by Aristotle. Here "democratic" is used as one item in a listing of undesirable forms of rule or government.

2 "... *obtained at the cost of blood*": Chydenius is misinformed here. The English freedom of the press gained in 1694 was not obtained at the cost of blood. Rather, the Licensing Order or Act of 1643 was allowed to lapse in 1694 as a consequence of the so-called Glorious Revolution of 1688.

3 "... *during the minority of the late King Charles XI*": King Charles XI (1655–97) of Sweden was only four years old when his father died. Before he ascended the throne in 1672 the state was ruled by a regency led by the Chancellor of the Realm (*rikskansler*) Magnus Gabriel de la Gardie.

4 "... *constitution in 1719*": refers to the new Swedish constitution of 1719 which replaced absolutism and laid the ground for the Age of Liberty. In principle it established a balance between the Estates and the King but in practice, from the 1730s, it implied that most power lay with the former. See the Introduction, pp. 6–7.

5 "*Then Swenska Patrioten*": "The Swedish Patriot", Swedish weekly periodical published in 1735. The censor at the time was Johan R. Rosenadler (1674–1743), professor Skytteanum (rhetorics and politics) at Uppsala. The publisher was anonymous but is sometimes held to have been the writer, politician and scientist Johan Browallius (1707–55). About Browallius, see note 6, p. 347.

6 "*Supplement to the High Exchange Rate*": the pamphlet *Bihang til Then höga wäxel-coursen och Låga handels-balancen, samt Dyra tiden...* was published anonymously in 1745 but is believed to have been written by Eric Salander (1699–1764).

7 "*Baron Hårleman's diary*": Superintendent Carl Hårleman (1700–53) was royal architect from 1741. Referred to here is Hårleman's *Dag-bok öfwer en ifrån Stockholm igenom åtskillige rikets landskaper gjord resa, år 1749*, Stockholm, 1749.

8 "*in oeconomicis*": on economic matters.

Commentary

Lars Magnusson

In the Introduction as well as in the commentary to the previous text, we have presented the background to and the initial stages of Chydenius's work in the Grand Joint Committee at the Diet of 1765–6 in pressing for a new ordinance on the freedom of printing and information. At a meeting on 26 August 1765 a Freedom of Printing Subcommittee, or the so-called Third Committee, was established. In practice it was dominated by Chydenius and the radical Caps from the Estate of Clergy. The preliminary report published above was the result of a decision made in the Committee on 18 December. While the result was a collective product, there is no doubt that Chydenius was its main author. However, it took some time for it to reach the Grand Joint Committee. Most probably Chydenius commenced to write the text very rapidly – spending lonely hours at his desk rather than celebrating Christmas and New Year's Eve, as most other members of the Diet did.

As we can see, this report does not really deal with the issue of censorship at all, or whether it should be retained or not. Rather, it presents arguments in favour of freedom of printing and information, referring to the principles of natural liberty. It also contains an outline of the history of the freedom to write and print in Sweden, or rather of the restrictions on that freedom. The report does not directly deal with the issue of access to official documents, although the Committee discussed the issue at length and even made a proposal concerning it. The report was signed by Gustaf Reuterholm (the Nobility), Carl Fredric Mennander (the Clergy), Erik I. Miltopaeus (the Burghers) and Henrik Paldanius (the Peasants) and sent to the Grand Joint Committee, which discussed it on 7 April.

The focus of this meeting was the specific issue of making the minutes of the estate meetings accessible by publication. In the heated debate the delegates of the Nobility in particular warned that printing would make it impossible for delegates to speak their minds openly. Moreover, they stated that accessibility would in the end lead to the English form of party parliamentarism (Whigs and Tories), which in Sweden was thought to be based upon the forbidden doctrine of principalship.[1] In the discussion, the right to publish Diet minutes was defended by Chydenius and some other members of the Estate of Clergy. Chydenius also referred to the discussions on the issue during the Diet of 1760–2, when Count Thure Gustaf Rudbeck, the head of the Cap government and the chairman of the Grand Joint Committee, had in fact spoken in favour of at least publishing *some* of the minutes from the Diet's proceedings. Rudbeck had vacillated earlier and was again uncertain of his opinion. He now pointed out that printing the minutes might be contrary to the Diet Act (*riksdagsordningen*), but when § 22 of the Act on request was read aloud, it became clear that the Act did not explicitly prohibit publication of the minutes.[2] This seemed to settle the matter, but at the last instance, in order to find a compromise, it was decided that the right to publish should be allowed only for minutes and documents produced *after* the new legislation on freedom of printing had taken effect. Hence, the possibility of publishing older documents with the aim of castigating old political sins – something that Chydenius, for example, had wished for – was effectively stopped.

Hence, an important step had been taken towards the launching of a new Act. The next step was to write the additional report (see pp. 237–50), and Chydenius seems to have commenced doing so soon after the meeting on 7 April. However, during the weeks that followed, Chydenius found himself in great trouble with regard to his pamphlet against the Caps' monetary and financial reform (see the Introduction, pp. 25 and 213–16). It cannot be doubted that his staunch defence at the April meeting of the right to publish political documents in order to enlighten the public discussion contributed to his expulsion from the Diet during the summer.

Notes

1 See the Introduction, p. 7. The doctrine of principalship (*principalatsläran*) was based on the notion that the delegates acted on behalf of their "principals", i.e. voters, and according to their instructions. During the 1740s there was a heated debate (*principalatsstriden*) in Sweden on whether the delegates were under an obligation to render account of their actions at the Diet and whether the voters could withdraw their authorization in the event of disagreement with the delegate. The theory of such an imperative mandate was expressly condemned at the Diet of 1746–7.

2 For this, see P. Virrankoski, *Anders Chydenius: Demokratisk politiker i upplysningens tid*, Stockholm: Timbro, 1995, p. 185f.

7 Additional report on the freedom of printing

Additional Report of the Third Committee of the Grand Joint Committee of the Honourable Estates of the Realm on the Freedom of Printing, submitted at the Diet in Stockholm on 21 April 1766

Since the honourable Grand Joint Committee has on 7 April last deigned to approve both the Committee's Report of 18 December 1765 and the attached draft of an ordinance and has moreover decided that the Committee should likewise communicate its thoughts concerning censorship and the printing houses and book trade in general before the honourable Grand Joint Committee submits the aforementioned approved Report to the honourable Estates of the Realm, the Committee has in view thereof addressed itself to these points.

The first, or how censorship should henceforth be conducted, has thus become the initial subject of deliberation by the Committee and has all the more required its most careful examination as the Committee has found censorship to be the principal issue in what has been referred to it for elaboration.

The Committee has to that end sought to ascertain the reasons why a *censor librorum* has in times past been regarded as necessary, among which were the following:

First, that the censor ought to read through the manuscripts intended for printing and examine whether they contained anything that might be contrary to religion, the political constitution and good customs and in consequence thereof notify the Royal Board of Chancery whether they were to be released for printing or be banned, as it was otherwise feared that harmful publications could be disseminated among the general public; second, to inspect the books and documents arriving from abroad, as to whether there were any among them that could be regarded as harmful to the state or religion, which he had to notify for proscription to the Royal Board of Chancery; third, to exercise supervision over the libraries in the kingdom and in particular the Royal Library here in Stockholm.

In addition, fourth, the censor has stated that he has been assigned the duty of allocating to authors useful subjects for elaboration and in so doing to select gifted writers and to encourage them to perform the work thoroughly, by which it was thought that a number of works of public utility could be published; while it was also the duty of the *censor librorum* to most carefully ensure homogeneity

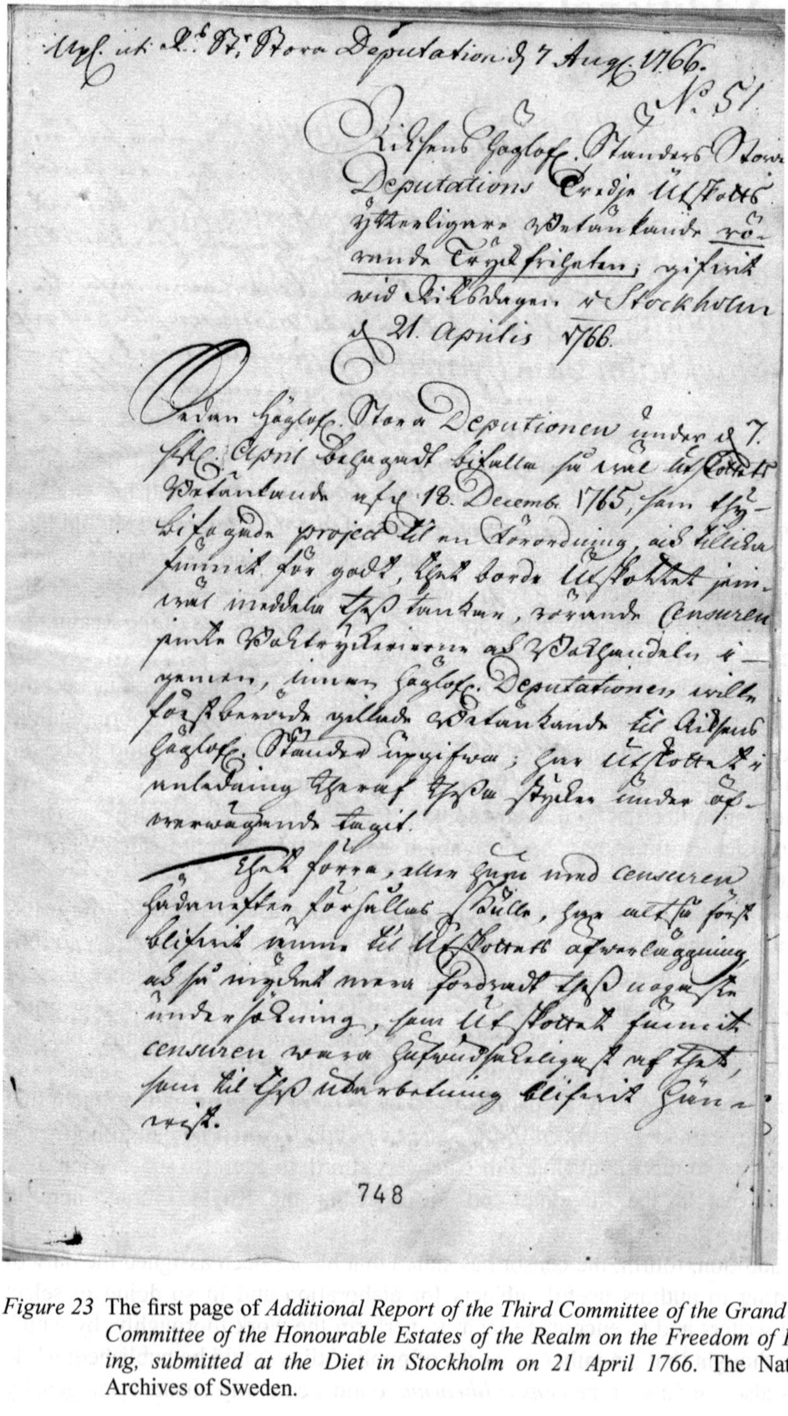

Figure 23 The first page of *Additional Report of the Third Committee of the Grand Joint Committee of the Honourable Estates of the Realm on the Freedom of Printing, submitted at the Diet in Stockholm on 21 April 1766.* The National Archives of Sweden.

everywhere in the actual orthography or manner of spelling in order to make the Swedish language clear and attractive.

But the Committee has furthermore considered whether some other more convenient solution, in closer accord with the security of a free nation, might not be adopted, whereby the same purpose could be achieved, more enlightenment be disseminated in the nation, the preconditions for literature be eased and promoted and, most essentially, the rights and liberties of the nation itself and of each citizen be best safeguarded.

In this respect the Committee has in particular taken into consideration whether one ought not in the case of publishing texts, as in any other business, focus primarily on the author and let each individual retain responsibility for his work, although in such a manner that in this, no less than in all other cases, he be guaranteed a lawful trial befitting a Swede.

It cannot in general be denied that, under the strict censorship of past times, some things were published that could have been expressly described as contrary to religion, the state and good customs, as it was precisely the censor in conjunction with the Royal Board of Chancery who had the sole right to accept or reject the works submitted, as they saw fit, and to act in relation to authors as both prosecutors and judges, which has caused a number of such works to be subsequently labelled as either permissible or harmful, though with the difference that at the Royal Board of Chancery the reasons for the ban have gradually been somewhat more fully recorded in its minutes, whereas the censor, simply by withholding his signature, could achieve exactly the same result. But that this was oftentimes founded on nothing more than a preference or whim can never be disputed when one considers that the censor has prohibited the printing of writings that the Royal Board of Chancery has regarded as innocuous and, vice versa, the Board has prevented ones that the censor has released for printing, while on occasion a work that has been published with the sanction of them both has nonetheless subsequently been confiscated as injurious *either by the censor or by the Board of Chancery*. Then there are manuscripts that at one point are suppressed yet at another are allowed to be published. Some have been approved with the imprimatur of the censor and yet, when already at the printer's, have nevertheless been banned despite the fact that the truths expressed could not throughout all this have been mutable and neither the laws nor the system of government have undergone any changes.

When the Committee actually looks into the issue itself, it appears, furthermore, that scarcely any work can be so carefully worded that it cannot be said to give rise to some offence or other against the system of government or to point to individuals and thus be labelled as subversive, not useful and dangerous, which are the usual terms with which both the censors and the Royal Board of Chancery have stifled many works, and that no law can be formulated so clearly that it may not in a hundred ways be distorted and misinterpreted when it is in the hands of a prosecutor who is also the judge in the case.

Laws and their observance are indeed often subject to arbitrariness among human beings, but to entrust the light of the nation, the most precious jewel of liberty, to the supervision of a single person cannot but be hazardous. Therefore, neither the advantage of human beings over innocent animals, namely their ability to communicate thoughts to one another, nor the civic right to enlighten the nation seem to be appropriately protected under censorship.

Next, as regards the censor's examination of foreign books, the Committee must state that no censors have so far conducted any foreign correspondence by which they would have been able to obtain the necessary information about the content of various foreign books, nor is it in any way possible, when they are inspected in the warehouse or are unpacked in the bookshops in the presence of the censor, to read through every copy of them, which has also led to a number of licentious works in foreign languages arriving from abroad, which have at times, as an offence against morals, been put on sale before the censor was aware of it and sometimes not been banned by the censor and the Royal Board of Chancery until they were actually on sale, a hazard that under normal circumstances can hardly be avoided. To that must be added that a *censor librorum* who resides in Stockholm cannot possibly prevent the importation of harmful books in the other staple towns in the kingdom and across other borders of the country to towns where there are no consistories, universities and grammar schools, and they are thus sometimes examined by relatively inexperienced inspectors.

Concerning the censor's supervision of the country's libraries, it is also quite impracticable for him to intervene in some way or other in any except the Royal Library here in Stockholm, to which the censors have paid the least attention, however, but which in addition does not lack the necessary staff to assist those who wish to use it for some purpose.

The Committee, furthermore, has no knowledge as to whether any subjects have been distributed for elaboration by the censor to authors chosen for their wit and talent, how successful that has been, and what benefit the public has derived from it. But the Committee wishes to declare that learned and astute writers in every branch of scholarship will never be lacking in the Swedish nation as long as literature is not kept in fetters by one or a few persons, and provided that the book trade is facilitated so that it can become profitable, the authors can gain some corresponding advantages, and outstanding talents can see their names immortalized. But the limited scope for ideas and reasoning, together with wretchedness and contempt, make learned and zealous men rarities among us, turning their best efforts into mediocre works, the nation becomes unwell and lethargic and it is pointless for a censor to arouse it from its torpor until the cause of its sickness is removed.

Truths exercise a persuasive power over the human heart if they are simply allowed to irradiate it freely and without constraint, but obscurantism and prejudices leave it unmoved.

Finally, as regards the regulation of orthography and the Swedish language by the censor, the Committee would point out, first, that such matters have never so far been undertaken by a censor, of which all Swedish publications that have been submitted bear incontestable witness; and, in truth, guardianship over the manner of writing and spelling the native language of this country would appear to be almost too great a task for a single censor in the entire country, as other learned men have not yet been able to agree upon this, and ought rather to be left to a scientific or literary academy, as the spelling could then eventually achieve an appropriate consistency. Apart from that, such supervision is inherently impossible, as a censor does not have the time to carefully scrutinize every character in the manuscripts received from all over the country and still less to involve himself in proof-reading, without which, however, this aim cannot possibly be achieved.

In regard to all this, therefore, the Committee, for its part, cannot find that what was intended by the establishment of censorship has been fully achieved thereby or that its continued existence is any longer necessary.

The Committee has not, however, left it at that but has further turned its attention to the harmful consequences that ordinary censorship involves for literature as well as for the country and for liberty, consequences that the Committee views as all the more distressing as it is able to assert with assurance that the reasons for the present poor condition of the country are principally due to obscurantism and secrecy and by no means to a lack of authors who have aspired to enlighten the nation. For it is an incontrovertible truth that, had printing been free, those evils could never have occurred that have reduced our country to insolvency and the causes of which have cost the honourable Estates of the Realm so much time to identify and such great effort to rectify during the present Diet.

As differences of opinion and party are almost inescapable in free states, and the censor therefore cannot but be more favourably inclined towards one of the parties, it is no less certain that he must also show greater partiality towards the publication of those works that support its opinions than those in which the faults of the party with which he sides are laid before the nation.

As long, therefore, as a censor has the right to inspect and examine all works that are to be printed in the country, he will always be able, either by bans or by making changes in the texts of authors, or even by merely delaying those that do not conform to his taste, to stifle many useful truths.

This will always be all the more dangerous to a state should it happen that the government, in some objective or other, has an interest contrary to that of the nation.

That such things have happened and may therefore happen again, of that the history of all free states provides the clearest evidence, and it is well known that when the English government wished to suppress the liberty of the nation, it decided to lay the foundations for that by appointing a censor and therefore worked assiduously to that end, nor would it have failed had not some enlightened and resolute patriots laid the consequences of it before Parliament and thereby blocked such a perilous attempt.

The renowned Mabbott[1] in England, who for a time occupied the office of censor, demonstrates this expressly when, on resigning his office before Parliament, he said that he by no means did so merely because he regarded his occupation as superfluous, as he was fully aware that the office of censor was not the only one in England that was regarded as of great importance but was nonetheless useless, but chiefly because he found it to be harmful both to authors and to the nation itself and that, in view thereof, the honour and authority that he possessed in that regard to act as judge of the thoughts and common sense of the entire nation could not flatter or persuade him to retain it any longer to the injury of his nation.

Nor has it escaped the attention of the Committee that the more honourable the position of censor was made and the freer the access he had to the records and most confidential activities of the members of government and the officials, the more concerned would they be in such a case to win him over to their side by whatever means, while he, on the other hand, would have all the less difficulty in making common cause with them as, precisely by so doing, he could most securely protect himself from prosecution by authors who could achieve nothing at all against such a united force. To believe, under such circumstances and when the interests of these two authorities may so easily coincide, that the liberty of the nation is well protected merely by the personal qualities and impartiality of the censor cannot but be hazardous at a time when legitimate complaints are so openly made against both senior and junior officials.

In this regard the Committee has indeed conceived that the security of subjects in a free nation ought to be founded on good and explicit laws but has, on the other hand, been persuaded by the records of every epoch that the execution of the laws depends chiefly on there being a relative equality or reciprocity between those who command and those who obey, for should the former possess a power many times greater than the latter, the execution would likewise always be to the advantage of the more powerful and the misfortune of the weaker.

Laws are nothing but words and sentences and never in themselves affect anyone; by a superior power they may therefore either be interpreted arbitrarily or left unimplemented or else, without any risk, be utterly transformed.

Although the Committee has not actually identified anything of that kind in Sweden, on such an important matter relating to the enlightenment and liberty of the nation it has not wished to conceal such great apprehensions from the honourable Grand Joint Committee when a law is to be enacted for the future.

Equally unfortunate consequences are viewed by the Committee as inevitable if breaches of the projected ordinance are to be examined and judged by a single designated court, such as the Royal Board of Chancery has hitherto been, and if authors are immediately summoned before higher courts without enjoying *beneficia juris et processus*[2] in this as in all other cases.

The Committee has therefore set aside all previously issued statutes, orders and ordinances on this matter that could give rise to any confusion and misinterpretation and has in addition drafted the ordinance concerning what should be regarded as lawful to print or not in such a short and simple form that it should be easy not only for an author to bring his work into conformity with it but even more so for magistrates in the ordinary lower courts in the country to base verdicts on it, as they will be the ones pronouncing judgment according to several more obscure laws in complicated cases, such concerning the welfare, life and property of citizens.

The Committee has furthermore considered what security the nation has derived or may in future derive against the dissemination of injurious works among the public from having a censor and how his responsibility might be defined.

It is an undeniable truth that both the censor and the Royal Board of Chancery have banned and sequestrated certain printed works that had been approved by the censor without the censor's being held to account for having approved them or in the slightest way compensating the author or the printer for their distress, and however much the law might increase the penalty for a censor in such an event, it is no less obvious that an author or printer will in vain seek redress from him if he enjoys the full support of the government and the officials.

Should the censor, on the other hand, whether through inattention or partiality, exemption from which is rarely the lot of mortals, allow writings that affront certain individuals to appear and the authors are allowed to evade responsibility by hiding behind the censor, not only will they be more audacious but the victim will have to sue the censor, which in the previously conjectured case, after a long and uncertain procedure, is likely to provide him with such limited redress that it will scarcely serve his purpose, whereas, according to the Committee's draft, the author will, under this ordinance, be accused by the affronted person in the appropriate court and will be held accountable just as in all other criminal cases.

Among the factors that in a remarkable manner promote enlightenment and literature in the nation, one is undoubtedly that authors are rewarded for their toil, while the prices of books nonetheless do not rise excessively, so that the book trade is consequently carried on with greater advantage both at home and abroad. In that regard, everything that unnecessarily increases the cost of any work also immediately inhibits the printing and sale of books, but as publishers or authors have been obliged, for the supervision and approval of their publications, to compensate the censor separately for his trouble, over and above the salary that he receives from the state, such things have not been able to occur without a significant burden being imposed on literature, nor can such things be prevented if the office of censor is retained, as long as the authors, in order to have their writings printed, are obliged in some respect or other to seek the favour of the censor, an obstacle to the Swedish book trade that the Committee has also believed it should remedy.

Nor, finally, can the Committee omit mention of the fact that belles-lettres itself and the cultivation of the Swedish language are not inconsiderably impeded when a single person, even the most literary one, has the right of oversight over all works that are published, whereby they are all in the main, as it were, cast from the same mould and the divergent gifts of thought and expression used by authors to persuade and captivate each in their own different way, competing with each other in freedom, are not a little restricted, and all the more so the more closely the censor adjusts them to his taste. It would otherwise be difficult

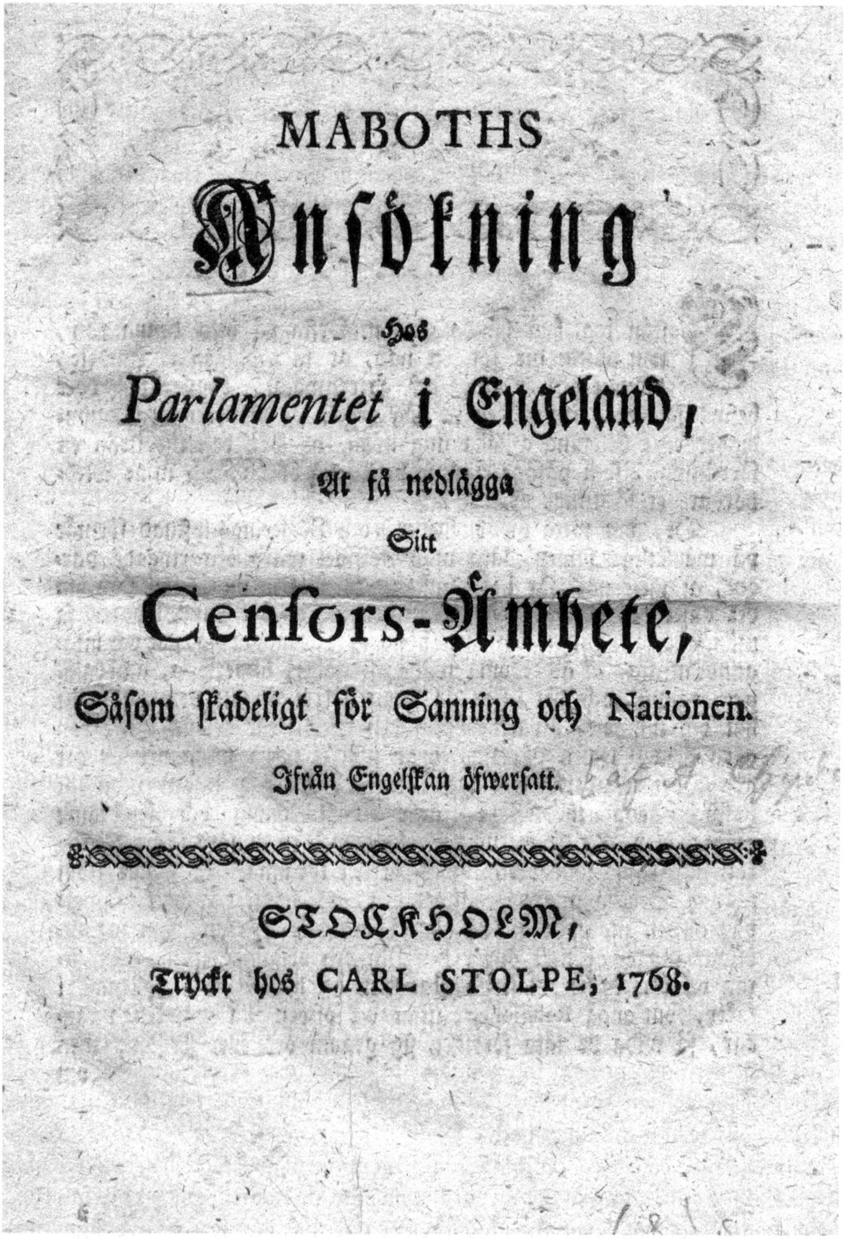

MABOTHS

Ansökning

Hos

Parlamentet i Engeland,

At få nedlägga

Sitt

Censors-Ämbete,

Såsom skadeligt för Sanning och Nationen.

Ifrån Engelskan öfwersatt.

STOCKHOLM,

Tryckt hos CARL STOLPE, 1768.

Figure 24 In 1768, Chydenius published a pamphlet dealing with Gilbert Mabbott's presumed petition to the English Parliament to abolish the office of licenser in the seventeenth century. Two years earlier, Chydenius had touched upon the same story when arguing for freedom of printing at the Diet. Kokkola University Consortium Chydenius.

to show any sufficient reason why Swedish belles-lettres down to the present time has resembled an infant rather than a fully developed body, and it has not yet been determined whether its growth in recent years may not be attributed to some leniency in the censorship rather than to the scrutiny that it has undergone thereby. It is at least certain that the freer printing has been in a nation, the more ingenious are the works that have been published there, to which the English ones in particular bear incontrovertible witness.

So many and, in its view, such very important reasons have inevitably and completely persuaded the Committee of the harmfulness of regular censorship in a free nation and that, whatever regulations concerning it may be adopted in future, neither learning, belles-lettres nor liberty itself can be well protected under censorship. In consideration of which the Committee, in all confidence, most humbly recommends to the honourable Grand Joint Committee that censorship or the office of censor, being useless, unnecessary and harmful, should henceforward cease entirely and the censor's salary be discontinued as soon as the present *censor regius* departs, either by promotion or death, thus saving the budget this expense.

In the first article of this ordinance, which has won the approval of the honourable Grand Joint Committee, a fine adapted to the nature of each offence is already imposed on those who publish or cause to be printed any harmful publications, which, in the event that a censor has permitted that by virtue of his imprimatur, ought in fairness to be claimed not from the author or publisher but from the censor.

The advantages of a freedom of writing and printing of that nature will, judging from what has already been stated, be all the more evident as precisely in that and in no other way the liberty of the nation may be preserved and the love of our propitious system of government be increased, as the experience of all ages bears witness to the fact that a free people has never thrown itself into the arms of autocracy unless it has been denied the opportunity to complain of its distress, and obscurantism and repression have brought it to despair. Only then will it be possible for Swedes, under the shelter of the law, to inform each other of the genuine interests of the country and for many prejudices to be banished that had, as it were, become rooted under the censorship and had undermined a great deal of the legislation issued by the Sovereign Power. Then good sense and talents could escape from their inappropriate reins and gain a wider sphere in which to strengthen each other; harmful and licentious writings could then with greater liability, and without simultaneously stifling the good, be restrained by the penalty imposed; innocence would then be protected by the law in every court and the spirit of vindictiveness find it less easy to exercise its influence throughout the country than in a single court, and the reciprocity that the Committee has outlined between plaintiffs and defendants would be most effective in associating with that law an unswerving observance.

The Committee is aware that this still arouses much opposition in our nation but has not on that account felt able to conceal the true context of the issue, as it is itself so utterly convinced of its utility and necessity.

The freedom of the nation is always proportional to the freedom of printing it possesses, so that neither can exist without the other. To the extent that a nation is free, its freedom of printing will be the same, but on the contrary, where printing is muzzled by some form of guardianship, it is an infallible sign that the nation is fettered, as one observes that even under autocratic governments where freedom of writing and of speech are tolerated, subjects enjoy more of their civic rights than in certain states where thoughts and reason have been curbed by restricting printing, although they are otherwise reputed to be free.

Nor has the Committee, in examining this subject, failed to take into account the main objections that may be made against the discontinuance of censorship, such as that it is unlikely that it can be implemented without the greatest hazard if a nation that has hitherto been subject to a censor should suddenly be freed from all supervision while not yet being sufficiently experienced and careful to correctly use such a freedom, which could soon be transformed into arbitrariness, or else that authors and printers might be deterred from publishing useful works by their liability for such works. But the Committee regards neither as a risk in this case, as the penalty laid down in an explicit ordinance must make the authors more careful than before, when they depended merely on the censor's signature without any enacted laws, while on the other hand the honourable Estates of the Realm themselves during this Diet, by publishing a number of tracts on a variety of subjects, have prepared the way for them to state without apprehension what they believe themselves entitled to in defence of truth.

To retain the office of censor because the nation is still unfamiliar and inexperienced is the same as to maintain the reason why it has hitherto been so and to prevent it from improving in the future. And albeit that a few small irregularities may occur in the works that are published after the abolition of censorship, it remains a fact that it has not been possible to avoid them hitherto, though they could not so easily be touched when under the protection of a prominent name. But when a greater purpose, which is the liberty of the nation, is to be achieved by the freedom of printing, it is not the time, in order to avoid small inconveniences that can never be prevented among human beings, to fail in a matter of such urgent concern for the future existence of the country and of liberty because it may appear dangerous to the honourable Estates of the Realm to leave the country and liberty subject to further hazards, when the transfer of censorship from the Royal Board of Chancery to the censor alone would be merely to transfer power from a collective authority into the hands of a single individual, and the effect and observance that one ought then to expect of even the best of laws may easily be perceived by anyone.

If, on the other hand, in order to forestall such inconveniences and in order that a censor should not be allowed to approve of and suppress whatever writings and works he wished, one were to insist that the authority of the censor should not be so extensive that he could positively prevent anything from being printed but could merely provide the authors with good advice and indeed have the right to expressly approve or disapprove of something in a text yet not have the power to prevent it from being printed if the author insists on it, in which case the printing would also be the responsibility of the author but not that of the censor, the Committee would observe in that regard that even such supervision would be not only futile but harmful.

It would be futile because an author who dares to print at his own risk that of which the censor has disapproved and thus puts himself at risk can then rather more easily answer at once for that which the censor had regarded as inoffensive. If the censor were to have no power to ban anything from being printed, he could not be held responsible for what he advises either, so that he might then all the more easily be moved by whims, and his rejection would impose a certain pressure on the judge to support his wishes against a defenceless author. And although good advice should never be despised and sensible authors are unlikely ever to ignore it, whether it is given by the person who has held the office of censor or someone else, there is still no reason why one single person in the entire country should become everyone else's adviser, or why other learned and honourable men should not equally enjoy the same right. There is thus greater reason to fear more harmful consequences from according such a right to a censor, for then learned and literary men might thereby be made to refrain from having works printed rather than accept advice and instructions from one to whom they regarded themselves as superior in learning and experience, in which respect the Committee is all the less likely to be mistaken as it is able with certainty to report that several learned men have already refused to submit their works to the scrutiny of the censor and have thus, though in breach of the censorship laws, had several editions of them printed here in Stockholm without his signature but could easily, by the renewal of this constraint, be deterred from honouring and benefiting their fatherland. Literature would then also, in the same way as before, be encumbered with a fee to the censor which could not be prevented by any prohibition; obstructions and delays for that which might, to some degree, be contrary either to the censor's interests or his opinions would, moreover, infallibly become the fate of many works; and, finally, if the offences of authors were to be adjudicated in some particular court that had the same outlook and interest as the censor, or they could in some way mutually influence each other, freedom of writing would survive in name only.

The Committee therefore believes that it is all the more urgent to use the present moment for the abolition of censorship and the defence of liberty, for which Providence itself has in an excellent manner recently prepared the way, as it might otherwise soon happen that the nation will be enveloped in a new fog when that which could now easily be achieved will at another time be quite impossible to carry out. Year and date as above.

On behalf of the Third Committee of the Grand Joint Committee of the Estates of the Realm.

Ut in protocollo,[3]

Christoffer von Kochen, Anders Ph. Forssenius
Leonard de la Rose and Johan Andersson

Notes

1 *"The renowned Mabbott in England"*: Gilbert Mabbott or Mabbot (1622–*c*.1670), newsletter writer and parliamentary licenser of newsbooks and pamphlets in England. Mabbott was a professional newsletter writer in the turbulent times of revolution, regicide and the interregnum of the 1640s and 1650s. In March 1645 he became deputy licenser but was dismissed, presumably for political reasons, only two years later. In September 1647 he was reinstated as licenser but he resigned or was dismissed in May 1649. The office of licenser was, however, not abolished, and Mabbott was succeeded by John Rushworth. Later on in life, Mabbott held the office of manager for licences of wine and strong waters in Ireland. In 1768, Chydenius published the pamphlet *Maboths ansökning hos Parlamentet i England att få nedlägga sitt censorsämbete, såsom skadeligt för sanning och nationen*, dealing with Gilbert Mabbott's presumed petition to the English Parliament to abolish the office of licenser, as it was harmful both to truth and to the nation. The pamphlet by Chydenius is stated to be translated from English, or Danish according to other sources, but no original can be found in Mabbott's name in English or Danish bibliographies. The original text by Mabbott, if there ever was one, is therefore presumed to be lost or part of a larger whole, and has not been found.

2 *"beneficua juris et processus"*: the right to be put on trial in order to defend oneself from accusations.

3 *"Ut in protocollo"*: according to the minutes.

Commentary

Lars Magnusson

This additional report was written in April 1766, most probably after the meeting with the Grand Joint Committee on 7 April referred to above, and presented during a meeting with the Third Committee on 21 April. The discussion at this meeting seems to a large extent have been focused on the issue of censorship – a theme which was not so much in focus in the last report, discussed earlier in April, as we saw. As Virrankoski shows, several of the more conservative members of the committee were not present, "thus making the position of the adversaries of censorship quite strong".[1] The censor, Niclas von Oelreich, was summoned to this meeting in order to present his views and arguments. Not surprisingly, he spoke in favour of censorship. His emphasis on the argument that censorship helped to improve and standardize the written Swedish language was perhaps more unexpected. Moreover, he stressed that although censorship sometimes can be "despotic", it also has good sides: excessive freedom to publish can endanger the public order. He also spoke against making the printer responsible for the publication – referring back to the memorial signed by Kraftman (in fact written by Chydenius) from the previous summer (see Chapter 5). Such an order would only lead many printers, through fear of being prosecuted, to abstain from publishing controversial texts, he argued. Hence, it would lead to even less freedom of printing. Chydenius changed his opinion on this matter in the additional report, possibly in part under the influence of von Oelreich. It was now suggested that only the writer should be held responsible, and this principle was also subsequently implemented in the final Act.

At this time, when von Oelreich's plea for the preservation of censorship seems to have created new proselytes, Chydenius interfered. While speaking favourably of von Oelreich as a person, he insisted upon the negative effects of the institution of censorship as such. The task of improving the Swedish language could not be put upon the shoulders of a single censor, but should rather be taken care of by a scientific or literary academy, he argued. He also spoke in favour of a system in which printers would be prosecuted at ordinary courts of law if they misused the freedom of printing and published texts offending private individuals. Here he also referred to the case of England and how the censor Gilbert Mabbott (see pp. 241–2) back in 1649 had voluntarily left his position, which eventually led – according to Chydenius – to the abolition of the institution of censorship in England. The message to von Oelreich was clearly put: in the name of freedom he too ought to resign from his position. Responding to Chydenius, von Oelreich changed the subject and stressed the need to censor blasphemous religious texts. However, as we have discussed, Chydenius had never intended to allow a total freedom to publish theological texts without their being censored by the Church authorities. Hence, von Oelreich's discourse here was beside the point and possibly indicates that he had problems in defending the old institution.[2]

The result of the discussion signalled a clear victory for Chydenius and his group: it was decided that the Committee would submit the additional report to the Grand Joint Committee and on the basis of it suggest a new Act that would ban censorship. What happened thereafter, we have already depicted. With Chydenius deported back to Alaveteli, there were a number of changes made to what in December 1766 became the new Act abolishing censorship (except for religious texts), and admitting an increased right to publish such political documents as until then had been considered to contain classified information. The Peasants, the Burghers and the Clergy supported the new Act, whereas the majority of the Nobles rejected it. With three estates against one, the new Act could be established. It was a grand victory for the radical Caps, but for Chydenius personally too. The result was the world's first Act combining freedom of printing with freedom of information.

Notes

1 P. Virrankoski, *Anders Chydenius: Demokratisk politiker i upplysningens tid*, Stockholm: Timbro, 1995, p. 187.
2 Ibid., p. 187.

Part III
Radical rector of Kokkola

8 Answer to the Question Posed by the Society of Arts and Sciences in Gothenburg

Whether Rural Trade Is Generally Useful or Harmful to a Country, and to What Extent It Contributes to the Promotion or Decline of Industry

By Anders Chydenius
Rector of Kokkola
Stockholm, Printed at the Royal Printing-Press, 1777.

Preface

I herewith present to you, dear reader, a treatise about the rural trade, as to whether it is useful or harmful to a country.

It is not the first time that I venture to defend the freedom of the people and my fellow citizens before a revered public.

The *Answer* that I submitted to the Royal Academy of Sciences in response *to its question concerning the cause of the emigration of Swedish people*[1] was printed in 1765.

Soon after that, I took up the defence of the natural rights of our maritime towns in the form of a treatise entitled: *Refutation of the Reasons Employed to Deny the Towns in Ostrobothnia and Västerbotten as Well as in Västernorrland a Free Navigation.*[2]

In the same year I ventured to defend freedom of trade in general in this country and demonstrated the unfortunate consequences of the Commodity Ordinance in particular in a tract entitled *The Source of Our Country's Weakness*,[3] of which the publisher, the late Director Salvius, within a fortnight printed two issues that attracted the particular attention of many people and was therefore described by the Royal Librarian Mr Gjörwell[4] as the most notorious tract to appear during the entire period of the Diet.

The author, who was at first anonymous, was thought to be a foreigner or a Swede bought by foreigners to betray his fatherland; the tract was therefore, apart from innumerable small pamphlets, attacked with extraordinary zeal in two more extensive treatises, of which the first was called *Circumstantial Refutation of the Treatise Called The Source of Our Country's Weakness*[5] and the second *Water Tests Conducted at the Same Source*,[6] and that with such vehemence that everyone proclaimed the defeat of the author, and his friends advised him, as the

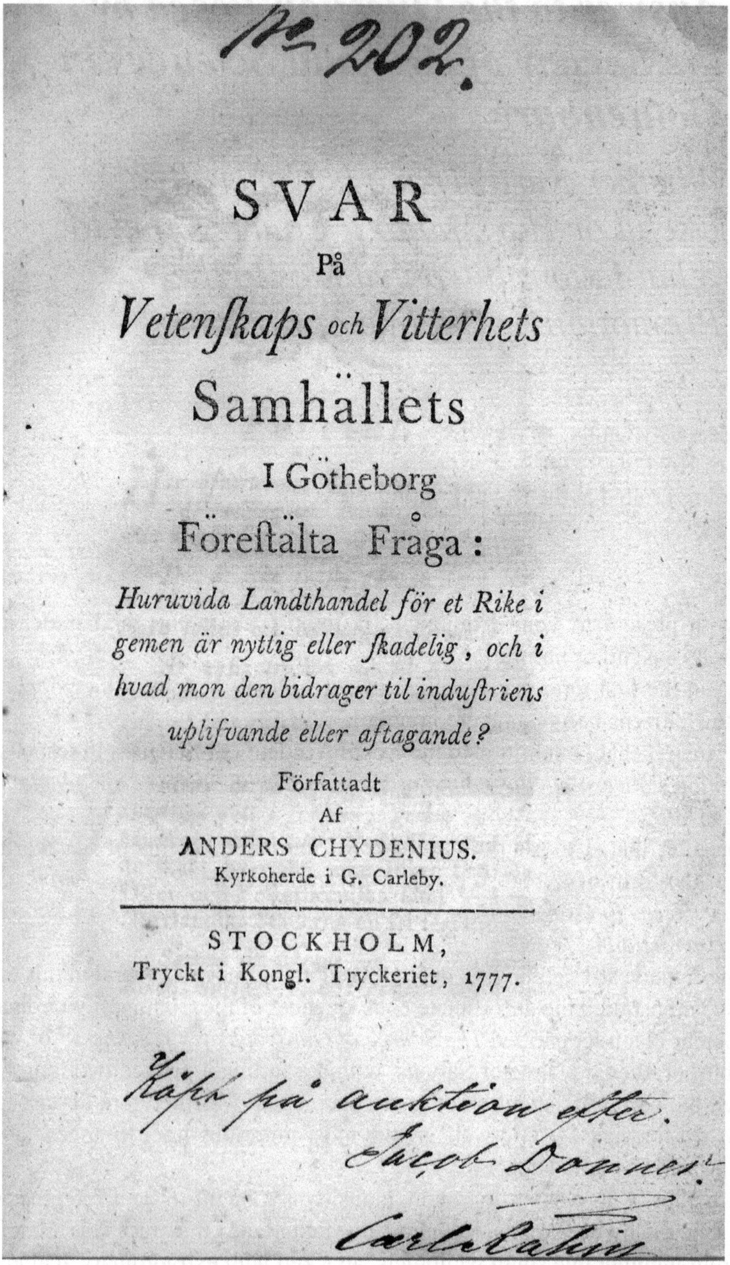

No. 202.

SVAR

På

Vetenskaps och Vitterhets

Samhällets

I Götheborg

Förestälta Fråga:

Huruvida Landthandel för et Rike i gemen är nyttig eller skadelig, och i hvad mon den bidrager til industriens uplifvande eller aftagande?

Författadt

Af

ANDERS CHYDENIUS.

Kyrkoherde i G. Carleby.

STOCKHOLM,

Tryckt i Kongl. Tryckeriet, 1777.

Köpt på auktion efter. Jacob Donner.

Figure 25 The title page of *Answer to the Question Posed by the Society of Arts and Sciences in Gothenburg: Whether Rural Trade Is Generally Useful or Harmful to a Country, and to What Extent It Contributes to the Promotion or Decline of Industry* (1777). Kokkola University Consortium Chydenius.

best way to save his honour, which under such circumstances might be entirely destroyed, never again to attempt to engage in that subject.

Despite that, however, I ventured to confront my powerful opponents, with no other protection than the naked truth, and, in order to prepare the ground for my intended response, had a tract printed called *The National Gain*,[7] following which, towards the autumn of the same year, my *Circumstantial Response* to the *Refutation* and to the *Water Tester* appeared. The effect of this was that, of my brave assailants, although they had casually spread innuendos and venom in various other tracts against the truth and its defender, none dared to extend their refutation into an attack on the foundation on which I had erected my edifice of liberty. I had in fact hoped they would, in order thereby to gain further scope to expand the concepts of freedom among our citizens and to convince them all the more fully of such a precious truth.

With calm restored on that front, the duty incumbent on me as member of the Diet led me to make some investigation of the finances of the kingdom and of the then so controversial redemption policy and the reduction of the rate of exchange, with its consequences for the whole economy, and I recorded my indefeasible thoughts on that subject, which I submitted the same autumn to the honourable Joint Banking Committee of the Estates of the Realm, with the express reservation that if the Joint Banking Committee did not wish to comment on them, I would then be obliged to present these thoughts of mine in full to the public, so that both contemporaries and posterity should see that I had no part in the so-called reduction of the exchange rate and that all the disadvantages that would be caused to the public thereby had been clearly foreseen and predicted. I often discussed these with the members of the Joint Banking Committee. I raised them during debates, but when that had no effect, I fulfilled my promise and ordered my thoughts in *A Remedy for the Country by Means of a Natural System of Finance*,[8] which I submitted to the consideration of my Estate, where it was examined by the deputies and, with the endorsement and permission of that Estate, printed in 1766.

Scarcely had that been printed when the alarm was sounded everywhere. I was summoned to appear before the honourable Secret Committee. My Estate revoked its endorsement, although it had been based on an examination by the deputies, and held it to be a very lenient punishment for my crime, which consisted in daring to consider means of preserving the realm, when the Estate declared me unworthy of its confidence.

Serious offences against the whole of Europe were seen in my tract. Delusions were read in every line and dangerous designs underlying the whole. It was publicly stated that I had been bought by an opposition party, the purchase sum being set at 70,000 or 80,000 *daler*. Fearsome formulas of apology were proposed and urged, and there was much talk of an arrest and even more.

The first edition was quickly sold out, however, and within three weeks of that, Director Salvius had already sold the following one, though without distinguishing them in any way on the title page, as it was feared that the entire tract would be confiscated and banned.

Finally, a starving hack[9] was hired to spew streams of venom over the author on behalf of the establishment, using the most offensive expressions of ferrymen's language, to vent the indignation of the party and to arouse among the unthinking mob, which was at that time used to carry into effect by its voice the decisions of the great men, an abhorrence and loathing for the truths that he had brought to light. I can now look upon the troubles that I suffered with all the more contentment as I have not needed to write anything in my defence, the upheavals of recent years having told in my favour, and His Majesty has based his Redemption Ordinance[10] in all essentials on the same fundamental truths, bringing blessed stability to the long-perturbed enterprise of the entire kingdom for all future time – a great encouragement for one who loves his native land to also venture something in the future for truths that are of such great benefit to our species.

During the same period the question of censorship, so important in every age for free societies, was discussed in the Grand Committee's Third Committee on the Freedom of Printing. There I also had the fortune to be able to speak out for liberty and to some extent, despite the active opposition of several important members, contribute to freeing it from its tutelage.

Moved by the same tender feelings for freedom and for the citizens, I have composed this little treatise. The reason for it is made clear by its title. The Society of Arts and Sciences in Gothenburg some years ago announced a prize question, to be answered, regarding the rural trade, which received no answers the first time round and was therefore set again as a competition subject for the year 1776, when this answer of mine was submitted. None of the answers received won the prize, however, but one was awarded the so-called *accessit*,[11] in addition to which the Society expressed itself favourably about this answer of mine and willing to publish it if the author himself would only make such changes as the Society would propose to him. The Society of Arts and Sciences also graciously informed me, under my motto, of these, which I have to the best of my ability sought to use to improve my treatise. But as I nonetheless apprehend that the Society may still on its part find many doubtful matters in it, which I, on the other hand, being ardent and sensitive in defence of liberty, would not wish to remove from this publication of mine, I have decided to present it on its own merits rather than be the cause of further trouble on account of it to such a venerable Society.

Most of all, dear reader, I prefer to leave my essay to your examination. I am quite prepared to be contradicted, but no other reasons convince me than those that palpably lead to the only true purpose of all political arrangements, the happiness of our species.

Kokkola
26 September 1777
Anders Chydenius

§ 1

Invited by a worthy Society, deeply moved by the fetters laid by human beings on humankind, despairing of my ability to remove them, yet owing a duty to attempt it, I take up my pen.

Being unconversant with the world, I thought that truths revealed by the defenders of humanity would produce conviction among a thinking people and extinguish the will-o'-the-wisps of ignorance and self-interest, but as many years' experience has taught me that arrangements that are most deleterious to humankind are for centuries upheld as fundamental truths and that whole continents are governed on the basis of prevailing delusions and prejudices, while truths designed for the salvation of our species are, on the contrary, banished, there seems to be little else left for those unfortunate enough to love humanity than to sigh over these fetters borne by their species and yet to conceal that within themselves in order not to be dismissed as heterodox by the entire society to which they belong.

But since people have begun to be able to breathe in the most powerful countries in Europe, when our Great Ruler has the acuity to penetrate the outer bastions of self-interest and his highest desire is to make people happy with his reign, all hope should certainly not be abandoned. I therefore venture to appear before such an honourable Society, to breathe pure freedom, to offer support for our oppressed species.

The Society of Arts and Sciences has proposed a question, *whether rural trade is generally useful or harmful to a country, and to what extent it contributes to the promotion or decline of industry*, and has encouraged its fellow countrymen to submit answers to it. I intend to defend you, oppressed *rural trade*, a small but indispensable part of the body of freedom, not because I have been bribed or enriched by you, but because you enrich people and provide them with their necessities and pleasures. Oh! persecuted rural trade, on whose destruction, along with that of their own species, a combination of forces has laboured for several centuries, that, having innumerable times been put on trial, condemned to be eradicated, tormented, fettered and restricted, yet still survives, to call you forth from your prison and to break the fetters that you have borne is my task on this occasion. I speak on your behalf with pleasure, though I shall be called a heretic, and am willing to be trampled on by our present era, provided that I can promote you for posterity.

§ 2

This name, so odious among us, comprises all the trade, apart from open fairs, that townsmen conduct in the countryside, in order to buy its various products and to sell to the country people what they need; or else when a countryman provides himself in town with all manner of goods for the country-dwellers and in return purchases the goods they have for sale, in order again to supply these to others.

It is this trade that is now at issue. Its very name is already odious to our general public, nor can its defender expect a better fate. As far as official reasons are concerned, it is clear that it is not only the laws of our kingdom that prohibit all trade in rural regions, while I also know of the complaints of many wise men on this subject. But as it is here neither a question of whether it is prohibited or not, nor a question of what great men have thought and said about it, but whether it is useful to a country or not, it should be possible to freely discuss the issue as such without touching upon the laws promulgated concerning it, either among us or elsewhere, and their observance.

§ 3

Rulers have for ages past wished to arrogate to themselves the right to prescribe to their subjects by legislation in what manner and by what rules they should support themselves and have, often by severe penalties, obstructed the rise of several branches of industry.

The very first Law-giver, the greatest of all, did indeed present an economic law to mankind, *to feed themselves by the sweat of their brows*, but it was also so general that it neither condemned one to follow the plough nor privileged another so that he could simply live on a gain acquired without labour. It was entirely unlimited with regard to where and in what manner human beings should support themselves around the globe, whether they lived together in towns and villages or by themselves in the countryside. To support life is the first requirement of nature, and it will tolerate no limitation, as it extends far beyond the ties that have bound societies together. The leaders of societies cannot possess rights over life, nor exclude any means by which it may be sustained. The practice of moral vices, being always and in all circumstances harmful to humankind, is the only one to which the Almighty has desired to set limits by threats and punishments, but not to any way of honestly obtaining one's food, clothing and comfort.

How, then, can rulers wish to arrogate to themselves a right that is beyond them? Nor do the wise leaders of our time do so, but petty princes dare to meddle in all manner of things that they do not understand, merely on the basis of their own or others' prejudices or the advice of venal ministers. They gather a large portion of their subjects into certain groups and grant them advantages at the expense of the others, advantages that they entrench with privileges by which some are enabled to gain a superabundance by indolence and idleness, while the rest end their lives prematurely, owing to unemployment and starvation, or else seek to preserve their lives by emigrating.

To guarantee a subject security for his life and property and to arbitrarily prohibit some means of protecting the former and acquiring the latter appears to be a political contradiction that ought not to be possible in a well-ordered society, as precisely such regulations often devastate towns and countries far more than a bloody battle, especially if they are carefully observed, which seldom happens, however, in view of the great havoc that would be wreaked by them.

The necessities of life are manifold. A single earner often has to feed five, six or seven persons. All possible expedients are necessary for a worker with a modest daily wage; if a single one is closed off and he flees the country or perishes in misery with his family, that should in truth be attributed to the prohibitions and to the person who has issued them.

The orthodox politicians of our time may say: why should he need to starve? He is able to earn a living for himself and his family by his labour. But what if that is not enough? He will have to redouble his diligence, they say. I reply: But if that is still not sufficient? Well, they say: he should cut his coat according to his cloth. But his and his children's stomachs will not endure that for many days: he has to think either of dying, stealing or fleeing – all of them hard choices.

I do not have time to pursue this proof further, but conclude it fairly with the preface of the young and enlightened King of France[12] to his new and blessed decree of freedom:[13] "Illusion or fancy," he says, "has so far prevailed with some that they have asserted the right to work to be a royal prerogative that the King could sell and the subjects ought to buy from him. We hasten to reject such a maxim. God himself, when he gave humankind needs and made it indispensable for it to seek the means to satisfy them through labour, has (N.B.) *given every human being as a possession that right to work; and this possession is the first, the most precious of all, the one that least of all can be restricted.*"[14]

Such a King, with his minister,[15] ought with good reason to be called great who has voluntarily relinquished an ancient right and a flattering control of the trades, who by this single decree, had it been carried into effect, would have benefited his subjects more than by distributing ten million *livres* annually to the poor.

From this the reader will already see how one should generally regard most of our economic laws, namely that they are hazardous steps towards the oppression of our species. Among these I include, with good reason, the prohibition against making it easier for the farmer to sell his goods by means of buyers in the countryside and through them obtain his requirements from the town, in the absence of which he is obliged to waste his valuable time on unnecessary journeys to town.

§ 4

Once that general foundation has been laid, we come closer to the rural trade that is here in question. We shall then soon see how, in the first place, it *markedly contributes to individual profit.*

From the yield of agriculture, the countryman has a variety of goods to sell, in larger or smaller quantities, such as grain, butter, tallow, beef cattle and others, or craft products such as textiles, stockings, all kinds of wooden goods and the like. On the other hand, his need for urban or mercantile goods is manifold, if not quite as extensive as in the towns, where extravagance prevails, though not much less where gentry reside in the countryside, although the country people themselves also require a number of things, such as salt, tobacco, iron and certain small-wares, etc.

Let us then imagine for a moment a rural area situated 6 *mil* from the nearest market town, inhabited by 100 farmers. One of them can, for example during the summer months, sell ½, another ¾, the third 1, the fourth 2, the fifth 3 *lispund* of butter every month, which is also the monthly requirement of the town either for its own needs or for onward sale. According to the regulations, each of these farmers should personally take his produce to the town and sell it in the market-place. For that purpose these farmers use three days every month for a journey to the town, which amounts to 300 days of travelling a month during the busiest season of labour, which, if valued at 10 *mark* each day, amounts to a sum of 750 *daler kmt*. Let the entire quantity of butter be 120 *lispund* a month, then the cartage cost for it, not including the obligatory carriage days owed to the more affluent, will be 750 *daler*. Let the market price be 12 *daler kmt*, though it is often less in smaller market towns, then the sum for the entire quantity of butter will come to 1,140 *daler*, and when the cartage costs, which, by the regulations, must amount to 750 *daler*, are subtracted from that, 690 *daler* will be the actual price that the countrymen receive for the 120 *lispund* of butter, or somewhat less than 6 *daler* per *lispund*.

It is objected to this that, despite the prohibition on rural trade, a countryman is nonetheless allowed to send his butter on commission with other people, when several can combine to entrust it to one who will carry it such a long distance. But what countryman would want to take such trouble on behalf of another? Or even if he could be persuaded to do so, how is he to draw up the account? Different quantities, of varying quality, at different prices and diverse weights, make it impossible for him to settle with several owners and for them to entrust their goods to him. But let us suppose that one man could carry the butter of two farmers and that the cost would thereby be reduced by half, then the cartage cost would still be at least 375 *daler*. That is something at least!

But let us now instead in our minds exempt this rural area from chapter 6 of the Commercial Code.[16] Three rural traders or buying agents visit this area and each buys 40 *lispund* of butter and collects it by means of 3 days' work per horse and man, altogether nine days' work, which at 4 *daler* a day amounts to a cartage cost of 36 *daler* for 120 *lispund*, over a distance of 6 *mil*. If they now pay 11 *daler* 16 *öre* per *lispund* out there, the country people will, instead of 690 *daler* net, receive *alterum tantum*,[17] namely 1,380 daler, the agents recover the cost of their days of carting and a small profit of 6 2/5 *öre* per *lispund*, or 8 *daler* a load, while the town still obtains these 120 *lispund* of butter for 12 *daler* per *lispund*.

But the profit of these agents will be even larger if they also carry with them tobacco and small-wares and supply the country-dwellers with those.

§ 5

Let us now, to extend the argument, take the example of another rural commodity, namely beef cattle, which are driven in to the towns in the autumn to be sold. Let the same 100 farmers have 50 larger and smaller animals for sale, some one and others two, or at most three. According to the regulations, each individual owner should drive his own cattle to market. Then he who has one small animal as well as the one who has three has to drive it the same 6 *mil*. That will then require two hands from each farm that has any beef cattle to sell. Let there be 40 such tenants, then 80 persons will be engaged in driving those cattle to town and selling them, including the return journey, and each of them then takes four days, amounting for the entire drove of 50 cattle to 320 days' work, which, reckoned at 2 *daler kmt* a day, amounts to an expenditure of 640 *daler*. Let 36 *daler* be the average price at which all of them are sold, which amounts to 1,800 *daler*. Driving them to town will then have consumed more than a third of the total value. Nor can anyone entrust his animal to a neighbour, considering the differences in quality and price, and the fact that they are not all driven there on the same day but as and when each individual has the time and opportunity.

Now let us again, in our mind, rescind the law prohibiting rural trade and allow a buying agent, whether farmer or townsman, to travel out there in the autumn and buy up all these 50 beef cattle, which would take him five days for the journey there and back. In order to bring the drove back, he hires three hands, who in four days get all 50 of them to the town, performing 12 days' work, which, added to the five of the agent, amounts to 17 days' work in all, producing, at 2 *daler* each, a sum of 34 *daler* spent purchasing the drove and getting it to the town, which produces a pure profit of 606 *daler* on this single commodity, by means of the rural trade, whether it is made by the buyer or the seller.

In the same way, one could demonstrate with regard to other products of the country what a remarkable profit accrues to individual people when they are sold through the rural trade. One could also make rough estimates from that as to the effect which that might have throughout the kingdom in a single year, but truth does not need to dazzle with impressive calculations; it presents itself best simple and naked; and I venture to assert that this proof is not much inferior to the mathematical ones in essence, even if the figures may be increased or diminished by various circumstances.

§ 6

It is the same with urban commodities. If no one in this village has the most necessary things – iron, steel, salt, tobacco, ribbons, needles, etc. – for sale, he who lacks any of these has to make a journey of three days for a *mark* of steel, a *vacka* of salt, a *skålpund* of tobacco, or whatever he is short of, which he could have used to work on his farm, had such goods been available there. It may be objected that the rural trader fleeces him, as he would find more favourable prices in town, but I reply: he can never fleece him so much that his three-day journey to the town, at 10 *mark*, or 2 *daler* a day, will not fleece him even more. For example, if he only needs 1 *skålpund* of tobacco, the rural trader cannot possibly raise the price of 1 *skålpund* of tobacco so much that he can charge 7 *daler* 16 *öre* for it. Yes, you say, if he had nothing else to buy than 1 *skålpund* of tobacco! It may well be that he has neither the money nor credit even for that but has to make his journey only for a few *aln* of tobacco. The reader will say: yes, but that seldom happens; he may often have several errands, with goods going to and from town carrying the cartage costs. Well, for that purpose he may go to town when it pays him to do so, but that does not always happen, for he can neither remember his needs nor always be aware of them in advance, nor always have the money to pay for them, except in instalments, and is therefore often forced, to his great annoyance, to go without some necessity, whereas he will get everything from the rural trader without effort and waste of time, at a reasonable mark-up.

§ 7

Various objections may be raised against these obvious truths. It is said that the example given of a region that lies 6 *mil* from a market town is not suitable as evidence of the utility of the rural trade in rural areas that lie closer to some town; and as few areas are as remote as that, the utility of the rural trade will also be rather limited. But against that I would argue, first, that in the less populated provinces of the realm there are whole parishes and villages that are situated 8, 10, 15 and 20 *mil* and more from the nearest market town, in which case the transport of the goods by the owner will be even more expensive than in my computation. Second, this calculation also applies to the rural areas that are nearer, only with a certain reduction in the expenses, always in proportion to their increasing proximity to the town, until it becomes almost negligible closest to the town, just as in a medium-sized town it is already reckoned a waste of time and expense in the case of various necessities to have to go to the other end of the town to fetch them.

It is also alleged against the rural trade that, as a result of such buying agents, the price of rural products is raised quite excessively for the town-dweller, when rural traders bid against each other for them and compete with one another, whereby the commodities required for the manufactures from the countryside are also made more expensive and their products correspondingly dearer, whereas those rural commodities would be available at lower prices in the marketplace. My response to that is: if the true interest of the kingdom as a whole consists in the availability of rural commodities at a reasonable price in the marketplace, then the conclusion is warranted, but if the countryman is as much a free Swedish subject as the town-dweller and the manufacturer, he would seem as entitled as them to seek the highest price for his commodities, and when that is denied him, every impartial person must conclude that he is deprived of the security and freedom that the King has sworn to secure for his subjects in their property, and then the name of freedom will have little meaning for him.

If the price of the country's produce rises owing to the rural traders, that will become the natural value of these commodities. And those manufactures that do not pay their way without depressing the price of rural commodities must always be harmful to the country. As rational people, those traders must expect to recover their costs; if they do not, then such agents will not trade for long but will soon be replaced by more circumspect rural traders. Whatever reduction in the price that the country people now receive for their commodities compared to what they would receive if buyers were allowed to visit them is the first loss that the rural population suffers in this connection. The second is the difference in the cost of cartage to the town when they themselves took their goods there and when the agent did so, which in the examples given amounts to a half and a third of the overall value of the commodity.

What is one to say about this? A ruler of an autocratic state has the power to impose on his subjects, for the support and security of himself and the realm, expenditure at such a level as he decides is necessary; but whether he is entitled to force them to sell their commodities below cost price and to squander half or a third of that for no good reason or on unnecessary journeys I firmly believe to be a question that those who surround the persons of princes should allow them to answer themselves. On my part I sincerely confess that in my view I cannot but ascribe that loss to the prohibitions issued against the rural trade, which is likely to amount to several millions annually if applied across the entire kingdom, a loss that, by allowing a free and unrestricted trade to anyone, even in the countryside, will immediately cease and, especially in the most remote areas, turn into a clear profit.

§ 8

Now that I have thus shown my reader in concrete terms what advantages accrue to individuals from the rural trade, the way also appears to be cleared to *demonstrate that it is useful to the country in general.*

By country we simply mean the inhabitants of the country. It has now been shown that the farmer benefits and that the towns do not suffer unreasonable and unfair losses but rather benefit through their buying agents; is the country then not bound to benefit from it? The matter is quite clear. Our regulated trade in Europe and our so-called useful commercial system has, judging from our first example, obliged many farmers to quite fruitlessly waste many days' work that could have been used to improve the land. I have shown that by means of the rural trade all such things may be eliminated to the great advantage of the country; who, then, does not see the utility of that to the country? Or when the individual gains, without depriving anyone of anything by cunning, force and deceit, then the country can only gain thereby. I do not wish to dwell any longer on this point, however, which should already be regarded by all thoughtful persons as axiomatic for our domestic economic system, but let us proceed.

§ 9

The country gains not only in so far as unnecessary journeys to town are eliminated; there is something here of far greater significance. The quantity of commodities always increases, as far as it is possible, to the extent that commodities are in high demand and command a good price. Among those who live far from the towns they are not sought after and they are therefore produced only in small amounts, so that those country people spend most of their time in idleness, apart from what they are forced to do by extreme necessity. Whoever travels through such areas will see the clearest evidence of that.

But where a rural trader travels from farm to farm, asks for all kinds of goods, pays a reasonable price for them on the spot and places orders for the same or other goods after a certain time, as well as supplying the needs of the country people, there the quantity of goods begins to grow and the population is given increasing employment from year to year.

As evidence of this I would refer to what a rural trader told me some years ago from experience: he said that he had conducted this prohibited trade for several years, travelled around in the most remote areas and annually bought from there and carried to the town 70–80 *lispund* of butter, from where barely a simple *mark* had previously been brought to the town; but as he once got into serious difficulties because of that trade and therefore decided not to take such risks with regard to the laws, he declared that no butter had since then arrived from that district in any town.

Another proof of the same thing: no provincial population in Sweden produces more handicrafts relative to its size than the inhabitants of Västergötland.[18] But why? Nor does any province possess as much freedom as this one. It is their peddling that has really made that people enterprising, which is nothing but a form of rural trade. And that the town has not lost anything by that is proved by the prosperity of the town of Borås itself, which, though located in a rocky and infertile region, is nevertheless able, due to that freedom, to rank next to Stockholm and Gothenburg, I believe, in payment of taxes to the government.

The parishes of Orivesi and Längelmäki in Häme, with several others around there, have never brought their cultivation of flax, though they have practised it since time immemorial, to such a height as these last 15 years, since the inhabitants of Ostrobothnia have begun to regularly seek out the flax and fetch it themselves, as, due to that, the sowing of flax has increased many times over. But I can solemnly assert that if the Ostrobothnians cease to engage in this rural trade and no other provinces sustain it beyond what they themselves carry to town, the entire linen industry will come to a standstill within a few years and the flax fields will lie as fallow as they did before.

§ 10

The rural trade has also in an excellent manner demonstrated its usefulness to the country, even in the case of the metalworking industry, of which I will only provide a single yet remarkable and persuasive example. Despite several commercial ordinances, the Swedish *Bergslagen*[19] enjoyed the freedom for domestic and foreign commercial agents to travel around the county conducting trade in all kinds of products of the country until the year 1699, when the late King Charles XII was persuaded by specious arguments to strictly prohibit this trade, whereby the agents were excluded and the price of iron fell within a few weeks from 31 or 32 *daler* to 22 *daler* per *skeppund*, and yet *Bergslagen* was unable to sell their iron. That led to such a change in the metalworking industry that the royal boards had to jointly approach the monarch with an earnest representation concerning the inevitable ruin of *Bergslagen* unless trade was restored there to its former freedom, which was also achieved on that occasion, to the salvation of *Bergslagen*, and the price of iron rose again to its natural level.

During the Diet of 1723, however, a new demand was presented for the expulsion of the agents from *Bergslagen*, although that was very strenuously opposed, especially by Assessor Swedenborg, who protested most earnestly against it in a solemn memorial of 13 April 1723[20] and predicted everything that later in fact happened. But despite that, the agents were excluded, with no opportunity of ever engaging in that enterprise again, and that had the unfortunate consequence that the price of iron immediately began to decline in 1725, and within five years it fell by as much as 10 *daler* per *skeppund* and remained at that losing level of between 36 and 40 *daler* for as long as 20 years, during which period no one would consider any representation about restoring the former liberty, after which they would finally rather accept a palliative than the correct cure in adopting the idea of the Board of Trade Counsellor and Knight Nordencrantz by establishing an Ironmasters' Association.[21]

§ 11

Such examples, such tangible proofs, ought to suffice to persuade every Swede of the great utility to the kingdom of the rural trade and soon lead to a relaxation of the bonds that have for a long time fettered Swedish enterprise, if monopolistic notions and prejudices were not partly imbibed among us with our mother's milk and partly also sustained by the self-serving aim of being able, by means of a kind of autocratic power, through certain associations, to depress the prices of agrarian products to their own profit, and that under the protection of the laws of the realm.

It is those very associations that we have to thank for all the most destructive monopolies that a Copper Company, a Tar Company, a Salt Office,[22] an Ironmasters' Association and an Exchange Bill Office have been able to create, causing an untold loss to the realm. For the same reason they have also laboured for centuries, with the influence they exert over the legislative authority, to restrict the rural trade, all under the glorious pretext of setting commerce in order, to the benefit of the kingdom (though in reality of themselves) – by means of all of which, however, they have often forcibly accelerated their own destruction, but always that of the kingdom. And I assure you that neither the most excellent answer to the question of the Society of Arts and Sciences nor any arguments can persuade self-interest in this case, unless great rulers and their wise ministers themselves take the matter itself under consideration and for the sake of liberty venture all for the salvation of their subjects, as it was recently, to the eternal honour of its King, necessary to do in France.*

---

* At the time of writing, Turgot had not yet fallen,[23] nor had the decree of liberty been rescinded.

§ 12

It is also quite certain that if all our restrictive laws had been observed to the letter, the present figures for the population and quantity of commodities in the country, and thus its real strength, would have been one-third lower than they are now. For that reason, one has been obliged, partly by means of new permits, to exempt a number of commodities from the general prohibitions and partly also by conducting some rural trade covertly, especially with regard to those aspects of it that have been seen to contribute directly to the pleasures and necessary requirements of the associations and of the legislative authority; little attention is paid to what the rest suffer.

One could see, and easily appreciate, that if the Butchers' Guild had not been allowed to send its agents out to buy beef cattle in the provinces, the towns could scarcely have been provided with enough meat. Had people from Västerbotten and Västernorrland not been given the freedom to travel around the county and buy the fowls that are to be carried to Stockholm, not many loads of fowl would have got there. Were fish-buyers, with their corves, not allowed to conduct rural trade, little of that commodity would be available. Nor could much fresh herring be salted in the salting-houses at Gothenburg and Marstrand unless rural traders who bought the commodity from the fishermen and sold it to the salting-houses were tolerated. For that reason, one has been obliged to meet these and other indispensable needs by making exceptions to the rural-trade law, which, although little attention is generally paid to this, I believe provides me with a new and irrefutable proof of the utility of rural trade to the kingdom.

When a shortage of some commodity is noticed or feared, the rural trader is allowed to set off to find it, pay for it and bring it back. What happens? If it is at all possible, he will not return empty-handed; in that way the rural trade has now supplied the town of Stockholm with many thousand loads of fowl, many thousand oxen and a daily supply of fresh fish, all of which will largely cease to appear the moment such rural trade is obstructed. As it is thus obvious that the rural trade and nothing else is able to provide such a large town with its basic necessities, no more powerful means can be imagined of encouraging industriousness and increasing the quantity of commodities than that very enterprise.

Yes! I am told, it may be useful in certain permitted sectors, but one must not for that reason draw the same conclusion about rural trade in general. But, dear reader, does it not deal in butter, tallow, handicrafts, flax, hemp and other things just as much as in oxen and fowl? Are they not also in demand? Do they not likewise form part of the overall amount of commodities in the country? One and the same means, namely the rural trade, cannot have self-contradictory effects: having on the one hand increased the amount of commodities, and thereby the strength of the kingdom, it must tend to have the same effect in all cases.

§ 13

But it is not only this, so to speak, condoned rural trade that mitigates the unfortunate consequences that are associated with observance of the law. Fortunately enough for the realm and its subjects, it is everywhere conducted covertly on a considerable scale, but above all where it is most indispensable, namely in the country districts that are remote from the towns. Their inhabitants cannot possibly survive without it or obtain their most essential requirements but would then either have to abandon their fatherland or die for want of their most basic necessities, as if in a wilderness. In such remote places, it is said, one ought to establish towns or small market communities, when the rural trade would cease. Who would oppose or obstruct that, if not the traders in the already existing towns, who would not then so easily be able to exercise their absolute control of commodity prices and at the same time impede an otherwise possible growth of commodities? But privileged towns can never be established in every village, whereas a rural trader or even two are indispensable there. However, this and other such inescapable breaches of the law create a contempt for the law that cannot be remedied for a very long time and destroys law-abidingness in its most essential aspects. And even if the enforcement of such laws were extremely strict, he who is subject to them will inevitably grumble when he is denied the most fundamental rights of nature. Unhappy is the nation that is bound with many such fetters! And unhappy the government that has to rule a people hemmed in on every side, without daring to liberate it!

§ 14

In order to settle such a fundamental issue as this one is, I request permission to take my reader somewhat further out into the world, to throw some light on the present issue from ancient or more recent events in other countries.

Board of Trade Counsellor Kryger demonstrates quite convincingly in his *Thoughts in Leisure Hours*[24] in what a short space of time the human population increased and occupied the world before the Flood and that no particular rights then existed among the inhabitants of the earth, but that everyone worked and sustained himself in any way he pleased. But in our own time, when there is so much concern for an increase in population, one prefers to deal with it by quite different means. I can only wonder what the first world would have looked like had one placed its inhabitants' occupations under guardianship, regulations and privileges, made some into merchants, others into manufacturers and others into farmers, prohibited rural trade, appointed public prosecutors, conducted trials, confiscated commodities, imposed fines and so on. I believe it would have been said a few centuries after the creation of the world what was stated at the beginning, namely that it was *without form and void* of human beings.

A learned Freemason[25] proves with quite persuasive arguments in a speech to his brethren that the amount of people and commodities in earlier times was greater than in our own; but then there were no such restrictions as those that have become firmly established in our own time. It is now believed, however, that the same purposes are achieved by constraint as then by freedom.

The Jews, who possessed a small region of the Promised Land, were quite numerous; their main occupation appeared, from the time of Solomon, to be commerce. They travelled around almost the whole world, selling their goods and exchanging them for others, and were thus also great rural traders.

But no nation is able to set us a better example in this respect than China, for it is undoubtedly the country with the greatest number of people and commodities in the world. The capital, Peking, alone is inhabited by more than one million people, or about 20 times as many as Stockholm. All the roads around it are as full of people as Skeppsbron in Stockholm in the summer. But their political arrangements have also given their trades the most extensive freedom and seek only to protect everyone from oppression.

Imagine what the situation would be after 20 or 30 years in the densely populated and industrious Holland if rural trade were prohibited and the distinction between urban and rural occupations carefully observed, some of the towns made into staple towns and everything organized on a strict guild system. I am sure that Holland would then already be a wasteland, in most places inundated with water, with little more than remnants of its former industriousness apparent to posterity, where it now extends in perfect prosperity, with every freedom of commerce, navigation and transport, enjoyed equally by Dutch farmers and burghers.

§ 15

With regard to commerce, Russia has for a long time been entirely free, and the rural trade constitutes one of the most essential occupations in that extensive country. Here the inhabitants move around like ants in order to assist each other. The rural traders have their districts, not by decree but according to convenience and by agreement. They come across the border into Ostrobothnia and Finland with such goods as they believe they can find a market for and look for furs and other things that suit their trade, which they pay well for and carry some way into Russia, where they sell their goods to another rural trader, and he to a third and so forth; and that at such a modest profit that a licensed trader among us would hardly wish to sell his commodity for so little gain, which all three rural traders share among themselves. Precisely under that freedom their crafts have reached a very high level. Their leather goods and yufts are matchless; their furs made at reasonable prices from hares' necks, squirrels' heads, the leg pieces of foxes and cats, etc. are sought in vain elsewhere; their soap is renowned; their gloves are good; their footwear the cheapest available in Europe. And those who have travelled there repeatedly have attested that as soon as one crosses the Swedish border, even in the most recently captured Lappeenranta (Villmanstrand),[26] the population is much larger than on our side, and that simply because of the freedom to live and improve themselves, although all the inhabitants would, in other respects, rather be Swedish subjects.

When I now add to that the provision, in the peace treaty most recently con- cluded with Turkey[27] by the Empress of Russia,[28] for a completely open and unrestricted freedom of enterprise, and other matters, I have to admit that I am not a little vexed by the fact that one of the hitherto less civilized nations in Europe has gained the honour of being among the first promoters of freedom, while Sweden will still probably have to labour for whole centuries or half- centuries under the bondage of trade associations.

Finally, the great King of France has also brought the issue so far that he has overcome parliament, guilds and craft societies when he succeeded in getting the decree of freedom registered,[†] which, among other things, declares: "Every person of whatever quality and rank he may be, including every foreigner, shall, without a certificate of naturalization, be permitted throughout the realm, and particularly in this city, to commence and practise such kinds of trade, art or craft, as well as several of them combined, as he himself thinks fit; to which end His Majesty entirely abolishes and removes all the master-hoods and guilds of the traders and craftsmen and nullifies all privileges, rules and regulations issued in respect of these, so that no burgher may be inconvenienced or hampered for their sake in the pursuit of his trade or craft."[29]

§ 16

Yes, my reader now says, that is how it began, but ah, how did the game end? To that I reply: that game of being able to enjoy freedom in everything, except vices, is not a new one; it is the oldest of all and has already been able to show its effect for several thousand years. It, and not constraints, has filled the world with people and supplied their needs; the same causes must in every age have the same effects.

Apart from that, we have quite new gratifying evidence of the effects of freedom in our time. I merely wish to cite a single case: from Florence the fol- lowing was recently reported on 15 April: "Within a few years the population here has manifestly increased. Wherever people may live without constraint and oppression, there they inevitably increase in numbers. That principle is constantly in the mind of our enlightened government. The grain trade enjoys an unrestricted freedom, and no individual is hampered in any useful enterprise. *Everyone acts and lives here as he wishes, under the protection of the laws.* The government is greatly concerned for the health of the people and by means of suitable regula- tions prevents the spread of all epidemics. During 1767 a great multitude of people died in Tuscany, some because they could not afford the extremely expen- sive grain, some because their health was affected by its spoiled condition.[30] The government, however, with the most laudable generosity, arranged from its own resources the importation from abroad and distribution among the people of grain worth more than 500,000 Roman *daler*. Since then the harvests have during

---

† That was the situation in France when I wrote this, but since then affairs there have taken on a quite different complexion.

several years been far worse than that, but Tuscany has nevertheless always had a surplus of grain, and that of good quality. Nor have any such general diseases ravaged the country. To what may one then attribute the amazing difference between these, in certain respects equivalent, periods? During the aforementioned year Tuscany was still subject to the restrictive principle in respect of all commerce that was then still common in Europe and especially with regard to grain, the transport and sale of which were burdened with the most intolerable obstacles. *During recent years our mild Sovereign*[31] *has removed all these fetters, and Tuscany has that freedom to thank for its present bliss.*"

What objections can one have to all this? The blessed effect of freedom has within eight years become so manifest that it is already obvious to everyone who has not become quite blinded by prejudices and self-interest. How long, then, shall Swedes argue about the means to make the country blissful? or how long shall the repressed freedom be trampled upon by self-interest and private aims?

§ 17

The reasons for the utility of the rural trade thus appear, on the basis of what has been adduced, both by rational deductions and from internal and foreign experience in earlier and more recent times, to have been so clearly demonstrated that there ought to be no argument against them. In order to decide this question fully it therefore seems appropriate to examine how legislators, in opposition to such obvious truths, have come to infringe the rights of nature.

In this connection I ought to note in particular that the reasons given for legislation are often quite different from its true incentives; both are worth knowing in the case of a law of this nature.

When regulations are issued against rural trade, the most common arguments used are the following: the most general and principal one is that, as urban and rural occupations naturally differ widely from one another, a careful distinction should be observed between them in a well-ordered state, so that the countryman does not engage in trade or the townsman occupy himself with purchasing the produce of the countryman and transporting it to the town, to the detriment of other townsmen, who could otherwise have obtained those commodities directly from the countryman himself. But I venture to ask at this point from where that difference is derived. Is it founded in nature or its laws? That can never be demonstrated. Or is it necessary to sustain societies? Have there not in every one of the ages of the world been fortunate societies in which that difference has not been observed? Is a townsman not often engaged in farming and cattle breeding, and that not only for his own requirements but also for the market? Why should the countryman then not be able to obtain townsmen's wares and also supply others with them, when the townsmen themselves are unwilling to provide them with such things to meet their needs?

To that one could indeed respond: in large towns, where commerce and handicrafts flourish, one observes that townspeople occupy themselves little or not at all with farming; and a countryman who is assiduous in farming is fully occupied with his work and does not have time to engage in rural trade, which would involve him in a harmful multiplicity of activities and waste his valuable time, which should have been applied to cultivating the soil. But to that I reply: that observation is quite correct with regard to populous towns and densely populated rural districts that are adjacent to the towns. Where people live close together, there multiple activities cease of their own accord and everyone concentrates on a specific occupation. That has happened in every age, but as soon as the laws ordain such things, that offends to a greater or lesser degree against the most sensitive right of nature; one man becomes dominant, another oppressed. And when such laws are applied in particular to the more sparsely inhabited provinces, one immediately inhibits the growth in population and commodities.

To banish the simultaneous pursuit of multiple occupations is the task of nature, not of political regulation. And the fear that freedom will create heterogeneity or disorder is in itself nothing but an idle fancy presented to legislators, in which I can scarcely credit that its own authors believe, although they wish to scare others with it, in order to entrench their exclusive privileges.

§ 18

The next reason given for such a restriction is that the rural trade reduces the business of the towns and hampers their supply. Let us see now what truth there is in that. Who are supposed to be obstructing the townspeople in the pursuit of their occupations? At present they have merchandise for sale in their shops, whereas they could otherwise lay up stores of commodities when and where they wished, including the countryside. It is certain that when some kind of commodity is always available, one will sell more of it than if it is only on sale from time to time, when a countryman goes to town. The rural trade must therefore inevitably increase and never reduce the business of the towns. And as little as it reduces their trades does it impede their supply.

It has been demonstrated above that the rural trade markedly increases the amount of commodities; if that is expanded, the supply must also expand, unless there is some locality with a greater need that is willing to pay more for it than the town does through its buying agents. If there is such a place, the townsman is not entitled to that commodity unless he pays as much as those who need it.

It is precisely that, you say, which often impedes the supply, namely that in a situation of free trading more buyers may, through a few rural traders, snatch away the commodity that the town, had it been alone, would otherwise have obtained at a better price. But I should note at this point that, as much as the townsman would have wished to get a better deal than the rural trader has offered, so much has the former sought to fleece the latter.

§ 19

It is further maintained that rural trade ought to be prohibited because, when wealthy rural traders buy commodities from the country people at a good price, they can store them for a time and thereby raise the prices. In response to which I again ought to say that no price rise can occur when everyone can buy freely and sell freely. In any case, such stores of commodities, when they are selling at too low a price, are not as harmful as self-interest in the first place makes them out to be. Under conditions of free trade they are storehouses that prevent famine; and while they do raise the cost of the commodity slightly a price that would mean selling at a loss, they also prevent an unconscionable price inflation in hard times and thus ward off both of these extremes.

Lastly, it is also alleged that the reason for this prohibition is to prevent the monopolies that townsmen exercise when they travel round the country buying commodities to sell them in the towns. How can that be plausible? If one or two were licensed to purchase all the rural commodities in certain parishes, that would sound convincing, but when all possess the same freedom to purchase whatever and wherever they wish, it becomes quite impossible for any kind of monopolies to arise.

So feeble are the reasons and so volatile the vapours displayed before princes and legislators when one wishes to restrict by legislation the rights of a people that are founded in nature.

§ 20

But when we look for the fundamental motive for prohibiting rural trading, we discover it primarily precisely in the desire, by means of associations, to force down the price of rural commodities. The traders easily grasp that when rural traders seek out commodities in the countryside, the countryman is entirely free to set a price on his commodity and either retain or sell it. But if he brings it to the town, travelling many *mil*, he is forced to sell it at the price that is offered there, as his loss would be even greater should he want to take his commodity home again.

This indeed may not have much effect on the price of necessities that are con-sumed in the town, as everyone bids for them according to his need for them. But with the goods that the town puts further on sale, it is quite a different mat-ter. There an association can buy up everything through a single man. It sets prices, in accordance with its own interests, which are by no means the highest ones possible; it is therefore a major objective, in their self-interested trading system, that the commodity should be brought in by the farmer himself and offered for sale in the marketplace, when they have both him and the commodity in their power.

An additional reason appears to be that the traders in the towns do not them-selves wish to take on the trouble of rural trading. It looks as if the guild traders of our time regard it as below their dignity to obtain anything by labouring and competing, as they believe that profit should come to them of its own accord. Such arrangements are desired and striven for by which everything may be gained without effort, by the sweat of oppressed fellow citizens. And as little as they themselves can be bothered with that trade, so envious are they also of him who aims to enrich the country thereby and earn himself a *styver* or two. They therefore rally their forces to get such laws promulgated and preserved that will most effectively and surely, under some good pretext or other, entrench such an unjust domination.

§ 21

It has been shown above what inconveniences, given the constraints and restrictive law, are directly involved in this matter. But apart from these, there are others that may not at first strike a reader but which are nonetheless as inescapable as the former and have such an impact that they are scarcely less important than the others and must therefore not be ignored.

Economic laws and restrictions, especially when they affect the first and most precious rights of nature, cannot but lead to innumerable breaches of the law, which occupy the courts of the kingdom to an incredible extent, create whole hosts of lawyers, waste the valuable time of workers and officials, set citizens against each other and everywhere impose intolerable expenses on them, for the conduct of their lawsuits.

We recently had an interesting reminder of this in the news from Paris on 22 April last: "In this city," it says, "there were formerly 118 kinds of master-hoods of craft guilds. Everything was subject to the guild ordinance, even the selling of bouquets, and there were regulations concerning the selling of flowers. The cooks were distributed between several guilds, of roasters, fricasseers, etc., and the slightest infringement perpetrated by one of the rights of another led to a legal dispute. One saw three guilds litigating about a foreman's whip. Other guilds wrangled about a ham that had been boiled by a roaster, lawsuits that cost the parties much money and waste of time."

Whoever reads the reports of proceedings in our lower courts, the records of the Board of Trade and the reports of the Council of the Realm fairly attentively, whoever has attended some of our past Diets and seen shoemakers and cobblers collecting large sums of money, each in order to win their lawsuit before the Estates of the Realm concerning whether or not cobblers should be allowed to make a curved incision in the heel leather and whether they should be allowed to make shoes with a mid-sole of leather or whether it must necessarily be made of birch bark; and another scarcely less remarkable one between gold-wire drawers and lace-makers, with others that must eventually become party matters, he must on the one hand smile at the folly of mankind and on the other hand weep at the exorbitant taxing of our industries due to all this.

The rural trade, the general freedom to trade in the countryside, may never have dared to stand up to the courts or Estates but has sought to assist humanity covertly and then to evade the penalty as best it could, though sometimes at a considerable cost. But the peddling trade of Västergötland, the only rural trade that may truly said to be protected by the law, has been attacked in almost every Diet by our guardians of order, and in 1766 it came close to being lost, which, had it happened, would have meant nothing less than the assured destruction of

half or two-thirds of the population and quantity of commodities in Västergötland. However, the preservation of that freedom cost the town of Borås large
sums of money.

See, dear reader, how heavy, how oppressive it is to bear the fetters of constraint, nor will they ever be removed by any other means than freedom. Where
that comes to prevail, there all disputes about benefits, innumerable lawsuits,
large perquisites and unwarranted victims will cease; judges will have more time
to devote to their true task of punishing vicious people and protecting those who
wish to live quietly and moderately; and people engaged in economic pursuits
will be able to retain for themselves and their children that which they have
obtained by their own efforts.

Here I must quote the words of a lover of freedom[32] from the publication *The
Source of Our Country's Weakness*, which was so heavily criticized during the
Diet of 1766. On page 5[33] he says: "Where would then", namely in a condition
of freedom, "all the disputes about urban privileges and rural trade be? Where
would the many customs regulations and burdensome tollgates then be, or the
expensive matters of staple towns, guild regulations, commodity ordinances and
retorsion acts, monetary regulations, finances, exchange rates, and a hundred
other things? Where then would all the lawsuits be that these have brought
about? Where all the prosecutors who have initiated them, all the lawyers who
have pursued them, all the judges who have presided over them, and, finally, all
the salaries, food, and paper that all of these have consumed in the process, all of
it a drain on the economy?"

§ 22

Such prospects must inevitably have led the Society of Arts and Sciences to
present this question to their fellow countrymen for an answer. Nor can he who
has thoughts only for the true interest of the fatherland find greater pleasure than
in submitting them to the public. But who is concerned for freedom? Everyone
is so entangled in regulations and the maintenance of order that I believe the
worthy Society will receive more replies opposed to rural trade than in favour of
it.

But as I know the enlightened Patron of the Society of Arts and Sciences and
his noble cast of mind,[34] I believe I may without misjudgment assume the
Society in general to be motivated by the same spirit of freedom.

Should freedom prevail on this occasion, as I hope, may the Society see fit
through its Director to present it to the Throne, but should servitude prevail and
freedom, the true one, namely that of the people, be trodden underfoot, then I
wish those shackles to be found a place of concealment, among mouldy piles of
paper, in the obscurest archive, so that they will not prepare an even harsher
prison for humanity, already oppressed for long enough.

Aurea Libertas toto non venditur auro.[35]

Ennius.[36]

Notes

1 *"The Answer..."*: see pp. 63–123.
2 *"Refutation of the Reasons..."*: see the Introduction, note 55, p. 56.
3 *"The Source..."*: see pp. 124–41.
4 Carl Christoffer Gjörwell (1731–1811) was a publicist and librarian first at the University of Greifswald (then in Swedish hands) and after that in Stockholm. He is most famous for the publication of more than 20 journals from the 1760s onwards dealing, for instance, with political issues. Through his many letters (altogether 80 volumes) he is an extraordinary source for historical inquiry regarding the Age of Liberty and the reign of Gustavus III.
5 *"Circumstantial Refutation"*: see note 6, p. 141.
6 *"Water Tests"*: see p. 139 and note 3, p. 141.
7 *"The National Gain"*: see pp. 142–69.
8 *"A Remedy for the Country..."*: see pp. 170–216.
9 *"a starving hack"*: refers to an anonymous pamphlet published in September 1766, *Rikets fördärf och undergång genom et konstladt och förledande finance-systeme, nyligen föreslagit såsom rikets hjelp, af riksdagsmannen och comministern magister Andreas Chydenius*. The writer was most probably Jacob Gabriel Rothman (1721–72), a former pro-sector in anatomy at Uppsala University. He seems to have been sacked from the university in 1755 for misconduct. See note 56, p. 349.
10 *"Redemption Ordinance"*: In 1776 a monetary reform was introduced which replaced the old, complicated system based on silver and copper *daler* with the *riksdaler*, divided into 48 *skilling*. The old banknotes were redeemed for half of their nominal value, or in practice their current value, and the currency was tied to a silver standard. In Chydenius's view the reform proved that he had been right in his *A Remedy for the Country by a Natural System of Finance* of 1766, which argued against any drastic revaluation of the currency. This reform rendered obsolete this old controversy, which had occupied so much of Chydenius's time during the Diet of 1765–6.
11 *"accessit"*: the runner-up prize; a prize awarded to a person judged to be next in merit to the actual winner.
12 Louis XVI (1754–93) was king of France from 1774 to 1792.
13 *"... this new and blessed decree of freedom"*: refers to the famous six edicts of Louis XVI's *contrôleur général des finances* (Minister of Finance), Anne-Robert-Jacques Turgot (1727–81), which were presented to the *conseil du roi* in January 1776. Here he suggested the abolition of the old feudal *corvées* and the guilds' privileges but also the taxation of all three estates of the realm, the right in principle of every man to work without restriction, easier naturalization of foreigners, a free trade in corn, religious tolerance and many other things. However, as his reforms seemed too radical to the Nobility, the Clergy as well as the rich merchants, he was dismissed by the king later that year. Of Turgot's enemies, Queen Marie Antoinette had the most influence on the king's decision.
14 *"Illusion or fancy..."*: the citation is from *Édit du Roi, portant suppression des jurandes* (Donné à Versailles au mois de févrïer 1776, registré le 12 mars en lit de justice), in A.R.J. Turgot, *Œuvres*, Nouvelle édition ... avec les notes de Dupont de Nemours augmentée de lettres inédites..., Tome Second, Paris, 1844, p. 306. Chydenius probably quoted a translation in a newspaper article.
15 *"his minister"*: i.e. Turgot.
16 *"... chapter 6 of the Commercial Code"*: This chapter in the Swedish Law from 1734 is called "Regarding rural trade", and it starts as follows: "Nobody in the countryside is allowed to put out merchant goods for sale, or travel with them from village to village..."
17 *"alterum tantum"*: double the sum; twice as much.
18 Västergötland is a county in south-west Sweden. See note 5, p. 164.

19 *"Bergslagen"*: most often refers to the mining and iron production district in the middle part of Sweden stretching from the county of Värmland in the west to Uppland in the east. Sometimes also synonymous with mining and iron production areas in other parts of Sweden (for example in Småland).

20 *"Assessor Swedenborg ... memorial of 13 April 1723"*: see p. 140.

21 *"... establishing an Ironmasters' Association"*: Nordencrantz was the initiator of the *Järnkontoret*; see the Introduction, p. 24.

22 *"Copper Company..."*: see note 62, p. 119.

23 *"... Turgot had not yet fallen"*: this means before 12 May 1776. The immediate cause behind Turgot's fall has been debated and is still not fully clear, although it is known that the Queen Marie Antoinette and court intrigue had something to do with it.

24 *"Thoughts in Leisure Hours"*: J.F. Kryger, *Tankar wid lediga stunder*, 3 vols, Stockholm, 1761–6. About Kryger, see note 2, p. 115.

25 *"a learned Freemason"*: refers to Montesquieu, who was a well-acknowledged Freemason. In his *Persian Letters* (*Lettres persanes*, letter CXII), Montesquieu proposed that the population of the world had once been ten times as large as it was in modern times.

26 *"Lappeenranta"*: as a consequence of the disastrous war with Russia in 1741–2, Sweden lost parts of Karelia to Russia, including Lappeenranta (Villmanstrand), in the Peace of Turku in 1743.

27 *"... in the peace treaty most recently concluded with Turkey"*: in 1774 a peace agreement was established between Turkey and Russia, which concluded a war between the countries that had broken out in 1768.

28 *"the Empress of Russia"*: Catherine II "the Great" (1729–96), empress of Russia from 1762 to 1796.

29 *"Every person of whatever quality and rank"*: refers to Turgot's six edicts; see note 13, p. 275. The text Chydenius refers to is published in Turgot, op. cit., pp. 311–12.

30 *"During 1767 a great multitude of people died in Tuscany"*: without doubt the spread of epidemic disease (contagious pneumonia) in Tuscany in 1767 was made worse by famine caused by bad harvests. It is often supposed that this had to do with restrictions on the trade of grain. As a consequence of the famine, the grain trade was opened in September 1767, after which conditions seem to have improved.

31 *"our mild Sovereign"*: refers to Leopold I (1747–92), Grand Duke of Tuscany from 1765 to 1790; also known as Leopold II when he was Holy Roman Emperor and king of Hungary and Bohemia, from 1790 to 1792.

32 *"a lover of freedom"*: this is of course Chydenius himself. The pamphlet was published anonymously and Chydenius seems to have wanted to preserve the secret. That the author was Chydenius was, however, commonly known already in 1765. Cf. his *Autobiography*, pp. 339–40.

33 *"On page 5..."*: see p. 126.

34 *"the enlightened Patron"*: refers to count Carl Fredrik Scheffer (1715–86), diplomat, Councillor of the Realm, politician and writer. See the Commentary to this text, p. 277, and the Introduction, p. 34.

35 *"Aurea Libertas toto non venditur auro"*: "Liberty could not be sold at any price".

36 Quintus Ennius (*c*.239 BC–*c*.169 BC) was a Roman poet.

Commentary

Lars Magnusson

In 1775 a learned society in Gothenburg, *Vetenskaps och Vitterhets Samhället i Göteborg*,[1] launched a contest for the best essay written on the topic of "whether rural trade is useful or harmful to a country". Forbidden rural trade implied any trade occurring outside the towns or the annual fairs. The farmers were allowed to exchange products with each other, but in order to sell them to others they had to take them to town. Correspondingly, the merchants in the towns were not allowed to trade in the countryside.

The society had been established in 1773 in order to stimulate particularly the natural sciences. Like most other learned societies at this time it also focused on belles-lettres. An overarching aim was the diffusion of useful knowledge, and for this purpose publication series were inaugurated and prize essay competitions launched. Like other academies during this period, it was keen to have a royal patron, or at least one from the highest nobility. From 1775 the patron of the Gothenburg society was Count Carl Fredrik Scheffer, a member of Gustavus III's council. As Virrankoski explains, it was to please Scheffer that the topic of rural trade was specifically picked out by the society.[2] He was perhaps the only "real" Physiocrat in Sweden at the time – familiar as he was with François Quesnay and his little group from his time in Paris as ambassador in the 1740s.[3] For the Physiocrats as well as for those who, in more general terms, proposed that agriculture was the most important sector of the economy, the development of rural trade was a cherished task. In France during the 1770s a discussion concerning Turgot's[4] initiative to make the corn trade free stirred up much controversy. Up to this time a general line of policy – in most countries, including France as well as the Swedish realm – had been to protect the population from the laws of supply and demand. A common view was that free trade in corn would inevitably lead to poor people starving in times of dearth and bad harvests, while corn-growers would be hurt by a fall in price when harvests were ample. In order to even out such cyclical effects, a system of regionally placed storehouses for corn was established in Sweden from the middle of the eighteenth century, and this system was still in operation during the first decades of the nineteenth century.[5] This arrangement was criticized by Scheffer and others inspired by Turgot's reforms and the Physiocratic doctrines. As we have seen, the critics included Chydenius (see p. 34). According to the reformers, a free market for corn was superior in order to reach those who needed it most badly, for example when a bad harvest hit a certain region. Even more so, by creating individual incentives, free trade would stimulate increased production of corn, which would make dearths more unlikely in the future.[6] When the Gothenburg society launched its competition for the best essay, it particularly wished to find arguments for the beneficial effects of a freer trade in agricultural products. It was no coincidence, of course, that Gustavus III's finance minister, Johan Liljencrants, the very same year had issued a new ordinance that made much of the corn trade free in Finland (almost immediately after Gustavus had proudly sent the text of the law to Turgot, the latter was, ironically enough, sacked from his post as French minister of finance). However, Scheffer without doubt played a pivotal role in respect of the new ordinance. Consequently, the Gothenburg society took the opportunity to launch a prize competition in order to show its members' warm support for the society's protector.

Apparently Chydenius had met Scheffer in person, or at least communicated with him by letter. Most certainly he had also read Scheffer's translation of some of the French Physiocratic texts, which had been published some years earlier, as well as the anonymous pamphlet written by him, *A Letter from an Inhabitant of Savo to One of His Patriotic Friends in Stockholm*[7] (1775), in which he argued in favour of free trade, with regard to both foreign and domestic trade, as well as of free enterprise. On the other hand, Chydenius's contribution to the prize competition repeats many of the standpoints from his older texts, especially voiced in the essay on the causes of emigration from Sweden written 13 years earlier, but also from texts written during the Diet of 1765–6. Most probably Chydenius reasoned that now, when the issue of freer trade again was on the agenda, it was the right moment to take the opportunity to intervene. It is not unlikely that he saw it as a possibility to return to the political scene.

In this essay he once again refers to natural liberty as a main argument in favour of free trade and enterprise. Moreover, as before, he points to the right that each citizen has under a free constitution to find the most suitable way to procure a living for himself and his family. As we can see, he does not restrict himself to talk about liberalizing the corn trade. Instead, his emphasis is on free trade and enterprise in general as a means to stimulate growth of rural and domestic industry. Such industry, most often referred to in the scholarly literature as "proto-industry", was widespread in the Swedish realm during the second part of the eighteenth century. Before the industrial revolution, proto-industry appeared in Europe mainly in two different forms: either organized in the form of putting out, with merchants from cities placing orders with producers, delivering raw materials and afterwards taking the finished products to markets; or in the form of a so-called buying-up system, in which the peasant-producers had control of all the stages from a raw to a finished ware sold in the marketplace.[8] Moreover, in the putting-out system the majority of workers were crofters or landless workers, many of them working as families. The second type of system production was more often organized within the household of landowning tenant farmers. Here the majority of the workforce was made up by members of the farmer's family but also included servants, most often females. While both of these variants existed in the Swedish realm – not least, the rural wool industry situated in Sjuhäradsbygden in the county of Västergötland in south-west Sweden was organized according to the former type at the end of the eighteenth century and during the first half of the nineteenth century, with merchants from Borås and Gothenburg serving as putter-outers (*Verlagers*); the "buying-up" system was the most prevalent, especially in more remote areas such as, for example, Ostrobothnia in Finland.[9] Hence, in such districts production of tar, rope, honey, tools made of wood and iron, boats and other items was carried out within the households of tenant farmers. To a large extent it was based upon natural resources more or less freely available in the locality (most of the woods were still common property), it was worked up by members of the household and put to market either by themselves or (illegally) with the help of neighbours or local pedlars who travelled to nearby towns or organized shipping to more distant ports. It was perhaps also the prohibition of such peasant shipping to Stockholm and other ports that had stimulated Chydenius to take part in the local discussion concerning the Swedish navigation laws before entering the Diet of 1765–6. His critical attitude towards city merchants is clearly spelled out in this text – even of merchants from the ports of Ostrobothnia, who had gained the lawful right to sell directly to foreigners only ten years previously. In relation to the peasant traders they were still monopolists suppressing the countryside, Chydenius insists.[10]

As in the case of his essay on the causes of emigration, Chydenius did not receive any prize. Perhaps – as Virrankoski supposes – its message was much too radical for the members of the learned society in Gothenburg. Although the society promised that the text would be printed in the future – with some unspecified "minor changes" – Chydenius chose to publish it himself. Since the mid-1760s Lars Salvius had died, and Chydenius's new printer was less well known but certainly had a pompous name: the Royal Printing-Press. On the whole, the publication seems not to have made much political impact. This is not especially surprising: much of the lively debate on economic issues had in fact disappeared with the passing of the Age of Liberty. After Gustavus III's coup in 1772 the discussion died out. While steps were taken in a more liberal direction by his government, the reform of a free trade in corn in 1775 was passed without any major public discussion of the kind that most probably would have taken place ten years earlier. Be that as it may, Chydenius did not contribute to Liljen-crants's ordinance on a free trade in corn, for the simple reason that it was published too late (and perhaps not widely read).

Notes

1 The society did not gain royal status until 1778. Since then the official name has been *Kungliga Vetenskaps- och Vitterhetssamhället i Göteborg* (the Royal Society of Arts and Sciences in Gothenburg).
2 P. Virrankoski, *Anders Chydenius: Demokratisk politiker i upplysningens tid*, Stockholm: Timbro, 1995, p. 292.

3 E.F. Heckscher, *Sveriges ekonomiska historia från Gustav Vasa*, II:2, Stockholm: Albert Bonniers förlag, 1949, p. 871f.; L. Magnusson, "Physiocracy in Sweden", in B. Delmas, T. Demals and Ph. Steiner (eds), *La Diffusion internationale de la Physiocratie*, Grenoble: Presses Universitaires de Grenoble, 1995, p. 381f; L. Herlitz, *Fysiokratismen i svensk tappning 1767–1770*, Meddelanden från Ekonomisk-historiska institutionen vid Göteborgs universitet, nr 35, Gothenburg, 1974.

4 About Turgot, see note 13, p. 275.

5 B.Å. Berg, *Volatility, Integration and Grain Banks: Studies in Harvests, Rye Prices and Institutional Development of the Parish Magasins in Sweden in the 18th and 19th Centuries*, Stockholm: Economic Research Institute, Stockholm School of Economics (EFI), 2007, p. 79f.

6 The standard work here is S.L. Kaplan, *Bread, Politics and Political Economy in the Reign of Louis XV*, 2 vols, The Hague: Nijhoff, 1976.

7 *Bref, ifrån en Sawolax-bo, til en des patriotiska wän i Stockholm*, Stockholm, 1775.

8 S.C. Ogilvie and M. Cerman (eds), *European Proto-industrialization*, Cambridge: Cambridge University Press, 1996, ch. 1.

9 L. Magnusson,"Proto-industrialization in Sweden", in Ogilvie and Cerman (eds), op. cit., p. 208f.

10 Virrankoski, op. cit., p. 295f.

9 *Thoughts Concerning the Natural Rights of Masters and Servants*

submitted by Anders Chydenius, Rector of Kokkola.
Stockholm, printed at the Royal Printing-Press, 1778.

To His Majesty the King.
Most Sovereign and Gracious King!

The virtue of loving one's neighbour and one's fatherland was breathing its last among Your Majesty's subjects at a time when all attempts to display it and benefit one's native land were regarded as crimes, but the more your subjects have become aware of Your Royal Majesty's great magnanimity and compassion for humankind, the more has social virtue begun to expand and flourish among us.

This inquiry is also a new shoot from that same withered plant, and as Your Royal Majesty is the Sun from whose delightful rays and warmth it has derived its whole existence, the entire credit for it therefore belongs to Your Royal Majesty.

These pages deal with a subject that is disdained by the oppressors of humankind but deserves all of Your Royal Majesty's high attention.

They concern the rights of the most humble but useful citizens, those who of all the inhabitants of Sweden bear the heaviest burdens, who by their diligence improve the soil of Sweden and by the sweat of their brow supply other citizens with necessities and comforts.

Their increase constitutes the natural strength of the realm, and it lies in the power of Your Royal Majesty's grace to promote it for these innocent subjects by means of letters of emancipation and to elevate your own true honour among contemporaries and for posterity.

Concern for the rights of the citizens has imposed upon me the role of spokesman for the servants in this kingdom, which I would not have regarded myself as able to fulfil in a worthy manner unless I had represented their oppression before the throne.

Most Gracious King!

Oh! Let a breeze of mercy from there console these most humble citizens and royal magnanimity restore their buried and stifled freedom!

TANKAR

Om

Husbönders och *Tienstehions*

Naturliga Rätt;

Upgifne

Af

ANDERS CHYDENIUS,

Kyrkoherde i Gamla Carleby.

STOCKHOLM,

Trykt i Kongl. Tryckeriet, 1778.

Figure 26 The title page of *Thoughts Concerning the Natural Rights of Masters and Servants* (1778). Turku University Library.

I remain with the most profound veneration,
Most Gracious Sovereign,
Your Royal Majesty's
most humble and obedient servant
and subject.
Anders Chydenius.
Kokkola
12 September 1778.

§ 1

In an age when great new discoveries are made in every realm of nature, when sciences are developed to an unusual degree, when intellectual and literary talents are promoted and art produces virtual marvels compared to former times, it is disconcerting that the most valuable of all, the rights of mankind, are neglected.

We ought not to deny that our age has also produced brilliant individuals who have raised themselves above the miasma of ignorance and self-interest that envelops the majority of our species and have seen and defended our general rights from a longer perspective, without prejudices and in a wider context, but oh! how few they are, and how little they have convinced their fellow men and those who have a common interest in the increase and improvement of mankind and moreover possess the ability to bring happiness to millions!

The argument here is about nothing less than the fundamental principles of the happiness of humankind. The moralists of our age have not yet arrived at a general consensus about these; still less have they been able to convey them to others and make them generally known. I do not deny that the general good has probably been the common aim of them all, but the means that they propose for achieving it directly contradict one another.

There are few who speak up for civic liberty, though most of them bear the leaf of liberty in their mouths, and the few who proceed along that path and regard human rights as the property of humankind in general are regarded by most people as defenders of licentiousness and as political free-thinkers. Others do, indeed, talk much about liberty but understand by that the liberties of certain groups of people or individuals and forget the most humble, who have not been fortunate enough to find their way inside the others' entrenchments but must naturally, the more those entrenchments are extended for the rest, become all the more crowded and pressed for space on our globe.

But then there are also those who can barely stand the name of liberty but conclude from the natural indiscipline of humankind, of which people in their wilfulness constantly provide the most deplorable tokens, how important it must be to regulate everything by legislation, down to the smallest details of their activities. They appear to believe that the Almighty was incapable of establishing humankind on earth with the ability to survive, multiply itself and live on earth unless they were to maintain the economic life of our species by means of privileges, guild regulations, bounties, overseers and bailiffs. For that purpose they toil with great care, write volume after volume about order, supervision and duty in the economic sphere; they stealthily lay their proposals before princes, in which they interpret small inconveniences as mortal dangers and the want of an extravagant profit for some prominent citizens as the ruin of society as a whole. They offer their services to princes and show how a state that in their view is facing imminent collapse may be preserved from ruin by means of new regulations and more order and supervision. Nor should one conceal the fact that there are some proposers of schemes among us who are extremely short-sighted, who simply dig around themselves as far as they can, like the mole, and regard the public sphere as fortunate enough as long as they themselves are able to extend their rights.

Given these circumstances, and as various reasons are advanced for the growth and continuance of the realm and the happiness of our species, it is not surprising that rulers, even in the more enlightened part of the world, fumble in the dark and, with the greatest zeal for the good of their realm, often pull down with one hand what they build up with the other. And the greatest of them, who really have raised themselves above vulgar prejudices and have reached the perfect state of loving people in general and endeavour to gain their affection, will confront almost insuperable obstacles in actually accomplishing that. Where will a ruler find advisers of such elevated, such noble opinions? If he does obtain them, then the powerful, whose interests are opposed to those of the general public, will endeavour to deprive him of those supports, by means of corruption or guile. Should he wish to suddenly remove the yoke of bondage from his subjects, he will often, even in absolute monarchies, be powerless to carry that into effect; should he do so gradually, his good intentions will be worn down by the complaints of those who regard themselves as unfortunate when they have lost their authority over the humbler ones and inwardly resent seeing those living free and contented whom they had regarded as born to toil for their desires, and at every step new obstacles will be placed in his way. Why, then, should one be surprised that so few princes accomplish such a great aim? That requires the most thorough belief in the foundations of the happiness of a people; it requires a natural energy and hardiness in order to overcome all the difficulties, but it also, finally, requires a penetrating genius, a fire, an unquenchable desire to serve people and strive for the true honour of princes, which by no means consists in laurels drenched in human blood or incursions into regions whose inhabitants have fallen on their borders, in defence of their former ruler's dominion over themselves, but in protecting the inhabitants of the earth from violence by their fellow beings, which entitles them to be rightfully reckoned among the gods on earth. This fire alone is what can make them indefatigable in labouring for such great aims.

But it is the duty of us who are subjects and are well intentioned towards our native land, it is our duty, I say, to draw forth from their secret places the fundamental principles of human happiness by means of publications *pro* and *contra*, if not to inform princes, then at least to mutually convince ourselves of the proper means of achieving that, so that, when the rulers adopt them, we will then be accustomed to high-minded ways of thinking and zealous to labour among the unthinking masses to persuade them of the purpose and effect of such measures.

With that innocent intention I have also taken up the pen on this occasion: the liberty of the most humble people has become the topic of my inquiry. I cannot speak on my own behalf in this matter, as I myself require 12 or 13 legally hired servants from year to year and ought therefore rather to play the same tune as a large proportion of other masters, but I would hold myself unworthy to be a subject of *Gustavus III* should I, against my own conviction, say nothing about the rights of the most humble, just as I willingly excuse those who from a lack of conviction attempt to stifle the small spark of liberty that the servants may still enjoy. Kind reader! Seek the truth and do not desist until you find and follow it.

§ 2

There have been many reasons in our time for thinking and writing about this subject. Whenever I look up the *Royal Ordinance on Servants and Hired Workers* of 21 August 1739 and its article 1, § 1, I cannot avoid shuddering on reading these words: *No vagrants, vagabonds, idlers or dependent lodgers ought to be tolerated in our country and our realm.* These and other insulting designations refer to none other than those who are not engaged under annual service contracts, and it is decreed with regard to them that they are outlawed within the borders of Sweden, as stated in § 2: *And no excuse shall be valid, whether for a farmhand, maid or any other servant fit for work, to evade an annual service contract for the sake of other employment that they may cite or allege as a pretext.* Paragraph 4 imposes a fine of 10 to 20 *daler* on those who harbour them and show some humanity towards these outlaws, and § 5 sets in motion the entire body of officials in the realm – census commissioners, county governors, magistrates, clergymen, churchwardens and sextons, deans and bishops, sheriffs, district police superintendents and parish constables, governors, public prosecutors, etc. – to seek out these unhappy people and send them to hard labour in fortresses and male and female penitentiaries and to annual service contracts.

The honourable Estates of the Realm themselves realized that this hue and cry after vagabonds would put them in fear and cause them to flee far away from such troubled regions, and therefore the officials are given new orders in article 8 to confine them strictly within the borders of the kingdom, and I venture to say that although this regulation has driven out several thousand Swedish natives and has prevented the immigration of many foreigners to take service among us, had this statute on servants been strictly observed everywhere, as regards vagabonds and a limited number of servants per farm and the prescribed hiring fees and yearly wages and other things, then Sweden would certainly have half a million fewer inhabitants than it has now, who have all the same been retained only by infringing a law that is highly praised by the majority.

When I look at the scheme elaborated during the Diet of 1766[1] in its Finance and Trade Committee, which in § 3 recommends the enrolment of all masters and servants; when I consider § 18 through to 27, which declares all those who have not accepted an annual service contract liable to a penalty or hard labour in female penitentiaries and on public works, and add to this that their period of freedom,[2] which was seven weeks under the previous ordinance, should now be shortened to 14 days, and if they had not found a new master during that period it stated that he who applies first shall then take such servants into his service, there can be no lack of reasons to inquire into a subject that so greatly affects our human rights and the growth of the entire realm.

But it is really more recent events that have brought this matter up for debate at this particular time. In Västernorrland, and in particular in the county of Gävleborg, a general complaint has arisen that there is a shortage of servants and that they are intolerably expensive to hire and, furthermore, lazy, wilful and reckless in their work, so that the residents feared that their farms would become wasteland, which has led to some county assemblies being convened and deliberations held on this subject, during which it has been proposed that certain wages should be paid to a farmhand and a maid, that masters and servants should be enrolled, and that those who wish to move should be distributed by lot among those who require them, as well as other things; and in some counties the governors, in order to obtain a more plentiful supply of servants for the inhabitants of the county, have adopted from the statute on servants the designations of outlawed vagabonds, vagrants and cottars and thereby procured for the masters a reasonably large haul of servants.

This would not, however, have been of any particular significance to the general public had not those masters who lived in neighbouring counties become aware of it and the public, having read the account of it in the *Transactions of the Royal Patriotic Society*,[3] become resentful that they had not been allowed to participate in the division of these spoils and thus appeared to be intent on demanding from their county governors a similar parcelling out of servants, on reasonable terms. Several complaints about it were published in the transactions of that Society, and there were even demands for assistance from that body. The newspaper *Dagligt Allehanda*[4] was inundated with cries of distress from masters who believed that all farming and rural crafts would now be doomed unless relief were soon at hand. No one listens, no one responds, everyone complains, until one person in authority imprudently unmasks the whole plan, loudly demands regulations that would give the masters scarcely less than *jus vitae et necis*[5] over their servants and proposes penitentiaries etc. by the farms. This was so harsh and so definite that I could not read it without horror, and it moved me so deeply that I was unable to leave it without a response, and as the opinion in all the papers was so general, I feared that new fetters were already being forged for humankind among us. To forestall these, should that prove possible, is the purpose of this publication, as well as to bring under scrutiny a subject on which the majority selfishly and unthinkingly drift with the current.

§ 3

There are three questions in particular on this subject that I have to answer: first, *should workers be forced to accept annual service contracts?* Second, *should they serve for a specific wage prescribed by law?* Third, *should they be distributed among masters by lot or some other form of compulsion?*

Regarding the first question, our entire general public responds to it with an almost unanimous *Yes*, so that in that respect I am outvoted many times over. How is it possible, everyone thinks, to have a household and require service without servants engaged under an annual contract? Unless it is the duty of workers to accept annual service contracts, the majority will be left without servants and the farms will become wasteland, for neither can one always obtain day labourers when one needs them, nor will it be possible for a householder to pay his employees day wages.

The second question will probably also be answered in the affirmative by the majority. The authorities, they believe, should indeed prescribe the annual wages for a farmhand and a maid, or else the servants will become so wilful that they demand and obtain exorbitant hiring fees and wages, so that a master cannot endure them and yet is forced, if no regulations prevent it, to pay them what they shamelessly demand, as he cannot do without them.

But with regard to the third question, not all masters or mistresses would agree to being assigned servants by lots or some form of compulsion, while others would on the contrary be the most fervent advocates of this proposition. Pious masters who deal with their workers in a kindly way and are therefore generally loved by their servants would far rather be allowed to look around and choose pious and diligent servants than let it depend on blind fate, whereas on the other hand nothing pleases some masters more than precisely this assignment by lot; they see themselves assured of workers by means of it, they do not have to take the rejects of others, they are spared the so-called haggling and the servants' demands for large sums in hiring fees and wages, as well as other freedoms.

But it is precisely these three questions that I have proposed to subject to a caring and impartial examination in this treatise, and you, dear reader, will be the judge as to whether I have built on firm foundations and whether I have established the truth or not. Lay aside all preconceptions while you read this; do not pass over the issues in a hurry but allow yourself time to think, for I assure you that, as a Swede, you cannot engage with a more worthy subject than this, which relates to the general rights of your own people, the growth and improvement of the kingdom and the well-being of every subject in the future.

In order to examine these propositions in the decisive and methodical manner that they deserve, it is not enough to look at the matter from one side alone. No! It has to be viewed from different perspectives and be understood in all its aspects. I must therefore first show whether obligatory annual service contracts, prescribed annual wages and a forced distribution of servants are compatible with the general rights of mankind. After that I shall investigate whether all this corresponds to the true interests of the kingdom and its inhabitants. Having proceeded that far, however, I also intend, finally, to propose correct and natural expedients for supplying the kingdom and its industries with sufficient workers.

That is the general approach of this little treatise as a whole! May my thoughts, however, be guided by Christianity and virtue! And my pen follow closely in the footsteps of truth!

§ 4

I shall thus first examine *whether it is compatible with the natural rights of mankind to force workers to accept annual service contracts.* The first right of nature is that people shall be able to live, dwell and reside on earth, maintain themselves and their families, marry and multiply. That right is therefore most forcefully entrenched in both the earlier and more recent fundamental laws of the kingdom of Sweden, in the statement that *the King shall not cause anyone to suffer injury in respect of life and honour, body and welfare, unless he be lawfully convicted and sentenced, and shall not dispossess or cause anyone to be dispossessed of any property, movable or fixed, without due judgment and trial.* Such is the letter of emancipation that Swedish kings have placed in the hands of each one of their subjects. Fortunate is the people in whose fundamental laws these words are not a mere formality but where the welfare and property of the subjects are likewise proclaimed to be inviolable!

In what does the welfare of the poor worker indeed consist if not in the freedom to dwell and reside on earth, maintain himself and his family, marry and multiply, the property of the poor man being little else than the freedom and ability to work and obtain for himself his daily necessities? If these rights were to be denied to him, or be restricted, and he be forced into some form of guardianship, however much the guardians may extol it as being to his advantage, it is clear that he has, to a greater or lesser degree, suffered injury in respect of his welfare and that he has been deprived of some part of his property or freedom to earn a living; then the letters of emancipation will become meaningless and lose some of their real value, just as the value of bonds diminishes when they are not redeemed by those who have issued them.

There is indeed one condition in this letter of emancipation (which is humanity's real guarantee of security from oppression), namely that they have not been convicted and sentenced for any crime, which gives my adversaries cause to assert: how can those be regarded as innocent whom the law has convicted of being vagrants, vagabonds and idlers, who have no lawful employment and ought therefore not to be tolerated anywhere in the realm? To that, however, I must first reply: This is the clearest case of *petitio principii.* You prove their criminality by the wording of the statute on servants, when the question actually before us is whether they are what that statute calls them. Let us therefore inquire into their criminality, in what it consists. You say: they do not accept an annual service contract but live in indolence, and in their indolence they become accustomed to all kinds of vices and debauchery, to drinking, whoring, stealing, and the like. Should such people not then be regarded as criminals, who may therefore with every justification be forced to accept an annual service contract? Here, I believe, lies the main strength of the argument (*nervus argumenti*) against me, in this portion. But, dear reader, may I now object: first, with regard to indolence, it is a crime that secular laws do not recognize or should not punish, as it soon penalizes its possessor with poverty and destitution, a penalty that is more protracted and harsher than bread and water in our legal code. What penalty does the lazy farmer and freeholder suffer for his indolence? The law does not punish him, but hunger and destitution will be his punishment, and he will finally be driven from his home and farm, as a sparrow is driven from the ear of grain, and that is punishment enough. If a businessman neglects his business, his punishment will be bankruptcy, so why should the humblest worker lose all his civic rights and be declared intolerable throughout the realm, or else become the prey of him who wishes to seize him? Or may I ask: who has examined and tested his indolence? In what court has the case been tried and judged? In my opinion, the party that want to have him in their service have pronounced the judgment, and how then can it be impartial? For that, you say, all that is required is that, as it can be proved that he does not have an annual service contract, he is able to be indolent whenever he wishes. Everyone else is also able to do so, yet they do not. *A posse ad esse, non valet consequentia.*[6] He may also in his freedom be far more assiduous than many who are in annual service and is thus the only one who is often wrongfully punished with outlawry for indolence.

But when he is unengaged, he indulges in debauchery and all kinds of vices, so that it is best for his own sake if he is placed in annual service, when he will not have the opportunity for such things. Is that not a strange kind of tutelage, to force workers into annual service, male or female penitentiaries, etc. before they have actually committed any offence, merely in order that they will not commit any? Imagine if you or I, dear reader, were to be suddenly removed by force from our homes, to be kept either incarcerated in a castle or in service with some gentleman, and we asked the officers of the crown who dragged us off: Why are we being subjected to this and deprived of our freedom, what have we done? And we were then told in reply: You may not have done anything yet, but in your freedom you may soon commit some offence, so that it is better for you and for the general public to forestall such things in this way. What would we think of that guardianship? We would cry *assault! assault! to arrest us before we have offended,* nor am I sure that it would in fact be anything else. The legally blameless worker, however, has to lose his freedom for a supposed possibility that he may commit some offence in the future. Is that not excessively harsh treatment for a freeborn Swede? I may well be told in response: it is not a mere supposition that they may in their wilfulness commit offences; it is a truth fully confirmed by daily experience that they really do often commit them. I concede that, but are there no other subjects who offend apart from them? Indubitably there are; and yet they are not punished before but only after they have offended. Why, then, should these most humble ones not enjoy the same right?

§ 5

Such unengaged workers, it is said, even if they have not committed any other crime, are of course, under our laws, criminal enough, as they have not accepted an annual service contract and are therefore justly liable to the penalty of labour on public works and in female penitentiaries that the law prescribes for them. Quite right, if such laws are regarded as equitable and unalterable, but as it is precisely the equity of those laws that is in question, nothing can be proved by that. If it is a crime not to accept an annual service contract, then that must apply to all, whoever they may be, for otherwise we lose all true notions of crime. But as no one can assert such a thing, as being in itself unreasonable, all criminality is likewise at once removed in respect of workers. And if it is ultimately to exist somewhere, it must be found in one's birth.

What kind of compulsion, then, do they have to complain about? They have no need to fear labour on public works and in female penitentiaries provided that they are willing to accept an annual service contract, and that cannot be regarded as compulsory, especially as they also possess under the law a right to change their employment once a year; that provides them with the food they need, mostly better than what they can obtain for themselves in their cabins; in addition, they have their yearly set of working clothes and moreover on top of that a fair wage for holiday clothes and other necessities, so that they are much better off in annual employment than when they remain unengaged.

To all this I reply that annual service contracts are indeed advantageous for the servants in certain cases, though not always, as long as they are allowed to remain on a natural footing, so that they are entirely voluntary, but when they become an unconditional obligation, and with a specific wage proposed by masters and established by the authorities, then the matter acquires a very different complexion. Freedom with dry morsels is often more attractive to a person than an abundance of food under the domination of someone else. There is a cost attached to being independent, but who would not prefer that, with a meagre income, to being comfortable as the servant of another? The servants, as inhabitants of the earth, naturally also long to be able to settle in some spot in the world and to live, if possible in a cabin or a crofter's cottage, as fate has not granted them more space, but when even that is denied them by the law, then we all realize that their freedom has disappeared.

§ 6

But that which makes forced annual service contracts particularly incompatible with the freedom that nature has vouchsafed them is that workers, precisely through them, are deterred and prevented from conforming to the Creator's own arrangement and the natural instinct to marry.

We are not speaking on this occasion of the harm caused to the kingdom by this constraint. Further on we shall examine that matter more closely, but now the only question is whether a law can be founded on natural equity that places obstacles in the way of nature's tenderest inclination and one that sustains our world. The statute on servants, you say, does not forbid marriage between servants? But, I answer, the designation vagabonds and vagrants does so by the injunction that such people, together with cottars, are not to be tolerated in Sweden. When a farmhand and a maid marry while in service, they generally lose some of the esteem in which they were previously held by their master and mistress. If their masters can find other servants, they will give them notice to quit at the latest by the following moving day, and no one wishes to employ them any more, except in cases of extreme necessity. These wretches are then left without a fatherland: according to the law, such people are not to be tolerated in Sweden: they are not allowed to live in one place, they are not allowed to wander around the country like tinkers. Someone may perhaps wish to employ the husband, but then he has to separate from his wife, who has no place of abode, often in the most troublesome circumstances. Will not that prevent marriages?

When birds mate, they immediately begin to jointly build their nest and take care of their brood. The propagation of their species tolerates not the slightest constraint: if anyone touches the nest and merely handles the eggs, they will desert it, or even if they do hatch them out, most of that brood will be lost. But if they are allowed to nest freely and in accord with nature, they will produce flocks of their species, which form a small society or household in themselves until they have grown to adulthood and move apart from one another. How, then, can the human species prosper under constraint? We count, we calculate, we decree, we regulate everything, as it is said, for the propagation of our species, but with all that our species melts away, and instead of inhabitants on earth we have a few figures on paper suggesting great possibilities, all of which, however, lack life and motion.

Which servants will then, under such harsh conditions, dare to think of marriage? Nothing but rash responses to the natural inclination may unintentionally lead them to take such decisions, which they soon regret and which are accompanied by so many difficulties.

A further objection to this is that, although the statute on servants bans cottars, there are other regulations that do allow and protect them. In addition, the authorities have, by granting remission of personal taxes to those who have several children, tried to encourage marriage, as it were by bounties, so that there should be no reason to complain on that score. But see, dear reader, how chaotic our political arrangements are: at one time a hunt is organized for them and they are turned into outlaws and lose their civic rights; at another time they are protected, and just when they have been granted protection and been allowed to settle down for a while, we decide to raise a hue and cry after them; and a little later we are again great patriots who take up their cause and arrange for them to receive bounties for their children. What kind of system is there in all this? And for that reason we have regulations for everything we wish and that we think will best suit every individual situation: if we want to liberate them, we take a letter of emancipation from one shelf in the archive of regulations and set them free, but if we think the circumstances require servants for ourselves or our friends, we take a whole bundle of condemnations of vagrants, idlers, etc. from another shelf and mobilize all the officers of the crown to force them into annual service. This inevitably leads to one county governor, who happens to lay his hands on the vagrancy bundle, going hunting in his county and the masters for the moment obtaining great hauls of servants, while the others have hit upon the letter of emancipation and, given the current scarcity, establish nurseries of people for later generations. What a muddle all this is, leading to a different administration in each county within one and the same kingdom and under one and the same mild ruler and identical laws. Whereas a law guaranteeing security from oppression for workers, one that for ever abolishes all constraints on their liberties and provides them in return with no other advantages, no bounties, than those the Lord of nature has granted them at birth, to be free inhabitants of the earth, with permission and security to take care of themselves and their families, marry and dwell on earth, is the only measure that will do everything that can and ought to be done in this regard and removes the weapons from the hands of their oppressors.

§ 7

Let us now follow nature further and consider to what extent certain legally pre-scribed annual wages for servants are compatible with the general rights of mankind.

When it comes to precedents in this respect in most of the states of Europe, I am certain that I have more opposed to me than on my side: I am drowning in nothing but regulations and tariffs everywhere, and aristocratic propositions have won such widespread acceptance among us that we scarcely believe the world could survive without them, still less any societies within it, and one only has to give certain groups of people and guilds the privilege of being able to harm their fellow citizens in order to make regulations and tariffs absolutely necessary if people are not to devour each other. Nor would I have been surprised had one established certain annual wages if the servants had constituted a particular guild, with the privilege of working only under their guild masters, so that none except them were allowed to hire themselves out, although in that case, too, I would not think tariffs advisable but the removal of the causes that necessitate them. But as the servants are almost the most defenceless of all, humanity demands of us that we protect their rights.

Nature makes them exactly the same as us at birth: their body posture when they at first lie in their cradle is identical with ours, their souls are just as rational as those of other people, which makes it obvious that nature's Lord has also accorded them the same rights that other people enjoy. Apart from security of life, the next is undoubtedly the one that protects our property, or the means whereby life is sustained. Our fundamental laws have also, without any excep-tion or qualification, defended these in respect of all legally blameless subjects. The servants must therefore also enjoy them to the same extent as other subjects in the kingdom. Where that does not happen, the right of nature has been violated and they have been deprived of their freedom.

A farmer is entitled to dispose of his property and to seek the highest price for his goods, and likewise the merchant, and a public official is legally entitled to let his tenant farmers take their rent-paying produce to whichever town within the local jurisdiction it will command the best price in, so why should the poor man, or the property of the humblest worker, be subject to tariffs and tutelage? The freedom and ability to work is his only property; if the laws ascribe a specific value to this, then he has lost the freedom that other inhabitants of Sweden enjoy.

That could happen, the reader will argue, if the wages were set at too low a level, but when they are established by law at a fair level and rather as high as possible, their freedom cannot suffer from that. But to that I reply: the freedom to personally dispose over one's property is in any case lost with prescribed wages, and that loss is in itself great enough, however highly it may otherwise be praised. Let us see, however, what advantages and fairness one may then expect in regard to the wages themselves. We would be excessively naive when saying or writing anything about human rights if we based our conclusions on the fine words of the laws and on the goodwill and conscience of our ancient legislators. Self-interest, partiality and ignorance inevitably underlie most economic laws, and it is with reference to these that their fairness or unfairness may also best be judged.

In each county, tariffs have been established with regard to what hired workers or servants may receive in annual hiring fees, clothing and wages, and the statute on servants of 1739, article 5, § 3 states expressly: *Should a master, under any pretext whatsoever, promise or pay, or hired workers demand and obtain, more in hire and wages, they shall both be liable to a fine of 20* daler smt, *payable in full to the informer.*

If we wish to correctly assess the fairness of this, we must first note the identity of those who have enacted these tariffs. The servants have not been consulted on the matter, still less has their opinion had any influence on it, and least of all have they been able to foresee various events in the future. Who, then, have instituted these laws? None other than the masters themselves. When we then consider that masters and servants have diametrically opposed interests in this regard, namely the master to obtain servants as cheaply as possible and the servant to obtain the highest price for his labour, it is not hard to understand whose advantage such tariffs have served. You object: the masters or legislators have most likely adopted a middle way, so that neither party suffers; such fairness has after all been demanded of the county governors and other officials who have drawn up these tariffs; but I answer: one cannot reasonably expect such fairness, still less presuppose it, as the matter essentially involves nothing else than awarding or depriving oneself of several hundred *daler* a year by means of such a tariff.

Ought such arbitrariness to be tolerated, then, you may be thinking, so that the servants will be able to raise their wages as much as they wish? Why do you call it arbitrariness? In that case your freedom to independently set a price on your commodity should also be called arbitrariness, and as unwilling as you are to lose that, so little should you also resent that the servants possess it. It is precisely the same with the wages of servants as with all other commerce, if both are free: where there is an abundant supply of some commodity and there are few buyers, the commodity will inevitably fall below its cost price; if there is an abundant supply of workers and few who need them or see any chance of profiting from their labour, day wages and annual wages will fall. But if there are many buyers and few commodities, their price rises and that increase procures a more abundant supply of them, as acquisitiveness brings them there far more quickly than a royal decree, and a shortage of workers, together with greater prospects of profiting from them, raises the day wage, remunerations and annual wages, because of which people are again tempted to earn money and are drawn there from other regions, where there is less profit and enterprise, by which a further increase is again checked.

But higher wages, after all, make the servants arrogant and luxurious, and in their arrogance they fall into debauchery and other vices, all of which would be avoided if they were instructed by the laws to live peaceably and modestly. My response is: luxuriousness is a natural result of wealth and prosperity, both among them and among us, but as little as we would put up with any obstruction by the governing authorities of our own progress and prosperity, so ill-advised and self-interested are also the barriers that we wish to set to the progress of these most humble workers, especially as their luxuriousness will, in any event, never equal ours. And it is quite certain that if they had their natural freedom, married and brought up children, all superfluity and the consequent luxuriousness would soon disappear, as they would willingly use their possessions to rear workers for us and our descendants. But with regard to their vices and debauchery, I fear that among a hundred masters there are more depraved ones than among as many servants, and that where, for example, one in ten of the depraved individuals among the servants incur penalties for their vices, barely one in a hundred of the masters, or at least those of higher rank and officials, will find themselves in that position. Is it not then a shame, is it not a manifest injustice, to deprive them of their freedom to improve themselves, merely because of the opportunities that will arise for them to commit offences in the process?

§ 8

Such is the general unfairness inherent in certain prescribed annual wages, but on closer inspection of the issue another emerges, almost more appalling than the former, namely that all farmhands are to have the same wages and all maids likewise, without regard to their loyalty, their diligence, their previously acquired knowledge and experience, and their varying physical strength and skills.

As great as are the differences in quality between animals of the same kind of which we make use, so great are certainly those between workers. What would the reader think, when horses are now bought at different prices, from 3 to 100 *riksdaler* each, if a regulation established the same price for all these animals, regardless of their size, quality and training, on pain of a heavy fine if anyone either demands or offers, pays or receives, anything above or below that? Or let us speak to a shopkeeper and suggest a regulation, procured by those who wish to buy a quantity of fine cloths, that all cloths that are otherwise sold at between 9 *daler* and 9 *plåtar* per *aln* should now command one and the same price, for example 12 *daler* per *aln*; would he not call that a manifest injustice? God preserve us from such a law! He who obtained some of the coarse cloth would, because of the regulation, pay 3 *daler* too much per *aln*, but all those who took some of the finer sorts would not pay a third or quarter of the value of the commodity. We might well reply to him: it is necessary to prevent the shopkeepers in that way from arbitrarily raising the price of their goods, so that they will not rapidly become wealthy and, owing to their wealth, luxurious; but he would probably respond to us and say: fine cloths can never be offered for sale at that price. If the price is set at a low level, the commodity will also be of a corresponding quality.

It is precisely the same with servants, labour being their commodity, on which the law has set a tariff, and how great is not the difference in their labour: one is busy early and late with his master's work, is proficient in his duties and is agile and physically strong enough to do whatever task he is set; whereas another, even if knocks and blows may keep him from idleness, is nevertheless unable either to perform his duties or to make headway with them and therefore does not earn his keep. What extreme unfairness is it not, on account of the statute on servants, to pay them the same wages? One is in all fairness receiving too much but the other too little.

This natural unfairness also has a deplorable effect on our servants, inducing in them slothfulness and carelessness: where virtue is not encouraged, where vice is favoured as much as virtue, there one is straining every nerve to create dissolute citizens.

Individual happiness and individual advantage is the true, the effective motive force in the activities of all free people, whereas knocks and blows are really appropriate to slaves. He is a wise ruler who recognizes the need to remove from acquisitiveness the aristocratic fetters in which the self-interest of some has confined them, but a great one if he has the ability to do so. Our statute on servants, with prescribed annual wages, is inevitably bound to create idlers and slack workers, whereas free labour contracts, on the contrary, encourage everyone to make themselves deserving of a greater reward through diligence and loyalty.

You will probably object: should the servants not be told that it is their duty, for the sake of God and their conscience, to be diligent in their tasks? Is it not an impure motive for diligence to display it for one's own advantage? To that I reply: however pure, however elevated the former motive force may be among those who have a lively understanding of the true power of Christianity, yet the latter is more down to earth and persuasive for physical human beings; it is nature's own and should thus not be condemned, as it is kept within bounds by virtue and by reasonable restraint on the part of other people. The former may act upon the human heart to its fullest extent, but the latter is inhibited by fixed annual wages, and the ordinance acts in direct opposition to it. In such an absurd manner do we hasten to achieve blissfulness, with sails set quite contrary to each other.

Why, says another, should we discuss fixed annual wages and their harmfulness at such length? Who has actually ever paid the servants on that basis? Who has been able to find servants at the prescribed wage level? Has not one after the other, even the originators and most ardent proponents of fixed annual wages, been obliged to pay wages as high as the servants themselves have been able to command? Why should one then complain about the unfortunate results of that which has never been implemented? Yes, dear reader! Here is a double cause for complaint: one is that the regulation in question actually has been observed in several places for a longer or shorter time, when it has necessarily exercised its effect, and has everywhere so to speak legitimized the same annual wages for vigorous and for lazy workers, a system that the latter have willingly obeyed and the former have been unable to escape, so that it is incredible how much harm it has already caused. The other reason is that however exposed this truth may be and fixed annual wages be directly opposed to all natural equity, yet there are, apart from a number of loudmouths, also some great and perspicacious men in the kingdom who with the best intentions continue to forge these fetters as fast as they are able to in the belief that should they manage to complete the new prison, which they do in all decency try to make as attractive as possible for their fellow beings, they will have performed a real service to humanity and the fatherland. Is it not, then, time to raise questions on this subject among the general public? Is it not, then, necessary to examine it?

§ 9

Now, to take another step forward with our subject. When the statutes on servants of 1723 and 1739[7] were promulgated, however great were the restrictions then imposed on their natural liberties, they did still retain that of being able at the end of the year to choose a master for the following one in a certain prescribed manner, but efforts are now beginning to be made, with increasing urgency, to limit that remaining small freedom. One constraint always makes another inescapable. It was realized that fixed annual wages could never be effectively established unless the servants also lost the freedom to seek work by themselves.

I recall that the scheme of 1766[8] already included an enrolment of masters and servants, and the new proposal, which has been put forward in certain counties and is being promoted by a number of people as a boon, stipulates the distribution of servants by lot between masters. The purpose of this, in my view, appears to have been threefold: first, to deter servants from moving, as they would have no freedom to make any plans themselves; second, to obtain servants for those with whom no one would otherwise serve without compulsion; and third, never to have to look for servants, or ever for that reason be placed in the situation of having to negotiate on hiring fees or annual wages but simply be able to follow the tariff established for that purpose by the masters.

Stop again for a moment at this point, dear reader, and consider humankind from the point of view of its natural freedom. What do you think of this blind-fold game? I imagine some men of authority sitting at the gambling table and the masters standing around them, most of them worried about whom they might now be taking into their service, with only the ill-tempered one, who had previously been left without, being confident of obtaining some prey by the throw of the dice, but the servants who were changing employment standing outside like flocks of sheep, in trepidation at their unknown fate, being distributed by numbers to their new masters, scarcely otherwise than slaves in the marketplace at Algiers who have to go where fate leads them. Do you not feel sympathy, dear reader, at this spectacle of oppressed humanity? Where is reason in all this? where is consideration? and where, finally, is the fair word *Freedom*? Everything has been transformed into a game of dice.

But let us consider the matter more calmly. Are not reason and examination the things that endow our species with a nobility that exceeds that of all other creatures? What was the Creator's purpose with them? Perhaps merely to serve others with them, while we play blind man's buff with our own welfare? No, but to seek to use them to promote our own true interest, in which serving our neighbour is also a great means, but not our purpose. The master does not tolerate his servant playing blind man's buff while he is at work, for that demands diligence, care and understanding; how, then, can one have such a hardened conscience as to force the servant to be blind with regard to his own future?

The master, you say, is as much in the dark with regard to the lot as the servant, not knowing whom he will have in his service either, so that it is as much a constraint on the master as on the servant. That is indeed truly the case, and for that reason I also do not understand how the masters can accept it without apprehension, excepting those who are generally notorious for their barbaric treatment of their servants and are therefore seldom or never able to obtain any servant by free choice, and if they do finally obtain one, he will certainly be of the worst kind, whom no master can cope with. For masters of that kind, the lottery is a wonderful thing, by which the non-virtuous is able to share the spoils equally with the virtuous, and that provides the chief incentive for the lottery.

You say: a master will soon come to be regarded as barbaric when he wants to keep the servants to their tasks, when they are not allowed to idle as they wish, and for that one is then not only to be disgraced but also placed in extreme difficulty in running one's farm. But I reply: when a master conducts his work in an orderly fashion, treats his employees as human beings, retains their love and respect and shows towards them, as towards other people, patience and mild-ness, he will not acquire such a reputation except from brutes, and they never have any credibility among the general public, only among mockers.

As clearly, therefore, as the lottery deprives virtuous masters and servants of their reasonable advantage of being able to seek each other out, it also at once removes the strongest incentives to virtue in both of them. According to this new plan, the masters have no need to fear that they will be left without employees towards the autumn. Their emotions with regard to their servants will thus become unbridled, on which the freedom of the servants formerly exercised a powerful check, one that is necessary for humanity, and the servants, who will then suddenly have lost every encouragement to diligence and virtue, will become despondent, slavish and desperate. Under this arrangement they will have no encouragement to be diligent, for all their efforts will be merely a duty that does not improve their terms by a hair's breadth, and their last remaining encouragement, that of at least being allowed to look for a virtuous master, will finally be removed from them here, while the lazy and dissolute one will be able to secure by insistent demands the same advantages as the willing one, unless the discretion of the master is to be restored, on the grounds that the master can reward his servant according to his deserts, in which case the prescribed wage will take a quite different form, namely that the most the master has to pay the servants is the wage prescribed in the tariff, though he may well pay less than that, as little as he pleases, on the grounds that the servant does not deserve more, and then the oppression will be doubled. Apart from that, it is not worth the trouble to be faithful and diligent. The lot determines his fate, and blind fate will forcibly stifle his desire for blessedness.

From such heavily oppressed souls one cannot expect any civic virtue, when the rod must become almost the sole motive force for their diligence and loyalty, in the same way as the methods applied to the dumb animals. You say: and there is unfortunately no morality among them. I answer: nor can it exist where every reason for it has so manifestly been removed.

§ 10

Having thus, in the foregoing, compared the main proposals in the projected and so insistently demanded ordinance on servants with the general rights of humankind, let us now, dear reader, change our point of view and look at this system of servitude from another aspect, namely: *to what extent may it be found to be compatible with the true interest of the kingdom and its inhabitants?* This is a yardstick by which our political arrangements in particular are to be compared and then judged to be acceptable or not. Here, however, I should observe from the outset that we must not stand too close to this subject of our inquiry, for if we get involved in small individual advantages and drawbacks, we will not be able to grasp the overall position and context of the matter, nor too far away from it, where the entire system fades before our eyes into an indistinct shadow.

It is precisely on this aspect of the matter that many masters in every estate confront me with a general outcry: "The kingdom must perish owing to the wilfulness and extravagance of the servants and their vastly inflated wages. We cannot obtain servants, they do not work diligently, nor can a farmer afford to pay such high wages. The farmland of the kingdom must therefore return to fallow, no land reclamation can be considered, and the owners will be forced to abandon their properties. Such a loss to individuals must become a loss to the general public and ultimately to the entire kingdom: is it not then time to consider a remedy before all is lost?"

That is how the situation looks when seen at close range, and such is the outcry that now drives forward the new ordinance on servants, and although there is much that one could say regarding each of these propositions, yet we may as well accept the truth of this and that the complaints are well founded, in order all the more effectively to get to the nub of the matter; but let us now step back a little, view the objective from a slightly greater distance and look for the real and natural sources of this evil, against which the protests are directed. We are then likely soon to discover that the cause of all this lies precisely in the regulations themselves and that the evil that is now to be remedied is a natural consequence of what has already been done and must become far worse should the published proposals be brought into effect. If this is found to be the case, one can only shudder at the thought of new fetters being prepared for the ruin of the kingdom: we observe the immediate evils, which are shortages and dearness, but we do not know their sources; we suggest remedies that will cure the evil by means of something far worse. Dear reader! lend your consideration to this matter and let love for humanity and truth make your conclusions unwavering. I dread the resort to blind blows in our enlightened times, which ought to be banished to the hideous bygone era of antiquity.

§ 11

But where are we to rediscover fundamental truths on which to base our proofs when, in truth, there are few things *in politicis*[9] that are not debated *pro et contra*? Ah, yes! I believe the truth may be accepted without proofs by all who understand political science that the true strength of a kingdom lies in the number of its working inhabitants. This proposition is also consistent with the genuine advantage of the masters, for when there is an abundance of workers there is always a way of getting the work done, but if they are not there or there are few of them, the work must of necessity be left either entirely undone or at least some part of it, so that those measures that increase the number of workers must also be the most useful ones for the kingdom and for its inhabitants generally, whereas, on the contrary, those measures are harmful that to a greater or lesser degree contribute to a diminution of workers. It therefore only remains to ask: how should those measures then be framed that serve or detract from such a high purpose?

As incontrovertible as it is that human beings naturally love freedom, so infallible is also the consequence that the more the laws promote and favour that freedom, the more will inhabitants assemble together to enjoy it, and, contrariwise, the more that freedom is restricted, the more will people flee such troubled regions. Reason must prove me right in this, and the slightest understanding of our own feelings will reveal these truths, and incontrovertible experience speaks volumes on this subject. Dumb animals, created for far less freedom than we were, nonetheless yearn for it: they flee localities where they are frequently hunted but flock together in large numbers in protected places. Human beings, the noblest inhabitants of the earth, relatively quickly filled the earth with people in their state of freedom, but constraints have harmed them so much that large regions are still left uninhabited after 4,000 years of occupation. Who will not agree that the freedom of residence has filled Brandenburg[10] with people and that Spanish inquisitions have denuded Spain of inhabitants? Truths that no person with common sense can call in question.

On this occasion the topic is not to show to what extent our laws generally or a number of them, in the name of promoting orderliness in our economic activities, lead to the destruction of the freedoms of the people and thereby to the ruin of the kingdom, matters that are well worth the attention of those in power but are regrettably so little investigated that mistakes are inevitable in almost every sphere. The statute on servants with the proposed additions to it will on this occasion be the sole subject of our inquiry, as to how far it is fully compatible, as many assert, with the true interest of the kingdom and its inhabitants or whether it is wholly opposed to it.

The matter does not require extensive investigation; it must be manifest from the foundations already laid. If there is anything in the statute on servants that makes the inhabitants of the kingdom into outlaws and fugitives, then it is obvious that it drives our workers away from the kingdom and is consequently in conflict with the chief interest of the realm. Let us listen again to article 1, § 1: *No vagrants, vagabonds, idlers or dependent lodgers ought be tolerated in our country and our realm, either in the towns or in the countryside.* Let us imagine all the officials of the Crown set to work under § 5 of the same article to seek out, seize and place them in service with masters, in military or naval service and in hard labour in fortresses and female penitentiaries; what anxiety and restlessness must that not cause among our workers? They seek shelter, they hide away, they live in fear in their cabins and look for some refuge on earth where they can earn a living for themselves in tranquillity.

Since earlier times, rulers have had the sense to amnesty those of their soldiers who have abandoned their posts and would otherwise, under the Articles of War, have forfeited their lives, in order to lure them back into the kingdom; but as yet no proclamation of amnesty has been issued in Sweden for legally blameless workers to live freely within the borders of Sweden; and what increase in inhabitants can one expect here, what accession of strength to the kingdom, what supply of workers, when this still remains undone among us?

Someone might wish to argue against me, I who talk so much about freedom, that as long as human beings were in their natural state, without societies, they were also entitled to such an extensive and, as it is called, lawless freedom, but as soon as one enters into social relations with other people, under a governing authority, one must of necessity surrender some of one's natural rights and submit to the laws of that society, and thus obedience to the laws cannot be termed constraint or bondage. I answer: that is correct, though with the qualification that, as the same amount of natural freedom does not have to be lost in every centralized society in the world, but more in one and less in another, as experience clearly shows, it is obvious that the most fortunate society must be the one in which the loss of natural freedom is the smallest, for people are drawn there in the greatest numbers, there they live most contentedly, and there the kingdom grows in strength as far as is possible, whereas, on the other hand, the more we must lose of our natural rights, the more constrainedly we enter into such associations, the more discontented will we be there and the sooner will we move away from there to another society, where there is more freedom.

But how much of the natural freedom has to be lost by subjects in order to ensure the successful continuance of a society is a question of the greatest importance to princes who wish to earn themselves a truly high reputation among people and make them pleased with their rule. I do not know whether it has been fully answered and elucidated by our great and philanthropic intellectuals. How, then, are rulers to guard against the greatest errors with regard to the rights of our species? All constraints that violate the latter will infallibly bring misfortunes on the kingdom and the citizens.

But as regards the freedom to reside and support oneself by one's labour, it is the first and most precious right of nature, most solemnly guaranteed in our fundamental laws, and therefore cannot be questioned in this context. We complain about emigration, which is also deplorable, but we have not yet placed the letters of emancipation of nature and our constitution in the hands of our fugitive workers in order to keep them here.

Is it any surprise that a perennial chasing around and hunting for workers has over long periods of time denuded us of people and provoked a general outcry over shortages and dearness? But it is even stranger that our legislators have considered the only remedy for those shortages to be the organization of even stricter hunts and harsher confinements, just as if, having fished out a small lake, one thought the correct remedy were to fish more often, as long as there was a single fish there, when there might be a real danger of losing the entire stock.

§ 12

However, we find an even more significant cause of the deplored shortage of workers in that same statute on servants, if we accept as a fact what was demonstrated above in § 6, that it is mainly annual service contracts that inhibit marriages.

The proposition that without marriages our species cannot survive possesses very nearly the same degree of certainty as that inherent in the mathematical axioms; as soon, therefore, as there is talk of a dearth of population, of a sparsely populated land, it seems to me that all rational thought must turn towards marriages, to see whether our political arrangements or their consequences offer some obstruction to this tenderest instinct of nature. If that is found to be the case, and, even with a troubling dearth of population, we still wish to defend them, we shall be working directly against the real means of remedying the evil and at the same time erecting insuperable barriers to the growth and strength of the kingdom and thereby increasing the complaints and distress of those who now suffer from a shortage of workers.

If a country does not have as many inhabitants as it is able to contain and are capable of supporting themselves there, one can safely say that it must be the fault of the government, not of nature. With regard to the propagation of the human species, nature is quite enterprising and generous, as with the other animals according to their kind, and ought therefore to entirely fulfil the blessing and purpose of its great Creator, to multiply and cover the earth. But when officials must spend their best years unmarried, because of a salary insufficient to provide maintenance for a wife, and the humblest workers toil under annual service contracts without seeing any chances of supporting a wife and children or having the freedom to build themselves a hut to live in, then it is not surprising that the growth of the kingdom will be slight and that masters make reasonable complaints about the scarcity of workers, but that this scarcity is to be overcome by even harsher constraints and greater obstructions to marriage is such a preposterous proposal that it will scarcely be able to gain any adherents among thoughtful individuals.

Now what do the proponents of the statute on servants reply to that? This statute, they say, has nothing to do with population growth but only with the appropriate use of the people for the benefit of the kingdom and the citizens; there are other laws intended to promote an increase in subjects, so there is no need for the supply of workers to run short on that account; but, dear reader! what is the good of thus using them appropriately when this very system so manifestly, as has now been demonstrated, disperses the existing workers and completely prevents the rearing of new ones? If other statutes, they say, promote the growth in population, then the ordinance on servants is useful for employing them correctly. But I respond, to the contrary, that when the statute on servants, in the form now proposed, destroys all freedom and security for workers, no other law can possibly promote their increase while this one exists; that is utterly impossible.

From where are workers to come? Who does not know that none arrive among us here from abroad, and in this country the nursery garden for people is obstructed by legislation; is our entire plantation not, then, bound to die out? It is also said: there is no real shortage here, if only proper use were made of the population; what that really amounts to is: if only I and someone else were allowed, with legal sanction, to arbitrarily take as many as we might need from some who could well do without them. In opposition to that, however, I wish to prove that there is an actual shortage of workers and servants here. That can be clearly seen from the agreement that masters in a certain county have mutually arrived at to reduce their requirement of servants – that is to say, not to enter in the register, in which the number of servants of each of them is recorded, as many as they would actually require – in order that other masters (N.B.) should not be left without any. If, after the enrolment of the servants who were everywhere sought out and recorded, no scarcity had been revealed, every master would have been allowed to record under his name as many as he wished to have, but as that is not permitted, there obviously is a shortage.

How, then, should this shortage be remedied and the kingdom be supplied with as many workers as are needed? We will have to wait a long time for those who are still unborn; what many a master probably thinks is that if no other expedients are possible to redress the shortage, the remedy is likely to come too late. That is what they thought when they drafted § 4 of the resolution of 1635[11] as well as when they promulgated the ordinance on servants of 1664.[12] The same approach was likewise adopted in the era of absolutism, of which the ordinance of 1686 provides incontrovertible evidence. That self-interested principle underwent no change during the so-called Age of Liberty in the drafting of the statute on servants of 1723, but on the contrary it became even more deep-rooted in 1739 and put out new shoots in 1766 in the scheme of the Finance and Trade Committee and is still poised to extend its sway, if that were possible, in the enlightened era of our *great* and *sagacious* Gustavus. How, then, should our dearth of population be countered?

Just imagine! If one had established a nursery for workers in the seventeenth century or if in 1739, instead of the statute on servants then issued, one had at least offered them protection, what a large number of servants would not already be available to us from their children and grandchildren, who are now largely absent and make the scarcity more severe as time passes? Sweden is just like a garden in which the gardeners never laboured to produce new saplings from seeds and never established a tree nursery. But that great achievement must indeed have been reserved by Providence for our *Great King* Gustavus to accomplish, for the happiness of contemporaries and posterity and the expansion and power of Sweden, in the face of every assault of self-interest.

I am not advocating any contrived arrangements; I am not alluding here to the establishment of new children's homes; I do not intend herewith to recommend any rewards for marriage or children; I speak only in favour of the one small but blessed word *Freedom*. I believe that nature, in this as in many other respects, left to itself, achieves far more than many artful and ingenious plans with which their inventors promise heaven and earth.

§ 13

With the truth revealed in this regard, as to whether obligatory annual service contracts may be beneficial for the kingdom, it now seems appropriate for us to examine whether fixed and prescribed annual wages for servants would be advantageous to the kingdom or not.

I can assert with full conviction in that regard that all tariffs, even the most essential ones, are nothing but unfortunate consequences of aristocratic combinations, which combinations, as long as they are protected by the laws and the governing power, would in the absence of tariffs be able to tax their fellow citizens excessively and without limits.

In most of the European states the governments have favoured such associations and have granted them exclusive privileges to provide the state and its citizens with certain necessities, by which they have eliminated all their rivals and are able under the protection of their rulers to act as arbiters of the prices of their commodities, to their own advantage and the oppression of their fellow subjects.

For that reason the tariffs have in turn become indispensable in order, on the other hand, to curb their selfishness, from which humankind may nonetheless suffer greatly, in so far as such associations are able to influence those who issue such tariffs. That is, one first establishes an aristocratic ascendancy and is then obliged to conduct an everlasting war against it.

But with the servants the issue is of quite a different nature. They are the most defenceless group among the subjects of a state, dispersed around the whole kingdom, without any guild ordinance, without spokesmen or any specific protection. No combinations are formed here, but each individual in his freedom simply follows his natural instinct to promote his own welfare. Just as the price of a commodity necessarily increases when a general shortage arises, the same happens with servants' wages: if there is a general shortage of servants, so that there are more who need them than will allow all to obtain as many as they desire, then they are eagerly sought after and bargained with, and then he who wishes to meet his requirement must offer a larger hiring fee and higher wage than the others. But the need for servants also depends on a number of accidental circumstances; if the masters have large incomes or are planning profitable land reclamations, they would rather pay high wages than forgo real profits from their labour.

In circumstances like these, such an increase in wages is not unreasonable, and, rightly, the poor worker is also able to enjoy some of the agreeable crumbs that fall from his master's table. Nor can it be harmful to the kingdom, as increased wages attract more workers to it, where, with improved earnings, they engage in work that manifestly contributes to the profit and power of the realm, rather than in less productive occupations.

It may well be the case, someone will say, that a few individuals in some rural area make a very good living and are thus able with their reasonable income to pay high wages. But there may be several hundred apart from them who possess neither the wealth nor an income that enables them to do so, and consequently all of these must suffer because of the others and pay as much as the wealthy ones if they are to obtain any servants, once the wealthy man has increased the wages. But I reply: no, they need not do so at all; and you will say: how, then, will the others obtain any, when he offers more? I answer: as long as he is making an offer, they cannot, but once he has fulfilled his requirements, they will obtain enough at the price that they can reasonably offer. But, the argument continues, they cannot avoid making an offer for fear of being left without; thus, the shortage is again the true cause of the increase, and that can only be remedied by a superfluity of people but in no way by means of tariffs, which, when the shortage is so severe, mean less than nothing.

On the other hand, however, if there is again an abundant supply of people and few who need their labour or consider it worth providing them with food and wages, then their remunerations and annual wages will fall in the absence of tariffs and regulations, of which we have the clearest evidence in the occasional years of general crop failure, when it may often happen that one has more workers than one is able to feed and set to work for their food alone, and there again no master is likely to be willing to pay according to the tariff.

§ 14

I therefore venture to assert that fixed annual wages are in themselves unfair and also have an effect on emigration; they utterly stifle all diligence, force the most virtuous citizens to break the law and, through law-breaking, create a contempt for the law that is most damaging to a state. The matter has far-reaching implications, but for the unbiased and thoughtful reader, for whom I write, I do not need to argue this at length.

Such legally prescribed wages must be unfair in several respects. I need say no more here about how unfair these wages must be, taking into account the variations in monetary values that have hitherto occurred among us from time to time, when since 1739 the *riksdaler specie* has risen from 9 *daler kmt* to 18 *daler*, whereby the servants, if the tariffs were the very fairest in 1739, have lost half of their annual wages, as the regulations in that regard have not changed in the slightest in line with the value of the *riksdaler* established for all time by our *great king*.[13] I merely wish to show that they cannot in themselves be other than unfair. For just as one and the same commodity commands quite different prices within one and the same county, the same labour also has quite a different value in different places. In one parish, where there are many opportunities for gainful employment, the day wages and remunerations rise steeply compared with the others, where there are few chances of paid work, and we have the clearest evidence of that in the fact that in one and the same parish in Finland the natural value of the day wage varies by almost 100 per cent. How fairly can one then impose a fixed value on labour throughout the entire county?

An unfairness must also arise from the fact that the earnings are not everywhere the same at all times. One parish, for example, that earns an income by shipbuilding from its forest has an excellent income in some years, when ships command a good price, and can therefore pay its hands high annual wages, which the others cannot, but when that source of income ceases, or all the forest in the parish has been felled, the day wage declines and with it the annual wage of the worker, during which time the saleable products of another parish may rise in price and in the same manner force up the remunerations for a while. How fair could fixed annual wages then be under such circumstances? Or how useful could they be to the realm? If it were possible to maintain low tariffs in such cases, that would cause an inevitable emigration from the country, in order to look for a better income among our neighbours.

But the damage done to the realm and its subjects in general by fixed annual wages, through suppressing the willingness to work, although least visible to an unreflecting public, is nevertheless the most serious one in the long term. The proposition to pay the same price for a good and a useless commodity, apart from being in itself extremely unfair, will also have the obvious effect of causing the commodity to deteriorate and making it virtually useless. That fixed annual wages for the servants will have the same effect is likewise evident. When diligence and eagerness are not rewarded or, even worse, are forbidden on pain of a stiff fine from being remunerated, they cannot exist in a society where such laws are observed, still less be increased to any degree. The matter has been clearly established above in § 8, and here I merely wish to express regret for the consequences of it for our kingdom. What, then, is labour without willingness? A concealed lethargy. What is willingness without encouragement and reward? A folly of working and striving to no purpose, being made a mockery of by the bad worker who, in sleep and idleness, to the chagrin of diligence, gathers as great a harvest as the hard-working one. Is it, then, not amazing to see in our laws that such a reward for diligence has for ages past been most strenuously precluded and how the legislative power has already for a hundred years busied itself with stifling the willingness to work of the Swedish labourer, merely in order to favour masters by means of low annual wages for their servants?

The trade balances never reveal how much the kingdom has lost by this,[14] but the loss must become insupportable. In this and other such regulations we may thus easily discover the natural reason why the Dutch and the English far outstrip the Swedes in all kinds of work, when even daily experience teaches us how work can be done as piecework in half a day, and often less, which otherwise generally takes a whole day.

Nor must I omit to mention here the damage that the kingdom and its inhabitants, both masters and servants, have suffered from the numerous lawsuits to which our previous statute on servants has given rise, both by prescribing certain annual wages and by the designation vagabonds and other circumstances, which on both accounts have cost the realm almost millions, have probably increased the fees of the courts considerably, but have also led judges either to pronounce judgments, according to the plain wording of the laws, that are quite contrary to conscience and equity, or else, in order to appease their consciences, to find ways of evading the issue, of which I may cite a single remarkable example. One such case, concerning an annual wage, had progressed as far as one of the appeal courts of the realm, where the case was submitted for the opinion of a member of the tribunal learned in the law, of wide renown and conscientious, who, in order to avoid pronouncing a judgment contrary to conscience and equity, adopted the expedient of declaring himself disqualified on the grounds that he had been obliged to infringe the same tariff; and I cannot without the greatest anxiety think of how the renewal of that statute, including the proposed lot-drawing and other constraints, will give rise to discord, lawsuits, breaches of the law and penalties, which have now in most places, as it were, fallen into abeyance and become ineffective owing to the inappropriateness of the previous one and its widespread infringement.

§ 15

It should in no way be a secret that the previous statute on servants of 1739 has for most purposes in practice become a dead letter now in most parts of the kingdom. But although I regard the breaches of the law as being of more advantage than harm to the realm, a true citizen cannot observe such transgressions of a clearly formulated law with complete equanimity, considering their effect on the nation's morals and opinions.

This law is for most purposes quite clear and comprehensible to the simplest citizens; nor can they generally have any other notion of crimes than that they consist in transgression of the laws, while one cannot expect them to differentiate between good and bad, useful and useless laws – a distinction that ought not even to exist in a well-ordered society. What happens then? They become aware that the most virtuous citizen, the most conscientious official, the truest Christian every year quite openly commits offences against this statute with impunity. I ask, what notion could our general public then have of crime and punishment? What ideas of virtue and of obedience to the laws will we be able to implant among the common people? And how much of either can we expect from them? And what crimes would they commit if they were to be made aware from such precedents how liable they are to penalties? When transgressions become unavoidable and are consequently not always followed by condign punishment, penalties will come to seem like persecution.

I cannot express how much this has troubled me as a clergyman, on whom it is incumbent to impress on my congregation not only a deep veneration for the authorities as such but also unqualified obedience to the laws of the realm, and how much it has distressed me, as a citizen, not only, despite the most sincere zeal for King and country, to be a transgressor of our laws but also to provide examples of law-breaking to my congregation and fellow citizens.

I have always wondered at the proficiency of almost everyone, especially under the former constitution,[15] in reshaping laws and issuing new ones, often in response to a particular event, and not infrequently in complete contradiction to each other, of which not one-tenth of the subjects of the kingdom could be aware and which not one in a hundred observed. Answer me then, dear reader, what veneration can subjects have for such laws, and what law-abidingness may one expect where numerous obstacles prevent their observance? Where royal decrees are daily infringed, the general public loses all respect even for the most necessary and salutary ones and believes itself to be equally entitled to transgress against everything, whereby all morality must disappear among the citizens. A lamentable condition for a kingdom!

The harm caused to the realm by such breaches of the law becomes all the greater and more significant the longer they occur. Several such transgressions turn law-breaking into a habit and have the effect of making the inhabitants of the kingdom lawless and unbridled, so that neither laws nor barriers can curb them. The meekest of lambs, having in their earliest years become gradually accustomed to leaping over enclosures, soon become habitually the worst fence-jumpers and most troublesome animals, whom no enclosures can any longer restrain. In the same way, our numerous laws, on which the aristocratic power has probably already been labouring for several centuries, have regrettably transformed the docile Swedish people into unrestrained transgressors of the laws.

§ 16

In this way, dear reader, I have now tried to persuade you to what extent most of the proposals made so far for a new statute on servants may be in keeping with a true civic liberty or the good of the realm. How far I have been successful in all of this your impartial opinion will decide.

However, a general public that complains about the wilfulness and mischief of the servants is unlikely to be content with my overthrowing the Golden Bull of the masters but believes itself entitled to demand from me a proposal for what in my opinion would be a better ordinance on servants, so that the public may ascertain whether I have been more successful in that respect than the earlier proponents. Nor should I deny my fellow citizens that justice, but I should also add in advance that my proposal is exceedingly simple and brief, the entire proposal being as follows: "That, as all the regulations concerning servants that have from time to time been issued cannot be considered as fully upholding the civic liberty rightfully due to Swedish subjects, nor as being conducive to the true purpose, which is the strength and improvement of the realm, His Majesty desires that all of them be, in all respects, repealed and declared void, except as regards the times for giving notice to leave and moving to other employment, which may be retained in future according to existing practice, and that every subject, servant as well as master, be allowed individual freedom to mutually agree, as they think best, either on an annual service contract or day wages, at such a price as they may arrange between themselves."

Behold! Here is the whole of my proposal, constructed on the foundations of true freedom. It stands all alone, with no support except the freedom on which it rests and a natural balance or reciprocity between masters and servants, without in the least favouring either or oppressing one more than the other.

Away with such a pernicious proposal, most of my readers will probably say. It is bound to put all masters in an extreme quandary, leave them without servants, oblige them to let their properties revert to wilderness or else, in the general disorder that may be caused by it, to sell their estates for half their value. I can well imagine that it would be a thunderclap for many masters, especially those who have now been working vigorously to forge new fetters for freedom, but that will not deter me from keeping closely to my conviction. I am already accustomed to such an outcry and have always noticed that aristocratic power is like a boil, or alternatively a precious jewel, and anyone who touches it is always assailed by a fearful roar that the entire kingdom is perishing, which should be interpreted to mean that *the aristocrats are losing some of their illegitimate encroachments, whereby the realm and the citizens will recover their rights.*

In that case, you say, annual service contracts will cease altogether and a farmer will always have to look for workers every day at an insufferably high day wage. No, dear reader! Annual service contracts freely entered into offer great advantages to servants as well, so that those who are unengaged and unmarried, having tried being unengaged for a year, are quite willing to accept an annual contract the following one. The day wage will indeed now rise to a high level during the busiest working period, when few day labourers are available, but if they increase in numbers, it will fall. The day labourer may indeed seem to receive a high day wage on one occasion, but he has to go without on another and consume his earnings. Workers hired for the year, on the contrary, receive their hiring fee, their working clothes, and so forth; they have free board all the year round, on both Sundays and weekdays, and generally receive a greater abundance of food from their masters than they could afford in their poverty at home, apart from an honest wage, freely negotiated for their year's work, which all told and in terms of money corresponds to a relatively high day wage throughout the year.

One small example may illustrate the matter more clearly: the Crown distilleries[16] are now hiring annually contracted hands in Vaasa (Vasa) with individual board, free lodging, firewood and heating and a few months of leave in the summer during the busiest working period, for a sum of around 720 *daler kmt* in wages and hiring fee, and if one were also to calculate the house rent and firewood in money, it would amount, close to a town where rent and firewood are expensive, to 90 *daler*, at least with the very stimulating dram of spirits that is likewise provided, which, added to his wage, amounts to 810 *daler*. Let two summer months of leave then correspond to 50 days of work, during which the hand, at least in our area, can earn himself a day wage of 3 *daler* 16 *öre kmt*, which adds another 175 *daler* to his wage and in combination with the latter constitutes an annual wage of 985 *daler kmt* all told, a sum that, evenly distributed over 300 working days a year, corresponds to a day wage of almost 3 *daler* 9 *öre* for each day throughout the year, which is in itself a high day wage, for if one takes 150 winter days, for which no more than 2 *daler* 16 *öre* can be paid, amounting to 375 *daler*, that annual wage will produce a day wage rising to about 4 *daler* 2 *öre* in copper coin for each summer day, which is already an excessive day wage. One nonetheless sees that many workers hand in their notice at the distillery and prefer to accept annual service contracts with other people for freely negotiated annual wages of up to 120 or 150 *daler kmt* a year, with 3 or 4 *plåtar* as a hiring fee, when they receive board and their usual working clothes.

From this calculation I conclude, first, that a worker hired for day wages is obtained far more cheaply than such annually contracted hands are now employed at the distillery. Second: when hands give up such obvious advantages for annual employment at a wage of 20 or 25 *plåtar*, with board throughout the year and their working clothes, the advantages of that can hardly be much less, when everything is carefully added up; and, third, that annual service contracts are not as advantageous for masters as it appears to us at first sight and that we should therefore, as masters, not be too afraid of getting the work done with day labourers; if they were to increase in numbers, the day wage would drop considerably, and I assure you that if all the food that the servants consume throughout the year, together with their working clothes and other such things, are carefully reckoned in terms of money, they would constitute a large sum. Yes, you say, they certainly would, so for that reason there should be a tariff, at least for their wages. But, dear reader, what are we to do with tariffs, which are in any case not observed, either by you or by me, when we really need servants, unless we also turn them into bondsmen and deprive them of all their liberty, as will happen with the assignment by lot, and that is again contrary to all civic feeling and love for humanity and will soon bring misfortunes upon our fatherland, as was shown above? Let us therefore for the present accept our lot, which is to pay our servants dearly; that is the natural consequence of their scarcity. We must regrettably reap what our forefathers have for centuries sown by their statutes on servants and by that dearness experience the shortage of workers that is a natural consequence of them.

§ 17

On the other hand, however, it is the duty of us who live in a more enlightened epoch, in which the voice of humanity has been able to reach the thrones of kings and gain a place in the hearts of great princes, to liberate ourselves from the well-deserved charges of posterity, which we can lay against our forefathers, and let our descendants with God's blessing reap the fruits of our ways of thinking, which are Christian and honourable for mankind.

The Royal Swedish Academy of Sciences adorns its Proceedings with the motto "*For Posterity*". It has lived up to it, as well. It is the duty of Swedes to work likewise for the same great purpose in this matter. Unless Sweden is for ever to toil in weakness and with a shortage of workers, we ought to be considering powerful means of aiding our fatherland. When we find that our weakness consists in a lack of working inhabitants, it is obvious that we should contemplate nurseries for people, not so much by establishing many children's homes, as experience throughout Europe has taught us that few of the children in them really become useful to the state, as most of them languish in overcrowding and unhealthy air, die or become dissolute citizens, still less by promoting sexual immorality, by which some waste their lives in vice, with very little increase in population and without taking care of their children, and others tear their marriage ties asunder, to the irreparable loss of their children in their upbringing, but by promoting Christian marriages among the workers. But the question is: how should that be done? By freedom, so that the authorities restore nature's letter of emancipation to the workers, of which they have hitherto been deprived by the statutes on servants.

In my candid opinion the general public ought first of all to be given quite a different definition of the term "vagabond", namely that it applies only to fit and able-bodied beggars who cannot be bothered to earn a living, whereas all those who honestly support themselves and their families, whether they live in crofts, cabins or as dependent lodgers, should now and for ever be placed under the particular favour and protection of the Crown, so that no one, whoever he may be, should be authorized to force them to become soldiers, sailors or saltpetre boilers or to accept an annual service contract, unless they agreed to that of their own accord. Next they should be told that His Majesty regards the marriages of farmhands and maids and other unengaged workers as of equal utility and advantage to the kingdom as those of freeholders, and that in order to promote them more effectively, His Majesty will as an incentive exempt them from one, two or three revenue taxes whenever they are able to prove by certificates at the census registration that they have entered upon marriage before either of them has reached the age of 30, a reward for marriage that could initially be granted for ten years, not because people, if they were free, would not consider marriage without rewards but in order all the sooner to eradicate old prejudices about the folly of unengaged workers marrying. In addition, they should be assured that they may not only with due permission settle in all Crown forest areas but also enjoy the gracious protection of His Majesty wherever they can come to an agreement with individual landowners to construct crofts and cabins for themselves or else live as lodgers with some freeholder; and finally, and most importantly, that they should have complete freedom to support themselves and their families by any kind of work and craft, apart from keeping a public house, that they themselves may wish to pursue, without any restriction.

By means of such a law, and in no other way, could freedom in my view be restored to our workers, and this is to my mind the natural ground plan for a most necessary nursery for our servant population. Here our great and beneficent King would have blessed scope, in accordance with his compassionate spirit, to invigorate and enliven those of his loyal subjects who otherwise, being situated too far from the throne, rarely come to feel the warmth of the sun that shines upon it. Here is an opportunity for a great achievement by a King in Sweden who cannot but be great in every respect. He occupies the Swedish throne, as the conqueror of aristocracy in the administration of the realm, but those same creatures of mischief still seek to exercise their ferocity towards the kingdom by oppressing its most humble subjects. The honour ought then to fall to Our Dear Anointed One to complete the victory. As the world must admire such noble-minded interventions, in the face of the grumblings of self-interest, and even the most humble happily bless *King Gustavus* and *Freedom*, our descendants, benefiting from a joyful harvest of that which the solicitude of our Gracious King has sown, will for centuries to come strew flowers on the beloved grave of him who, by his wisdom and a charitable heart, has been able to curb the ravages of self-interest.

I have not been able to proceed further on this occasion. I am deeply concerned for my fatherland and my heart bleeds for its wounds, content if I have been able to encourage my fellow countrymen to examine this subject, but happy if I have been able to provide the slightest grounds for redress!

Notes

1 "... *the scheme elaborated during the Diet of 1766*": as Pentti Virrankoski notes, Chydenius here remembers incorrectly, as the mentioned "scheme" was quite liberal in its tone and critical towards harsh measures against the unemployed (P. Virrankoski, *Anders Chydenius: Demokratisk politiker i upplysningens tid*, Stockholm: Timbro, 1995, p. 297f.).

2 "*their period of freedom*": according to the statute on servants of 1739, a servant

wishing to leave his or her master had to find new employment during a seven-week period before 29 September. See also note 12, p. 115–16.

3 *"Transactions of the Royal Patriotic Society"*: this society was founded in 1766 under the auspices of King Adolphus Frederic in order to support the arts and trades of Sweden as well as its industriousness. Its members during its first decades of existence were made up of industrial leaders, politicians, noble landowners and learned men with a patriotic zeal for reforming and developing the Swedish economy. From the start, the Patriotic Society published a monthly journal called *Hushållnings-Journal*.

4 *"Dagligt Allehanda"*: the first Swedish daily newspaper, which started in 1769 and existed until 1849.

5 *"jus vitae et necis"*: "the right over life and death".

6 *"A posse ad esse, non valet consequentia"*: "From a thing's possibility, one cannot be certain of its reality".

7 *"statutes on servants of 1723 and 1739"*: see the Commentary, pp. 313–14.

8 *"the scheme of 1766"*: see p. 286 and note 1, p. 311.

9 *"in politicis"*: see note 49, p. 118.

10 *"... freedom of residence has filled Brandenburg"*: during the seventeenth and eighteenth centuries, monarchs in Brandenburg-Prussia were generally inclined to encourage immigration of economically productive elements, particularly peasants, into the more backward and underpopulated areas of the state, especially after the Thirty Years War. Alongside this, Frederick II ("the Great", 1712–86) established religious tolerance, which made it possible for other worshippers to reside in Brandenburg, and particularly in Berlin. Frederick was an enlightened monarch who combined paternalism with liberal reforms such as freedom of the press, religious tolerance, individual protection against the law, including the abolition of torture, and making death sentences legal only with his personal sanction.

11 *"the resolution of 1635"*: the first so-called *Landshövdingsinstruktion* (Instruction for county governors) was issued in 1635. It states that the county governor is responsible for the "unemployed and vicious persons" who do not have a master.

12 *"the ordinance on servants of 1664"*: the first statute on servants was passed in 1664 and revised in 1686, 1723 and 1739, the content being basically the same. See the Commentary, p. 313.

13 *"... the value of the* riksdaler *established for all time by our great king"*: refers to the minting reform of 1776, when the monetary system was totally renewed. A sole silver (specie) standard was introduced and *riksdaler* became the main currency.

14 *"The trade balances never reveal..."*: a common type of critique among English economic writers from the 1690s onwards towards the idea of basing English trade policies upon the balance of trade. As stated by Charles Davenant and others during this time, it was almost impossible to calculate the trade balance for a particular time or moment. See L. Magnusson, *Mercantilism: The Shaping of an Economic Language*, London: Routledge, 1994, p. 116f.

15 *"the former constitution"*: refers to the constitution during the Age of Liberty, 1719–1772.

16 *"Crown distilleries"*: in 1775, Gustavus III enacted an ordinance that prohibited home-distilling of hard liquor (*brännvin*) and instead decreed the establishment of Crown distilleries. See p. 351.

Commentary

Lars Magnusson

This tract was published by the Royal Printing-Press in Stockholm, most probably in November or December 1778. Its publication is directly connected with the fact that Chydenius in the autumn of this year once again was appointed as a delegate of the Estate of Clergy in the forthcoming Diet. The notice of call for a new gathering of the Diet was sent out on 9 September and, as we can see, the foreword to the tract was signed on 12 September. During the next month, elections were held, which eventually (and not without the usual complications[1]) led to Chydenius being appointed as a delegate from Ostrobothnia. When he arrived in Stockholm on 12 November, the Diet had already started, and shortly afterwards his tract on the natural rights of masters and servants was published.

It is clear that the intention of writing the tract was to use the new Diet as a platform for pushing for reform – the abolition of the Statute on Servants and Hired Workers (*tjänstehjonsstadgan*). While regulations concerning servants have a long pedigree in Sweden, all the way back to the medieval county laws (*landskapslagar*), the first "modern" statute was inaugurated in 1664.[2] However, as the Swedish economic historian Gustaf Utterström explains, it was not until the Age of Liberty that these regulations reached their zenith.[3] Two regulations were issued during this period, in 1723 and in 1739. As in many other parts of Europe at the time, statutes and ordinances of this kind were proclaimed in order to combat vagrancy and begging – practices that during this period were endemic in most societies and occurred both in the towns and in the countryside. In addition, the aim was to guarantee that agriculture and industry, including the always highly esteemed iron industry, were furnished with enough hands. The statute of 1739 – which Chydenius refers to – was especially rich in detail. It not only stated that it was unlawful and punishable to be a vagrant and without a master – to be without lawful protection (*laga försvar*) – but also regulated the employment relationship between the master and the servant. With regard to the master, it was ordained that he should treat his servants well and keep them for at least one year. Moreover, he was only allowed to employ and keep a certain number of workers on his farm or on his premises. With regard to servants, the statutes of 1723 and 1739 included certain wage tariffs (in coin and kind): an employer who offered wages above this level could be fined. Moreover, servants had no right to move to another county, but had to seek a new employer within Ostrobothnia, for example, if they wanted to move for some reason.

As has been pointed out, this regulative order implied that servants and hired workers were kept in very servile conditions. They were dependent upon their masters, who also had the right to administer corporal punishment. This right was preserved until as late as 1858; the statute as such was finally abolished in 1885. During the Age of Liberty it was defended as a necessary means to overcome the problems caused by a small population. According to this view, without such legislation, servants and workers would instead put themselves up as crofters or even free labourers. This danger was especially acute given the abundance of available land in the Swedish realm; the statute of 1723 in particular explicitly referred to a lack of hands after the devastation of the Great Northern War. The strict prohibitions against the splitting up of farms (*hemmansklyvning*) that were in effect until 1739, as well as against the increase of crofters, were based upon the same arguments. A constant fear, especially during the 1730s, was that servants would flee to the towns. Stockholm was considered to be a particular magnet. The capital city received a constant inflow of people who more or less illegally had left their old masters in the countryside. Even in the 1760s – as we have seen – emigration out of Sweden, for example to Denmark, was still considered such a severe problem that the Royal Academy of Sciences launched an essay competition in order to find a remedy.

Although Chydenius was probably the most outspoken enemy of this system, he was not by any means the only one. In 1772 the Royal Academy of Sciences published a text, which Chydenius most probably had read, written by the Uppsala adjunct in economics Anders Gustaf Barchaeus (1735–1806) who spoke in favour of radical reform. In the same year a committee was formed by the Estates which suggested that the statute of 1739 should be abolished and instead argued for the establishment of free contracts between masters and servants without restrictions on mobility. However, after the mid-1770s more reactionary ideas were again voiced. In 1777 a decision was taken in the county of Gävleborg that the statute of 1739 should be fully enforced, not least the wage tariffs (after a period of more slack practice). Moreover, the servants should be counted and then distributed among masters according to certain criteria. The background to this draconian decision was that the masters of Gävleborg felt that several years of good harvests had created such a demand for more agricultural workers that the masters were forced to increase wages rapidly in order to employ enough hands.

It was this decision that triggered the heated debate taking place in periodicals such as *Dagligt Allehanda*, *Stockholms Posten* and *Hushållnings-Journal* (the last published by the Patriotic Society, *Patriotiska sällskapet*). Chydenius's first contribution to the debate was a letter to the editor published in *Dagligt Allehanda* on 11 August 1778 under the signature "Prodromus". His arguments here are largely the same as in the longer tract published later in the autumn: the system of sharing out servants was both cruel and against the principles of natural right. For these reasons, the whole system of restricting the freedom of servants should be scrapped, the author argued. The opinions presented in the article, and especially in the tract, provoked a large number of interventions, and Chydenius himself wrote several responses during the first eight months of 1779 – this time under his own name.[4] As Virrankoski has pointed out, Chydenius's critics mainly argued that it was the workers' duty to serve their masters so that agriculture could prosper. Higher wages would only lead to increased idleness and to workers spending their money on drink. Moreover, Virrankoski has proposed that one of the anonymous critics of Chydenius, signing himself "Sincere & Moderate", was none other than his friend the historiographer royal Anders Schönberg. Schönberg as well as others most likely felt that Chydenius had gone too far in defending the human rights of servants – a fanatic for democratic principles once again.

In the tract *Thoughts Concerning the Natural Rights of Masters and Servants*, its author without doubt develops views that were not common at the time. His fierce attack on the view that servants were morally inferior and needed a paternal hand particularly stands out in this context. Economic literature at the time, both in Britain and on the Continent, was full of moralist proclamations of the same kind as when the Irish economist Richard Cantillon (*c*.1680–1734) stated that poor people receiving a slight rise of income would multiply "as mice in the barn". In general, workers were supposed to behave according to the "theory of a backward-sloping demand curve for labour"; that is, they would diminish their work effort if their wages were increased.[5] Moreover, Chydenius's condemnation of the use of corporal punishment was quite advanced for the period. As was discussed in the Introduction, his more humane attitude followed from his very consistent interpretation of natural rights doctrine (as well as from his faith). However, to this must be added his almost innate sympathy with ordinary people, the peasants and servants from his home provinces of Ostrobothnia and Lapland.

We have already argued that the result of Chydenius's campaigning for the establishment of a free contractual relationship between masters and servants must have been a disappointment – this especially as a joint committee of the Estates in 1772 in fact had recommended a withdrawal of the old statute. In accordance with his wish, in 1778 Chydenius became secretary of the committee that was to put forward a new proposal. It was known that Gustavus III and his government (in practice, Permanent Secretary Johan Liljencrants[6]) were in favour of a reform creating free contracts between masters and servants. However, after a good start everything went wrong. The proposal issued by the king was voted down in three of the estates (the Clergy, the Burghers and the Nobility). Only the Peasants supported it. We can only speculate about the reasons for this outcome. On the one hand the proposal might have seemed too radical, even for those who disliked the extreme position taken by the authorities in Gävleborg. Where indeed would such a system of free contracts lead? Hence, the estates at the same time saw the opportunity to send a clear signal to Gustavus III that they wished to be more involved in decisions of this kind. Such new laws should, according to the fundamental laws of 1734, be decided on by the estates, they argued. At this point, Gustavus III retreated. The issue must be further investigated, he stated – and the statute on servants (or most parts of it) survived for another hundred years.

Notes

1 P. Virrankoski, *Anders Chydenius: Demokratisk politiker i upplysningens tid*, Stockholm: Timbro, 1995, p. 306.
2 See B. Harnesk, *Legofolk: Drängar, pigor och bönder i 1700- och 1800-talens Sverige*, Umeå Studies in the Humanities 96, Umeå, 1990, p. 32f.
3 G. Utterström, *Jordbrukets arbetare: Levnadsvillkor och arbetsliv på landsbygden från frihetstiden till mitten av 1800-talet*, del I, Stockholm: Tidens förlag, 1957, p. 249.
4 The debate continued for at least another year after this, but Chydenius did not take part in it, although some of the later contributions were directly addressed to him.
5 A.W. Coats, "Changing Attitudes to Labour in the Mid-Eighteenth Century", in A.W. Coats, *On the History of Economic Thought: British and American Economic Essays*, vol. 1, Routledge: London, 1992, p. 63f.
6 Concerning Permanent Secretary Johan Liljencrants, see the Introduction, note 127, p. 58.

10 *Memorial Regarding Freedom of Religion*

By Anders Chydenius, Dean and Rector of Kokkola.
Stockholm. Printed at the Royal Printing-Press, 1779.
Submitted to the most Reverend Estate of Clergy on 11 January 1779.
Read to the most Reverend Estate of Clergy on 18 January 1779.

At a time when the inhabitants of Sweden, under the rule of a gentle and wise King, are almost the only people in Europe to enjoy perfect internal and external peace, we cannot but be profoundly moved by the terrible wars, horrendous events and persecutions that are now rapidly spreading in several parts of the world.

Could anything then be more well advised, more in accord with a righteous Christian love for humankind as a whole, more suited to the noble spirit of unity and liberty that befits a fortunate nation and to the true interest of our blessed but underpopulated fatherland than that we, at just such a juncture, should tenderly open our arms to all those unfortunates who already are or may in future be deprived of a sanctuary in their native countries and therefore yearn to move elsewhere in search of some protection from violence and oppression for themselves, for their wives and children, and for their property?

Those who mock our Christian faith, who, by their unbridled freedom of thought, have sought to tear apart all moral philosophy that is consonant with the Word of God and with common sense, have both in this and other countries, though often without reason, sought to cast a dark shadow of intolerance over the Spiritual Estate as being a main cause of the frequent oppression of humanity and the obstruction of the growth and improvement of countries. Would it not then be worthy of the most Reverend Estate if, precisely in an auspicious era, when the Estates of the Realm have been enabled to transfer the weight of the administration of the realm onto the shoulders of their gracious and wise King,[1] it were able to persuade the whole world of the zeal with which the clergy of Sweden mildly and patiently desire to follow the elevated and holy example of their head, the Saviour of the whole world?

We are fortunate to live at a time when the gentle hand of Providence, during a period of blessed internal calm, has vouchsafed us a great blessing in our Royal Family, which awakens in all our hearts, in addition to heartfelt joy, a mutual

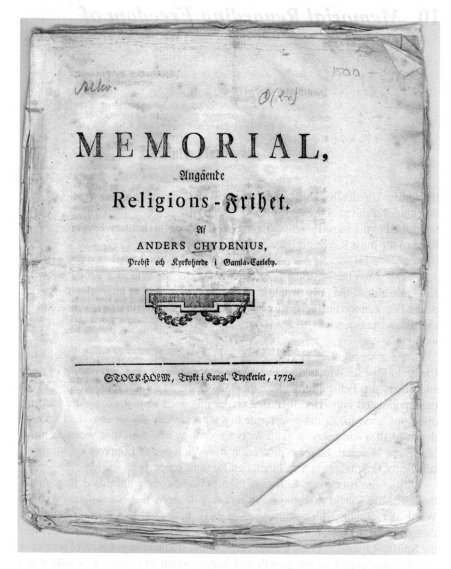

Figure 27 The title page of *Memorial Regarding Freedom of Religion* (1779). Kokkola
     University Consortium Chydenius.

emulation to accomplish works of charity and noble deeds; could any aim, then,
be worthier of the most Reverend Estate than to likewise diligently strive on its
own part towards such blessed ends?

His Royal Majesty has at this juncture opened his tender heart to many
wretches and unfortunates within the borders of the Kingdom of Sweden by
His gracious and recently issued Proclamation of Amnesty.[2] Would it not
then be an adornment to the most Reverend Estate if it were to seek to persuade

His Majesty by humble representations to extend a General Decree of Peace to such fellow beings, even beyond the borders of the Kingdom, who, without having forfeited their civic rights through any vices, have nonetheless been deprived of a fatherland by oppression and persecutions, so that Sweden may become a longed-for refuge for them all and the lofty name of our Most Gracious King become as beloved to them as it already is to all his loyal subjects?

There is not a Swedish citizen who does not know how willing His Majesty is to show mercy to unfortunates. And, as love and compassion in all respects are incumbent upon those to whom the holy ministry of preaching has been entrusted, and as it is certainly the duty of our Estate to set a good example to others in that regard, a humble statement by the most Reverend Estate on this matter would also certainly not fail to influence a King whose great magnanimity can only view with gracious pleasure every proposal that will promote the progress of the Fatherland and the salvation of humanity.

Our native land suffers from an overall deficit of population. Farmers complain about the shortage of labourers, factories and workshops lack craftsmen, and a general outcry is heard from masters regarding the expense of engaging servants. It will inevitably take a long time before native Swedes can satisfy all these deficiencies. Has not the right time arrived, then, to simultaneously lift the barriers and welcome useful people to increase the strength of the Kingdom and ease our burdens?

The prejudices that led to efforts to eradicate heterodox opinions by means of constraint of conscience and persecutions have, thank God, long since been dispelled, and it is precisely our Evangelical co-religionists,[3] especially in the southern countries of Europe, who have been the most pitiable victims of such efforts.

Actual experience and universal history provide incontrovertible proof that, with the blessing of God, mildness, patience, enlightenment and gentle instruction are the only means by which people who have gone astray may truly be converted. And may any such lack of faith in God's revealed Word and our holy Evangelical doctrine be banished from all of us who constitute the clergy of the Kingdom of Sweden that might cause us to fear some alteration in them merely because a few strangers might settle among us, including some of other religions, who, if they do not immediately accept our faith, quietly and peacefully worship the Eternal and Almighty God, our common Father, each according to his own conviction. No, Stockholm has not become Calvinist, although members of the Reformed Church have conducted public services here for several years. Denmark is not Jewish, although that unhappy people lives there in peace and publicly attends its synagogues. Prussia is not Roman Catholic,[4] although these and all other foreign believers are free to practise their religion there.

In view of all this, I most humbly request permission to propose that the most Reverend Estate, in consultation with the other respective Estates, would think fit to humbly propose to His Royal Majesty that he may graciously decree:

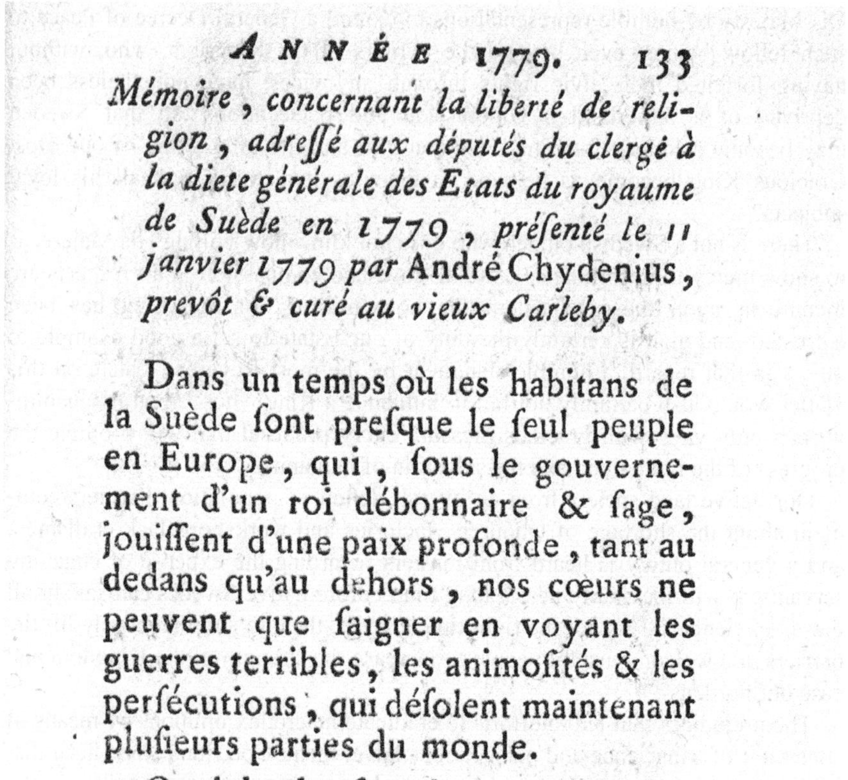

Mémoire, concernant la liberté de reli-
gion, adreſſé aux députés du clergé à
la diete générale des Etats du royaume
de Suède en 1779, préſenté le 11
janvier 1779 par André Chydenius,
prevôt & curé au vieux Carleby.

Dans un temps où les habitans de
la Suède ſont preſque le ſeul peuple
en Europe, qui, ſous le gouverne-
ment d'un roi débonnaire & ſage,
jouiſſent d'une paix profonde, tant au
dedans qu'au dehors, nos cœurs ne
peuvent que ſaigner en voyant les
guerres terribles, les animoſités & les
perſécutions, qui déſolent maintenant
pluſieurs parties du monde.

Quoi de plus ſage dans ce moment;
quoi de plus digne de cette charité
véritablement chrétienne, qui s'étend
à tous les hommes en général; quoi
de plus conforme à ce généreux eſprit
d'union & de liberté, qui ſied ſi bien
à un peuple heureux; quoi de plus
convenable enfin aux véritables inté-
rêts de notre patrie comblée de biens,
mais dépeuplée, que d'ouvrir préci-
ſément dans cette circonſtance, avec

Figure 28 By order of King Gustavus III, Chydenius's memorial on religious freedom was rapidly translated into French; it was published or referred to in at least five French newspapers and periodicals during the spring of 1779. The first page of *L'année Littéraire,* Tome second, Lettre V, 1779. National Library of Sweden. Photo Jens Östman.

1   That all foreigners, of whatever age, civil status, sex or creed they may be, who hereafter wish to immigrate to Sweden and its subordinate provinces to reside there and support themselves by honest work, shall be entirely free to do so, at least in the larger staple towns of the Kingdom, with the most gracious assurance of the same royal patronage and protection as all other subjects of the Swedish Realm, from the day on which they swear allegiance to His Royal Majesty, which might be done in the Magistrates' Court of the first town in which they arrive. And to that end not the slightest difficulty shall be imposed at the borders concerning passports, but it shall merely be recorded which of them have been provided with these and which not. However, the King's peace shall not extend to those who, within a certain time after their arrival, are found to have fled their home countries because of serious crimes.

2   That all arriving foreigners shall be assured by His Royal Majesty of complete freedom of conscience for themselves, their children and descendants, and each be permitted to practise his own religion quietly and without being allowed to cause offence to our native communities, though with the strictest proviso that they neither secretly nor publicly seek to inveigle anyone into apostasy from the pure Evangelical Lutheran doctrine, on penalty of confiscation of all their property and permanent expulsion; as also, that no one of a foreign religion shall, in accordance with the constitution of the realm, be allowed to occupy any higher or lower office. The difficulties that may arise with regard to their marriages, infant baptisms and education would, in my humble opinion, be most advantageously overcome if all marriages between a follower of a foreign religion and an Evangelical Lutheran were sanctioned by a wedding according to our Church rituals, while it should be obligatory for all children that result from these marriages to be baptized by our clergy in accordance with the Statute on Religion, be brought up in our Evangelical Faith and remain in our Congregation. But that all who are born into another religion on both their mother's and their father's side likewise be allowed to be brought up in their own religion.

3   That all immigrants, whether foreigners or Swedes who, for various reasons, have previously emigrated, shall be allowed, in town or country, wherever they are able to settle with the appropriate permission, to individually practise, without any restriction, some craft, trade, art or science by which they are able and willing to support themselves and their families in accordance with the statutes and regulations that His Royal Majesty shall think fit to promulgate, and that they shall not, on the other hand, be burdened with heavier imposts than native Swedes incur in pursuit of their occupation.

The advantages of such a charter of freedom would seem obvious.

The sacred name of our Great King would thereby come to be revered among most nations in the world. All who are oppressed, all unfortunates would bless the mildness of our Sovereign and hasten to seek shelter under His wings, and the Kingdom would gain a very rich harvest from the bloody wars of other nations that would consist of a multitude of working citizens. Agriculture, factories and craft production could be developed to a higher level and the burdens of the State, borne by a greater number of shoulders, become more tolerable for its previous inhabitants.

Sweden would then also have the pleasure of seeing those of its children who, for a variety of reasons, have emigrated, who still think with affection of their fatherland, returning in large numbers to share the joy with their brethren and reap the blessings of the felicitous era of Gustavus III.

Nor is this a new issue. Wise rulers have well understood how to increase the strength and reputation of their realms by such immigration. Prussia would never have become such a powerful kingdom so rapidly without it. The Grand Duchy of Tuscany,[5] a Roman Catholic state, owes its rapid progress to a general freedom of religion and commerce. France, which is so deeply in thrall to Catholicism, already appears to be considering toleration for Protestants, and even the remotest part of the world has, by tolerating various religions, attracted many thousands of families from Europe. At this precise moment the time appears to have come for Sweden to likewise win such blessed spoils by means of the same liberty.

Moved by the misfortunes of my fellow beings and concerned for the progress and strength of my native land, I have, with the most profound reverence for our pure and Evangelical faith and the sincerest good intentions, expressed my thoughts, which I most humbly submit to the careful and considered examination of the most Reverend Estate, and I rejoice to be allowed also to present them for the most enlightened scrutiny of our mild King, who is certainly destined by High Providence to become a blessed protector of all oppressed individuals and to make his Kingdom great and his subjects happy.

Anders Chydenius

Notes

1 "*... transfer the weight of the administration*": refers to the "revolution" of 1772 with the new constitution by which Gustavus III transferred most of the power from the estates to himself.

2 "*Proclamation of Amnesty*": proclamations of amnesty and pardon for soldiers who had fled their duty were issued at several times during the Age of Liberty and the reign of Gustavus III, including in 1779. They offered pardon to a returning soldier who otherwise would have had to face the death penalty for desertion. In 1779 there was a more general amnesty issued in favour of persons who had been sentenced to death, whose penalty was instead commuted to a prison sentence. We do not know whether Chydenius is referring here to the said proclamation or to the amnesty for the latter.

3 "*Evangelical co-religionists*": refers especially to Calvinists.

4 On Prussia, see note 10, p. 312.

5 "*Grand Duchy of Tuscany*": the Grand Archduke at the time was Leopold I (1765–90). See notes 30 and 31, p. 276.

Commentary

Lars Magnusson

If Chydenius made little headway in reforming the conditions for servants and workers, his contribution to the Diet of 1778–9 was still considerable. We showed in the Introduction that Chydenius became a leading figure at the Diet – he is also quite detailed on this matter in his autobiography (p. 343) – in respect of the case for religious tolerance and freedom.

Ever since the sixteenth century, religious unity within the realm had been regarded as a basic condition for the continued existence of the state and of the Church in Sweden. This unity was emphasized in every constitution, accession charter and statute on religion. In matters of religious doctrine, Sweden clearly moved towards a more orthodox standpoint during the seventeenth century, and the new conservative Church law that was inaugurated in 1686 led to a stricter enforcement of Lutheranism. After the great wars at the beginning of the eighteenth century the Royal Proclamation against Conventicles was issued in 1726, which forbade religious congregations outside the official places of worship. The purpose of this prohibition was to keep the spread of Pietism within bounds and to restrain its manifestations among Swedish subjects.

The question of religious tolerance had arisen in Europe during the Age of Enlightenment, and in the Swedish realm the demands on increased religious tolerance were in particular connected to economic arguments. The country needed experts, especially in the growing mining industry, and skilled workers at the ironworks, and therefore professionals were recruited in Holland and England. The immigrant workers were often adherents of Calvinism or the Anglican Church. In principle, it was forbidden for non-Lutherans to hold religious services in their homes or at other premises, but during the seventeenth century Calvinism had in practice been tolerated as numerous Walloon workers immigrated to work at the Swedish ironworks. Generally they were able to hold their own religious services in the remote areas where the ironworks were situated. Small Calvinist congregations had also become established in Gothenburg and Vadstena by the end of the seventeenth century.[1] In Stockholm the emergence of rich Calvinist merchants at the end of the seventeenth century made the issue even more acute. As Fredric Bedoire has shown, in the case of Stockholm they were officially forbidden to organize services of their own, but in practice control seems to have been lenient.[2] Immigrating Huguenots were indeed a source of income for the Swedish Crown; so why not be more ready to admit them?

By a royal decree in 1741, Anglicans and French Calvinists were granted the right to form congregations of their own and practise their religion. The Hat government had been under strong pressure on this matter from rich merchants, particularly in Stockholm, the so-called *Skeppsbroadeln*. As a consequence, French, Spanish and Austrian Catholics were also allowed to hold private congregations. In 1775 even a small group of Jews were allowed into the country by special permission from the finance minister, Johan Liljencrants. Jews were not, however, given permanent right of residence until a new edict was inaugurated, in 1782. The strong insistence on religious unity was gradually loosened as more immigrants moved to the country. The Estate of Clergy, however, maintained its strong resistance and tried on several occasions to have the royal decree of 1741 revoked.

Religious tolerance was of course one of the most important issues for those inspired by the Enlightenment movement. This was also the case with King Gustavus III, who aspired to become an enlightened monarch, and his inner circle of politicians. Among others, the historian Sven Göransson has guessed that the monarch was the initiator of the new ordinance, but it is an overstatement to say that Chydenius acted as an agent for the king.[3] However, as we have noted, there might also have been other reasons for Chydenius's collaboration with the king (see pp. 44–9). The question of whether Chydenius acted on the basis of personal conviction in this matter or on the orders of the king is much debated. If we look at the personal experiences Chydenius had had with religious separatism within his own congregation and in the vicinity of Kokkola, there is every reason to believe Chydenius had strong personal motives to work for increased religious tolerance. Among the religious separatists in Ostrobothnia the deplorable fate of the Eriksson brothers and their followers, who had been banished and forced to leave the country in the 1730s, must have had the strongest influence on Chydenius in his youth. The Eriksson brothers roved from place to place along the coasts of the European continent for almost 15 years before they were allowed to settle in Skevik, on Värmdö outside Stockholm. In the administration of his office, Chydenius met with strong opposition from Moravian Brethren within the congregation. In the case of Anna-Stina Silahka, a member of his congregation who had started to preach the gospel on her own, Chydenius showed how leniency, patience and gentle teaching were the only practicable approaches with which to meet the separatists. Persecution or moral and religious constraint only made matters worse.[4]

In his autobiography, Chydenius depicts how in December 1778 he wrote a first draft of the memorial on religious freedom. After showing it to a few friends and conferring with them, he decided to show it to the king and seek his approval. If the king did approve, Chydenius could be sure of royal protection from the persecution the memorial without doubt would inflict on him personally. In fact, the king approved of the idea, unsurprisingly as he had granted both Catholics and Jews in Swedish Pomerania certain privileges a few years earlier, and Chydenius and a group of like-minded friends went ahead and drafted the final version of the memorial.

As Georg Schauman has shown, there are some differences between the original and the final version. The conclusions are basically the same: devotees of other religions (including Jews) should be able to live and work in Sweden, enjoy the same legal protection as other inhabitants and have the right to practise their religion. These privileges would be granted to everyone wishing to move to Sweden without regard to social class, age, gender or confession as long as he or she took an oath of allegiance to the Swedish king and refrained from trying to convert others. Withdrawn from the final version was the suggestion that immigration of foreign worshippers could be a means to populate wasteland areas and that the immigrants thus through "diligence and hard work" would contribute to the enrichment of the realm – a pet idea of Chydenius, as we have seen.[5] Instead, another economic argument for making immigration easier was added: in a more general sense it could contribute to economic development and growth. The view that countries like the Netherlands and England had become more prosperous because of their generous attitude towards the immigration of foreign worshippers, while for example France had declined, was in fact common in the political discussion on economy during most of the eighteenth century (Anders Nordencrantz had already spoken in favour of it in his *Arcana*, published in 1730). Here, of course, the Edict of Nantes and the establishment of Huguenots in countries with which France competed in trade and industry were often used as a main illustration. In order to mitigate the severe criticism the memorial would without doubt meet in the Estate of Clergy, concessions were made regarding the upbringing of children resulting from mixed marriages. Such children were to be baptized according to Lutheran ceremonies and brought up as Lutherans. Foreign worshippers were also denied access to both higher and lower official posts within the administration.

The final memorial was without doubt a collective product even though it was Chydenius who signed it and delivered it to Archbishop Mennander on 11 January 1779. During the same time at least three other memorials on religious freedom were either submitted to the Estates or printed. Archbishop Mennander was reluctant at first, but eventually he had to bring up the proposal for discussion in the Estate of Clergy. In the discussions on 18 and 19 January, both the memorial and its author were condemned in quite strong language. For example, the bishop of Visby, Gabriel Lütkemann – as Chydenius tells us in his autobiography (p. 343) – was astonished that such a proposal had been put forward by a clergyman. In the other estates, however, a majority seem to have been in favour of the proposal. In the Estate of Nobility a landlord and colonel from Skåne, Hans Ramel, had prepared a similar memorial on religious freedom (how familiar he was with Chydenius's text we do not know). In the end it was only the Estate of Clergy which under strong protest voted against the proposal.

Chydenius's memorial, which during the discussions in the Estates only existed in handwritten copies, was printed on 23 January 1779 – in fact only three days before the king very suddenly, and to everybody's surprise, dissolved the Diet. The actual new Ordinance on Religious Freedom was not inaugurated until 24 January 1781 (on King Gustavus III's birthday, to mark its importance), but Chydenius's contribution in December 1778 and January 1779 in bringing about the ordinance was without doubt considerable, even though modern research has played down his role somewhat.[6]

King Gustavus III made sure Chydenius's memorial and the decision taken by the Diet were made known throughout Europe. The Swedish ambassador in Paris was instructed to have the memorial translated into French, and it was in fact published in at least five French newspapers and periodicals during the spring of 1779. Translations of the Ordinance into Latin and German were also made and distributed all over Europe as political propaganda for the king. During his travels in Europe during 1783 and 1784, Gustavus III was able to stand out as the enlightened monarch he wished to be, elevated above the shackles of faith.

It is of course accurate that the new ordinance did not bring total freedom of religion in the Swedish realm. To begin with, freedom of religion was only granted to foreign immigrants. Swedish citizens were still forbidden to become proselytes of foreign religions, and the Proclamation against Conventicles from 1726 was still in force with respect to radical Pietism. Moreover, although the so-called Jew edict of 1782 gave Jews the right to live in Sweden, they were only allowed to settle in Stockholm, Gothenburg and Norrköping. Neither were they allowed to become members of town guilds or to employ Swedes in their service.[7] It has also been argued that the position of Catholics in fact worsened after 1781, as they were now forced to become Swedish citizens.[8] However, the pope in Rome, Pius VI, thought otherwise, as in 1780 he sent a letter of thanks to the Swedish monarch. The ordinance was undoubtedly a step towards increased religious tolerance in the spirit of the Enlightenment, and Chydenius had contributed to it in a very active way.

For Chydenius personally the matter without doubt had a darker side. By at least some of his clergymen colleagues he was looked upon as something of a traitor. Moreover, his cooperation with the king on this matter cemented the view of Chydenius as a more loyal Gustavian than perhaps he was. In the end we are left with the question of why he thought that pursuing religious freedom was worth its undoubtedly high price. Was it only for opportunistic political reasons that he collaborated with the king on this issue? We will never know for sure, but on the basis of his personal experience and general attitude towards freedom in other areas of life, we can say that Chydenius most probably regarded religious tolerance as the most effective method to preserve the unity of his own Church, not least in his own Ostrobothnia, where the number of Pietist devotees was on the increase. In the long run it might endanger peaceful communion if religious separatists were met by excessively harsh methods. The case of the Eriksson brothers gave lamentable evidence of this possibility. The Ordinance on Religious Freedom was a conscious breach with the conception that religious unity was a precondition of the continued existence of the state and of the Church. For Chydenius, constraints with regard to religion or faith were just as unacceptable as constraints in other areas of life, and therefore had to be fought against regardless of the price.

Notes

1 H.R. Boudin, "Valloninvandringen som religiös migration", in A. Florén and G. Ternhag (eds), *Valloner – järnets människor*, Hedemora: Gidlunds förlag, 2002, p. 76.
2 F. Bedoire, *Hugenotternas värld – från religionskrigens Frankrike till skeppsbroadelns Stockholm*, Stockholm: Albert Bonniers förlag, 2009, p. 185f.
3 S. Göransson's review of Arne Palmqvist's *Die römisch-katholische Kirche in Schweden nach 1781*, vol. 1, in *Kyrkohistorisk Årsskrift*, Uppsala, 1955, cit. from Virrankoski, p. 321.
4 I am much indebted to Gustav Björkstrand and thank him for providing me with valuable information on Chydenius's views on religious separatists in Ostrobothnia.
5 Cited in G. Schauman, *Biografiska undersökningar om Anders Chydenius*, Skrifter utgifna af Svenska Litteratursällskapet i Finland 84, Helsinki: Svenska Litteratursällskapet i Finland, 1908, p. 321.
6 P. Virrankoski, *Anders Chydenius: Demokratisk politiker i upplysningens tid*, Stockholm: Timbro, 1995, p. 315f.
7 H. Valentin, *Judarnas historia i Sverige*, Stockholm: Bonnier, 1924, pp. 190–2.
8 Virrankoski, op. cit., p. 318.

Part IV

Autobiography of Anders Chydenius

11 Autobiography submitted to the Society of Arts and Sciences in Gothenburg

Anders Chydenius was born on 24 February[1] 1729 (Old Style)[2] in the parish of Sotkamo, 2 *mil* from Kajaani (Kajana). His father was the Rector and Dean of Kokkola, Jakob Chydenius, who was then Chaplain in Sotkamo but in 1734 became Rector of Kemin Lappi and of Kuusamo and was transferred from there in 1746 to the parish of Kokkola, where he died in April 1766. My grandfather was the Rector of Rymättylä (Rimito), Anders Chydenius, M.A., the son of a farmer of that parish. The name of my mother was Hedvig Hornæa, daughter of the late Rector and Dean of Eurajoki (Euraåminne), Samuel Hornæus.

Next to God, I have a loving father to thank not only for life and its sustenance during my childhood and youth, which most parents provide for their children, but rather for untiringly instructing me from my tenderest years. He did not follow the usual path of merely burdening the memory of his children during their instruction. He taught them to think and at the same time to let the light of reason incline their hearts to virtue and piety.

For two years, under the supervision of a loving father, I received private tuition. For two years I attended the lower grammar school at Oulu and studied for one year under the personal guidance of the then Headmaster at the Tornio (Torneå) state secondary school and later Rector and Dean in Oulu, Mr Johan Wegelius,[3] with whose testimonial I left in December 1744 for the Academy in Turku, together with my older brother, the gifted Assistant Master Samuel Chydenius,[4] M.A., who sadly was drowned in the Kokemäenjoki, and was enrolled in January 1745 as a student there, where I received instruction in philosophy and Latin composition during the first year from the then Assistant Master but now Archbishop, the Right Rev. Carl Fredrik Mennander,[5] though I improved myself most of all through the daily company and discourses of the gifted Master Nordstedt with my brother, to which I always listened with the greatest pleasure. In 1750 I attended the seat of learning at Uppsala and in 1751 also defended my brother's dissertation, *De navigatione per flumina et lacus patriæ promovenda* ("On the promotion of navigation on domestic rivers and lakes"). In 1753 I returned to Turku, having received a call to the newly established chapel at Alaveteli in the parish of Kokkola, to serve as their local minister, being also ordained as such in March by the then Bishop of the Turku diocese, the Right Rev. Johan Browallius,[6] and, with the full approbation of my

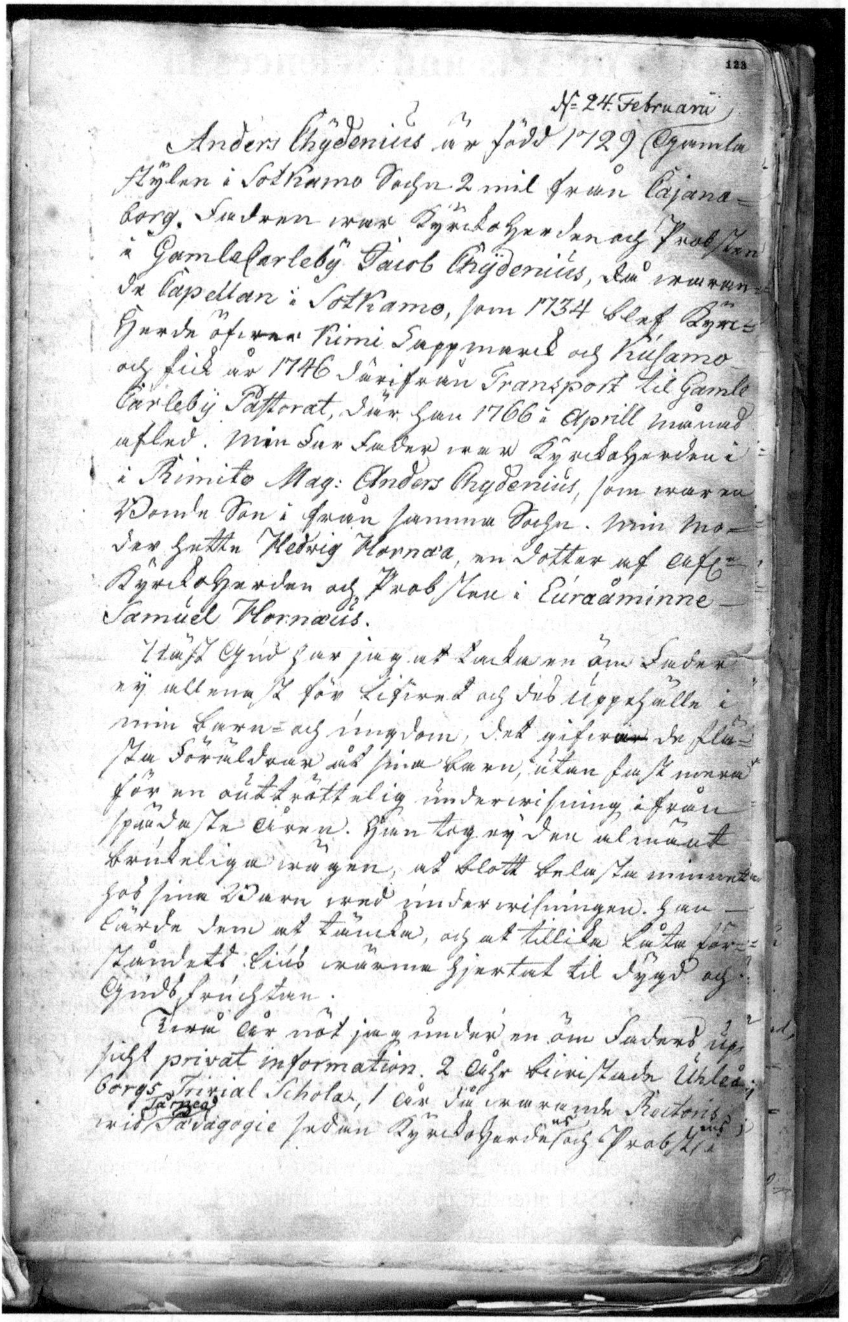

Figure 29 The first page of Chydenius's autobiography (1780). The Royal Society of Arts and Sciences in Gothenburg.

superiors, produced the usual *specimina academica* for a Master's degree,[7] which I was awarded the following year in my absence. My dissertation consisted of a few pages concerning American birchbark boats, with the late Dr Kalm[8] acting as praeses. In the summer of that year I took up my duties at Alaveteli. In that small chaplaincy of 30 *rökar* I worked for 17 years without any thought of promotion and still less troubling my superiors with any application for that purpose, and I would probably have remained there until my death had my father not on his deathbed, shortly before he died, instructed me by letter to apply for the Kokkola parish in succession to him and to be the guardian of my two under-age half-siblings and maintain my stepmother, though I was not nominated to that post until two years later, when my father's successor, Rector Johan Haartman, was transferred to the parish of Vöyri (Vörå).

Both the urban and rural congregation then unanimously declared their confidence in me and requested from the Consistory that I be sent there as a nominee, which I was also granted once I had passed my pastoral examination, and in the election I received an almost unanimous invitation and was in 1770 officially appointed to the parish of Kokkola, which I took over in May of that year and have now been in charge of for almost ten years, with which work I intend to continue as long as God grants me life and health, without seeking any greater earthly advantages during the remaining days of my life. In 1778, during the last Diet, I was honoured by the Right Rev. Bishop Haartman,[9] at the request of a majority of members of the most Reverend Estate of Clergy, without the slightest action on my part, with the title of Dean and was officially appointed as Dean on 24 February last and at the same time granted a doctorate of theology by His Majesty, which was conferred on me by the Archbishop of the Realm, the Most Reverend Dr Carl Fredrik Mennander, on 6 June last.

I sincerely confess that I am undeserving of all the Lord's kindness, which he has shown my unworthy self in manifold ways, not the least of which is that the Lord has vouchsafed me a good, loving and faithful spouse, as I entered upon marriage in October 1755 with Miss Beata Magdalena Mellberg, daughter of the tradesman Olof Mellberg from Pietarsaari. Being childless myself, I have regarded it as my duty to bring up the children of others, among them in particular my half-sister Helena, who in the autumn of 1777 married the Headmaster of the school in this town, Master Johan Kreander,[10] my half-brother Adolph Chydenius, who died this autumn in Oulu from an epidemic of dysentery, and my sister's son Johan Tengström,[11] who is still studying at the Academy in Turku and holds out the joyful hope that my expenditure and toil on his upbringing will not have been in vain.

As brief as the account of my life is, as simple has my mode of life likewise been so far, and I also sincerely wish that it will involve nothing else out of the ordinary, even if this mortal frame were to be granted a few more active years, than that I be allowed, whether as part of or outside of my official duties, to do some good and defend innocence and that I shall close my eyes in the bosom of my dear Saviour.

But if the Royal Society of Arts and Sciences also requested from me some account of my studies, my writings and my experiences as a member of the Diet, I ought to likewise try to be candid in that regard.

At the universities my studies were miscellaneous; I dabbled a little in a variety of subjects, which was also to some extent required for the degree for which I was studying. Apart from the philosophical sciences, I was very interested in mathematics, especially geometry, astronomy, gnomonics,[12] mechanics and some algebra. But since I entered upon the pastoral profession, which is inherently precious though despised by many, including clergymen, the study of the practical doctrine of salvation has been my principal occupation. I have sought to establish the most certain and manifest theoretical truths as the foundation of the Christianity of my parishioners, and ever since I attempted at the university, in the enthusiasm of my youth, to follow all kinds of fine theological distinctions as well as to split hairs myself by the rules of logic and metaphysics and found, both in discussions and in my own reflections, that I did not know in the end to which straw I should cling with my own conviction, I have stepped back from those dizzying heights and resolved, in accordance with Paul's instruction to Titus, ch. 1, v. 9, to hold firm to the sure word as taught, which has led me to ask myself when I hear or read such subtleties: *Quis est usus huius loci practicus?*[13] And when the Lord granted me the grace to preach, not merely in order to say something but to convince my parishioners and to move them, I soon found how inappropriate that stilted erudition was in the pulpit and that a priest could never be as simple as he ought to be even in genteel urban and academic parishes. For if the purpose of a sermon were either to persuade the congregation of one's wide reading or to show, by such a learned sermon, that one regards the congregation as people who are able to grasp and understand such a learned piece of work, then subtleties and grandiloquence might be tolerated, though they will always amount to charlatanry, but if it is to persuade and move, change and improve the progress towards Christianity and virtue, then the reasons for that should be as simple, the means as comprehensible and the incentives as powerful as possible, whereas the elevated learning is, on the contrary, nothing but an obscuring fog for a pilgrim who longs for the goal of blessedness.

Catechization, by which I do not mean some perfunctorily delivered sermons on the catechism or some formally conducted household examinations but all the oral instruction by which a priest should, through conversations, instil and implant in his parishioners of all ages the necessary and infallible grounds of the correct doctrine of salvation, for a living Christianity, is what I have found to be the hardest and most responsible of all my official duties. It requires a plainness and simplicity that must almost presume nothing to be familiar, and, although I do in some degree possess the gift of intelligibility, I often find myself at a loss in this regard, despite all my efforts. It requires an order in which the truths are joined together by unforced links and flow from one another; it requires a pure and unforced faculty of thinking and constant reflection, if leaps from one thing to another are not to make a farrago of it all; and lastly, it also requires a spark of the celestial flame in one's heart, that is, a divinely inspired longing to liberate one's own soul and the souls of those who listen to us. We must keep before our eyes on the one hand the sanguinary judgment that awaits us if we fail to proclaim all God's counsels to our congregation, namely that he is cursed who does the work of the Lord with slackness etc. (Jer. 48:10) and, on the other hand, our reward of grace (Dan. 12). The eternal bliss of our congregation should also be very close to our heart, so that we simultaneously enlighten, persuade and move our congregation by means of our catechization: *hoc opus hic labor.*[14] For that there are a number of opportunities, apart from the regular catechetical meetings: as, in particular, when instructing the young people as they are being prepared to receive their first Communion, when people move into the parish and again when they leave it, as well as when visiting the sick, if they are not too infirm. Such opportunities I have always eagerly sought to make use of and have most often felt a particular blessing from God in doing so.

But that is not all: the Lord likewise, through the powerful effects of His grace on myself and my communicants, opened a new door to make my office more fruitful when I began, for their individual instruction and devotion, to use the Sunday afternoons for some godly conversations and instructions, at first with them and, at the persistent request of others in my congregation, with all those who wished to attend such devotional exercises, in which the previously delivered sermon is generally explained and more closely applied to the consciences of those present for chastisement, counsel and consolation. I have now continued with this for more than 15 years, and a large part of my congregation has also frequently but quite freely participated in these devotional exercises in my house, often to the number of 200–300 individuals, which are always concluded with an evening prayer adapted to the theme, after which I have offered open access for private conversations to those who desire it. In order not to be impeded in this, I immediately declared on taking up my parochial duties that I would refuse to pay or receive any visits on Sundays other than those that are conducive to some improvement in Christianity.

Apart from this principal occupation of mine, I have also sought to be useful to my fellow beings in other ways. I had indeed studied chemistry a little at Uppsala, though without any application to medicine; but during the first years of my ministry, being far removed from any physicians in the countryside, I began, following the printed account of the curing of children's diseases issued by the Royal Medical Board,[15] to practise the cures on the children of my parishioners. The household remedies of Assessor Haartman[16] and the *Parish Pharmacy* of Assessor af Darelli,[17] which were published soon after that, guided me progressively in the science, so that I began to study chemistry in order to prepare drugs. I made up my mind, wrote off for equipment and raw materials and set up a small chemical laboratory, in which I eventually advanced so far that I myself produced *mercurius sublimatus corrosivus, mercurius dulcis,* calomel and other mercurial compounds, *spiritus nitri fumans, spiritus salis* and *spiritus salis ammoniaci,*[18] *liquidus Hoffmanni*[19] and others and prepared all kinds of medicines with them. I improved no less in the knowledge and use of all kinds of resinous solutions, made experiments with them in different solvents and had enough patients on whom to practice my medicines and rarely bought anything except *simplicia*[20] from the pharmacies.

I assiduously read Archiater Rosén von Rosenstein's anatomy[21] and also began to conduct surgical procedures, to excise cancerous tumours and sebaceous cysts, often in quite dangerous places, and in particular to operate on the eyes[22] and make incisions in the eyelids of those with ulcerating eyes, with almost unbelievable success.

After many trials I invented an eye-water that somewhat resembles that of Mrs Segercrona[23] but which excels it in many respects and is specific enough for most weak and bleary eyes.

I had time to occupy myself with such things as long as I was chaplain of a small chapel, but when I took over the parish of Kokkola my official duties also became too extensive and unremitting for me to be able to continue with that, except that I have now and then been obliged to perform operations on those with weak eyesight and occasionally to write prescriptions for some of my parishioners to the pharmacy in Vaasa or Kokkola, owing to the lack of any reliable medical practitioner any closer than 14 *mil* from here.

There was nothing with which I was less acquainted than politics when I became a clergyman, but the newspaper *Riksdagstidningar* that was published during the Diet of 1756 first inspired me to give some thought to the Swedish political practice and our political regulations, and when Board of Trade Counsellor Nordencrantz presented his detailed memorial[24] to the Estates of the Realm in 1761 during the Diet and it soon came into my hands, together with other writings of his concerning the rate of exchange, I was stimulated to learn more about such subjects. I found this author in possession of so much knowledge and so many comments *in politicis*,[25] with such a wealth of ideas, that, despite his style being rather heavy and full of repetitions and although a partisan rancour also reveals itself in them in many places, there was nonetheless an abundant store of topics here to attract the full attention of an inquiring reader and of fundamental truths *in politicis* that sound reflection and a heart well disposed towards the fatherland could not but approve of and accept.

With such information provided for me by Mr Nordencrantz concerning humankind and its abuse of power, about the English execution of the law as compared with our laws and their administration and abuse, as well as some general notions regarding our country's financial system, rate of exchange and the like, with such a grounding I travelled to the Diet of 1765 as the parliamentary delegate of the chaplains and then had the opportunity during such a protracted Diet both to increase my knowledge through reading and conversations and also to reinforce it by experience.

Husbandry has also been a subject of not inconsiderable interest to me, in which the late Lieutenant-Colonel Boije's farming manual[26] has been my tutor, as the one that most closely follows nature. At my new chaplaincy in Alaveteli, which was built in 1753 beside a waterfall on quite an appalling stony slope, I established a small kitchen garden and orchard, surrounded it with stone walls, laid it out in regular terraces towards the river with a dam that conducts the water from the waterfall to the garden, improved a fairly watery marsh first into arable and then into meadow land, constructed barns for leaf-fodder and began to annually gather a crop of leaves according to the instructions of Mr Boije, but endeavoured in particular to acquire and maintain a flock of genuine Spanish sheep and to that end ordered mature sheep, rams and ewes from the aforementioned Lieutenant-Colonel and tended them in exactly the manner prescribed by him in his farming manual, with the successful result that the cloth I produce from this flock rivals our finest Swedish cloths in softness. Among my farming activities the fact should also be included that on the land of my present rectory I have turned a stony slope into an arable field and surrounded it with a stone wall, raised earthen banks around meadows to a length of several hundred *famn*, built a large cowshed, a stable with room for ten horses and a cook-house, all constructed of granite, and a brick-built brewhouse and bakery, for which labour and expenditure on an official residence His Majesty has also graciously freed me from all personal taxes for myself and all my household.

Literary exercises have attracted me since my student days and I have constantly read all kinds of belles-lettres with critical attention and sought to improve myself in that regard both in my writings and in sermons and speeches on several ceremonial occasions. My aims in this respect have always been a facility of syntax and expression, persuasiveness and grace, and however paradoxical I have often appeared to be in my propositions, my rather idiosyncratic style of writing has nonetheless won favour with the public, far beyond what I could have expected or surmised.

On the other hand, I have paid no attention at all to legal matters and practical jurisprudence, and have always regarded a small loss as preferable to gains achieved by means of a factitious lawsuit.

Now a few words about my writings.

No Swede of an intellectual bent can have had less expectation of ever becoming known as an author in his native country than I. My limited knowledge, my quiet and secluded way of life and yes, I ought to candidly confess it, my complete detachment from the wider world, having decided to examine my own sinful heart in a remote corner of the world and in my ministry to benefit the flock entrusted to me by heaven, my heartfelt contempt for flattering fame, had put far from my mind the thought of ever writing anything for the general public or of holding any office of greater consequence than the modest position that I initially occupied. But the ways of Providence with my unworthy self have been quite different from what I could have imagined.

Compelled by my friends to embark on the first essays, they have been received with attention and satisfaction by fellow citizens, who have consequently imposed more upon me and have obliged me to increase my limited knowledge by some further reading and reflection. Continuing approval of my efforts, and the zeal that I developed in the course of them to attempt to do some good, have subsequently imposed that on me as a duty, indeed as one of my noblest pleasures. But my main task, my busy and responsible ministry, has in this regard always obliged me to keep to the circumscribed and brief disquisitions that have rarely been produced during the daytime or normal working hours but always in the silent midnight hours, which most people spend unproductively, if not in vices then in the lap of sleep on the couch of indolence. It may well be profitable to be a writer in Germany, France and England, even with a modest talent, but in Sweden it is always a pure loss. I ought not, however, to conceal what I have received as an author *pro labore*.[27] The late Director Salvius[28] paid me 700 *daler kmt* for my circumstantial response to the refutations of *The Source of Our Country's Weakness*[29] and 400 *daler* for my piece on finances. Before God and my conscience, that is all the wealth I have earned as a writer.

In 1750, when the happy news was expected of the safe delivery of Her then Royal Highness,[30] the present Queen Dowager, which occurred with the birth of Prince Frederic Adolphus, I was obliged during that celebration to deliver a speech as a student in the synodal auditorium in Kokkola, by which I proved to the complete satisfaction of the audience the *Prosperity of the People of Finland under the Crown of Sweden*.

I responded in the usual manner under a motto to three of the prize subjects proposed by the Royal Academy of Sciences and twice competed for the highest prizes. The first was economic, concerning the cause of moss-growth on meadows and how it might best be prevented, on which occasion only the fact that my response arrived two or three days too late disqualified me from receiving the gold medal that would otherwise have been my due. The response was printed together with the prize-winning response and another one, by Rector Hederström I believe, and each of us was awarded an *accessit*.[31]

The second was mechanical: whether our ordinary carts can be improved such that one can as easily carry 70 *lispund* on them as at present 40. Here the late Superintendent Faggot[32] and Dr Gadolin[33] became my competitors, and the former won the prize, being not only a member of the Academy but also having relatives in the Royal Academy of Sciences, though with what justice those in the know will be best able to judge, especially if it was the case that the question had been proposed in the Royal Academy of Sciences by himself or his friends. In any case, the Academy again, as on the previous occasion, awarded me as well as Dr Gadolin an *accessit* and decided to print both contributions along with the prize-winning response. However, Gadolin then withdrew his response, so that mine follows that of Mr Faggot.

The third was political, on the cause of the emigration of Swedish people and how it may be prevented. There I was also one of more than 30 competitors. On the response to this I incontrovertibly worked the hardest compared to the previous ones, but for that very reason it was most unlikely to be considered: the descriptions were too candid, far too graphic; they were unsuitable. A patriot was at that time barely allowed to think about the injuries suffered by the country, much less talk and write about them,[34] as such things were unheard of unless it was done in order to support the aims of some noble gentleman or to pull the rug from under one party or another, but it was nevertheless printed in 1765, at my own expense and with a dedication to the Estates of the Realm.

When the question concerning the establishment of more staple towns in the kingdom that had been seriously raised during the Diet of 1756 was carried to extremes during the subsequent Diet of 1762 by the distribution of several barrels of gold[35] by the opposing parties but was nonetheless brought to a halt, the then Deputy Governor of Ostrobothnia and Chief Judge Johan Mathesius[36] decided not only to unite the towns of Ostrobothnia more closely with the surrounding rural regions at a general provincial assembly at Kokkola in 1763 in the interval between the Diets, in order that they should work together at the following Diet for the previously requested freedom of navigation, but also to arm themselves against the opposition that might be raised against the change by the merchants of Stockholm and Turku. I was also urged on that occasion by some friends in Kokkola to contribute to such a good cause on behalf of that town by means of some treatise[37] and was for that purpose informed of the arguments that the merchants of Stockholm had adduced against it at the last Diet, which were so powerfully formulated that they could not be weakened by a few brief memorials, and whose arguments I regarded myself as powerless to refute. Yet, compelled by my friends, I decided to make an attempt, in which I succeeded so well during its implementation that no one has ever since dared to confront or respond to the arguments advanced there. The treatise was audacious and I wished to remain anonymous, but no one at the assembly was courageous enough to present it. I therefore had to appear myself and read it out before the entire gathering, with the lively approval of most of the audience, which, because of envy, very nearly caused me to be arrested that same evening, had not some well-wishers, entirely without my knowledge, been able to prevent that. This treatise was subsequently printed in 1765 at the expense of the town of Kokkola under the title of *Refutation of the Reasons Employed to Deny the Towns in Ostrobothnia and Västerbotten as Well as in Västernorrland a Free Navigation*,[38] and was distributed free of charge to all the Estates.

The late Director Salvius, as an investor in the metalworking industry and the iron trade, had learned from long experience how oppressed that branch of the economy was, because the buyers of the products of the mining districts were few and combined, and advances were almost unobtainable. He knew that the Commodity Ordinance of 10 November 1724 and its elucidation of 28 February 1726 were the real causes of the foreign buyers being driven out of the iron trade and how the prices of salt and grain (those commodities that are indispensable in all commerce) have thereby been raised. He liked my style and asked me to think about the subject and gather material on it and write something. The subject was at first quite alien to me, but the access that I had as a member of the Fisheries Joint Committee to the records of the Royal Board of Trade soon enlightened me on the subject; in the same year of 1765 my disquisition on the subject was printed under the title of *The Source of Our Country's Weakness*, which struck the general public as so paradoxical and attracted so much attention that two large editions were issued within a few weeks, there was great agitation everywhere and vengeance was called for against the initially unknown author.

The enemies of free navigation had commissioned a defence of servitude for this Diet as well, entitled *Indefeasible Thoughts on the Establishment of Five New Staple Towns in the Northern Provinces of the Realm*,[39] a reserve defence that they nonetheless withheld until my *Refutation* had been printed, in which all their arguments had already been confronted and demolished. They must quickly have realized that it was therefore quite useless in that form as a reply to my treatise, but as the manuscript must have cost them a tidy sum, which they did not wish to lose so suddenly, and as they either found no one willing to reply to my treatise or else thought that he would cost them too much, they nonetheless decided to have it published, though the time and circumstances were so unpropitious, and let it have what effect it could; I therefore penned some *Remarks*[40] on it, which are printed at the end of *The Source of Our Country's Weakness*.

Little critiques of *The Source*[41] began to fly like swarms of birdshot, but they were merely harbingers of two general salvoes that were then fired off against it one after the other, the first under the title of *Circumstantial Refutation of the Treatise Called The Source of Our Country's Weakness*,[42] the author of which remains unknown to me, although I have heard two prominent names mentioned, the second entitled *Water-Tests* conducted at that *Source*,[43] composed by the learned and literary Secretary of the 50 Aldermen of the City of Stockholm, Mr Edvard Runeberg; both were received with such great acclaim by the friends of the Commodity Ordinance that they thought the author of *The Source* would never again dare to make an appearance unless he wished to be laughed to scorn by the general public.

I then first wrote a short piece entitled *The National Gain*, which was printed at my own expense by Director Salvius and was intended as a preparation for my response to the critiques, and soon afterwards my *Circumstantial Response*[44] to both the *Circumstantial Refutation* and the *Water Tester* was printed, for which Salvius was again my publisher, by which my opponents became aware that my gun was more heavily charged than they had imagined, after which *Response* on my part there was a general silence on that subject.

That same year, towards autumn, the Secret Committee requested from the plenary assemblies complete authority, when putting the financial operations in order, to adopt whatever regulations and measures it thought fit, without the knowledge of the plenary assemblies, which, although completely contrary to the instructions given to the Secret Committee, was nonetheless universally approved, for the majority had faith in the Joint Banking Committee.

A few weeks after such complete authority had been granted, so much money vanished from the Bank under the greatest secrecy that even its members,[45] with their unlimited authority, fell into some irresolution and perplexity as to how the plan for gradually restoring the exchange rate could best be achieved. That induced in me, who was not a member of the Secret Committee, great apprehension and anxiety for my fatherland, the welfare of which I thus saw had been placed at risk in complete silence, and I began to ponder the matter and gather information, for I shuddered to think of the consequences of a restoration of the exchange rate. I therefore briefly set down my thoughts, which I personally handed to the Speaker of the Nobles in the Joint Banking Committee with a humble request that the Joint Committee should consider them, as I would otherwise be obliged to lay the matter before the public in all its vivid complexion, so that it would realize in future that I had had no part in the unfortunate consequences of a restoration of the exchange rate.

Board of Trade Counsellor Nordencrantz[46] was the mentor of the Joint Committee in the plan of restoration that it adopted, and Colonel Gyllensvaan,[47] the Chamberlain Baron von Essen[48] and Captain Baron Cederström[49] were its most active members. I waited, I demanded a response, when they finally undertook to persuade me of my error at the home of member of the Joint Banking Committee in the presence of a number of people, but my arguments were in my view far too solid to be disproved and my conviction thus shaken. I expressed myself heatedly at one point about the adopted plan in a conclave with the Speaker of the Nobles; but that was of no avail, and I therefore carried out my promise and wrote the piece called *A Remedy for the Country by Means of a Natural System of Finance*, which is no less notorious than *The Source*. I decided at first to remain anonymous and thus the first *sextern*[50] passed the censorship and were printed, but when the censor, in conversation with the Speaker of the Nobles, General Rudbeck, happened to mention that work, which was at the printers and which the Speaker was curious to see, the censor himself fetched the manuscript from the printer and showed it to him. Then the censor was ordered to prevent its printing but also to summon the author through Director Salvius, upon which I was told by Mr von Oelreich[51] that the treatise would not be allowed to be printed but that the Speaker had promised to honourably compensate the author for the trouble he had taken. I then took back my manuscript and kept very quiet until the fire had died down, when I went to the late Bishop Serenius[52] and told him that I had written something on financial matters and wondered whether he would present it to the Estate or suggest deputies who would scrutinize it. I was in very good standing with him at that time and he was immediately prepared to propose in the Estate that it be submitted to auditors whom I designated: these were the Deans Wijkman,[53] Kröger[54] and Högström.[55] However, the scrutiny was mostly left to the last of these, who presented the Estate with his opinion that he had not found anything in my treatise except what had previously been argued for and against in printed publications and proposed that it should be printed, which was approved.

No one else in the Estate knew what the treatise contained; those of the predominant view trusted their friends, who had scrutinized it, but the others began to oppose its being printed. I was therefore obliged to show the manuscript to some of them and assure a few doubting fathers by means of a trusted gentleman that they had nothing to fear from it, when the endorsement of the Estate was approved on 11 June 1766, whereby the Estate permitted that treatise to be printed. Salvius was given the manuscript and continued day and night with the printing that had begun earlier, and in no time at all the banned item was in everyone's hands; gentlemen bought 40, 50 or up to 100 copies at a time and sent them to the provinces. I will never forget Permanent Secretary von

Oelreich's description of the members of the Joint Banking Committee two days after it had appeared: *They curse*, he said, *and they read*. As soon as it appeared, I distributed unbound copies free of charge to all the members of my Estate, most of whom, from both parties, sincerely thanked me for it at the next plenary session, but it was not long before the tide turned and the ruling party directed all their weapons against me as a seditious and perfidious man.

Heated debates about me and my treatise took place in the Secret Committee. The Chamberlain Baron von Essen set the tone of the persecution with a memorial in the Estate of Clergy, in which he asked whether the endorsement of the Estate signified assent. I was called in for interrogation by the Secret Committee, where several insidious questions were put to me one day, with great severity in the morning, with a beguiling courtesy in the afternoon. In the evening before the last plenary session that I attended during that Diet, I was treated as a traitor to my country even at the club and the most merciless drafts of a retraction were read out to me, which I was expected to sign, and the most mendacious calumnies were hurled at me by those who a few days earlier had been my greatest friends and supporters, and the following day I was voted out of my Estate. I was threatened with arrest or even worse and was advised to escape, but I remained in Stockholm for five weeks without anyone laying a finger on me, and finally went to see the Speaker of the Nobles and asked whether there was any objection to my returning home. Board of Trade Counsellor and Knight Nordencrantz told me that he had been requested to write a refutation but claimed to have replied: no! For that purpose a certain Rothman[56] was ransomed from the debtor's prison, who made such a masterly job of it that, although the censor deleted whole pages of sheer abuse from the manuscript, there was still nothing else left in what finally remained to be printed, a tract that I deliberately left unanswered. The terrible drop in the exchange rate in 1767 and the general distress caused by that throughout the country and the destruction of the party before the following Diet have been the best refutation of it.

On the happy day for all inhabitants of Sweden when the crown was placed upon the head of our Great King and the town of Kokkola wished to emulate other subjects in expressing its joyful reverence for its King, I was chosen to be their spokesman and delivered a speech[57] in which I sought to demonstrate how Gustavus III had then already demonstrated his greatness both within and outside the realm, which was then, at the request of my friends and supporters, printed the same year by Director Salvius.

In 1776 I submitted to the Royal Society of Arts and Sciences in Gothenburg my response to its prize question *concerning the rural trade*,[58] which I subsequently had with a short preface printed in Stockholm in 1777 by the Secretary and Knight Fougt and at his expense.

In the summer of 1778 so much began to be written in *Dagligt Allehanda* about a new statute on servants, and many people made such harsh, such preposterous proposals that one could not but shudder at them, and apart from that a regulation on the casting of lots had already been passed in one county, though its implementation was prevented by our humane King. These severities stirred me to the defence of liberty. I therefore wrote about the natural rights of masters and servants, with a humble dedication to His Majesty; the Secretary and Knight Fougt[59] was again my publisher. The piece appeared, and the many debates to which it gave rise in *Dagligt Allehanda*[60] and *Stockholms Posten*[61] show what attention it had aroused. The conflict still continues and is unlikely to cease until His Majesty personally settles the matter.

I should finally also mention among my writings the memorial[62] that was submitted at the beginning of 1779 to the most Reverend Estate of the Clergy *concerning freedom of religion*, which was soon afterwards printed by Secretary Fougt. The procedure on that occasion was as follows. In consultation with a few friends[63] I drafted that memorial as early as the beginning of December, then conferred about it with several members of my own Estate, who fully approved of the idea and advised me to present it to the Estate. But when I realized that it could arouse excessive opposition among some members and an intense persecution of myself, I decided to let His Majesty first read it in person, with a humble request that, should His Majesty approve of the idea, he would then also strongly support it before the Estates of the Realm and protect the author against persecution. I was most graciously assured of this and the memorial was presented to the Archbishop, who did not, however, submit it to the Estate until the matter was raised in the Estate of Nobility in the form of another memorial and was taken up for debate in the other Estates. The matter was tabled in the Estate of Clergy one day, and the following day it was debated with uncommon vehemence by Bishops Benzelstierna,[64] Celsius[65] and Lütkemann,[66] of whom the last also referred with bitterness to the author, when the Chief Court Chaplain von Troil, the Cathedral Dean Dr Fant and I had also put ourselves down to speak in defence of the freedom of religion, but the proceedings were conducted through all kinds of objections in such a way that none of us was allowed to say a single word and the question was dismissed with immense passion, although it was approved by all the other Estates the same day.

A reliable anecdote regarding this treatise. When His Majesty observed the vehemence against me in the Estate of Clergy and the indifference and steadiness with which I confronted it, he observed: "I am fairly audacious as well, but I would never have dared to do what Chydenius did." It was indeed true that almost all my adherents in the Estate wavered and withdrew and I stood alone when the heat was greatest, although others had previously been as zealous and active in the matter as I was.

This account of my writings has included most of my experiences as a member of the Diet, in which they presumably occupy their rightful place, but there are also a few events that are worth recording for posterity, which illuminate the history of this era and will probably be looked for in vain elsewhere.

As soon as I was admitted to the Estate of Clergy as the individual delegate of the chaplains at the Diet in 1765, I drew up and presented to my Estate a memorial regarding the appointment of impartial members to the most important joint committees, by which everyone seemed to be amazed but of which no notice was taken, as it directly contradicted the lists that the Electors were then already preparing. I sought and gained the acquaintance of my teacher, the polymathic Nordencrantz, who entirely approved of the content of my memorial.

But I worked on nothing as assiduously during this Diet as on the freedom of writing and printing. The writings of Nordencrantz had already opened my eyes so far that I regarded it as the most precious possession of a free country. It was also very acceptable to the party[67] that had for so long been subordinate and was now for the first time in power, which desired to uncover the secrets that had been concealed by the previously ruling party, under the rule of which they had for so long been oppressed. I therefore drew up a memorial on the subject, which I communicated to the late Bishop Serenius, who introduced me to the late Court Councillor Arckenholtz,[68] who had just arrived in Stockholm, in order to confer with him about this. After several conversations and deliberations I rewrote my memorial and asked Bishop Serenius to take the lead on such an important matter by adding his signature to the memorial. He looked over it and shortened it but inserted at the end of the plan of liberty that one should not be allowed to write anything concerning the state, by which I was highly incensed, as with these few words everything that the friends of repression and secrecy could ask for was already conceded, and declined to have anything to do with it. He regretted that the matter was rather sensitive and met with opposition but then asked me to write as I wished under my own name, which I did and submitted it to all the Estates, to which, however, an honourable member, Schoolmaster Kraftman,[69] lent his name, without knowing who had written it.

The Estates referred this matter of the freedom of printing to the Grand Joint Committee to be elaborated by a special Committee, of which I and Archbishop Mennander and the then Dean and now Bishop Forssenius[70] were members of our Estate. The issue was divided into two separate parts, the first being to define what it would be lawful to print and what unlawful, the second dealing with the censorship or the legal tribunal before which the case would be examined. On the former, all the members were agreed, but not on the second. If freedom of writing and printing becomes a main pillar of liberty under all regimes that protect it, if most of Sweden's misfortunes in the recent past have arisen from obscurantism and delusion, it is worthwhile for posterity to know about the small coincidences by which it has been granted here, as if by a lucky chance of Providence, to the inhabitants of Sweden – anecdotes that will never otherwise reach the hands of our historians.

I saw clearly that the most extensive freedom to choose any subject on which to write would mean nothing as long as its application were to depend on the arbitrary will of a single person, namely the censor, over whom either a ruling party or ministry or ruler would be able to exercise control, and I therefore firmly proposed to have the censorship in all political cases entirely removed, but my influence with the most important and enlightened members was relatively slight. I therefore turned to the delegates of the Estates of Burghers and of Peasants and persuaded them to make common cause with me. Through my supporters I also worked upon the Dean, Bishop Forssenius, so that he too declared that he was opposed to censorship. The question had already been raised in the

Committee and tabled, and at the following session the question was raised again by Burgomaster Miltopæus,[71] who asked to hear the opinion on the matter of the *censor librorum*, Permanent Secretary von Oelreich, who best understood the advantages and disadvantages of the censorship. Mr von Oelreich, who had a seat on the Committee not as a member but as an expert adviser, first spoke gracefully about the great importance of the freedom of writing and printing, yet he nonetheless regarded it as hazardous to leave the works that were to be published without any censorship, believing that the censor should have his hands tied by formal instructions, so that he did not arbitrarily prevent the authors from having their works published, but he feared that there would be an unbridled frenzy of book-printing if the censorship was completely abolished. I for my part could not but praise the Permanent Secretary's great merits in the office of censor, who had allowed so much more enlightenment to reach the nation than all the others that have held that office in Sweden, but I also pointed out the peril to the nation and to liberty of such a guardianship, which might soon fall into less worthy hands, and urged him, like Mabbott[72] in England, to make his name immortal and renounce censorship altogether and leave it in the hands of a free nation and under the surveillance of the law. The debates on this became extensive on both sides. An adjournment was requested in the matter, but I maintained that the case should be decided according to the established practice of the Diet.

The members were of different minds, so a vote was taken in the Committee. Our permanent chairman, Chief Judge Baron Reuterholm,[73] was not present on that occasion, so Lord Chamberlain Baron von Düben[74] acted as chairman when the Estates of Peasants and of Burghers voted against the office of censor. Bishop Mennander was not present, Bishop Forssenius dared not reject it outright, whereas I took the same stand on the issue as the aforementioned Estates. The majority of the Nobility, on the other hand, were in favour of maintaining the censorship, resulting in two Estates being opposed to it, the Estate of Clergy ending up with *paria vota*[75] and one being in favour of retaining the office of censor. The report of the Committee was consequently to be drawn up against censorship, which I undertook to do and luckily just managed to get it approved by the Committee before I was voted out of the Estate a few days later. The entire issue thus depended on the absence of a single member of the Estate of Clergy who was also in favour of a censor, which could have meant two Estates against two, when no report could have emerged. Chief Judge Baron Reuterholm did afterwards draft a separate motion in favour of censorship, which most of the members signed, but fortunately it was so prolix and so convoluted that when it was read out along with the report in the Grand Joint Committee the members tired of listening to it, and those in favour of the freedom of writing could easily see that it would hardly be protected with so many subtleties and reservations, so that the report was finally unanimously accepted, first in the Grand Joint Committee and then by all the Estates. Thus, liberty at last prevailed and the Swedish wit happily escaped from an oppressive guardianship, and although dangerous intrigues have since then been conducted to destroy this most precious aspect of liberty, it has nonetheless been most solemnly confirmed – praise be to

Providence and our Gustavus – by our Most Gracious King, who is not willing to rule with obscurantism. May Swedes make worthy use of it and may it always radiate light, truth and virtue around the Throne and in the hearts of all citizens, to make the reign of our clement King a great one and his subjects happy under his sceptre!

Together with a parliamentary delegate from Raahe, I composed a separate motion for the Joint Mining Committee against the transfer of the forge tax,[76] which was also approved by the Estates of the Realm, whereby an attempt was obstructed to gradually turn the whole country into a mining region and imperceptibly subordinate the allodial rights of the country people to the privileges of the metalworking industries.

I likewise composed a separate motion against the Ironmasters' Association, which was at first approved by the Estates of Burghers and of Peasants but was taken up again after my departure from Stockholm as a result of powerful pressure from the Nobility, by which it was finally brought to a standstill.

Appointed by the chaplains in Ostrobothnia, I also attended the Diet of 1769 but, owing to certain secret machinations, I was not accepted by the Estate of Clergy. However, in Norrköping I received a summons from the *Consistorium Ecclesiasticum* in Turku to take a pastoral examination and immediately travelled there and was nominated, following an interview concluded to the satisfaction of my superiors, to the position of Rector of Kokkola.

Last year, 1778, I was again honoured with the majority of votes to be the individual parliamentary delegate of the clergy in Ostrobothnia and attended that first notable Diet since the change in the constitution, at which I finally received the favour of being allowed a private audience with our Great King and in the course of it to candidly present the most pressing concerns of my native region.

I am profoundly grateful that I have by my modest endeavours for King and Country won the special favour of my dear King with an express assurance of all possible promotion and favour in whatever I might wish for. For although I have never been one of fortune's favourites or aspired to official honours and do not in my occupation lack an income that, with a contented mind, will suffice for earthly happiness, and although I never intend in that respect to seek or accept any promotion, such a high and gracious offer is nonetheless in itself something on which I set infinite value.

Kokkola, 14 February 1780
Anders Chydenius

Notes

1 "*24 February*": as Georg Schauman has shown, a more likely date is 26 February. See G. Schauman, *Biografiska undersökningar om Anders Chydenius*, Skrifter utgifna af Svenska Litteratursällskapet i Finland 84, Helsinki: Svenska Litteratursällskapet i Finland, p. 9.
2 "*Old Style*": refers to the Julian calendar, which was used in Sweden until 17 February 1753, when it was replaced by the Gregorian calendar.
3 Johan Wegelius (1693–1764) was rector in Tornio from 1725 and dean in Oulu from

1757. His main work as a religious writer was a postil in Finnish, *Se pyhä ewangeliu-millinen walkeus* (1747–9). He was influenced by, for example, the Pietists and the Moravian Brethren.

4 Concerning Samuel Chydenius (1727–57), see p. 15.

5 Carl Fredrik Mennander (1712–86) was bishop of Turku from 1757 to 1775 and Swedish archbishop from 1776 to 1786. He was a member of the Royal Academy of Sciences from 1744 and a member of all the Diets from 1756 to 1778. During the Age of Liberty he was acknowledged as a leading Hat.

6 Johan Browallius (1707–55) was a natural scientist, theologian and politician (a Hat). He became professor of natural history in Turku in 1737, professor of theology in 1746 and bishop of Turku diocese in 1749.

7 *"Master's degree"*: Chydenius became *filosofie kandidat* in Turku in 1753.

8 Pehr Kalm (1716–79) was a botanist and economist, best known as one of the so-called apostles of Carolus Linnaeus. As such, he took part in Linnaeus's scientific journeys through Sweden (Västergötland and the county of Bohus) and was sent to North America in 1748–51. He was appointed to the Royal Academy of Sciences in 1746 and became professor of economy in Turku the year after. See also pp. 15–17.

9 Jakob Haartman (1717–88) was professor first of philosophy and then of theology at Uppsala University. In 1776 he was appointed bishop of Turku.

10 Johan Kreander (1752–79) was the headmaster in Kokkola from 1776 to 1779.

11 Johan Tengström (1757–1821) was the youngest son of Chydenius's sister Maria through her marriage with Johan Tengström the elder, deacon and schoolmaster, and helper of Chydenius in Kokkola. Johan the younger became rector at Vaasa and Mustasaari (Korsholm). Chydenius supported him financially during his upbringing.

12 *"gnomonics"*: the art of constructing and using sundials.

13 *"Quis est usus huius loci practicus"*: "What is the practical use of this passage?"

14 *"hoc opus hic labor"*: "this is the task, this is the difficulty".

15 *"Royal Medical Board"*: the *Collegium Medicum* was founded in 1663 in order to ameliorate the standard of medical practice in Sweden, to supervise medical doctors, to promote teaching in medicine and to combat quackery.

16 Johan Haartman (1725–87) was a physician and medical doctor in Uppsala in 1749. The same year, he was appointed as "provincial medical doctor" in Turku. From 1765 he was professor of medicine at Turku and the same year became a member of the Royal Academy of Sciences. He was the first to practise vaccination against smallpox in Finland (see pp. 2 and 19 for Chydenius's activities in this field) and wrote well-known instructive books on medical issues.

17 Johan Anders af Darelli (1718–88) was a physician and writer. His name by birth was Darelius but when he was ennobled in 1770 he took the name af Darelli. The work referred to is *Socken apothek och någre huscurer, utgifne under kongl. Collegii medici öfwerseende och besörjande*, Stockholm, 1760.

18 *"mercurius sublimatus corrosivus, mercurius dulcis, calomel and other mercurial compounds, spiritus nitri fumans, spiritus salis and spiritus salis ammoniaci"*: these are different chemical substances and compounds made from mercury, nitric acid, hydrochloric acid and an ammonium salt, used as medical cures.

19 *"liquidus Hoffmanni"*: the so-called Hoffmann's drops, or *liquor anodynus mineralis Hoffmanni*, were a mixture of alcohol and ether and a well-known remedy in the eighteenth century for several sicknesses, including heart and stomach problems.

20 *"simplicia"*: simple ingredients.

21 Nils Rosén von Rosenstein (1706–73), a medical doctor, was professor of medicine at Uppsala University from 1740 first in anatomy and botany but later only in anatomy (when Linnaeus received the chair in botany). He was appointed *Rector Magnificus* of Uppsala University in 1747 and head physician (*Archiater*) at the royal court. Among many other things he is remembered as the instigator of scientific paediatrics in Sweden. The work that Chydenius is referring to is most probably *Compendium*

anatomicum, eller En kort beskrifning om de delar, af hwilka hela menniskians kropp består..., Stockholm, 1736.

22 *"... to operate on the eyes"*: it is believed that Chydenius performed eye operations to remove cataracts during his time in Alaveteli.

23 *"Mrs Segercrona"*: Chydenius was proud of the eye drops or eye-water he had developed to cure sore eyes. Mrs Segercrona has not been identified with certainty.

24 *"detailed memorial"*: most probably Chydenius is here referring to Anders Norden-crantz's famous *Til riksens höglofl. ständer församlade wid riksdagen år 1760. En wördsam föreställning uti et omständeligit swar på de oförgripeliga påminnelser...*, Stockholm, 1759. On Nordencrantz and Chydenius, see pp. 19–21 and 25.

25 *"in politicis"*: see note 49, p. 118.

26 Carl Gustaf Boije (1697–1769) was an officer and writer. The text referred to is *Säkra rön och påliteliga medel til wälmågo och förmögenhet, eller den igenom många års egna försök förfarna Swenska landthushållaren...*, Stockholm, 1756, which was widely known at the time.

27 *"pro labore"*: for the work, for my effort.

28 Lars Salvius (1706–73) was a book printer, publisher of journals and an economic writer. He was one of the first to openly criticize the Hats' regulative economic policies in favour of, for example, the manufactures. See pp. 34–5.

29 *"... my circumstantial response"*: refers to *Omständeligt swar, på den genom trycket utkomne wederläggning af skriften, kallad: Källan til rikets wanmagt, jämte anmärkningar öfwer de wid samma källa anstälda wattu-prof*, Stockholm, 1765.

30 *"Royal Highness"*: in 1750, Queen Lovisa Ulrika of Sweden (1720–82) gave birth to Prince Frederic Adolphus (1750–1803), the younger brother of Gustavus III and Prince Charles (later Charles XIII). King Adolphus Frederic had died in 1771.

31 *"accessit"*: see note 11, p. 275.

32 Jacob Faggot (1699–1777) was a scientist, statesman and chief land surveyor in Sweden. From 1739 he was a member of the Royal Academy of Sciences. See note 39, p. 117.

33 Jakob Gadolin (1719–1802) was a scientist and politician. In 1753 he became professor of physics and nine years later (1763) professor of theology, both at Turku. In 1788 he became bishop of Turku. Gadolin wrote several works on mathematics and natural history. He was also a member of most Diets from 1755 to 1800 and during the 1760s was still regarded as a staunch Hat supporter. From 1751 Gadolin was a member of the Royal Academy of Sciences.

34 *"... much less talk and write about them"*: that is, before the passing of the ordinance on freedom of writing and printing in 1766.

35 *"several barrels of gold"*: most likely Chydenius here is simply referring to an excessive amount of money which was used as bribes, but since a barrel of gold (*en tunna guld*) was used as a measure equalling 100,000 *daler smt*, it is possible that he had a more specific amount in mind.

36 Johan Mathesius (1709–65) was the second oldest of the famous Mathesius brothers, who had great influence on politics in Ostrobothnia and also on the political thinking of Anders Chydenius (see the Introduction, p. 22). Johan Mathesius was a staunch supporter of the Caps and was imprisoned for political reasons during the 1740s. He was appointed county secretary in Ostrobothnia in 1745 and acted temporarily as vice county governor in 1763.

37 *"some treatise"*: see the Introduction, p. 21.

38 *Wederläggning af de skäl, hwarmed man söker bestrida öster- och wästerbotniska samt wäster-norrländske städerne fri seglation*, Stockholm, 1765.

39 *"Indefeasible Thoughts..."*: an anonymous pamphlet, *Oförgripeliga Tankar om Fem Nya Stapel-Städers inrättande i Rikets Norre Provincer*, Stockholm, 1765. According to Virrankoski, the author was Eric Schröder, former secretary for the burghers in Stockholm. P. Virrankoski, *Anders Chydenius: Demokratisk politiker i upplysningens tid*, Stockholm: Timbro, 1995, p. 125.

40 *"Remarks"*: refers to *Påminnelser Wid de af Trycket nyligen utkomne Oförgripeliga Tankar om Fem Stapel-Städers inrättande i rikets Norra Provincer*, pp. 27–35 in *The Source*. The *Remarks* are not published in this volume.
41 *"Little critiques of* The Source": there were at least nine printed responses to *The Source*. See p. 139.
42 *"Circumstantial Refutation..."*: probably written by Bengt Junggren. See p. 139 and note 6, p. 141.
43 *"Water-Tests"*: see p. 139 and note 3, p. 141.
44 *"Circumstantial Response"*: Chydenius's pamphlet *Omständeligt swar, på den genom trycket utkomne wederläggning af skriften, kallad: Källan til rikets wanmagt, jämte anmärkningar öfwer de wid samma källa anstälda wattu-prof*, Stockholm, 1765.
45 *"its members"*: that is, the members of the Secret Committee.
46 *"Nordencrantz"*: see above, pp. 25, 38–40.
47 Fredric Gyllensvaan (1723–87) was an officer and politician. He became a colonel in 1772 and was dismissed in 1776. He was active in the Estate of Nobility from 1760 onwards, a well-known Cap who served as one of the leaders of the attack upon the old Hat regime and the directors of the Bank of the Estates, especially during the Diet of 1765–6.
48 Fredric Ulric von Essen (1721–81) was a landlord, the chamberlain of Prince Gustavus (later Gustavus III) and a politician. He was one of the most important leaders of the Cap party during the Diets from 1755 onwards. See p. 213.
49 Anders Cederström (1729–93) was an officer and politician, a fervent Cap in the Estate of Nobility and one of the Estate's trustees in the Board of Governors of the Bank after 1766.
50 *"sextern"*: a quire consisting of six sheets of paper folded in two (= 24 pages).
51 *"Mr von Oelreich"*: see the Introduction, p. 8.
52 Jacob Serenius (1700–76) became bishop in the diocese of Strängnäs in 1763 and was a leading Cap politician in the Estate of Clergy.
53 Casper Wijkman (1718–80) was a clergyman and leading Cap politician. He was a delegate for the Clergy in the Diets of 1760–2, 1765–6 and 1771–2.
54 Carl Kröger (1711–73) was a clergyman and politician. When he attended the Diet of 1765–6, he was dean of Västra Göinge in southern Sweden.
55 Pehr Högström (1714–84) is probably today the best known of this trio mentioned by Chydenius. Högström was a clergyman in Lapland and served as a missionary among the Sami population. From 1742 he was rector at the newly established parish of Gällivare. As a delegate of the Estate of Clergy he was a member of the Diets in 1755–6, 1765–6, 1769 and 1771–2. He was a member of the Royal Academy of Sciences and became a doctor of theology in 1772.
56 Jacob Gabriel Rothman (1721–72) was a medical student at Uppsala and an adventurer. The Swedish title of the anti-Chydenius pamphlet was *Rikets fördärf och undergång genom et konstladt och förledande finance-systeme*, Stockholm, 1766. In 1768 Rothman published another work, *Philolalus Parrhesiastes secundus, eller Pratsjuke Fritalaren den andre*, which gained him the designation "abominable free speaker" by Carl Christoffer Gjörwell.
57 *"... delivered a speech"*: this speech was given in Kokkola the day before Gustavus III's coronation on 29 May 1772. It was later published under the title *Tal hållet vid vår allernådigste konungs, konung Gustaf III:s höga kröning, den 29 maji 1772*, Stockholm, 1772.
58 *"... my response"*: published here, pp. 253–80.
59 Henrik Fougt (1720–82) was a book printer in Stockholm. From 1769 he held the privilege of being allowed to print all royal ordinances, which led him to name his printing-house "The Royal Printing-Press of Stockholm".
60 *"Dagligt Allehanda"*: see pp. 314–15.

61 The newspaper *Stockholms-Posten* was founded in 1778 by Johan Henric Kellgren, a poet and writer, Johan Christopher Holmberg, a bookseller, and Carl Peter Lenngren, secretary to the Board of Trade. It was published from 1778 to 1833.

62 *"the memorial"*: published here, pp. 317–27.

63 *"... a few friends"*: it is unclear exactly which friends (in the Estate of Clergy) he had conferred with – perhaps the two he mentions below: the cathedral dean in Västerås, Johan Michael Fant, and the Chief Court Chaplain, Uno von Troil. (See also Virrankoski, op. cit., p. 318f.).

64 Lars Benzelstierna (1719–1800) was bishop of Västerås, professor of theology in Uppsala and a member of most of the Diets from 1755 until his death.

65 Olof Celsius (1716–94) was a clergyman, historian and politician, and cousin of the great natural scientist Anders Celsius. He became professor of history in Uppsala 1747 and after that he served as bishop of Lund from 1777. He was a member of the Swedish Academy from 1786. Starting out as a loyal Cap, he later became a steadfast royalist.

66 Gabriel Lütkemann (1723–95), a clergyman and politician, was appointed court chaplain in 1744, superintendent in 1758 and bishop in the diocese of Visby in 1772. As a member of the Estate of Clergy he visited most of the Diets from 1755 onwards.

67 *"the party"*: the Caps.

68 Johan Arckenholtz (1695–1777) was an official and historian. He was put in prison by the Hat government in 1741 and after two years' imprisonment he was sent abroad and not allowed to enter Swedish territory again. During the period 1746–66 he was court librarian and court councillor in Hesse-Cassel (the landgrave of Hesse-Cassel was the Swedish king, Frederic I). After the dethronement of the Hats he returned to Sweden. His most important historical work was *Mémoirs concernant Christine reine de Suède...* (4 vols, Amsterdam, 1751–60).

69 Anders Kraftman (1711–91) was rector and schoolmaster at Porvoo gymnasium. At the Diet of 1765–6 he was the delegate from the diocese of Porvoo in the Estate of Clergy and was also a member of the Secret Committee.

70 Anders Forssenius (1708–88) was bishop of Skara from 1767 and a member of many Diets as a delegate of the Estate of Clergy.

71 Erik Miltopaeus (1718–84) was burgomaster of Tammisaari in Finland.

72 *"Mabbott"*: see note 1, p. 248.

73 Gustaf Gottfrid Reuterholm (1721–1803), official and politician, was chairman of the freedom of printing committee in 1765–6.

74 Karl Vilhelm von Düben (1724–90) was a diplomat, official and politician. At the time in question, von Düben was court chancellor (*hovkansler*), not lord chamberlain (*hovmarskalk*).

75 *"paria vota"*: a tied vote.

76 *"forge tax"*: a tax paid by iron forges for their yearly production of iron. The iron forges were forges where pig iron was transformed into forge iron. The forge tax determined the amount of forge iron the forge was allowed to produce.

Commentary

Lars Magnusson

This text, which Chydenius wrote on request by the learned society in Gothenburg, the Royal Society of Arts and Sciences (*Kungliga Vetenskaps- och Vitterhets-samhället i Göteborg*), when he became a corresponding member, was finished on 14 February 1780. As we saw, it was this society that some years earlier had so kindly received his prize competition essay on rural trade. After his return home from the stormy Diet of 1778–9, he might have felt that this was a good opportunity to explain himself and the positions he had taken on different political issues over the years. His work in bringing about the memorial regarding freedom of religion had not, as we saw earlier, made him very popular – to say the least – among his fellow clergymen. Moreover, he might have wanted to clarify his relations with King Gustavus III. There may be several reasons for this. First, there might have been opportunistic motives. In order to emphasize the great favours he had done for the king – not least at the last Diet – he might have searched for protection and support, especially at a time when many were critical of him. After all, sometime in the future another bishopric might become available; as Virrankoski has shown, there was, for example, a discussion in the mid-1770s whether the wide-stretching diocese of Turku should be divided into two.[1] In such a situation, royal support for his candidacy would not be unwelcome. On the other hand, one might speculate that another motive may have been just as important. After the Diet of 1778–9, growing opposition towards the king was noticeable. He was accused of despotic tendencies in his treatment of the estates – as we have seen, he dissolved the Diet after only a few months, with unclear motives. What made him particularly unpopular was the prohibition of the free distilling of hard liquor (*brännvin*). In 1775 an ordinance had been introduced that made the production and selling of hard liquor a state monopoly. Especially during 1779, many reports of protests came in from different counties, and there was fear of a more general uprising in the countryside. This was made worse in September 1779 by the warning that any attempts at private distillation would be severely punished.[2] In Stockholm the periodical *Sanning och Nöje* ("Truth and Enjoyment") was particularly critical of the king, and there was an apparent risk that a more restrictive policy on the press and printing might be introduced at any day. After all, in the spring of 1779 the critical *Stockholms Posten* had already been subject to censorship.[3] Moreover, a new ordinance on the freedom of printing was issued on 6 May 1780, which declared that libellous publications from then on would be severely punished. In contrast to the previous ordinances of 1774, and indeed of 1766, it was now the printer instead of the author who was fully responsible. Without doubt the motive behind this shift was to deter book printers from publishing critical texts. However, this aim seems not to have succeeded, because of a peculiarity in the law. The fine was quite low for the first offence against this law, but it increased rapidly for the second and third time. Hence, as von Vegesack claims, the period after 1780 in fact saw a rise in the number of journals and tracts dealing with political matters. Printers were willing to take the risk, and authors could always shift to a new publisher if the first one was sentenced.[4]

Against this background of threats towards the freedom of printing in 1779 and 1780, it is perhaps not peculiar that Chydenius in his autobiography provides an account of his role in putting through the reform in 1766. On this issue in particular, but also regarding his role during the Diet of 1765–6 as well as the (coming) ordinance on religious freedom, he wanted to set the record straight. Who knew what would come later in a situation of political turmoil? Hence when at the end of the text Chydenius praises Gustavus III for his confirmation of a liberality with regard to the press, it is largely a rhetorical trick: it is a warning to the king and at the same time a statement on Chydenius's commitment to the ordinance of 1766.

Another highly relevant question here, of course, is the extent to which we can put our trust in this autobiography as a reliable historical source. There are some instances where he gets the historical facts wrong for one reason or another. In a more general sense the text must of course be read as a personal defence. Like any other author, Chydenius is writing with a purpose; he has a message for the reader. He is looking to be saved from harsh judgment by posterity and tries to present himself in the most favourable light possible. However, here as always, Chydenius shows his political aptitude. He is worried about the future. There might not be many alternatives – a new regime based upon more power to the nobles and the rich would be even worse – but his great hopes connected with King Gustavus III had at least partly been shattered. At this moment of increasing social tensions and possible threats to freedom of expression, he is eager to pinpoint the reforms for a just order founded on the principles of natural liberty on which he had worked.

Notes

1 P. Virrankoski, *Anders Chydenius: Demokratisk politiker i upplysningens tid*, Stockholm: Timbro, 1995, p. 339f.

2 C.T. Odhner, *Sveriges politiska historia under konung Gustaf III:s regering*, vol. II, Stockholm: P.A. Norstedt & söner, 1896, p. 142f.

3 T. von Vegesack, *Smak för frihet: Opinionsbildningen i Sverige 1755–1830*, Stockholm: Natur & Kultur, 1995, p. 91.

4 von Vegesack, op. cit., p. 95.

Appendix 1
Monetary terms

The history of the Swedish monetary system in the pre-industrial era is very complicated, and characterized by non-uniformity. Multiple monetary standards and currency units were used simultaneously and varied even locally. Consequently, there were also several exchange rates, and there was often a clear discrepancy between the official and the market rates. The picture given here is simplified and focuses mainly on the period 1719–76 and on terms used in this volume.

Since the seventeenth century the monetary system had been based on the bimetallic (silver and copper) standard up to the minting reform of 1776, and two units of account, *daler kopparmynt* (*kmt*) and *daler silvermynt* (*smt*), had a central role in everyday economic operations. In 1745 notes were made non-convertible into copper plates (*plåtmynt*) and a paper standard was, de facto, introduced. Consequently, *plåtmynt* disappered from the circulation and banknotes took its place.

In the minting reform of 1776 the monetary system was totally renewed: a sole silver (specie) standard was introduced and *riksdaler* became the main currency.

For more detailed information, we recommend R. Edvinsson, T. Jacobson and D. Waldenström (eds), *Historical Monetary and Financial Statistics for Sweden: Exchange Rates, Prices, and Wages, 1277–2008*, Stockholm: Ekerlids, 2010, on which this presentation is mainly based.

Currencies

Carolin (pl. caroliner)

Two *marks* in actual silver coin. In 1716–76, 1 *carolin* was officially equal to 25 *öre smt*. Over the period 1719–76, the market rate for *carolin* varied between 25 and 57.5 *öre smt*.

Daler (silver coins)

Originally a silver coin minted in Sweden since 1534. To distinguish it from the unit of account called *svensk daler*, the silver coin was called *slagen daler*, later *riksdaler*.

Daler (unit of account)

Since the late sixteenth century, the *daler* had also been a unit of account, equal to 4 *marks*, and called the *svensk daler* (Swedish *daler*). In the beginning of the seventeenth century, as the bimetallic standard (silver and copper) was introduced, *svensk daler* bifurcated into two units of account:

Daler silvermynt (*daler smt*)
One *daler smt* = 4 *mark smt* = 32 *öre smt*.
Daler kopparmynt (*daler kmt*)
One *daler kmt* = 4 *mark kmt* = 32 *öre kmt*. In the eighteenth century (until 1776), 1 *daler smt* = 3 *daler kmt*. *Daler smt* and *daler kmt* were the main currency units up to 1776; banknotes, which were the main legal tender from 1745 to 1776, were usually denominated in *daler kmt*.

Dukat (pl. dukater)

Originally an imported gold coin, minted in Sweden from 1654. One Swedish *dukat* was worth around 2 *riksdaler* (*specie*). Played only a minor role in domestic payments.

Mark (silver coins)

See *carolin*.

Mark (unit of account)

As in the case of *daler*, the *mark* bifurcated into two different units during the seventeenth century:

Mark silvermynt (*mark smt*)
One *mark smt* = ¼ *daler smt* = 8 *öre smt*.
Mark kopparmynt (*mark kmt*)
One *mark kmt* = ¼ *daler kmt* = 8 *öre kmt*.

Riksdaler (specie)

Originally an imported term used for the silver *daler* (*slagen daler*) with a stable fine silver content (*riksdaler specie*). It was mainly used in foreign trade. Officially, 1 *riksdaler* was equal to 3 *daler smt*; after 1777, 1 *riksdaler* = 72 *mark kmt* = 6 *daler smt*. Over the period 1719–76, the market rate of the *riksdaler* varied between 34 and 108 *mark kmt*. After 1777, the *riksdaler* was the main currency unit, based on the sole silver standard. See *daler*.

Skilling

Introduced in 1777. 1 *riksdaler* = 48 *skilling*.

Öre courant (silver coins)

The *öre* was used as a currency unit from the Middle Ages until 1776. One *öre* = 1/8 *mark*. In the seventeenth century, *öre courant* became the term for the actual silver coin. Over the period 1719–76, the market rate of the *öre courant* varied between 3 and 6.5 *öre kmt*.

Öre (unit of account)

As a part of the *mark* and *daler* account systems, the *öre* bifurcated in the seventeenth century into two separate units:

Öre silvermynt
One *öre smt* = 1/8 *mark smt* = 1/32 *daler smt*.
Öre kopparmynt
One *öre kmt* = 1/8 *mark kmt* = 1/32 *daler kmt*.

Other monetary terms

Agio

The percentage of charge made for the exchange of paper money into cash, or for the exchange of a less valuable metallic currency into a more valuable; hence, the excess value of one currency over another.

Bank transfer note

The issuing of *banco-transport sedlar* began in 1701. In the beginning, the note had the character of a deposit receipt, and had to be transferred (reassigned) from the old to the new owner every time it was used as a method of payment. However, in the course of time these regulations were laid aside and notes were more and more used in the same way as today. In 1745 notes were made non-convertible into copper plates (*plåtmynt*) and a "paper standard" was, de facto, introduced. Together with small coins, bank transfer notes were in practice the only method of payment in use up to 1776.

Devaluation

During the eighteenth century the concepts of falling and rising exchange rates were often reversed compared to how we see matters today. Today we would speak of a revaluation, since as a result of this "devaluation" the value of money increases.

Fyrastyver

Unofficial name for the silver coin minted as 4 *öre* with the nominal value of 6 *öre courant*.

Hamburg riksdaler

The foreign exchange rate of Swedish currency was most often announced in *Hamburger Reichsdaler Banco*. In practice, it was often used as equivalent for the *riksdaler specie*.

Pjäs (pl. pjäsar)

Unofficial name for a silver coin minted as 5 *öre* with the nominal value of 6 *öre courant*.

Plåt (pl. plåtar)

1   Coins minted in square copper plates in general (*plåtmynt*), used between 1644 and 1776. Denominated in *daler smt*.
2   *Plåtmynt* minted as 2 *daler silvermynt*.

Remit a bill of exchange

To send a bill of exchange as a payment to somebody.

Remitter

A person who sends or intends to send a bill of exchange to somebody (the payee) as a payment. For this purpose, the remitter has to buy a bill of exchange from the drawer of the bills.

Sexstyver

The same as *pjäs*.

Slant (pl. slantar)

A copper coin with the designated value of 1 *öre smt*.

Styver

Up until 1776, the unofficial name for 1 *öre courant*.

Tale-value

The Swedish term *räknevärde* is translated in this volume as "tale-value". *Räknevärde* implies that money is valued by tale (by counting pieces or coins taken at their nominal value), not by weight (by their intrinsic value). The use of *räknevärde* illustrates the complexity of the Swedish monetary system: as everyday monetary operations were mainly based on different units of account, there was a need for a term that could express nominal and relative values. In Chydenius's texts, *räknevärde* often refers to the nominal value determined by a government decree, which could differ from the market value and/or the face value physically marked on a coin or a note. Sometimes *räknevärde* can also be translated as "unit of account".

Tunna guld (pl. tunnor guld)

Barrel of gold. A unit of account, equal to 100,000 *daler smt*.

Vit styver

Vitten, unofficial name for 1 *öre smt* up until 1776.

Örtug

1   A silver or copper coin minted in the Middle Ages and the sixteenth century and valued at ½ *öre*.
2   A unit of account used up until the sixteenth century: 1 *örtug* = ⅓ *öre* = 1/24 *mark*.

Appendix 2
Measurements and weights

Linear measures

Aln (pl. alnar)
Ell; 1 *aln* = 0.59 m.

Famn (pl. famnar)
Fathom; 1 *famn* = 3 *alnar* = 1.78 m.

Mil
The Swedish mile; 1 *mil* = 6,000 *famnar* = 18,000 *alnar* = 10,688 m.

Weights

Lod
1 *lod* = 1/32 *skålpund* = 13.2 g.

Mark
1 *mark* = ½ *skålpund* = 212.5 g.

Skålpund
1 *skålpund* = 32 *lod* = 425 g.

Lispund
1 *lispund* = 1/20 *skeppund* = 20 *skålpund* = 8.5 kg.

Skeppund

1 *skeppund* = 20 *lispund* = 400 *skålpund* = 170 kg.

Cubic measures

Stig (pl. stigar)

Chaldron, an old measure for charcoal. The number of barrels counted into 1 *stig* varied locally and over the course of time between 12 and 24 barrels of 160 litres each.

Vacka

Old measure used especially for grain. Its size could vary from *c*.5 to 25 litres. The *vacka* was sometimes equivalent to the Swedish *skäppa*, an equally unstable unit of measurement for grain, although *skäppa* more often varied between 25 and 35 litres. The word *vacka* is of Fenno-Ugrian origin and was mainly used in Finland.

Units for taxation purposes

Rök

Originally the same as one household. Together with *mantal*, used as an assessment unit for taxation purposes.

Glossary

Academy in Turku *Åbo Academie* or *Academien i Åbo*, the old university in Turku, which was established in 1640 and moved to Helsinki in 1828. Not to be confused with the current universities in Turku, Åbo Akademi University and the University of Turku, established in 1918 and 1920 respectively.

Age of Liberty *Frihetstiden*, the period 1719–72 in Swedish history. The term was used at the time as well as in retrospect.

Appropriations Committee *Bevillningsdeputation*, one of several committees during the Diets. Dealt with all matters in connection with taxation and appropriations.

Bank of the Estates *Riksens ständers bank* or *Ständernas bank*, established in 1668 and later known as the Swedish National Bank.

Board of Chancery *Kanslikollegium*, the most central civil service department and the hub of all administration in Sweden, established in 1626. Had various fields of responsibility at different times, but often dealt with issues related to foreign policy and domestic affairs such as postal services, schools, universities, archives and libraries.

Board of Mining *Bergskollegium*, a central civil service department within the Swedish administration from 1637 to 1857, mainly dealing with matters related to mining and the metalworking industry.

Board of Trade *Kommerskollegium*, a central civil service department within the Swedish administration, established in 1651 and mainly dealing with matters related to commerce, industry and shipping.

Board of Trade Counsellor *Kommerseråd*, since 1682 a title for one of the highest officials within the Board of Trade.

Board of War *Krigskollegium*, a central civil service department within the Swedish administration from 1630 to 1866, mainly dealing with matters related to the Swedish armed forces.

Burgomaster *Borgmästare*, the mayor of a town.

Caps *Mössorna*, one of the two political factions or "parties" in Swedish politics during the Age of Liberty.

Commodity Ordinance *Produktplakatet*, an ordinance passed in 1724, resembling the English Navigation Acts.

Council of the Realm *Riksrådet or Riksens råd*, the King's Privy Council, which during the Age of Liberty mainly consisted of the highest officials within the realm. The Union and Security Act of 1789 gave the King the right to determine the number of Councillors. As Gustavus III set the number at zero the Council of the Realm was in practice abolished.

Dean *Prost*, a member of the clergy, usually a rector (see this word), exercising supervision over the ecclesiastical matters within a deanery.

Diet *Riksdag*, recurrent assembly of the four estates in the Swedish realm.

Estates of the Realm *Rikets ständer*, the four estates in the Swedish realm: the Nobility, the Clergy, the Burghers and the Peasants.

Exchange Bill Office(s) *Växelkontor* (*wäxel-contoir*), refers to a group of influential merchants who during the years 1747–56 and 1758–61 were commissioned by the state and with financial aid from the same to try to improve the value of Swedish money. The operations of the *wäxel-contoir* in 1758–61 failed completely and contributed to the defeat of the Hat party in the Diet elections of 1765.

Farmhand *Dräng*, male servant employed on a farm.

Fisheries Joint Committee *Fiskerideputation*, one of many committees that functioned during the Diets. In 1765–6, Chydenius was one of the most active members of the Fisheries Joint Committee, which this time prepared a new ordinance on fishing.

Freedom of writing and printing *Skriv- och tryckfrihet*, the concept was expanded during the Diet of 1765–6, thanks largely to Chydenius, and also included public access to official documents and papers. It was also originally a larger concept than freedom of the press, as handwritten material was also subject to censorship.

General Appeals Committee *Allmänna besvärsdeputation*, one of the committees during the Diets, dealing with general grievances and appeals submitted to the Diets.

General grievances *Allmänna besvär*, complaints submitted during the Diets by the towns, by the rural population or by some other interest group about an unsatisfactory state of things they wished the government to correct or alleviate.

Grand Joint Committee *Stora deputationen*, a joint committee functioning during the Diets of the 1760s, dealing with constitutional matters but lacking the right to make decisions.

Great redistribution of landholdings *Storskiftet*, an important reform introduced in 1757, when all landholdings were to be surveyed and redistributed. The aim was to combine formerly scattered landholdings in larger patches in order to facilitate the use of more rational methods of agriculture.

Hats *Hattarna*, one of the two political factions or "parties" in Swedish politics during the Age of Liberty.

His Royal Majesty *Kungl. Maj:t*, the king and his council, the government (seldom referring to the king as a person, as his power was nominal during the Age of Liberty).

Ironmasters' Association *Järnkontoret*, an association established in 1747, not a public authority. Its main task was to keep the export price of Swedish iron and steel high.

Maid *Piga*, female servant employed on a farm.

Manufactures Office *Manufakturkontoret*, a department subordinate to the Estates of the Realm between 1739 and 1766. Its main task was to give economic support to the manufactories in the country by lending them money and by issuing bounties. It formed an essential part of the Hats' economic policy, and was dissolved when the Caps took over power at the Diet of 1765–6.

Rector *Kyrkoherde*, a vicar in a congregation or parish.

Retorsion Act *Retorsionsplakat*, a navigation act passed in 1725 by the Dutch in revenge for the Swedish Commodity Ordinance.

Royal Medical Board *Collegium Medicum*, an organization for medical practitioners established in 1663. Its aim was to improve medical standards and combat quackery.

Rural dean *Kontraktsprost*, a member of the clergy, usually a rector, exercising supervision over the ecclesiastical matters in a rural deanery, a division of a diocese.

Rural trade *Lanthandel* or *landsköp*, a forbidden form of buying and selling in the countryside. *Lanthandel* was, however, fairly common, as it was an important source of income for people in rural areas and supplied them with many of their necessities.

Salt Office *Saltkontor*, an office for the salt trade established by wholesale dealers and shipping companies, which operated from 1750 to 1762. The Salt Office was allowed to charge a certain fee on imported salt against having salt in stock and selling it at a fixed price.

Secret Committee *Sekreta utskottet*, the committee during the Diets in which the most important matters were discussed, such as foreign policy, national defence and banking. The Peasants were excluded from the Secret Committee, which as a rule had 100 members (50 from the Nobility and 25 each from the Clergy and the Burghers). The Secret Committee was abolished in 1772 after the coup.

Sovereign Power *Högsta Makten*, the government.

Speaker of the Nobles The Speaker of the Nobles was also *lantmarskalk*, Marshal of the Diet, the highest official at the Diet.

Staple and non-staple towns *Stapelstäder* and *uppstäder*, two categories of Swedish towns, respectively with and without the right to trade directly with foreigners and export domestic products to foreign ports.

Tar Company *Tjärkompani*, a company or association of merchants with the privilege of being able to buy and export all tar produced within the country or within certain provinces.

Third Committee *Tredje utskottet* or *tryckfrihetsutskottet*, a subcommittee to the Grand Joint Committee during the Diet of 1765–6, dealing with the freedom of writing and printing.

Wäxel-Associerade *Växelassocierade*, the individuals who had taken part in the operations of the Exchange Bill Offices. Many held these "exchange associates" responsible for the deplorable economic state of the Swedish realm.

Anders Chydenius's central writings

Americanska Näfwerbåtar, Åbo, 1753.
American Birchbark Boats.

Svar På samma Fråga (Om bästa sättet at upodla Mosslupna Ängar), Stockholm, 1762.
A Response to the Question Regarding the Best Ways and Means to Cultivate Moss-Covered Meadows.

Svar på samma Fråga (Angående Kärrors Förbättring), Stockholm, 1764.
A Response to the Question Regarding the Improvement of Carts.

Wederläggning Af de Skäl, Hwarmed man söker bestrida Öster- och Wästerbotniska Samt Wäster-Norrländske Städerne Fri Seglation, Stockholm, 1765.
Refutation of the Reasons Employed to Deny the Towns in Ostrobothnia and Västerbotten as Well as in Västernorrland a Free Navigation.

Swar På den af Kgl. Wetenskaps Academien förestälta Frågan: Hwad kan vara orsaken, at sådan myckenhet Swenskt folk årligen flytter utur Landet? och genom hwad Författningar det kan bäst förekommas? Stockholm, 1765.
Answer to the Question Prescribed by the Royal Academy of Sciences: What May Be the Cause of So Many People Annually Emigrating from This Country? And by What Measures May It Best Be Prevented?

Källan Til Rikets Wan-Magt, Stockholm, 1765.
The Source of Our Country's Weakness.

Memorial om tryckfriheten, 1765.
Memorial on the Freedom of Printing (manuscript in the National Archives of Sweden).

Den Nationnale Winsten, Stockholm, 1765.
The National Gain.

Omständeligt Swar, På den genom Trycket utkomne Wederläggning af Skriften, Kallad: Källan til Rikets Wanmagt, Jämte Anmärkningar Öfwer De wid samma Källa anstälda Wattu-Prof, Stockholm, 1765.
A Circumstantial Response to the Refutation of the Treatise Entitled: The Source of Our Country's Weakness, and Remarks on the Water Tests Conducted at the Same Source.

Riksens Höglofl. Ständers Stora Deputations Tredje Utskotts Betänkande, angående Skrif- och Tryckfriheten; gifwit wid Riksdagen i Stockholm then 18 December 1765.
Report of the Third Committee of the Grand Joint Committee of the Honourable Estates of the Realm on the Freedom of Writing and Printing, submitted at the Diet in Stockholm on 18 December 1765 (manuscript in the National Archives of Sweden).

Anwisning Til Swar, På de Magist. Chydenius förestäldte 14 Frågor, Rörande Källan til Rikets Wanmagt, Stockholm, 1766.
Advice as an Answer to the 14 Questions presented to Chydenius, M.A., regarding The Source of Our Country's Weakness.

Riksens höglofl. Ständers Stora Deputations Tredje Utskotts ytterligare Betänkande rörande Tryckfriheten; gifwit wid Riksdagen i Stockholm d. 21. Aprilis 1766.
Additional Report of the Third Committee of the Grand Joint Committee of the Honourable Estates of the Realm on the Freedom of Printing, submitted at the Diet in Stockholm on 21 April 1766 (manuscript in the National Archives of Sweden).

Berättelse Om Chinesiska Skrif-Friheten, Stockholm, 1766.
Account of the Chinese Freedom to Write.

Rikets Hjelp, Genom en Naturlig Finance-System, Stockholm, 1766.
A Remedy for the Country, by Means of a Natural System of Finance.

Maboths Ansökning Hos Parlamentet i Engeland, At få nedlägga Sitt Censors-Ämbete, Såsom skadeligt för Sanning och Nationen, Stockholm, 1768.
Mabbott's Petition to the English Parliament to Abolish His Office of Licenser, as Harmful both to the Truth and to the Nation.

Tal Hållet Vid Vår Allernådigste Konungs, Konung Gustaf III:s Höga Kröning, Den 29 Maji 1772, Stockholm, 1772.
Speech on the Occasion of the Coronation of Gustavus III on 29 May 1772.

Svar På Vetenskaps och Vitterhets Samhällets I Götheborg Förestälta Fråga: Huruvida Landthandel för ett Rike i gemen är nyttig eller skadelig, och hvad mon den bidrager til industriens uplifvande eller aftagande? Stockholm, 1777.

Answer to the Question Posed by the Society of Arts and Sciences in Gothenburg: Whether Rural Trade Is Generally Useful or Harmful to a Country, and to What Extent It Contributes to the Promotion or Decline of Industry.

Tankar Om Husbönders och Tienstehions Naturliga Rätt, Stockholm, 1778.
Thoughts Concerning the Natural Rights of Masters and Servants.

Memorial, Angående Religions-Frihet, Stockholm, 1779.
Memorial Regarding Freedom of Religion.

Självbiografi, 1780.
Autobiography (manuscript in the Royal Society of Arts and Sciences in Gothenburg).

Predikningar öfver Tio Guds Bud, in *Homiletiska försök*, vols III–IV, Uppsala, 1781–2.
Sermons on the Ten Commandments.

Predikningar öfver Andra Hufvudstycket i Catechesen, in *Homiletiska försök*, vol. VI, Stockholm, 1784.
Sermons on the Second Main Part of the Catechism.

Förslag til Lappmarkernes uphjelpande, 1794–5.
A Proposal for the Improvement of Lapland (manuscript in the Finnish Economic Society).

Om Saltpetter-Sjuderierna, särledes i Österbotten, in *Skrifter af Sällskapet för Allmänne Medborgerlige kunskaper*, vol. II, Stockholm, 1795.
On Saltpetre Houses, especially in Ostrobothnia.

Finska lantbrukets upphjälpande, 1799.
The Improvement of Finnish Agriculture (original manuscript lost, a transcript printed in 1908).

Tankar om Koppympningen För Finlands Allmoge, in *K. Finska Hushållnings-Sällskapets Handlingar* 1, Åbo, 1803.
Thoughts on Inoculating against Smallpox for the Finnish People.

Bibliography

Arnberg, J.W., *Anteckningar om frihetstidens politiska ekonomi*, Uppsala: W. Schultz förlag, 1868.

Bedoire, F., *Hugenotternas värld – från religionskrigens Frankrike till skeppsbroadelns Stockholm*, Stockholm: Albert Bonniers förlag, 2009.

Berch, A., *Inledning til almänna hushålningen*, Stockholm, 1747.

Berch, A., *Tal om den proportion, som de studerande ärfordra til de ledige beställningar i riket…*, Stockholm, 1749.

Berg, B.Å., *Volatility, Integration and Grain Banks: Studies in Harvests, Rye Prices and Institutional Development of the Parish Magasins in Sweden in the 18th and 19th Centuries*, Stockholm: Economic Research Institute, Stockholm School of Economics (EFI), 2007.

Boudin, H.R., "Valloninvandringen som religiös migration", in A. Florén and G. Ternhag (eds), *Valloner – järnets människor*, Hedemora: Gidlunds förlag, 2002.

Brolin, P.-E., *Hattar och mössor i borgarståndet, 1760–1766*, Uppsala: AB Lundquistska bokhandeln, 1953.

Chydenius, J., *Sednare delen, om gamle Carleby, med wederbörandes minne, utgifwen af præses, Jacob Chydenius…*, Åbo, 1754.

Coats, A.W., *On the History of Economic Thought: British and American Economic Essays*, vol. 1, London: Routledge, 1992.

Cormack, E. (ed.), *The Linnaeus apostles: Global science & adventure. Europe, North & South America*, vol. 3: book 2, *Pehr Kalm*, London: IK Foundation, 2008.

Edvinsson, R., Jacobsson, T. and Waldenström, D. (eds), *Historical Monetary and Financial Statistics for Sweden: Exchange Rates, Prices, and Wages, 1227-2008*, Stockholm: Ekerlids, 2010.

Eek, H., "1766 års tryckfrihetsordning, dess tillkomst och betydelse i rättsutvecklingen", *Statsvetenskaplig Tidskrift*, 1943, pp. 185–222.

Ekegård, E., *Studier i svensk handelspolitik under den tidigare frihetstiden*, Uppsala, 1924.

Fischerström, J., *Påminnelser wid Sweriges Allmänna och enskylta Hushållning*, Stockholm, 1761.

Forsman, K., "Studier i det svenska 1700-talets ekonomiska litteratur", in *Skrifter utgivna av Svenska Litteratursällskapet i Finland*, vol. 312, Helsinki, 1947, pp. 78–262.

Forsskål, P., *Thoughts on Civil Liberty: Translation of the Original Manuscript with Background*, Stockholm: Atlantis, 2009.

Frängsmyr, T., "Den gudomliga ekonomin: Religion och hushållning i 1700-talets Sverige", *Lychnos*, 1971–2, pp. 217–44.

Frängsmyr, T., *Wolffianismens genombrott i Uppsala: Frihetstida universitetsfilosofi till 1700-talets mitt*, Uppsala University, 1972.

Gadd, C.-J., *Det svenska jordbrukets historia*, vol. 3: *Den agrara revolutionen 1700–1870*, Stockholm: Natur och Kultur, 2000.

Gadd, P.A., *Tal om finska climatet och dess följder, i landets hushållning*, Stockholm, 1761.

Haakonssen, K. and Horstbøll, H. (eds), *Northern Antiquities and National Identities: Perceptions of Denmark and the North in the Eighteenth Century*, Copenhagen: Det Kongelige Danske Videnskabernes Selskab, 2007.

Harnesk, B., *Legofolk: Drängar, pigor och bönder i 1700- och 1800-talens Sverige*, Umeå Studies in the Humanities 96, Umeå, 1990.

Heckscher, E.F., *Ekonomi och Historia*, Stockholm: Albert Bonniers förlag, 1922.

Heckscher, E.F., *Sveriges ekonomiska historia från Gustav Vasa*, II:1–2, Stockholm: Albert Bonniers förlag, 1949.

Herlitz, L., *Fysiokratismen i svensk tappning 1767–1770*, Meddelanden från Ekonomiskhistoriska institutionen vid Göteborgs universitet, vol. 35, Gothenburg, 1974.

Herlitz, L., "Anders Nordencrantz", in *Sveriges Biografiska Lexikon*, vol. 27, Stockholm, 1990–1.

Hildebrand, B., *Kungl. Svenska Vetenskapsakademin: Förhistoria, grundläggning och första organisation*, Stockholm: Kungl. Vetenskapsakademien, 1939.

Hont, I., "The Language of Sociability and Commerce: Samuel Pufendorf and the Theoretical Foundations of the 'Four-Stages Theory'", in A. Pagden (ed.), *The Languages of Political Theory in Early-Modern Europe*, Cambridge: Cambridge University Press, 1987.

Hont, I., *Jealousy of Trade: International Competition and the Nation-State in Historical Perspective*, Cambridge, Mass.: Harvard University Press, 2005.

Horn, C., *Ödmjukt memorial af fri-herre Christer Horn til Högloflige Ridderskapet och Adelen angående Högloflige Secrete utskottets til Riksens Högloflige Ständer upgifne berättelse om Banco-förwaltningen*, Stockholm, 1766.

Johnson, E.A., *Predecessors of Adam Smith: The Growth of British Economic Thought*, New York: Prentice-Hall, 1937.

Junggren, B., *Omständelig wederläggning af skriften, kallad: Källan til rikets wanmagt*, Stockholm, 1765.

Kaplan, S.L., *Bread, Politics and Political Economy in the reign of Louis XV*, 2 vols, The Hague: Nijhoff, 1976.

Knif, H., "Den farliga staden: Anders Chydenius och Stockholm", in M.-C. Skuncke and H. Tandefelt (eds), *Riksdag, kaffehus och predikstol: Frihetstidens politiska kultur 1766–1772*, Stockholm: Atlantis, 2003.

Krieger, L., *The Politics of Discretion: Pufendorf and the Acceptance of Natural Law*, Chicago: University of Chicago Press, 1965.

Kryger, J.F., *Tankar om swenske fabriquerne upsatte af Johan Fredric Kryger*, Stockholm, 1755.

Kryger, J.F., *Tankar wid lediga stunder*, andra delen, Stockholm, 1763.

Lagerroth, F., *Frihetstidens författning: En studie i den svenska konstitutionalismens historia*, Stockholm: Bonnier, 1915.

Leuhusen, C., *Tankar om de rätta och sanskyldiga Medel Til Sweriges Wälmåga*, 2 vols, Stockholm, 1761, 1763.

Liedman, S.-E., *Den synliga handen: Anders Berch och ekonomiämnena vid 1700-talets svenska universitet*, Stockholm: Arbetarkultur, 1986.

Lindberg, B., *Naturrätten i Uppsala 1655–1720*, Uppsala: Acta Universitatis Upsaliensis, 1976.

Lindroth, S., *Svensk lärdomshistoria: Frihetstiden*, Stockholm: Norstedt, 1978.

Magnusson, L., "Mercantilism and 'reform' mercantilism: The rise of economic discourse in Sweden during the eighteenth century", *History of Political Economy*, vol. 19:3, 1987, pp. 415–33.

Magnusson, L., "Corruption and Civic Order: Natural Law and Economic Discourse in Sweden during the Age of Freedom", *Scandinavian Economic History Review*, vol. 37:2, 1989, pp. 78–105.

Magnusson, L., *Mercantilism: The Shaping of an Economic Language*, London: Routledge, 1994.

Magnusson, L., "Physiocracy in Sweden", in B. Delmas, T. Delmas and P. Steiner (eds), *La Diffusion internationale de la Physiocratie*, Grenoble: Presses Universitaires de Grenoble, 1995.

Magnusson, L., "Proto-industrialization in Sweden", in S.C. Ogilvie and M. Cerman (eds), *European Proto-industrialization*, Cambridge: Cambridge University Press, 1996.

Magnusson, L., *An Economic History of Sweden*, London: Routledge, 2000.

Magnusson, L., *Äran, korruptionen och den borgerliga ordningen*, Stockholm: Atlantis, 2001.

Magnusson, L., *The Tradition of Free Trade*, London: Routledge, 2004.

Malmström, C.G., *Sveriges politiska historia från Konung Karl XII:s död till statshvälfningen 1772*, del III, 2. uppl., Stockholm: P.A. Norstedts & söners förlag, 1897.

Manninen, J., "Anders Chydenius and the Origins of World's First Freedom of Information Act", in J. Mustonen (ed.), *The World's First Freedom of Information Act: Anders Chydenius' Legacy Today*, Kokkola: Anders Chydenius Foundation, 2006.

Metcalf, M.F., "The First Modern Party System? Political Parties, Sweden's Age of Liberty and the Historians", *Scandinavian Journal of History*, vol. 2, 1977, pp. 265–87.

Nokkala, E., "Debatten mellan J. H. G. von Justi och H. L. von Heß om frihetstidens författning", *Historisk Tidskrift för Finland*, issue 1, 2009, pp. 20–55.

Nordbäck, C., *Lycksalighetens källa: Kontextuella närläsningar av Anders Chydenius budordspredikningar 1781–92*, Åbo: Åbo Akademis förlag, 2009.

Nordencrantz, A., *Oförgripelige tankar, om Frihet i bruk af förnuft, pennor och tryck, samt huru långt friheten derutinnan i et fritt samhälle sig sträcka bör, tillika med påfölgden deraf*, Stockholm, 1756.

Nordin, J., "Frihetstidens radikalism", in M.-C. Skuncke and H. Tandefelt (eds), *Riksdag, kaffehus och predikstol: Frihetstidens politiska kultur 1766–1772*, Stockholm: Atlantis, 2003.

Nyström, P., *Stadsindustriens arbetare före 1800-talet: Bidrag till kännedom om den svenska manufakturindustrien och dess sociala förhållanden*, Stockholm: Tidens förlag, 1955.

Odhner, C.T., *Sveriges politiska historia under konung Gustaf III:s regering*, vol. II, Stockholm: P.A. Norstedt & söner, 1896.

Ogilvie, S.C. and Cerman, M. (eds), *European Proto-industrialization*, Cambridge: Cambridge University Press, 1996.

Palmén, E.G., *Politiska skrifter af Anders Chydenius: Med en historisk inledning*, Helsinki: G.W. Edlunds förlag, 1880.

Petander, K., *De nationalekonomiska åskådningarna i Sverige: Sådana de framträda i litteraturen*, vol. 1, Stockholm: P.A. Norstedt & söner, 1912.

Pocock, J.G.A., *Barbarism and Religion*, vol. 1: *The Enlightenments of Edward Gibbon, 1737–1764*, Cambridge: Cambridge University Press, 1999.

Rabbe, F.J., "Anders Chydenius", in *Finlands minnesvärde män: Samling af lefnadsteckningar*, vol. 2, Helsinki: J.C. Frenckell & Son, 1857.

Roberts, M., *Swedish and English Parliamentarianism in the Eighteenth Century*, Belfast: Queen's University, 1973.

Roberts, M., *The Age of Liberty: Sweden 1719–1772*, Cambridge: Cambridge University Press, 1986.

Rothschild, E., *Economic Sentiments: Adam Smith, Condorcet and the Enlightenment*, Cambridge, Mass.: Harvard University Press, 2001.

Runeberg, E.F., *Wattu-prof wid Källan til rikets wanmagt*, Stockholm, 1765.

Salander, E., *Tal, om slögder, hållit för kongl. vetenskaps academien af Eric Salander...*, Stockholm, 1754.

Schauman, G., *Biografiska undersökningar om Anders Chydenius*, Skrifter utgifna af Svenska Litteratursällskapet i Finland 84, Helsinki: Svenska Litteratursällskapet i Finland, 1908.

Schauman, G., *Studier i Frihetstidens nationalekonomiska litteratur: Idéer och strömningar 1718–1740*, Helsinki, 1910.

Scheffer, C.F., *Bref, ifrån en Sawolax-bo, til en des patriotiska wän i Stockholm*, Stockholm, 1775.

Schück, H. and Warburg, K., *Illustrerad svensk litteraturhistoria: Romantiken*, Stockholm: Hugo Gebers förlag, 1929.

Schumpeter, J.A., *A History of Economic Analysis* [1954], London: George Allen and Unwin, 1968.

Skinner, Q., *Visions of Politics I: Regarding Method*, Cambridge: Cambridge University Press, 2002.

Stenhagen, P., *Tankar om Nödwändigheten af Stapel-Städers anläggande i Sweriges Norra Orter och i synnerhet Öster- och Wästerbottn*, Stockholm, 1762.

Stridsberg, O., "Hattarnas och mössornas ställningstaganden till tryckfrihetsfrågan på riksdagarna 1760–62 och 1765–66", *Historisk Tidskrift*, vol. 2, 1953, pp. 158–66.

Sundberg, G., *Partipolitik och regionala intressen 1755–1766: Studier kring det bottniska handelstvångets hävande*, Studia Historica Upsaliensia 104, Uppsala, 1978.

Swedenborg, E., *Oförgripelige Tanckar om Swenska Myntetz Förnedring och Förhögning*, Stockholm, 1722.

Thanner, L., *Revolutionen i Sverige efter Karl XII:s död: Den inrepolitiska maktkampen under tidigare delen av Ulrika Eleonora d.y:s regering*, Uppsala: Almqvist & Wiksell, 1953.

Tilas, D., *Anteckningar och brev från Riksdagen 1765–1766*, del II, Stockholm: Norstedt, 1974.

Tuck, R., *Natural Rights Theories: Their Origin and Development*, Cambridge: Cambridge University Press, 1979.

Uhr, C.G., *Anders Chydenius 1729–1803. A Finnish Predecessor to Adam Smith*, Meddelanden från Nationalekonomiska institutionen vid Handelshögskolan vid Åbo Akademi, nr 6, Åbo: Åbo Akademi, 1963.

Utterström, G., *Jordbrukets arbetare: Levnadsvillkor och arbetsliv på landsbygden från frihetstiden till mitten av 1800-talet*, del I, Stockholm: Tidens förlag, 1957.

Valentin, H., *Judarnas historia i Sverige*, Stockholm: Bonnier, 1924.

Vegesack, T. von, *Smak för frihet: Opinionsbildningen i Sverige 1755–1830*, Stockholm: Natur och Kultur, 1995.

Virrankoski, P., "Anders Chydenius and the Government of Gustavus III of Sweden in the 1770s", *Scandinavian Journal of History*, vol. 13, 1988, pp. 107–19.

Virrankoski, P., *Anders Chydenius: Demokratisk politiker i upplysningens tid*, Stockholm: Timbro, 1995.

Winton, P., *Frihetstidens politiska praktik: Nätverk och offentlighet 1746–1766*, Studia Historica Upsaliensia 223, Uppsala, 2006.

Index of names and places

338, 345; English 90, 108, 110, 128, 132–5, 140, 149, 154, 159, 306
Ennius, Quintus 274
Eriksson brothers 51, 324, 326
Essen, Fredric Ulric von 213–14, 341–2
Estonia 133
Eurajoki (Euraåminne) 331
Europe 13, 23, 33–4, 46, 48, 67, 73–4, 79, 85, 103, 126, 132, 135, 142, 144, 147–9, 173, 175, 177, 180, 207, 226, 255, 257, 263, 268–70, 278, 292, 310, 313, 317, 319, 322–3, 326

Faggot, Jacob 20, 122, 338
Fant, Johan Michael 343
Finland 1–3, 6, 14–15, 22, 26, 32–4, 52–53, 81, 131, 139, 156, 226, 268, 278–9, 305, 338
Finlay, Richard 24
Fischerström, Johan 37, 51
Flavius Caesar Vespasianus Augustus, Titus 105
Florence 269; Florentines 78
Forbonnais, François Véron Duverger de 37
Forsman, Karl 34, 37, 42
Forssenius, Anders 344–5
Forsskål, Peter 26
Fougt, Henrik 342–3
France 7, 44, 47, 53, 135, 166, 208, 259, 265, 269, 277, 322, 325, 338
Frederic Adolphus 338
Frisia: Frisians 78
Frängsmyr, Tore 41
Fyris river 12

Gadd, Pehr Adrian 105n4, 140
Gadolin, Jakob 338
Geijer, Erik Gustaf 47
Geneva 40
Germany 338
Gibbon, Edward 43
Gjörwell, Carl Christoffer 253
Godfred, King of Denmark 78
Gothenburg 121, 134, 264, 266, 277–9, 323, 326, 331, 351
Gournay, Jean Claude Marie Vincent de 37
Great Britain 226
Greece 70
Grill, Claes 24
Grill, Johan Abraham 24
Grotius, Hugo 6, 40–1
Gulf of Bothnia 30
Gustavus III 8, 12, 27, 29, 33, 46–7, 49, 52–3, 121, 226, 277–9, 281, 285, 303, 311, 315–16, 322, 324, 326, 342, 351–2
Gustavus IV 52, 226
Gustavus Vasa 132, 135, 175
Gyllensvaan, Fredric 341
Gävle 27, 30, 47
Gävleborg, county of 286, 314–15
Göransson, Sven 324

Haartman, Jakob 333

Haartman, Johan (assessor, later Professor of Medicine) 335
Haartman, Johan (rector) 30, 333
Hamburg 23, 193
Hamilcar (Barca) 74
Hamina (Fredrikshamn) 6
Heckscher, Eli F. 1–2, 14, 33, 35, 37, 40, 139
Hederström, Hans 338
Helsinki (Helsingfors) 6
Helvétius, Claude Adrien 35
Hesselberg, Peter 121
Hobbes, Thomas 43
Holland 126, 128, 152, 154, 268, 323, 325
Homer 70
Horace *see* Horatius Flaccus, Quintus
Horatius Flaccus, Quintus 70
Horn, Christer 39, 215
Hornæa (Hornæus), Hedvig 15, 331
Hornæus, Samuel 331
Hostilius, Tullus 75
Hume, David 23, 34–5, 41, 43, 168
Hårleman, Carl 232
Hälsingland 155
Häme (Tavastland) 157, 264
Högström, Pehr 213, 341
Höpken, Anders Johan von 26, 33, 51

Ingria 133
Isabella Clara Eugenia 77
Israel: Israelites 70

Jacob, the grandson of Abraham 73
Jennings, John 24
Johnson, Edgar Augustus Jerome 36
Julius Caesar Augustus, Gaius 76, 160
Julius Caesar, Gaius 76, 105, 159, 160
Junggren, Bengt 139
Junius Brutus, Lucius 75, 108

Kainuu (Kajanaland) 3
Kajaani (Kajana) 331
Kalm, Pehr 12, 15, 17, 333
Karelia 157
Karlskrona 232
Kellgren, Johan Henrik 44
Kemin Lappi (Kemi Lappmark) 3, 331
Kierman, Gustaf 24–5, 215
King, Charles 34, 36
Klingenstierna, Samuel 41
Kokemäenjoki river (Kumo älv) 15, 331
Kokkola (Gamlakarleby – today Karleby) 3, 15, 17- 19, 21–2, 30, 46, 49, 52, 256, 283, 324, 331, 333, 336, 338–9, 342, 346
Kraftman, Anders 26, 226, 249, 344
Kraftman, Johan 37
Kreander, Johan 333
Kryger, Johan Fredrik 14–15, 33, 41, 43, 63, 122, 267
Kröger, Carl 213, 341
Kuusamo 3, 331
König, Christian 26, 140

Index of subjects

absolutism 230, 303; *see also* monarchy;
    arbitrary despotism 44; enlightened 44, 46–7;
    fall of 8, 215
absolutist government 228
academic career 92
access to official documents 25, 226, 235
Act on freedom of printing *see* Ordinance on
    Freedom of Writing and Printing
actor publicus 225
administration: enlargement of 83
Age of Liberty 8, 12, 14, 29, 33, 41, 43–4, 46–8,
    121, 186, 213, 227, 279, 303, 313–14;
    condemned 48; critique against 44; economic
    policy during 12; semi-democratic 46
agio 174, 180, 203, 204
agriculture 3, 6, 80, 105, 108, 121, 133, 144,
    147, 150, 156, 232, 259, 277, 313, 315, 322;
    in Africa 82, 135; constraints on 80–6; crisis
    in 12; disfavoured 34, 36; economists friendly
    to 37; given preference to 80; growth of 12;
    improvement of 9, 12, 32, 131; new methods
    and practices in 8; people working on 83;
    Physiocrats 168; preferred over manufactories
    36; reforms of 166; regulation of 37; respect
    for 107; state support for 37
Anglicans 323–4
annual service contract 285–8, 290, 301–3,
    308–10; negotiated freely 308
Appropriations Committee 167, 210
aristocracy 224; associations of 303;
    condemnation of 47; conqueror of 311
aristocratic: ascendancy 304; fetters 295;
    government 228; power 307–8; propositions
    292
associations 266; against rural trade 272;
    aristocratic 303; influence on legislation 265;
    monopolistic 265, 272; servants have none
    304; use autocratic power 265
atheism 44, 107
Atlantis 34
autocracy 219, 221–2, 245
autocratic: governments 246; power 265; state 263

balance of power theory 46
Bank in France 208

Bank of the Estates 22–5, 40, 95, 102, 159,
    179–82, 184, 187–94, 196–205, 208–9,
    214–15, 340; the Crown is the greatest
    borrower 192; funds of 189, 192; in the hands
    of banknote capitalists 193; loans of 88, 176;
    loans to the Crown 194; management of 187;
    not legally obliged to honour its notes 180;
    not responsible for promissory notes 181;
    secrecy of 181, 204; victim of banknote
    capitalists 191
bank transfer notes 159, 180; against property
    179; against ready money 179
banknote capitalists 187, 193–4, 209; exploit the
    state 191
banknotes 21, 95, 96, 181–200, 202–3, 208–9;
    see also bank transfer notes; borrowed by the
    Crown 193; coming into circulation by loans
    188; conversion of 187, 198–9, 203;
    conversion rate of 187; debasing of 208;
    equivalent to *riksdaler* notes 203; fixed value
    of 202; lying idle 207; not honoured with coin
    180; over-issuing of 39; planned conversion
    rate of 187; redemption of 203–4; reduced
    conversion rate of 188; reducing the amount
    of 25, 199, 215; rising value 189; security and
    convertibility of 203; stock of 197–200; the
    only available currency 184
bar iron 132, 146
barbarians 70
barbarism 98
barbarous customs 66
beggars 208, 310
belles-lettres 243, 245, 277, 337; Swedish 245
belletrists 44
bills of exchange 134, 159–60, 163, 176, 181,
    187–9, 196, 202, 206; drawers of 206;
    remitters of 206
bliss 68, 270, 335
Board of Chancery *see* Royal Board of
    Chancery
Board of Trade *see* Royal Board of Trade
Board of War *see* Royal Board of War
bonds 23, 198–200; of the Bank 199, 202–3
book trade 237, 240, 243
Bothnian trade prohibition 6